Contents

Preface

'In examinations those who do not wish to know ask questions of those who cannot tell.'

SIR WALTER RALEIGH

'That state of restful coma that . . . dons dignify by the name of research.'

HAROLD LASKY

'For every person who wants to teach there are approximately thirty who don't want to learn much.'

W.C. SELLAR and R.J. YEATMAN

In rewriting this book I have continued to defy all three of the views expressed above. Initially the aim was to pull together into one source a rather disparate range of topics and material which I felt should be available in one place to students embarking upon graduate or postgraduate courses in apparel studies. In so doing I have assumed that the students want to learn what I believe they need in order to embark on careers in the industry and that they would welcome a text which made revision for examinations relatively easier. I have also taken the stance on research philosophy that research is a good thing and that students should be encouraged to continually pose the question 'how do we know that?' The positivist research ethic has been adhered to wherever possible and its corollary that scientific research findings should be regarded as the most important underpinning of any conclusions I have drawn.

This has uncovered some interesting gaps in our knowledge, particularly in relation to global statistics of production and consumption, and has highlighted problems in dealing with issues related to achieving an understanding of the so-called fashion process. These gaps remain unfilled.

I have also attempted to locate discussion of the sector firmly within the context of the wider economics research base – reflecting a view that the industry is not so special or different from other branches of light engineering that it has to be treated as some sort of special case. This is not to deny that the sector has at least one unique feature – its labour intensity – which has largely conditioned its global configuration.

My view of what should be included has been formed by some twenty years of experience in teaching graduate and postgraduate programmes which contain substantial elements of economics and, in effect, reflects what might best be described as the Hollings view of what students destined to work in the clothing industry need to know. Hollings introduced the first UK graduate programme in clothing studies in the early 1980s and it quickly became apparent that the existing literature on the economics of the industry (as opposed to design and textile technology, for example) was somewhat limited. Therefore, we started to generate our own literature in an in-house journal which has evolved over time into the *Journal of Fashion Marketing and Management,* now in its tenth year, which aims to fill a gap between journals dealing with design issues and those dealing with textile science subjects.

The second edition brings up to date all the statistics, especially those confirming the downturn in activity in the UK after 1998. The year 2005 sees the final demise of the system of quota control which had been in place since 1974 and provides a good platform from which to assess its impact in the light of a review of EU textile/apparel policy. Finally, the continued expansion of production in China can be brought into sharper focus.

The main themes of the first edition were largely confirmed by the passage of time, e.g. offshore production is now the norm and the only remaining issues are 'where' and 'how'; there is little talk of 'hidden costs'; China has emerged as the major player; the removal of the Multi Fibre Arrangement (MFA) did result in a surge in imports and the period after 1998 did turn out to be, as predicted, a second watershed for the evolution of the UK apparel sector – the prediction that employment would fall to 75,000 by 2005 was wrong but only in the sense of being too optimistic. These developments will have important consequences for the range of and type of skills future employees in the sector will require and will, I believe, make the topics covered in this text even more important in the future. Clearly it is not possible to cover all topics exhaustively in that many, such as supply chain management, have entire books devoted to them but I believe it has been possible to incorporate the main implications for the apparel industry into the relevant chapters. Each chapter ends with a reference list which should enable the reader to take things further if they desire to do so.

Richard M. Jones
Manchester

Acknowledgements

I believe that the need for a textbook covering the range of issues included here has been recognised since the early 1980s within the Department of Clothing Design and Technology as it developed degree-level courses preparing students for a career in the apparel sector. However, until now the conditions to allow the preparation of such a text have not existed. Therefore, the most important contribution to acknowledge is that made by my Head of Department, Catherine Fairhurst, for creating the timetable environment which allowed me sufficient time to prepare the initial manuscript.

It follows from this that a debt of gratitude is owed to all the other staff in the Department who covered various activities for me. A particular debt is owed to a number of colleagues – both inside and outside my own University – who read early drafts of various chapters of the first edition. I would like to thank Professors Ian Taplin (at Wake Forest University) and David Jeremy (at MMU); Andrew Godley (at Reading) and Gaynor Lea-Greenwood (MMU) for their efforts.

An enormous vote of thanks must go to Richard Miles, Senior Publisher at Blackwell Publishing, for supporting both the initial project and the production of this edition. I would also like to thank my colleague Dr S.G. Hayes for assisting with the updating of the statistics in Chapters 2 and 10.

Finally, my sanity was preserved by long walks with Dino the Dog, without which I would probably not have reached the end of the task.

Chapter 1

What is the Apparel Industry?

A. *Introduction: the textile–apparel pipeline*

The textile–apparel pipeline is a series of interrelated activities which originates with the manufacture of fibre and culminates in the delivery of a product into the hands of the consumer. Figure 1.1 illustrates the pipeline. The focus of this text will be that part of the pipeline contained in the highlighted box – the manufacture of garments. This area of activity can itself be subdivided into various stages (see Fig. 1.1). In many respects the crucial element is assembly – the sewing process – because this constitutes some 30% of the total cost of a garment and has remained obstinately resistant to automation. It is no exaggeration to say that this single fact is the defining feature of the apparel manufacturing process.

The issue of the relationship between the words 'clothing', 'garment', 'apparel' and 'fashion' will be dealt with below. The word 'pipeline' implies that there is a logical connection or progression between the stages of the process of converting an input into a product for the final consumer. The term 'supply chain', in contrast, will be reserved for situations in which companies, although legally independent, have agreed to work together to achieve a common goal. It is clearly possible for a pipeline to exist but not to be organised into a supply chain. Indeed, it could be argued that for many years, the failure of the UK textile and apparel manufacturing sectors to achieve meaningful co-operation was a significant factor in the evolution of the two sectors.

In the words of the UK Fashion Report (EMAP, 1998/99, p. 154):

> 'The main dynamic holding the industry back is the largely adversarial relationship of manufacturers and retailers. This inhibits best practice and generates supply chain inefficiencies which contribute to the lack of a competitive edge.'

Briscoe (1971, p. 1), for example, talks of 'these industries' and emphasises that the 'clothing industry has fared differently' from the textile industry. The whole tenor of her introductory chapter to the major UK textbook on the sector stresses the difference between the textile and clothing industries rather than

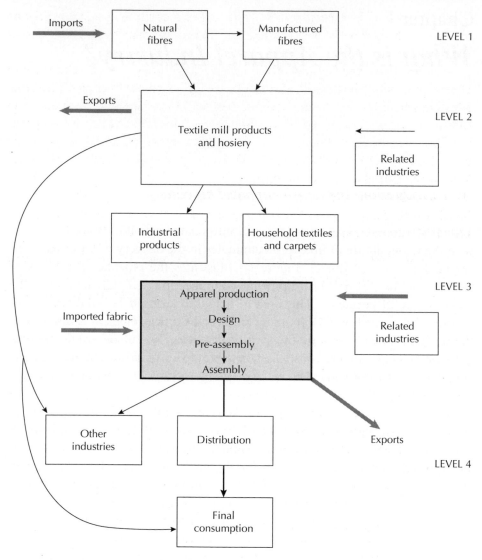

Fig. 1.1   The textile – apparel pipeline.

their inter-connectedness. A more modern view would stress the importance of all levels in the pipeline working together to achieve competitive advantage in world markets. In respect of the way in which, historically, the various levels of the pipeline have failed to co-operate in the UK the Briscoe view is, somewhat paradoxically, probably correct.

Therefore, while the focus of this text will be the garment manufacturing cell within the pipeline, attention will be continually focused on the issue of pipeline management and, in particular, upon efforts to reduce the length of the pipeline in terms of the number of days taken to move a product concept from one end of the pipeline to the other.

A highly simplified version of the progression through the pipeline would consist of Level 1 (the manufacture of fibre) which becomes the input into Level 2 within which fabric is manufactured then sold to companies manufacturing industrial textiles, household textiles or apparel (Level 3). The completed product then has to be distributed to the final consumer in a variety of ways: in the case of the apparel manufacturing industry this process is usually achieved via some form of retailer or distributor in Level 4.

In practice the picture is somewhat more complex. For example, there can be a link between the natural and man-made fibre cells at Level 1. Similarly, as the OECD (1983) pointed out:

> 'Technological change has blurred the distinction between these processes. In some cases . . . the basic processes of yarn and fabric production have merged. In other cases, such as seamless hosiery fabric, production has incorporated the product assembly stage.'

Hence hosiery production is often (in the UK) classified within the primary textile sector. Finally, there is no requirement for all four levels to be within any one country – nor is there any need for any one level in a given country to be linked solely with the other levels in the same country. Raw materials at Level 1 may be imported as they were historically in the UK (see Table 1.1). Fabric may be exported and a classic example would be cotton cloth from the UK prior to World War I. At Level 3 fabric may be imported while the finished product may be exported.

Table 1.1   Imports of textiles (£ millions) 1800–1980.

Year	Raw cotton	Raw wool
1800	1.8	0.5
1829	7.3	0.7
1850	21.5	2.0
1854/56	22.5	7.0
1900	41.0	22.7
1913	70.6	35.6
1930	45.0	43.5
1950	160.6	196.2
1970	50.3	92.6
1980	72.8	197.9

Source: Mitchell, B. (1988) *British Historical Statistics*, Cambridge
University Press, Cambridge, p. 462.

B.   *Are clothing and fashion synonymous?*

A number of words can be used to describe the sector which is the subject of this book, e.g. clothing; garments; apparel or fashion. The latter word has, to many commentators, a rather special meaning being associated with art, creativity or uniqueness. Let us start by examining some generally accepted definitions of the word 'fashion'.

According to Sproles (1981) fashion is:

'a temporary cyclical phenomena adopted by consumers for a particular time and situation.'

Easey (1995, p. 1) argues that 'fashion involves change, defined as a succession of short term trends' while Rogers and Gamans (1983, p. 7) define fashion as 'any form, custom or style'. Rath (1994, p. 17) considers fashion to be 'a look or style that is popular at a given time' while Stone (1990, p. 53) talks about 'the style or style of clothing . . . worn at a particular time by a particular group of people'. Nagasawa *et al.* (1995, p. 175) regard fashion as 'a process in everyday acts of appearance management'.

These definitions all stress the twin features of acceptance and change. It is the fact of change which produces so many problems for clothing manufacturers but as Easey (1995, p. 1) emphasises, the role of change in fashion markets is crucial when he argues that:

'[the] industry has a vested interest in developing new products for the customer at the expense of existing items: this process is known as planned obsolescence.'

This seems a long way away from the concept of creative design or art for its own sake. Easey (1995, p. 2) argues that the idea that fashion garments should be viewed as an art form is held more strongly in France and Italy than in the UK. As Jones (1997, p. 5) observes:

'the study . . . of clothing manufacturing occupies, in the UK, a somewhat uneasy middle ground position between textiles at one end of the supply chain and the more traditional fashion design school which approaches the subject from an art-based tradition or culture.'

In the UK this dichotomy may have its origins in the historical evolution of design education, e.g. in Manchester it was determined in 1853 to locate design education in the Manchester School of Art. This was seen (Fowler & Wyke, 1993, p. 10):

'as a victory for those who believed that the school's future lay in providing a more general art education than in the teaching of design skills. This direction was followed despite the fact that the initial impetus to the opening of a design school in Manchester in 1838 owed its origins to a concern over British industry losing markets to foreign competitors because of poorly designed products.'

The boundaries of the 'fashion' sector stray way beyond the garment market, e.g. in the watch market the success of the Swatch watch owed much to its repositioning as a trendy, fashion item. In 1999, Swatch had gone as far as to collaborate in the production of a small car. Is this now also part of the fashion industry?

The majority of garments sold do not fall into the 'art form' category. Nor can, by definition, all garments be, at any one time, 'fashionable'. On the other hand, most of us do change our clothes long before they are functionally worn out. From this point of view most garments are probably influenced to a greater or lesser degree by trends which have filtered down from the high fashion zones. Therefore, the argument over the extent to which there is a 'fashion industry' inside 'the clothing industry' is, while not uninteresting academically, probably something of a straw man or blind alley in terms of promoting an understanding of the current and future problems of the industry as part of the pipeline outlined in Fig. 1.1. Accordingly, in the remainder of this text the words 'clothing', 'garment', 'fashion' and 'apparel' will be used as if they were interchangeable and the word 'apparel' will be used henceforth to represent them all.

C. The importance of apparel manufacture to and in the textile pipeline

As output flows through the pipeline it should be possible to identify the relative importance and role of the various elements within the pipeline itself. This exercise can be conducted both on an historical basis and in current terms. In practice it is extremely difficult to identify the relative size of the various elements in the pipeline on a historical basis because most textile histories tend to concentrate on the cotton textile sector and, secondly, the Census of Production did not start until 1907. As Briscoe (1971, p. 2) notes, information on clothing 'is more difficult to obtain'.

Figure 1.2 attempts to summarise the historical importance of the primary textile and apparel manufacturing sectors to the UK economy in terms of measures of output, employment and trade. On the basis of these figures – and recognising that the measures are not perfect – a tentative conclusion would be, first, that the primary textile sector was approximately twice as important to the UK economy as apparel manufacture and, second, that the role played by the apparel sector in the UK economy as a whole had, by the 1960s, become rather

Nineteenth century

1812	Textiles	= 7–8% of output (D + C)
1820	Textiles	= 4% of output (M + D)
1830	Apparel	= 2% of exports (B)
	Cotton	= 50% of exports (B)
	Cotton	= 48.5% of exports (R)
1934/6	Apparel	= 438,000 jobs (G)
1836	Textiles	= 11% of output (D + C)
1851	Textiles and apparel	= 21% of the occupied population (D + C)
1870	Textiles	= 9% of output (B; D + C)
1871	Textiles and apparel	= 18% of occupied population (D + C)
	Apparel	= 540,900 jobs (G)

Twentieth century

1907	Textiles	= 2.3% of output (M + D)
1911	Apparel	= 800,000 jobs (G)
1913	Textiles and apparel	= 35% of exports (B)
1923	Textiles	= 1,312,000 jobs (B)
	Apparel	= 651,000 jobs (B)
1924	Apparel	= 25% of output (B)
1925	Textiles	= 5.2% of output (B)
1931	Apparel	= 708,000 jobs (G)
1935	Textiles	= 3.5% of output (B)
	Apparel	= 2.1% of output (B)
1951	Apparel	= 609,000 jobs (G)
1954	Apparel	= 470,000 jobs (C)
1958	Apparel	= 411,000 jobs (C)
1962	Apparel	= 1.1% of output (B)
1963	Textiles	= 2.6% of output (B)
1969	Textiles	= 580,900 jobs (B)
	Apparel	= 390,000 jobs (B)
1973	Textiles and apparel	= 2.2% of output
1996	Apparel	= 1.7% of output; 3.8% of employment and 2.2% output

Sources: B = Briscoe, L. (1971) *The Textile and Clothing Industries of the UK,* Manchester University Press.
C = Clayton, D. (1999) private correspondence with author.
D + C = Deane, P. & Cole (1969) *British Economic Growth 1688–1959.*
M + D = Mitchell, B. & Deane, P. (1962) *Abstract of Historical Statistics.*
R = Rose, M.B. (1991) *International Competition and Strategic Response in the Textile Industries Since 1870,* Frank Cass.
G = Godley, A. (1996) The Emergence of Mass Production in the UK Clothing Industry, in Taplin, I. & Winterton, J. *Restructuring Within a Labour Intensive Industry,* Avebury.
Note: 1996 figures from Table 2.2 are based on percentages of manufacturing totals.

Fig. 1.2   Historical estimates of the importance of textiles and apparel in the UK economy.

trivial on an output basis at around 1% of GNP. Its importance as an *employer* was, of course, always more significant given the labour-intensive nature of the production process.

As Godley (1996, p. 15) demonstrates, the clothing industry was, in historical terms, of major importance:

'. . . as a source of employment . . . especially of female labour. The clothing industry for most of this period (1851–1951) was the second most important source of non-agricultural female labour. However, the trends are fairly clear. The clothing industry's *importance to the economy was slowly declining* [author's emphasis] – from just under 2.5% of the population in 1851 to . . . only 1.4% of the population in 1951.'

As Deane and Cole (1969) pointed out in the mid-nineteenth century the textile and clothing sectors provided jobs for 10% of the population, or 21% of the occupied population. Estimates of employment between 1861 and 1939 have been given in Table 1.2, while the relative size of the elements of the pipeline in terms of exports are shown in Table 1.3. Even then, however, Mitchell & Deane (1962, p. 191) concluded that the impact of textiles 'on the national economy was still small in absolute terms'. The share of national output accounted for by clothing and textiles is shown in Tables 1.4 and 1.5. In terms of gross output, Godley (1996) concluded that in current price terms the output of the sector had risen approximately sevenfold between 1907 and 1954, but that most of this increase had been caused by inflation. In real price terms (column RP(a) in Table 1.4) the increase was only 150%. On the basis of the 1980 real price series

Table 1.2   Employment in the textile pipeline (thousands of people).

	Cotton	Wool	Silk	Linen	Clothing
1806[1]	274				518
1835[2]	455				
1862[1,2]	219	55	31	33	
1896[1]	533				706 (1891)
1907[1,2]	577	261	29	151	796 (1911)
1923[2]	568 (1312[T])	269	37	82	580[2]
1930[2]	564	240	78*		708[1] (1931)
1932[2]					605[2]
1938[1]	378				
1940[2]	383	231	80*	77	
1947					551[2]
1950	316	222	105*	66	548[2] (1951)
1958	952[T]				
1960[2]	285[T]	204	40**		387[2] (1961)
1965	829[T]				563
1970[2]	172+	159	53**		
1978[2]	92+ (490[T])	79	38**		378[2]
1981[2]	175[T]				296[2]

Sources: (1) Mitchell, B. & Deane, P. (1962) *Abstract of British Historical Statistics*, Cambridge University Press, Cambridge.
(2) Mitchell, B. (1988) *British Historical Statistics*, Cambridge University Press, Cambridge.
Notes: * Silk and man-made fibres.
** Man-made fibres only.
+ Spinning and weaving of cotton.
[T] All textiles.

Table 1.3   Exports from the textile pipeline (£ millions).

Year	Cotton	Wool	Man-made fibres	Linen	Silk	Hats, apparel, etc.
1814	20.10	6.4		1.7	0.5	—
1829	17.4	4.7		1.8	0.3	1.0
1850	28.3	10.0		4.8	1.3	2.5
1900	69.8	20.2		6.2	2.1	8.0
1920	401.4	139.3	3.0	9.5 (1913)	2.1 (1913)	13.3 (1913)
1930	87.6	35.5	5.9	6.3	1.3	
1940	49.3	24.2	7.6			
1950	126.7	82.8	45.7			7.7

Sources: Mitchell, B. & Deane, P. (1962) *Abstract of British Historical Statistics*, Cambridge University Press, Cambridge.
Mitchell, B. (1988) *British Historical Statistics*, Cambridge University Press, Cambridge.

Table 1.4   Gross output (£ millions) of the textile pipeline.

Date	Clothing			Textiles		TCL			FDT	Chemicals
	CP	RP(a)	RP(b)	CP	RP(a)	CP	RP(a)	RP(b)	CP	CP
1907	96	193	1,778	336	676	458	921	8,481	283	90
1924	178	156	1,447	762	668	987	865	8,024	670	220
1930	176	169	1,556	431	414	659	633	5,832	662	199
1935	173	179	1,765	443	459				665	206
1945	527	252	2,648	1,479	708				2,644	
1948	324	155	1,434			1,968	942	8,708	2,632	762
1951	479	186	1,736						3,819	1,283
1954	504	199	1,833						3,235	1,663
1963						3,204	10,369		5,347	2,900
1970						4,420	11,946		9,157	5,158
1979						12,093	13,173		30,579	27,624

Sources: 1907–45 Mitchell, B. & Deane, P. (1962), p. 270.
                1948–54 Godley, A. (1996), p. 10.
Key: FDT = Food, Drink, Tobacco.
                TCL = Textiles, Clothing, Leather.
Notes: (1)   RP(b) 1980 real prices, author's own calculations based on data from *The Economist* (1995), *Economic Statistics* 1990–1983.
                (2)   RP(a) used the 1938 deflator in Godley (1996).
                (3)   The percentage shares of all UK production were in current price terms as follows:

	1907	1963	1970	1979
Clothing	5.4	NA	NA	NA
TCL	19.0	9.3	8.6	5.9
FDT	16.0	15.5	17.8	15.0
Chemicals	5.1	8.4	10.0	13.5

the increase is just over 100%. In order to consider the period after 1954 it is necessary to move to the combined Textiles, Clothing and Leather series. The real increase between 1948 and 1963 was similar to the current price increase at 150% while the increase between 1963 and 1979 was about 400% in current terms but only just over 100% in real terms.

Table 1.5   Net output (£ millions) of the textile pipeline.

Date	Clothing			Textiles		TCL			FDT	Chemicals
	CP	RP(a)	RP(b)	CP	RP	CP	RP(a)	RP(b)	CP	CP
1907	40	80	741	95	191	141	284	2,611	87	27
1924	73	64	593	221	194	308	269	2,504	172	73
1930	77	74	681	147	141				187	77
1935	79	83	806	157	162		249	2,541	203	89
1945	210	101	1,055	484						
1948							733	3,243	525	269
1963							1,236	4,000	1,292	1,068
1970							1,838	4,968	2,485	2,031
1979							5,131	5,589	8,359	9,084

Sources: 1907–45 Mitchell, B. & Deane, P. (1962).
1948–79 Mitchell, B. (1988) as Table 1.2.
Key: FDT = Food, Drink, Tobacco.
TCL = Textiles, Clothing, Leather.
Notes: (1)   Real prices computed using data in *The Economist* (1995), *Economic Statistics* 1990–1983.
(2)   RP(a) used the 1938 deflator in Godley (1996).
(3)   The percentage shares of all UK production were in current price terms as follows:

	1907	1963	1970	1979
Clothing	5.6	NA	NA	NA
TCL	13.3	8.6	8.4	6.0
FDT	12.2	9.0	11.4	9.8
Chemicals	3.8	7.4	9.3	10.6

In terms of net output the apparent fivefold increase in apparel production between 1907 and 1945 again turns out to be largely an illusion caused by inflation. In real terms (both price series) the increase was about 140%. In the period 1948–1979 the current sevenfold price increase falls to a rise of about 200% when the effect of inflation is removed.

Historically the woollen industry was initially predominant within Level 1 of the pipeline. In Berg's (1994, p. 40) words:

> 'The woollen industry still dominated the whole industrial sector at the beginning of the nineteenth century and was still more important in terms of value added than the cotton industry until the 1820s.'

By 1831 cotton had overtaken wool in importance. In more modern times the trend has been for the importance of man-made fibres to increase relative to that of the natural fibres, e.g. OECD (1983, p. 38) reported that by 1979 man-made fibres were responsible for 67% of world fibre production as compared to cotton at 24% and wool at 4%. In the UK, man-made fibre production is classified in official statistics as part of the chemical industry.

In the UK (see Table 1.6) the textile sector – Level 2 – is some 59% bigger than the apparel sector – Level 3 – in terms of turnover and some 79% bigger in terms of Gross Value Added. Nevertheless, the apparel sector compares very favourably with some other elements of the pipeline such as fibres and carpets. The

Table 1.6   Relative size of elements of the textile-fashion pipeline, 2003 (£ millions).

	Turnover	Gross Value Added
Apparel (SIC 18)	4,430	1,506
Textiles (SIC 17)	7,031	2,689
Preparation and spinning of fibres	611	197
Weaving	863	334
Man-made fibres	490	214
Carpets	874	274
Hosiery	269	105

Source: ONS, Annual Business Inquiry, 2004.

significance of the apparel sector is confirmed below in the examination of sales from one level of the pipeline to another but this has not been reflected in the sector securing influence within the pipeline which is retailer led.

The relationships between the various elements of the pipeline can be explored by examining sales from one level to the next. According to Briscoe (1971, p. 49) the destinations of woven cloth and man-made fibres (by area) were 41% to clothing, 28% to household textiles and furnishings and 31% to industry. (These figures applied to 1968.) Taylor (1990) quotes a figure for EU fibre consumption (for 1987 and by weight) of 27.4% for clothing, 18% for carpets and household uses and 54.6% for industry. The Sector Review (ONS, 1999a, p. 8) for the textile sector states that 'the markets for textiles are varied with no single dominant player' but that the largest consumer of textile products (outside the textile sector itself) is the clothing sector which takes 22% of intermediate demand for textiles. The purchasers of textile products in the UK are shown in Table 1.7. It can be seen that 70% of the output of the primary textile sector (the second level)

Table 1.7   Purchases of the output of the textile sector (% of total demand), 2002.

	%
Intermediate demand of which	30
Intra textiles	31
Apparel	**22**
Motor vehicles	6
Furniture	7
Retail and wholesale distribution	8
Final Demand	70

Source: ONS, Input–Output Tables, 2002. Available electronically only at www.statistics.gov.uk/inputoutput – Detailed and Summary Supply and Use Tables, Table 3 'Combined Use' Matrix.

Notes: (1) Intermediate demand is demand from other industries as opposed to Final Demand which is demand from consumers.

(2) The average split for all industry is 43% to Intermediary Demand and 57% to Final Demand.

Table 1.8 Purchases of the output of the apparel sector (% of total demand), 2002.

	%
Intermediate demand of which	6
Public Administration and Defence	19
Health and Veterinary	14
Social Work	6
Recreational Services	7
Retail and Wholesale Distribution	4
Hotels	6
Education	7
Final demand	94

Source and Notes: as Table 1.7.

in our pipeline goes to final demand and 30% to other industries as intermediate demand. Of the intermediate demand some 22% still goes to the apparel cell in our pipeline diagram. This is more than double the percentage directed into any other industry. Therefore, the apparel industry is of great importance within the textile pipeline. However, it must be stressed again, that this does not necessarily mean that the interests of the cells within the pipeline are synonymous with one another. As Moore (1999, p. 261) puts it:

'The textile manufacturers have always presented their case as if they had a common cause with the clothing producer. This is incorrect; protection in the textile industry raises the price of cloth, the input into the clothing industry.'

Ninety-four per cent of the output of the apparel sector goes into final (consumer) demand – albeit via the distribution sector. Sales to other industrial uses (intermediate demand) are rather rare with the only sectors representing substantial markets being health and public administration and defence (see Table 1.8).

Finally, it must be recognised that consumer goods markets are virtually the *raison d'être* of the apparel pipeline. The health of the sector depends almost exclusively on trends in the apparel market – industrial sales are extremely insignificant. On average, for all industry, final demand takes only 57% of output. Therefore, the apparel sector is disproportionately vulnerable to the vagaries of the fashion market (see Chapter 10). It does not, of course, follow from this that companies in the apparel manufacturing cell of the pipeline will hold the dominant position. This position is held by the retailer, as will be shown in Chapter 2 (D, vi).

The timing of interactions between the various cells in the pipeline is driven by the demands of the final marketplace. In Forza & Vinelli's (2000, p. 139) words:

'The decisions and activities of the textile-apparel chain can be examined by referring both to the characteristics of the physical activities of transformation and to the length of time required for them.'

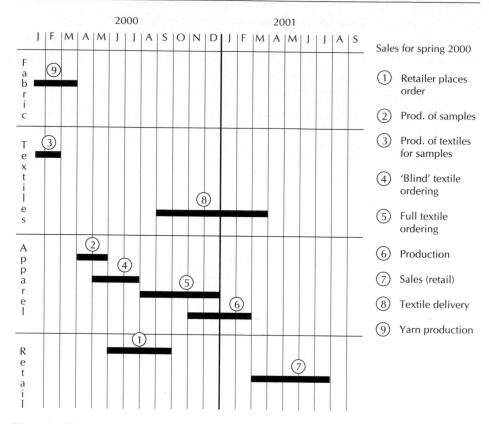

Fig. 1.3   The production stage chart (based on Forza & Vinelli (2000)).

This is facilitated by an examination of the traditional Production Stage Chart (PSC) – see Fig. 1.3. The major feature is that there is an extremely large gap between the placing and receiving of an order by the retailer. In addition, future orders must be placed before final current sales levels are known. If deliveries to the retailer are scheduled for (say) early 2001, then garment manufacture will typically begin in autumn 2000 and fabric production in spring 2000. It is clear that the system contains many built-in sources of error and potential waste. The attempt to modify this traditional scenario, consequent upon the adoption of Quick Response strategies, will be considered in Chapter 8. As KSA (2005, p. 5) observe 'the long-established method of sampling and forward ordering . . . is increasingly being replaced with different forms of speed sourcing, where lead times are measured in days.' This is considered in more detail in Chapter 7.

It has to be repeated at this point that there is no necessity for the entire pipeline to be located in any single country. The primary textile sector supplying the UK apparel cell in the pipeline could be anywhere. In fact, the import penetration rate in the UK textile sector is (ONS, 2004a) quite high at 66% while 49% of its output is exported. The consumer could also be anywhere – some 20% of the output of the UK apparel sector is exported (ONS, 2004a). There is even no real need for all the elements *within* the apparel cell in Fig. 1.1 to be in the same place. Increasingly the activities within the total pipeline will be geographically dispersed across national boundaries.

As will be seen in Chapter 3, there has been a massive global shift of apparel production to the so-called developing regions. In addition, the assembly operation within the apparel production cell of the pipeline has been moved offshore by many UK and Western European apparel producers (see Chapter 8). In fact, this internationalisation of the pipeline has always been the case. The explosive growth of the Lancashire cotton industry in the nineteenth century was based on imports of raw cotton from India and America (see Table 1.1). Additionally, as Briscoe (1971, p. 14) points out, the expansion of the textile sector was linked to exports, so that by the 1880s, 80% of cotton cloth was exported. Saul (1960, p. 34), in his analysis of UK trade between 1870–1914, shows that even in 1913 Britain was still responsible for 60% of world trade in cotton goods.

Clearly, the initial growth of an apparel manufacturing sector in the UK was promoted by the earlier expansion of the primary textile sector. This was true, for example, in the USA where Dickerson (1995, p. 32) states that:

'The American apparel industry did not begin to develop, at least to a significant degree, for nearly a century after textile production was industrialised.'

And also in the UK where, as Briscoe (1971, p. 14) notes, the clothing industry:

'changeover to the factory system came later and was associated with the introduction of the Singer sewing machine into England in 1851.'

However, as has been noted, most of the cotton cloth produced in the UK was exported. Rose (1991, p. 3) noted that the British cotton industry was:

'throughout the nineteenth century export orientated so that in 1882–84 UK cotton piece goods represented 82% of total world exports of those products.'

The divide between local elements within the textile/apparel pipeline seems to have evolved very early and to have persisted throughout the years. Dupree (1996, p. 273), in an analysis of the industry between the wars, singled out the fact that

'there were separate associations for spinning, weaving and manufacture . . . (and that) these groups knew each other only slightly and there tended to be hostility among them'

as one of the weaknesses of the sector. It could be argued that one of the weaknesses – both historically and currently – of the UK-based textile–apparel pipeline was that it never really possessed the characteristics of a co-operative supply chain. Relations between the levels in the pipeline were, and still often are, adversarial rather than collaborative. Morrison (1996, p. 243) wrote of the lack of integration of spinning and weaving in the late nineteenth century, describing 'a fight for the meagre spoils'.

Fraser (1948, p. 103) stated that apparel manufacturers of the day complained that: 'wherever we can we buy locally but this is seldom possible', while Levitt (1996), writing about the 1980s, commented that:

> 'most manufacturers complained that home suppliers were unable to meet prices or deadlines or just did not exist.'

Miles (1968, p. 94) wrote that the changes taking place in the outlets for textile products were having an impact on the industry itself in that

> 'about 50% of Lancashire fabric produced goes to the clothing industry and here it meets strong foreign competition in the market selling to industrial customers (the apparel manufacturers) who regard fabric as their main raw material'

and as a *cost to be minimised*. The same author (1968, p. 81) showed that from a position of having a positive trade balance in cotton cloth in 1959 the UK had moved to a negative balance by 1966 as UK apparel manufacturers increasingly switched to external suppliers. As late as 1990, Haines (1990, p. 4) still felt justified in arguing that feedback

> 'from apparel manufacturers and fabric suppliers to date shows a clear need for greater co-operation between the two sectors of the industry'

while Howarth (1990, p. 34) complained that:

> 'co-operation between manufacturing and textile companies along with common planning and EDI communications are noticeably lacking in the UK.'

In the 1990s the battle ground had seemingly moved to Level 4 in the pipeline, with Banning (1994, p. 44) writing that:

> 'the relationship between the manufacturer and retailer for the past thirty years has been largely a matter of "dog eat dog".'

It is interesting to note that Rose (1991, p. 175) traces the origins of retail power back to the 1880s, when 'manufacturers and retailers began to forge direct links'. Historically, the apparel manufacturing cell continued, in Levitt's words (1996, p. 154):

> 'to flourish . . . despite the decline in the cotton industry so that whilst the cotton industry steadily declined, clothing production expanded until the 1960s.'

The relative survival (in employment terms) of the apparel manufacturing sector in comparison to the textile industry is well illustrated earlier in Table 1.2.

Table 1.9 Output changes in the UK apparel sector (1948–1958, £ millions).

Year	Clothing
1948	216.3
1950	227.4
1955	306.5
1958	293.1

Source: *Annual Abstract of Statistics*, 1959.
Notes: (1) In this table 'Clothing' is defined as outerwear, underwear and gloves (excluding fabric gloves).
(2) The output of socks and stockings rose from £587.8 millions in 1948 to £638.9 millions in 1958 in current prices.
(3) In terms of real (1980) prices the figures are £957 million in 1958 and £1014 million in 1958 so that the percentage growth is reduced from 36% in current terms to 6% in real terms.
(4) The author is grateful to David Clayton of the University of York for providing this data.

As Godley (1996, p. 10) observes, the gross output of the clothing sector rose from £135 million in 1907 to £198 million in 1995 although by the early 1950s the industry's importance as an employer was already slowly declining. The dramatic collapse of both output and employment in the UK apparel industry post 1998 in documented in Chapter 2.

Output growth from 1948 to 1958 is shown in Table 1.9. This stagnation (and decline 1955–8) effectively predates any massive surge in imports which did not really occur until the 1970s and 1980s (see Table 1.10). It could, of course, be argued that the fate of the entire pipeline in the UK would have been different if the various elements had behaved more co-operatively. This issue will be considered in more detail in Chapter 7.

The pipeline relationships described above have been evaluated in terms of a sales relationship between the various cells. However, as Hunter (1990, p. 150) points out:

'the pipeline is not only a marketing and manufacturing pipeline, it is also a technical pipeline – the sectors are connected in all respects.'

The major technological advances of the 1950s were made upstream (at the fibre end of the chain) and have moved progressively downstream through the textile mill cell (in the 1970s); the apparel sector (in a more limited fashion) in the 1980s to the information technology revolution in retailing in the 1990s. As Hunter (1990, p. 150) observed:

'as the focus of technology moves downstream it has placed increasing demands on the upstream supplier.'

Table 1.10   Imports of apparel into the UK.

Year	£ millions (current prices)	Index (1950 = 100)
1920	15.7	144
1930	21.6	198
1935	8.5	78
1937	10.9	100
1947	6.1	56
1948	5.2	48
1949	6.4	59
1950	10.9	100
1951	11.2	103
1952	8.4	77
1953	8.6	79
1954	13.4	123
1955	18.4	169
1956	23.3	214
1957	26.2	240
1958	29.9	274
1959	41.3	379
1960	58.1	533
1970	170.4	1,563
1975	629.0	5,771
1980	1,584.7	14,539

Sources: (1) *Annual Abstract of Trade of the UK*, Vol. 1, 1947–1959, HMSO, London.
   (2) For other years outside 1947–1959, see Mitchell, B. (1988) *British Historical Statistics*, Cambridge University Press, Cambridge, p. 479.

Notes: (1) Apparel here is defined as Clothing, Footwear, Travel Goods and Bags.
   (2) The author is grateful to David Clayton of the University of York for providing much of this data.
   (3) In real terms (1980 prices) the increase was from £30 millions in 1947 to £46 millions in 1950; to £49 millions in 1954 and then up to £144 millions in 1959.

The same author illustrates this effect by reference to the incompatibility between the traditional fabric defect and shade variability and the inventory requirements and automated cutting implications of modern Quick Response strategies.

D.   The size and importance of the apparel manufacturing industry within the UK economy

(i)   An historical perspective

The main focus of this text is to be forward looking. However, it will be useful to review the evidence for the decline of the pipeline in the UK for two reasons. First, because any realistic attempts to formulate potential future policies must be grounded on an informed view of how the present situation has developed.

Second, because the literature is dominated by the history of the primary textile sector (and more especially by cotton textiles), it is important, from the point of view of this text with its emphasis upon the apparel manufacturing sector, to obtain a clear view of the relationship between the two sectors. The historical development of the textile and apparel manufacturing sector has been copiously documented elsewhere (Baines, 1966; Edwards, 1967; Kerridge, 1988; Rose, 1991; Singleton, 1991; Godley, 1996 and Rose, 1996) and will be referred to only briefly here. As Dicken (1998, p. 233) notes, the textile industry:

> 'was the archetypal industry of the industrial revolution of the eighteenth and nineteenth centuries in Britain. In some senses that industrial revolution was a textiles revolution.'

Similarly, Dickerson (1995, p. 22) observed that textile production

> 'became one of the earliest large scale economic activities that led the industrialisation process centuries ago.'

The clothing manufacturing industry developed later than the primary textile industry within the pipeline. In Briscoe's (1971, p. 8) words, 'the . . . cotton industry was the spearhead of the industrial revolution by which the . . . factory system was established' in the eighteenth century while the clothing industry's change-over to the factory system came later in the mid-nineteenth century, as has been observed above.

Unfortunately (from the point of view of the evolution and eventual decline of the UK industry) the same process of industrialisation was followed by many other countries. In Dickerson's (1995, p. 40) words, 'many additional countries imitated England . . . in using the textile sector as the first industry through which to pursue economic development'.

The reasons underlying this sequential process are well known: the industries in the textile pipeline are relatively simple technologically and they are relatively labour intensive (especially clothing production) and do not require vast injections of capital at initial stages. In Singleton's (1997, p. 31) words, the textiles industry 'is usually the first industry to become developed because it requires only modest amounts of skill and capital.'

There is, therefore, as Briscoe (1971, p. 2) says: 'a close association between industrialisation and the growth of the textile industry'.

The textile and apparel industries are, therefore, extremely attractive to developing countries seeking to industrialise. In addition, the textile–apparel pipeline has always been characterised by a strong element of international activity. Dicken (1998, p. 233) comments that these industries 'were perhaps the first manufacturing industries to take on a global dimension. They are the most geographically dispersed of all industries.' The fact that apparel production, particularly at the sewing stage, remains a labour intensive operation has been in large part responsible for the structural decline of the sector in most advanced countries.

Taplin & Winterton (1996, p. 2) in their major review of the reaction of developed countries to competition from low-wage regions observe that:

'clothing manufacture in the high wage economies is often regarded as a "sunset" industry undergoing rapid restructuring . . . leaving garment production to the newly industrialised low wage countries as part of an international division of labour.'

These issues will be considered in more detail in Chapter 3. At this point it is sufficient to note that apparel production has declined significantly in most developed countries. According to Briscoe (1971, p. 1) the peak of UK-based textile production was achieved in early 1913 with output falling by 27% by the early 1960s. The apparel manufacturing industry developed later as a factory-based industry in the UK, being associated essentially with the widespread introduction of Singer sewing machines from about 1850.

Statistics harder to obtain for apparel production but the same author concludes that employment in the UK apparel sector fell from 580,900 in 1923 to 390,000 in 1969. Godley (1996, p. 12) concluded that the gross output of the sector rose from £135 million to £198 million between 1907 and 1955 and that 'the emergence of mass production in the clothing industry was a phenomenon of the 1880s and 1890s rather than the 1930s and 1940s'. A number of indicators of the importance of textiles and apparel sectors over time have been summarised earlier in Fig. 1.2.

The role of the apparel industry in the UK economy is, therefore, historical rather than modern. Godley's (1996, p. 15) conclusion that the industry's 'importance to the economy was slowly declining (by 1951)' has been noted above. This decline essentially predated the emergence of large-scale imports in that the UK became a net importer of apparel in 1960. A watershed in the evolution of the industry was reached in the 1970s and early 1980s when, according to Winterton & Barlow (1996, p. 25) import penetration 'was perceived as a major problem'. It will be argued in Chapter 2 that the period 1995–2005 represented a second watershed when both output and employment collapsed together on a previously unprecedented scale. The most interesting question now is what the next stage of the evolution of the sector will look like – how will global sourcing be organised and what role will be left for apparel manufacturers based in the UK?

(ii)   The current situation

Table 1.11 summarises the relative importance of the sector in the UK in 2002. It can be seen that the industry accounts for only 2% of all manufacturing employment (which is itself as will be seen below a shrinking sector) and only 1% of the output. It is also responsible for under 2% of UK exports. Somewhat unexpectedly this figure equates to that achieved in 1830 when, according to Briscoe

Table 1.11   The relative importance of the apparel manufacturing industry within the UK economy (2002).

	Percentage of all manufacturing				% of exports
	Employment	Turnover	GVA	Investment	
Apparel	2.0	1.0	1.1	0.1	
Motor Vehicles	2.7	6.3	5.3	3.0	
Chemicals	7.2	10.8	11.4	15.7	
Food, Drink and Tobacco	14.0	17.0	14.4	18.6	
Pharmaceuticals	2.4	3.4	4.7	0.5	

Source: ONS Annual Business Inquiry (2004). The export figures were calculated from ONS UK Trade with the
    World (OTS A) (2003).

(1971, p. 77), clothing provided 2.0% of all UK exports in value terms – this equality may, in fact, be more coincidental than meaningful as the early figure predates the emergence of factory-based clothing production. The long-term trend in UK apparel exports is shown in Table 1.12.

At this point it is advisable to recognise that the observed fluctuations in the size and importance of any manufacturing industry in the UK have to be assessed within the context of changes that were taking place in the UK economy as a whole. Three such changes stand out. First, the relative decline in the importance of the *entire* manufacturing sector has to be recognised. Mathias (1969,

Table 1.12   UK apparel exports (including footwear) in £ millions.

Year	£ millions (current prices)
1959	46
1964	59
1970	157
1975	319
1980	938
1985	1,342
1991	2,238
1994	3,218
1997	3,864
1998	3,511
1999	3,336
2000	3,236
2001	3,186
2002	2,938

Source: *Annual Abstract of Statistics* (various issues).
Note: In real terms (at 1980 prices) the increase between 1975 and 1985
    was positive but smaller than recorded above. The increase after
    1987 would disappear if real (1987) prices were applied but this
    may not be sensible given the price deflation in the apparel
    market in recent times.

Table 1.13   Jobs by industry/sector 2003.

	Workforce jobs (thousands)	% change since 1998
Agriculture/forestry/fishing	233	−27.6
Real Estate	3,752	+9.6
Manufacturing	3,501	−16.6
Construction	1,145	+4.3
Services of which:	20,712	+10.5
Hotels/restaurants	1,818	+15.7
Transport/communications	1,549	+9.4
Finance	1,050	−25.3
Public Administration/education/health	6,561	+12.5
All jobs	25,794	+5.0

Source: ONS (2004b) *Annual Abstract of Statistics*, HMSO, London.

p. 223) produces data which demonstrate that the peak year for manufacturing as a sector in the UK economy occurred in 1861 at 41%. By 1907 the share of activity represented by manufacturing was down to 37%.

In terms of the UK's relations with the rest of the world the relative contribution of the manufacturing sector and other sectors is also illuminating. The current account was roughly in balance in the late 1990s. Trade in manufactured goods comprises the largest element of the current account and has been in deficit since 1983. Income from investment, by contrast, has been in surplus since 1946 while the service sector has had a positive balance since 1966. In 1998, the balance on trade in goods was a negative £20,865 millions, while that on services was a positive £12,253 millions (UK *Balance of Payments*, *Pink Book*, ONS, 1999a,b).

In 2003, of the just under 26 million people economically active in the UK only 13.6% were employed in manufacturing. As can be seen from Table 2.3 in 2002 the sector produced only 1.1% of the UK's Gross Value Added. Moore (1999, p. 23) noted that employment in 'manufacturing began to fall in 1966 at an accelerating rate . . . [and that it] declined precipitously over the three years 1979–82 when a fifth of manufacturing jobs disappeared.'

Table 1.14 reflects research by Rowthorn & Wells (1987) who, when writing about the de-industrialisation of Britain, pointed out that not only did the manufacturing sector lose 2.8 million jobs in the UK between 1966 and 1984, but that the percentage decline in the sector in the UK between 1950 and 1981 was much higher than in most other developed countries. His conclusion was (p. 248) that the UK's postwar decline in manufacturing employment 'has been an example of "negative de-industrialisation" (i.e. due to poor performance rather than inevitable structural change) compounded by the effect of changes in trade specialisation' but that, in the final analysis:

Table 1.14   Changes in employment by sector 1959–1981 (%).

Agriculture	−50.3
Manufacturing	−25.0
Private services of which	+22.9
Insurance/banking	+107.4
Public services	+60.0

Source: Rowthorn, R.E. & Wells, J.R., *De-industrialisation and Foreign Trade*, Cambridge University Press, Cambridge, p. 13.

'a large reduction in manufacturing employment was inevitable in postwar Britain, since the country was already on the verge of economic maturity in the 1950s. Manufacturing employment was bound to decline over the coming decades, no matter how bad or good the performance of British industry.'

Secondly, over the period 1950 to 1980 the UK's relative position in the world league table of manufacturing economies slumped drastically. A large number of factors have been held responsible for this decline, e.g. poor industrial relations; a failure of the banking system to support the manufacturing sector; the inadequacies of the education system and a cultural bias against manufacturing as a career; and government failure to support the sector. Owen (1999), in the latest review of the decline of the UK as a world power, points out that the UK share of world exports of manufactured products fell from 24.6% in 1950 to just 9.1% in 1973. However, his conclusion was that none of the conventional explanations was the central cause of this collapse. Owen (1999, p. 460) isolates the two primary causes of the UK's failure to compete effectively as being the decision 'to opt out of European integration in the 1950s' and the devotion of 'insufficient priority to competition as the main driver of higher productivity'.

Finally, as Eltis *et al.* (1978, p. 11) pointed out, there was in the UK between 1961 and 1975 a substantial collapse in the so-called 'market' sector of the UK economy in that 'employment outside industry increased by over 40% relative to employment in industry . . . and that this increase was most rapid in the public sector.'

The apparel manufacture sector falls, of course, within the 'market' sector of the economy. It is important, therefore, to be realistic in assessing the role of the sector and to recognise that even in historical terms the apparel manufacturing cell of the textile pipeline never was (other than in employment terms) a particularly major contributor to the UK economy. That role belonged – at least until just prior to the First World War – to the primary textiles element of the pipeline. As Briscoe (1971, p. 77) points out, in 1830 primary textiles accounted for some 67% of total UK exports and, in 1913, just over 30%. The UK clothing industry never was the dominant element in the pipeline other than in employment terms. It could well be that the tendency to use the word 'textiles' to encompass all the

Textiles and clothing	UK manufacturing sector
Inevitability of rapid industrialisation in other countries due to the labour-intensive nature of the sector and its role in the industrialisation process.	Inevitability of the production cycle in countries at varying stages of development.
	Poor productivity growth relative to other countries.
Lack of investment in new technology and in training.	Lack of investment; lack of support from the financial institutions.
Poor industrial relations.	Poor industrial relations.
Entrepreneurial failure; complacency; poor strategic choices made.	Short-sighted and inadequate management.
Too great a concentration on the wrong markets and on too low-quality products.	Loss of captive markets and complacency.
Lack of protection from 'unfair' import competition.	Lack of government support.
Lack of co-ordination in the supply chain; too great a reliance on the large retailers.	Failure of the educational system both in terms of general standards and in terms of a bias against manufacturing.

Fig. 1.4   The reasons for the decline of the UK industry.

products in the pipeline has produced not only a somewhat distorted view of the historical importance of the apparel sector, but also of the timing and extent of its decline. The major element whose spectacular collapse after 1913 has been taken as indicative of the demise of the UK textile sector as a whole was cotton textiles.

Many explanations have been advanced for the decline of the primary textile sector in the UK. There is, in fact, a relatively close correlation between the list of factors held to have been responsible for the textile sector and those responsible for the decline (in world terms) of the UK manufacturing sector as a whole – see Fig. 1.4 for a summary. In the case of the primary textile sector most commentators have isolated two factors. First, there was an over-concentration on low-quality goods and on one export market (India). Morrison (1996, p. 249) emphasises that increasingly in the late nineteenth century 'British exports were directed to less developed economies with lower consumer incomes and a predominant demand for coarse counts (low quality)' while Dupree (1996, p. 270) points out that in 1913 45% of UK cotton exports went to India and that, additionally,

'the Lancashire export trade in cotton piece goods was dependent in general on the bulk production of relatively low quality cloth – just the kind of product that was most exposed to competition from newly developing local industries in its overseas markets'.

Owen (1999), in his examination of the textile sector, also places some emphasis on the incorrect selection of markets, especially India, but contends that the main two pillars of the industry's response to low-cost competition turned out to be mistaken, *viz.* reliance upon protection and the attempt to generate scale economies through mergers in the 1960s. This latter policy was, according to Owen (1999, p. 76):

> 'based on a misreading of the market . . . Instead of a growing demand for standard, mass produced fabrics, European consumers wanted more differentiated, more colourful and more stylish fabrics. This called for flexibility . . . and quick response to changing fashions'.

Although Owen's analysis makes little reference to apparel manufacturing (other than as a consequence of demergers in the textile conglomerates) the same conclusions can be applied to apparel manufacture in that (Owen, 1999, p. 87) the dominance of the multiple retailers, especially Marks & Spencer, 'made it difficult for manufacturers to establish their own brands' and 'tended to reinforce the industry's attachment to long runs of relatively undifferentiated products'. Both of Owen's conclusions are supported by Moore (1999, p. 372) who also argues that de-industrialisation in the UK:

> 'was accelerated by Britain's entry to the EC . . . because imports from the other EC Member States ousted her home produced goods from her own market . . . so far from participating in a rapidly growing market, her rate of growth fell'

and (Moore, 1999, p. 266) that:

> 'the result of the domination of the market by large retailers meant a concentration on long runs of standardised products . . . in direct competition with imports from low wage countries'.

Second, most experts stress the role of what might be called the development cycle hypothesis – that most nations go through a cycle in which first agriculture and then manufacturing decline as the tertiary service sector expands. This view is, for example, reflected in the words of Singleton (1991, p. 231) when he wrote that Lancashire:

> 'dominated the world market for cotton textiles in Victorian times, largely as a result of its early industrialisation. But Britain possessed no unique advantages as a cotton textile producer. It was *inevitable* [present author's emphasis] that production facilities would be established overseas as the countries began to develop a manufacturing base'

Table 1.15   The relative size of the apparel and textile sectors 1923–1978 (employment in thousands).

Year	A Textiles	B Apparel	B as a percentage of A
1923	1,312	580	44
1932	1,271	605	48
1947	820	551	67
1958	952	648	68
1965	829	563	68
1971	681	510	75
1978	490	378	77

Source: Mitchell, B.R. (1988), *British Historical Statistics*, Cambridge University Press, Cambridge.

or in Briscoe's words (1971, p. 3):

'it will be argued that the growth and decline of the British textile industry is a reflection of the industrial development, first of Britain and then of overseas countries'.

In a similar vein Morrison (1996, p. 264) argues that Lancashire's problem in 1914:

'was in many ways over-development rather than under-development. There was no realistic way in which the cotton industry could be maintained at the size it had achieved'.

The clothing industry, in contrast, continued to expand for some 40 to 50 years after the decline in the primary textiles sector set in. In Levitt's words (1996, p. 183) 'whilst the cotton industry steadily declined, clothing production expanded until the 1960s'. This is demonstrated by the relative size (in employment terms) of the two sectors computed in Table 1.15.

As has been seen above (Table 1.10), imports of clothing into the UK did not really take off until the mid to late 1950s, at which point output was (Table 1.9) more or less constant. There is, somewhat unfortunately, a gap in the literature between the period up to the early 1950s which is well covered by Godley (1996) and the post 1980s, which is covered by Taplin & Winterton (1996). However, little seems to have been written about the experiences of the apparel manufacturing sector in the 1960s and early 1970s, other than as an element of changes made by the major textile conglomerates. It is generally accepted in the literature that the main cause of the industry's problems (that is, decline) was competition from imports. For example, Winterton & Barlow (1996, p. 34) wrote that:

'import penetration . . . has clearly had an enormous impact on the clothing industry in the UK. The global pressure has created successive crises which have been reflected in the long-run trends in output and employment'

Table 1.16   Net output of UK apparel sector 1954–1991.

Year	Output (£000)
1954	211,383
1958	233,155
1963	282,790
1973	458,702
1978	1,218,200
1983	1,560,000
1987	2,191,800
1988	1,430,600
1989	2,520,500
1990	2,622,600
1991	2,423,000

Source: Derived from Winterton (1996) in Taplin, I.M. & Winterton, R. (eds), 1996, *Restructuring Within a Labour Intensive Industry*, Avebury, Aldershot.

Notes: Winterton used a 1973 price deflator to obtain the real value outlined in the text. The application of a 1980 price base produces real values of £768,665 million in 1954 rising steadily up to £990,717 million in 1973. The late 1970s and early 1980s saw a fairly steady level of output followed by a substantial rise to £1,939,646 million in 1987 and a small decline to £1,180,209 million in 1991.

adding conclusively that:

'the crisis in the UK clothing industry can be directly attributed to the increase in imports'.

The same author does give net output data for the apparel sector for the period 1954 to 1991 which is produced in aggregate form in Table 1.16. Winterton & Barlow's (1996, p. 35) conclusion is that in terms of real output there was a 6% fall between 1954–63; a substantial rise (45%) between 1963–73; a fall in the 1970s followed by a large (34%) rise between 1983 and 1987. It has to be pointed out that these figures are not totally compatible with the official series of output figures for 1978–1998 supplied to the present author by the ONS and reproduced as Table 2.1 in Chapter 2. In this series the increase between 1983 and 1987 was only 12%.

In terms of employment Winterton & Barlow (1996, p. 35) identify the start of the 1970s as: 'a watershed which was followed by a steady decline. The fastest rate of decline occurred between 1978 and 1983, when employment fell by 31%.'

In this case the official series (see later, Table 2.1) confirms Winterton & Barlow's conclusion. As has been suggested above it is one of the main theses of the present text that the late 1990s represent a second watershed – but that in this case it is reflected in a decline of *both* output and employment. This theme will be developed further in Chapter 2.

Table 1.11 clarified earlier the position of the apparel industry relative to a selected number of other sectors, all of which might be regarded by an impartial observer as being significantly more important than apparel manufacture as contributors to the overall economic well-being of the nation. These facts are not stressed in order to minimise the problems caused to the industry in the UK by the rise in imports and reduction in employment which has occurred over the last 20 years (see later, Tables 2.1 and 2.5) but simply to place subsequent discussion of strategic responses which might be adopted into a realistic context. This completes the review of the evolution and decline of the textile–apparel pipeline in the UK economy. However, before proceeding to conduct (in Chapter 2) an examination of the structure of the modern apparel industry in the UK, it will be useful to review the theoretical basis upon which that examination will be carried out.

E. Examining an industry – a theoretical base

The aim of this book is to describe the current state of the UK apparel manufacturing sector; to identify its role in the textile–apparel supply chain; to explore the forces which have brought the industry to its present position and, finally, to explore and examine potential future strategies which will possibly condition the shape and size of the industry in the next decade. The development or evolution of an industry over time can be described statistically in terms of fluctuations in output and employment. Its performance can be described in terms of trends in prices, consumption, investment and trade. The shape of the industry can be analysed in terms of trends of various measures of specialisation, concentration and the size distribution of firms, for example. The danger of simply amassing statistics is that the observer will not be able to make any sense of an unstructured mass of data. The usual solution to this problem is to adopt some form of model within which facts can be assembled.

A number of competing models or frameworks exist which could be utilised in this task. First, there is the standard classical supply and demand model derived from traditional theoretical micro-economics. The role of this model is extremely controversial. The model is based upon a number of simplifying assumptions which cause its critics to describe it as being irrelevant in the real world. The supporters of the model argue that the only way to judge the validity of a model is to test its predictions – and they claim that the model can be shown to be correct in its predictions in thousands of instances. The model, in brief, forecasts price movements which follow from changes in the supply and demand for a product at an *aggregated* level, e.g. if the cotton crop fails supply falls and cotton prices rise. The role of this paradigm is controversial and is, in part, tied in with the equally controversial role of positivism in the natural sciences (see Section F). Supporters of the model argue that the task of a positive statement is to make correct predictions about the consequences of changes in circumstances (Friedman, 1962) while critics of the model point to the lack of realism in its assumptions. The model can be shown (Jones, 1976) to 'work' at a certain level of aggregation and will be employed in the present text to analyse such issues as the importance of tax on children's clothes and the impact of the legal minimum wage upon employment levels.

Second, and perhaps more promisingly, there is the industrial organisation (or industrial economics) model usually referred to as the Structure–Conduct–Performance (SCP) model. This has a number of attractions, not the least being that it can be used in both an analytical and a descriptive manner. This model has been developed within that branch of economics known as industrial economics or industrial organisation. According to Hay (1991, p. 3) 'the delineation of a specific area of economics under the title "industrial economics" is a phenomenon only of the last fifty years'. A review of the history of industrial economics is clearly beyond the scope of the present text and is covered thoroughly in Scherer & Ross (1990); Hay (1991); Martin (1993) and Stead (1996).

The modern evolution of industrial economics contains two threads – the provision of a framework within which to collect data and the development and refining of theoretical models which offer an improvement on the traditional microeconomic theory of the firm. In the words of Hay (1991, p. 17), the subject:

> 'is concerned not simply within adding descriptive material, or with elaborating largely deductive or prior theories, but with developing theories which recognise and incorporate the complexities of the real world . . .'

Much work in industrial economics has been concerned with statistical testing of associations between elements of industrial structure – notably the degree of concentration – and aspects of performance such as profits. Martin (1993) derides the adherents of this approach as 'regression runners'. In practice the results of the regression-based research have tended to be somewhat inconclusive, as will be seen in Chapter 2. In Hay's words (1991, p. 18) there remain very considerable uncertainties and 'relatively few concrete conclusions'. In addition, much of the work has, as already stated, been concerned with the impact of high degrees of seller concentration upon such issues as prices, profit margins and research activity. Much of this work is not immediately relevant to the apparel sector in which concentration levels remain very low. Nevertheless, as Scherer & Ross (1990, p. 6) conclude, there is a second use for the SCP model in that 'the paradigm is useful as a kind of hat rack for organising relevant facts'. It is from this standpoint that it is, therefore, useful to begin with the standard diagrammatic exposition of the model as is shown in Fig. 1.5. This framework will

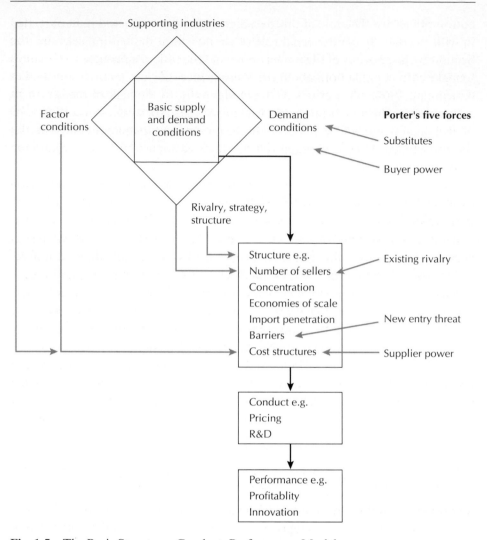

Fig. 1.5   The Basic Structure–Conduct–Performance Model.

provide a useful starting-point for the subsequent analysis of industrial structure in Chapter 2.

Two problems remain, namely that the role of international trade does not feature prominently in the model, and that, at least superficially, the model does not allow much role to the individual firm. For example, Scherer & Ross (1990, p. 1) state that the model 'has little to say directly about how one organises and directs a particular enterprise'. At first sight this could be seen as implying that the firm has no important role in the model. This would be a defect in examining potential strategies for the future. However, such a pessimistic view is not justified because while the industrial economics model may not be of use in analysing any *specific* firm, it is clear that the role of the firm as such has emerged in an enhanced position from the most recent research. Hay (1991, p. 261), for example, concludes his exhaustive review of the field with the statement that the conduct element in the SCP model has been driven into the foreground because it seems to play a greater than anticipated role in setting entry conditions and in uncovering the correct concentration to profit relationship. Therefore, the firm emerges as of much greater importance than before. Firms can no longer be viewed as merely units in the structure of an industry, passively accepting the constraints on performance which that structure determines. Rather they emerge as active players.

The second problem is more real – the relative lack of attention paid to international events in the model. It is significant that, in drawing a conclusion on the relationship between structure and profits, Hay (1991, p. 60) comments that 'a number of additional variables . . . and probably international trade are all important variables'. Martin (1993, p. 14), in his dauntingly rigorous review of the subject, comments that 'the intellectual apparatus of international economics is the jewel in the crown of economic theory' and does review the interaction between industrial and international economics in the sense that trade theories have borrowed from the former concepts of imperfect competition. However, even then the implications for the standard model of industrial economics (as described in Fig. 1.5) of introducing the international dimension are not explored. Stead (1996) incorporates a chapter on international trade in his survey of industrial economics, but is mainly concerned to explore explanations of the so-called intra-trade phenomenon (see Chapter 3). In the apparel industry (in which trade flows are a major influence on events) this is a significant weakness of the SCP model. For example, Singleton (1997, p. 1) shows that trade in textiles and clothing is conducted on a vast scale and accounted for nearly 10% of world manufactured exports in 1993.

One reaction would be to simply insert trade flows into the top box of Fig. 1.5, for example, as inputs into supply; or into the second box, in the case of trade barriers, as elements of barriers to entry. However, this does not give sufficient weight to trade influences in the industry. Therefore, another reaction might be to identify an alternative model which does give the required weight to the international dimension. Such a model can be found in the work of Porter (1998). This is usually called the 'diamond framework' and suggests that four factors determine the success of particular locations in promoting successful companies – demand conditions, factor conditions, the presence of related industries and rivalry between existing industries.

The Porter model starts with an analysis of industrial structure as outlined in the Five Forces Model which is represented by the right-hand component of Fig. 1.5 which makes the links between the five forces and the standard industrial economics framework clear. Porter (1998, p. 35) argues that the 'strength of the five competitive forces is a function of industry *structure*' (author's emphasis) and that these 'five competitive forces determine industry profitability'. The analysis is, therefore, rooted in the structural concept and there are clear points of contact between the two models as are shown in Figure 1.5 by the arrows connecting the two models.

In the Porter framework the Five Forces Model is utilised to explain the average level of profitability in an industry or sector. It indicates the ability of a sector to capture profits in the supply chain. In Singleton's words (1997, p. 3): 'the overall condition of the industry affects the prospects of individual firms'. In essence the model indicates the potential of a sector to capture a share of the profit generated within a pipeline. This is of particular interest to the present inquiry and will feature prominently in Chapter 3. The links between the Five Forces Model and the traditional SCP model are shown in Fig. 1.5. In Porter's view (1998, p. 34) the *industry structure* in which the firm competes is one of the major factors underlying competitive strategy.

The success of companies is, however, in part dependent on the selection of the correct strategy – within the confines set by the Five Forces Model. This is explained by the concept of Generic Strategies which identifies the choice between low use or product differentiation and broad or narrow market focus strategies as being crucial for success. It has already been noted that most commentators accept that one reason for the collapse of the cotton textile sector was that the UK industry concentrated for too long on low price/quality products.

The Five Forces Model is, therefore, essentially a structural concept and not in any real conflict with the SCP paradigm as such. It is, therefore, included on the right hand side of Fig. 1.5. However, it is in the final step in the construction of the Porter model that the previous absence of an international dimension is overcome. Porter argues (1998, p. 53) that: 'these principles of competitive strategy apply whether a firm is competing domestically or internationally'.

The vital international dimension is introduced via the so-called Diamond Framework which incorporates factor conditions, demand conditions, the strength of supporting industries and firm structure and rivalry. A basic issue is the role of place (Porter, 1998, p. 1):

> 'Why does a nation become the home base for successful international competitors . . . or . . . why are forms based in particular nations able to create and sustain competitive advantage?'

The four broad attributes of the Diamond noted above (Porter, 1998, p. 71) 'shape the environment in which local firms compete that promote or impede the creation of competitive advantage'.

The Diamond Framework overlaps both the basic conditions element of the SCP model and a number of the structural conditions traditionally included in that model as is shown in Fig. 1.5. The home base is seen as (Porter, 1998, p. 106) 'the location of many of the most productive jobs, the core technology and the most advanced skills . . . while the ownership of firms is often concentrated at the home base, the nationality of shareholders is secondary'.

However, it is vital that companies have a wide view of locational possibilities for different stages of the production processes so that they can, as required, negate any deficiencies of the Diamond Framework in their home base and reinforce the Diamond Framework through the use of other locations in which the advantages are greater.

The link between the Five Forces Model and the Diamond Framework is to be found, first, in a number of shared concepts such as domestic rivalry which appears both in the Five Forces Model and in the Diamond under the heading of Firm Strategy and Rivalry (Porter, 1998, p. 120), but, secondly, and more importantly in the concept of competitive advantage in that the basis structure (as expressed by the Five Forces Model) sets limits to the emergence of competitiveness in an industry. However, competitive advantage can also be created by international (as well as domestic) activity and it is this role of the nation in the evolution of international competitive advantage which is captured by the Diamond Framework (Jones, 2001).

This is not to say that there are no tensions between the two models, e.g. in the Five Forces Model fierce domestic rivalry erodes profits whereas in the Diamond Framework vigorous domestic rivalry creates competitive advantage. It must also be acknowledged that the Porter models have not been accepted uncritically. The concept of generic strategy has been criticised by, for example, Hendry (1990) and Hines (1999) on the grounds that there is very little empirical support for the concept; there are problems of defining the industry boundaries within which firms are competing and that differentiation itself is a difficult concept to define. The distinction between cost- and differentiation-based strategies is not always easy to maintain in practice.

Nevertheless, the present author believes that the model expressed in Fig. 1.5 will be the best framework within which an analysis of the UK apparel sector in the late 1990s can be conducted.

The SCP model will, accordingly, be utilised (in Chapter 2) as a *descriptive* device. In Singleton's words (1997, p. 3):

> 'the diamond is a *taxonomy* rather than a theory. It assists the investigator to arrange the evidence . . . The inclusiveness of the Diamond Framework does, however, mitigate against the adoption of iconoclastic explanations'.

This approach, therefore, accords with the decision to apply the traditional SCP model also in a large descriptive role.

The Porter model will be adopted in order to introduce the vital international dimension. There is, it must be admitted, an element of pragmatism involved in reaching these decisions in that at least two major studies of the textile–apparel supply chain have adopted the Porter model (Singleton (1997) and Koshy

(1997)), while Owen (1999) adopts a Porter-like stance in his analysis of UK industrial performance. The so-called 'double diamond' model (Moon *et al.*, 1995) has not been adopted as it seems to the present author to underplay the role of trade as outlined in the original Porter model.

F. Research philosophies

The examination of the UK apparel manufacturing sector which follows in subsequent chapters must, by definition, call upon the results of much previous research into various aspects of the industry's performance. The sector has been studied, over the years, from a variety of perspectives reflecting an equally wide range of research philosophies. The term 'research philosophy' refers to the general research methodology adopted in a piece of research.

The general approach adopted, in so far as it is possible, in the present text will be the so-called 'positivist' or 'logical empiricist' approach. In brief, the positivist approach attempts to utilise quantitative rather than qualitative data; tries to carry out controlled experiments or statistical tests; prefers an objective to a subjective view of events and chooses to test ideas using numerical research techniques. There is, as would be anticipated, a close link between positivism and quantitative analysis. In fact the two words are often used by commentators as if they were interchangeable – Bryman (1998, p. 40) for example, states that positivism 'reveals itself in quantitative research in particular in the emphasis on facts which are the products of observation'.

The positivist model is also closely aligned with the notion of causality, i.e. that certain events are caused by changes in various factors. This approach is widely used in industrial economics. An extreme view (but one that is widely held) is that, as Keat & Urry (1975, p. 7) express it: 'There is only one logic of science to which any intellectual activity aspiring to the title of "a science" must conform – that is positivism'. Adherents of this point of view argue that correct ideas can be defined as those which can be shown to have empirically refutable consequences.

In general terms this is the approach that will be adopted in the present text. However, in the context of the apparel industry it is not possible, or maybe even desirable, to adopt a rigidly extreme position regarding the admissability of other research paradigms. Apparel has a social context and dimension. Sociological research does tend to lean more heavily on alternative approaches such as phenomenology and ethnography. This is a somewhat controversial area of discussion as it can perfectly legitimately be argued (Hammersley & Atkinson, 1995, p. 10) that people 'do behave differently according to context'. Accordingly, alternative research modes such as the aforementioned approaches of ethnography and phenomenology might be appropriate. This conflict between competing research philosophies becomes most apparent in the area of fashion theory – see, for example, Chapter 10.

Finally, it has to be acknowledged that because, in industrial economics, controlled experiment is hardly ever possible, great reliance is thrown upon statistical investigations and interpretations. There is no concealing the fact that such tests are fraught with difficulties as, for example, statistical definitions change over time and data comparability becomes controversial. The current UK industrial statistical framework is described in Appendix A in which the PRODCOM system and the current Standard Industrial Classification are described.

References

Baines, E. (1966) *History of Cotton Manufacturing in Great Britain*. Frank Cass, London.

Banning, W. (1994) The Manufacturing and Retailing Conflict. *World Manufacturing Clothier*, **75**, 44–45.

Berg, M. (1994) *The Age of Manufacturing*. Routledge, London.

Briscoe, L. (1971) *The Textile and Clothing Industries of the UK*. Manchester University Press, Manchester.

Bryman, A. (1998) *Quantity and Quality in Social Research*. Routledge, London.

Deane, P. & Cole, W.A. (1969) *British Economic Growth*. Cambridge University Press, Cambridge.

Dicken, P. (1998) *Globalshift: Transforming the World Economy*. Paul Chapman, London.

Dickerson, K. (1995) *Textiles and Apparel in the Global Economy*. Prentice-Hall, New Jersey.

Dupree, M. (1996) Foreign Competition in the Inter War Period. In: *The Lancashire Cotton Industry* (Ed. M. Rose), pp. 265–96. Lancashire County Books, Preston.

Easey, M. (Ed.) (1995) *Fashion Marketing*. Blackwell Science, Oxford.

Edwards, M.M. (1967) *The Growth of the British Cotton Trade*. Manchester University Press, Manchester.

Eltis, W. & Bacon, R. (1978) *Britain's Economic Problem*. Macmillan, London.

EMAP Fashion (1998/99) *The UK Fashion Report*. Market Tracking International, London.

Forza, C. & Vinelli, A. (2000) Time Compression in Production and Distribution within the Textile Apparel Chain. *Integrated Management Systems*, **11.2**, 138–46.

Fowler, A. & Wyke, T. (1993) *Many Arts – Many Skills*. Manchester Metropolitan University Press, Manchester.

Fraser, G.L. (1948) *Textiles by Britain*. Allen and Unwin, London.

Friedman, M. (1962) *Price Theory*. Cassell, London.

Godley, A. (1996) The Emergence of Mass Production in the UK Clothing Industry. In: *Restructuring Within a Labour Intensive Industry* (Eds I. Taplin & J. Winterton), pp. 8–25. Avebury, Aldershot.

Haines, P. (1990) Improving the Link Between Fabric Suppliers and Garment Manufacturers. *Clothing Technology Centre*, **11**.

Hammersley, M. & Atkinson, P. (1995) *Ethnography – Principles and Practice*. Routledge, London.

Hay, D.A. (1991) *Industrial Economics – Theory and Evidence*. Oxford University Press, Oxford.

Hendry, J. (1990) The Problem with Generic Strategies. *European Management Journal*, **8**, 443–51.

Hines, T. (1999) *Management Information for Marketing Decisions*. Butterworth-Heinemann, Oxford.

Howarth, J. (1990) Information Technology in Overdrive. *Apparel International*, **18.4**, 33–5.

Hunter, A. (1990) *Quick Response in the US Apparel Industry*. Textile Institute, Manchester.

Jones, R.M. (1976) *Supply in a Market Economy*. George Allen and Unwin, London.

Jones, R.M. (1997) Editorial. *Journal of Fashion Marketing and Management*, **1.1**, 5–6.

Jones, R.M. (2001) Porter's Clusters, Industrial Districts and Local Economic Development. *Journal of Fashion Marketing and Management*, **5.3**, 181–87.

Keat, R. & Urry, J. (1975) *Social Theory as Science*. Routledge, London.

Kerridge, E. (1988) *Textile Manufacture in Early Modern England*. Manchester University Press, Manchester.

Koshy, D.O. (1997) *Garment Exports – Winning Strategies*. Prentice-Hall, New Delhi.

Kurt Salmon Associates (KSA) (2005) *Global Sourcing Reference*, 7th edition. ITSA, Manchester.

Levitt, S. (1996) Clothing. In: *The Lancashire Cotton Industry* (Ed. M. Rose), pp. 154–76. Lancashire County Books, Preston.

Martin, S. (1993) *Advanced Industrial Economics*. Blackwell Publishers, Oxford.

Mathias, P. (1969) *The First Industrial Revolution*. Methuen, London.

Miles, C. (1968) *Lancashire Textiles: A Case Study of Industrial Change*. Cambridge University Press, Cambridge.

Mitchell, B.R. & Deane, P. (1962) *Abstract of British Historical Statistics*. Cambridge University Press, Cambridge.

Moon, H.C., Rugman, A.M. & Verbeke, A. (1995) The Generalized Double Diamond Approach to International Competitiveness. In A. Rugman, J. Van Den Broeck and A. Verbeke (Eds), *Research in Global Strategic Management: Vol 5: Beyond the Diamond* (pp. 97–114). JAI Press, Greenwich, CT.

Moore, L. (1999) *Britain's Trade and Economic Structure: The Impact of the EU*. Routledge, London.

Morrison, A. (1996) Indian Summer. In: *The Lancashire Cotton Industry* (Ed. M. Rose), pp. 238–65. Lancashire County Books, Preston.

Nagasawa, R., Kaiser, S. & Hutton, S. (1995) Construction of an SI Theory of Fashion. *Clothing and Textiles Research Journal*, **13**, 172–84.

OECD (1983) *Textile and Clothing Industries – Structural Problems and Policies in OECD Countries*. OECD, Paris.

ONS (1999a) *Sector Review*. HMSO, London.

ONS (1999b) *Balance of Payments, Pink Book*. HMSO, London.

ONS (2004a) *Annual Business Inquiry*. HMSO, London.

ONS (2004b) *Annual Abstract of Statistics*. HMSO, London.

Owen, G. (1999) *From Empire to Europe*. Harper Collins, London.

Porter, M. (1998) *The Competitive Advantage of Nations*. Free Press, New York.

Rath, P. (1994) *An Introduction to Fashion Merchandising*. McGraw Hill, New York.

Rogers, D.S. & Gamans, L.R. (1983) *Fashion: A Marketing Approach*. Holt, Rinehart & Winston, New York.

Rose, M. (1991) *International Competition and Strategic Response*. Frank Cass, London.

Rose, M. (1996) *The Lancashire Cotton Industry*. Lancashire County Books, Preston.

Rowthorn, R.E. & Wells, J.R. (1987) *De-industrialisation and Foreign Trade*. Cambridge University Press, Cambridge.

Saul, S.B. (1960) *Studies in British Overseas Trade*. Liverpool University Press, Liverpool.

Scherer, F.M. & Ross, D. (1990) *Industrial Market Structure and Economic Performance*. Houghton Miflin, Boston.

Singleton, J. (1991) *Lancashire on the Scrap Heap*. Oxford University Press, Oxford.

Singleton, J. (1997) *World Textile Industry*. Routledge, London.

Sproles, G. (1981) Analysing Fashion Life Cycles – Principles and Perspectives. *Journal of Marketing*, **45**, 116–24.

Stead, R. (1996) *Industrial Economics*. McGraw Hill, London.

Stone, B. (1990) *Fashion Marketing*. McGraw Hill, New York.

Taplin, I. & Winterton, J. (1996) *Restructuring Within a Labour Intensive Industry*. Avebury, Aldershot.

Taylor, M. (1990) *Technology of Textile Properties*. Forbes Press, London.

Winterton, R. & Barlow, A. (1996) Economic Restructuring of UK Clothing. In: *Restructuring Within a Labour Intensive Industry* (Eds I. Taplin & J. Winterton), pp. 25–61. Avebury, Aldershot.

Chapter 2

The Apparel Industry in the UK – Current Size and Structure

A. The current size of the sector

The experience of the period 1978–2004 is summarised in Table 2.1 in terms of output and employment. Although this table is presented as an index so as to highlight trends, it can be noted that the official number of employees in the sector in 1998 was 118,547 as compared to 294,157 in 1978, and that by 2005 it had fallen to 46,000. A full set of figures, together with an explanation of their sources is given in Appendix B.

It can be seen from Table 2.1 that it was possible to argue, for the period 1978–1988 at least, that while employment was falling this did not necessarily represent the demise of apparel production in the UK because output was not on a consistent downward trend. In this respect the UK apparel industry seemed to have been adopting different strategies to many of its continental neighbours such as France, Germany and the Netherlands. Scheffer (1992, p. 193), for example, argues that it is possible to identify quite different approaches to the same problem in these countries, with Germany concentrating on offshore production while the UK stuck somewhat rigidly to producing long runs for major retailers.

However, Table 2.1 seems to reveal a new scenario post 1994 in that both employment and output seem to be in parallel decline. This is more clearly seen in Fig. 2.1. It will, therefore, be one of the main themes of this text that the UK had, in the mid-1990s, entered a new phase in the evolution of apparel manufacturing – one in which the UK had caught up with continental neighbours (such as France, Germany and the Netherlands) in the development of offshore production and in which, as a result, the gap between the UK-based apparel industry and the apparel industry **in the UK** will become progressively wider. In other words, it appears increasingly probable that the mid-1990s was emerging as a second watershed in the evolution of the sector. In contrast to the period between the early 1970s and the late 1980s when there was (Winterton & Barlow, 1996, p. 27) a 'profound operational restructuring which has involved both a dramatic contraction (in employment) and an increase in value added per worker', a new

Table 2.1 Indices of output and employment, UK apparel sector, 1978–2004 (1985 = 100).

Year	Output	Employment
1978	105.4	133.6
1979	107.0	133.0
1980	96.0	117.0
1981	88.7	103.7
1982	88.6	98.5
1983	91.6	97.0
1984	94.9	97.4
1985	100.0	100.0
1986	101.0	98.0
1987	102.0	98.5
1988	100.0	98.4
1989	96.6	94.0
1990	97.4	85.0
1991	88.0	71.2
1992	90.3	66.8
1993	90.0	70.3
1994	94.0	67.7
1995	91.4	65.7
1996	89.5	63.9
1997	83.9	60.9
1998	77.8	56.3
1999	70.5	49.0
2000	69.7	47.4
2001	61.2	43.2
2002	55.7	38.2
2003	52.8	24.8
2004	45.6	21.0
2005	N/A	17.8

Source: Appendix B.

Note: (1) The conversion to a 1985 base was made by the author in the belief that this gives a more realistic picture of the changes that have taken place.

scenario has developed in which both employment and output have moved into parallel decline as the rush offshore gathers pace.

It seems likely that the somewhat pessimistic view expressed by Winterton & Winterton (1997, p. 27), while startling enough in itself, almost certainly does not represent the end of the story:

'The trend of employment in UK clothing is particularly striking. The overall trend is downwards, but for a temporary upturn after 1983 . . . Between 1973 and 1993 employment declined by 53%. The latest figures suggest that the decline in clothing employment has accelerated, with the rate of attrition increasing after 1988'.

The latest employment figure for 2005 (see Appendix B) is, as has been noted, 46,000. This compares with a peak figure (Godley, 1996) of 796,300 in 1911.

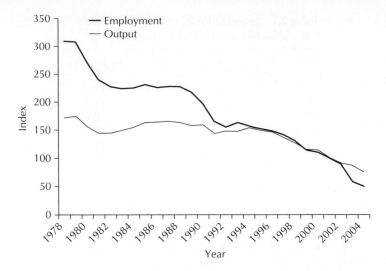

Fig. 2.1   Trends in output and employment.

Table 2.2   The size of the apparel manufacturing industry in the UK.

	1998	2000	2003
Enterprises (number)	7,630	6,330	4,838
Turnover (£ million)	6,945	5,574	4,430
Gross value added (£ million)	2,723	2,171	1,506
GVA per head (£)	17,019	16,829	23,531
Employment (000)	160	129	64
Wages (£ million)	1,666	1,206	854
Wages per head (£)	10,413	9,349	13,344
Net capital expenditure (£ million)	132	58	45
NCE per head (£)	825	450	703

Source: Annual Business Inquiry available from www.statistics.gov.uk.
Note: Data on sales, net and gross output are no longer available.

Between 1994 and 2004 employment fell by 69%. This decline has been accompanied by two notable changes: first, the traditional dominance of the labour force by female employees has disappeared (Labour Market Trends, 2005) and, second, the size distribution of companies appears to have changed.

Table 2.2 shows absolute size of the apparel industry (in terms of enterprises, output, employment and capital expenditure) while its relative importance is given in Tables 2.3 and 2.4. Apparel manufacture, in 2005, provided 1.4% of all jobs in the UK manufacturing sector. This compares with the Food and Beverages Industry at 13.5% and the Motor Vehicle Industry at 6.1% (ONS, 2005a). Clearly the 'importance' of the entire textile pipeline as an employer (as shown in Fig. 1.1) was much greater. The manufacturing sector, it should be recalled, was responsible for only 12.5% of all employment in the UK in 2004. In terms of

Table 2.3   The relative importance of apparel manufacturing in the UK (% of UK).

	A		B		C
	1996	2002	1996	2002	2004
Apparel (DB 18)	3.8	1.6	1.8	1.1	1.4
Motor Vehicles (DM 34)	5.8	6.0	6.8	5.3	12.1
Chemicals (DG 24)	6.3	6.7	11.0	11.4	18.6
Food and Beverages (DA 15)	11.5	13.3	12.5	13.6	5.2
Pharmaceuticals (DG 24.4)	1.5	2.2	3.0	4.7	7.5

Sources: ONS (1996) PA 1002 Manufacturing Summary Tables; 2002 from www.statistics.gov.uk/abi; 2004 ONS
Business Monitor, M 10 (June 2005).
Notes: A = Employment.
B = Gross Value Added.
C = Manufacturing Exports.

output, the apparel manufacturing sector, in 2002, contributed only 1.1% of all manufacturing value added – whereas the Motor Vehicles' share was to 5.3% and that of Food and Beverages was 13.6%. The labour-intensive nature of apparel production (which will be discussed more thoroughly below and in Chapter 4) is hinted at by the figures for capital investment in Table 2.4. The figure of £45 million in 2003 (Table 2.2) represents only 0.7% of the total for all manufacturing. Capital expenditure per head in the apparel sector in 2003 amounted to approximately £703 against the average for the manufacturing sector of £3,633. In the Food, Motor Vehicles and Chemical sectors respectively, the figures were £4,782, £8,484 and £8,460 (Table 2.4).

The Annual Business Inquiry tables also reveal some of the other problems which underlay the performance of the sector in the UK. As can be seen in Table 2.4 the industry, by a wide range of accepted measures, does not appear in a good light, e.g. the average employment cost in 2003 was 56% of the average;

Table 2.4   Operating ratios (2003).

Measure	All manufacturing	Apparel	Motor Vehicles	Chemicals	FBT
GVAPH (£)	40,553	23,531	35,158	65,426	43,882
TPH (£)	126,640	69,219	314,284	211,787	159,684
NCEPH (£)	3,633	703	8,484	8,460	4,782
ECPUT (£)	18.9	19.3	10.1	15.6	13.5
CCPUT (£)	2.9	1.0	2.7	4.0	3.0
PPUT	0.8	1.4	0.3	0.5	0.6

Source: ONS (2003) *Annual Business Inquiry* available at http://statistics.gov.uk/abi.
Notes: (1)   GVAPH = Gross Value Added Per Head.
(2)   TPH = Turnover Per Head.
(3)   NCEPH = Net Capital Expenditure Per Head.
(4)   ECPUT = Employment Costs Per £100 of Turnover.
(5)   CCPUT = Capital Costs Per £100 of Turnover.
(6)   PPUT = People Employed Per £100 of Turnover.
(7)   FBT = Food Beverages and Tobacco.
(8)   Average employment cost was £24,030 p.a. and £13,343 in apparel.

turnover per head achieved was 55% of the average and only 22% of that achieved in the motor vehicle industry. Many of these features are linked: the low level of output and the low level of investment all reflect the relative lack of technological sophistication in the sector.

These statistics are not provided in order to paint the industry in a poor light, nor to imply that, for example, the operatives do not work hard. The facts noted here help to explain why the industry has declined in the UK and make it quite clear how daunting a task is faced in endeavouring to survive within a UK base. Government support is, for example, linked to the perceived 'importance' of the sector – and yet by most measures the apparel manufacturing sector appears either to be somewhat insignificant or to be lagging behind other industries. The motor vehicle industry, for example, exported £20,696 million of product from the UK in 2004 whereas the apparel sector exported £2,343 million. Exports per head were over six times greater than in the apparel industry (ONS, 2005b).

It is probable that figures like this weigh heavily with governments when they have to decide whether or not to support an industry – as was the case with the Rover plant in the Midlands in 2005. Additionally, despite the fact that the industry's wage level is low by UK standards (as can be seen above), it is relatively high by Asian standards. Therefore, the ability of the industry to make itself more attractive to employees is very severely restricted. The figures for capital investment reflect the labour-intensive nature of apparel production – especially at the assembly stage. The cost structure of the sector is considered in greater detail in Section D below, but it can be noted at this point that the degree of labour intensity in the industry is one of, if not the, defining feature of the sector without reference to which the recent experience of the industry cannot really be understood.

Although there is always a danger of confusing short-term trends with significant long-term breaks in a sequence of events, the argument being advanced is that apparel production, in the late 1990s, exhibited a significant failure to recover output post 1990 (itself a recession year) against a background of overall recovery in the UK economy – see Table 2.5 – and that this failure is indicative of a long-term break with trends exhibited in the recent past. This conclusion would be supported by the following evidence: an examination of pronouncements in the trade press in the period from autumn 1998 through to autumn 1999 in which a number of major apparel manufacturers, often under pressure from retail customers, announced closures of capacity in the UK and an increase of offshore activity; that output has fallen by 53% since 1990; that employment has fallen by 75% since 1990 and by 63% since 1998; that the rate of import penetration (see Chapter 5) has reached 92% and is on a rising trend, and the number of enterprises in the sector fell by 44% between 1995 and 2003 (ONS, 2004). There is no way of establishing what fraction of the industry's decline is due to companies ceasing to trade as opposed to apparel production.

Table 2.5   Index of production 1993–1998 (1995 = 100).

Year	All manufacturing	Clothing
1993	99.0	93.0
1999	98.9	115.3
2002	96.9	91.0
2003	97.4	86.4
2004	98.8	74.5

Source: ONS (1998), *Sector Review: Clothing Leather and Footwear Goods*
  and *Labour Market Trends* various issues.
Notes: (1)   1993 based on 1995 = 100.
        (2)   1999–2004 based on 2001 = 100.

One would not have to be a subscriber to the view of economics as the dismal science to envisage a scenario in which a combination of cheap imports from Asia, the entry of China into the WTO, the final removal of quotas, and a change to off-shore production superimposed upon an already severe decline experienced in the period 1994–2004 all combined to produce an extremely difficult situation for UK-based apparel manufacturers. At the very least it would be quite a different industry to that which existed 25 years ago. It might be objected that all industries can expect to face different circumstances as time moves on – the question is how severe are the differences and how well placed is the industry to deal with them. These are the sorts of issues to be examined in subsequent chapters.

As has been noted (from Table 2.1), employment has fallen more or less consistently year on year from 1978. As Winterton & Barlow (1996, p. 35) observed:

'employment in the clothing industry had declined to 42% of the 1954 level by 1991 . . . and the plateau period at the start of the 1970s formed a watershed which was followed up by steady decline. The fastest rate of decline occurred between 1978–1983, when employment fell by 31%. After a slight upturn in the period 1987–88 the decline has continued'.

These trends are reflected in Table 2.1. The trend in output has followed a far less predictable path and has *not* been in a consistently downward direction. After a period of decline between 1954 and 1963 there was a 45% increase between 1963 and 1973 (Winterton & Barlow, 1996, p. 35) and another substantial increase between 1983 and 1987. The link between output and employment is, clearly, productivity or output per head.

The issue of the trend in output per head (productivity) can be examined from two angles: (a) the trend in productivity within the industry itself; and (b) the trend in productivity relative to the average trend in all manufacturing.

The second issue can only be examined in the official statistics from the point of view of textiles, clothing, leather and footwear as one sector as against manufacturing as a whole and the results are given in Table 2.6. Unfortunately the series has been re-based five times over the period 1970–2004.

Table 2.6   Productivity in the UK apparel sector.

	All manufacturing	Textiles, leather and clothing
A 1975 = 100		
1970	89	84
1972	96	93
1973	104	101
1975	100	100
1976	105	105
1977	107	107
1978	108	110
1979	109	113
1980	105	105
1981	109	111
1982	115	113
B 1980 = 100		
1978	103.4	103.7
1980	100.0	100.0
1981	103.5	106.5
1982	110.4	112.2
1983	119.8	121.2
1984	126.4	125.0
1985	130.6	128.4
1986	133.8	131.2
C 1985 = 100		
1980	76.6	77.9
1982	84.5	87.4
1984	97.0	97.4
1985	100.0	100.0
1986	103.5	104.4
1987	109.8	102.0
1988	116.2	102.9
1989	120.9	107.7
1990	122.8	109.7
1991	124.6	114.1
D 1990 = 100		
1986	84.6	91.9
1988	94.2	95.3
1989	98.1	94.5
1990	100.0	100.0
1991	101.2	99.3
1992	105.8	101.2
1993	109.8	98.5
1994	115.1	97.8
E 2001 = 100		
1998	112.7	149.2
2000	104.8	118.2
2003	90.9	76.1

Source: A–D Employment Gazette; E from *Monthly Digest of Statistics* and *Labour Market Trends* various issues.

Table 2.7   Long run productivity trends (1975 = 100).

	All manufacturing	Textiles, Clothing; Leather & Footwear
1970	89	84
1975	100	100
1980	105	105
1982	116	118
1984	132	131
1985	138	134
1990	168	142
1994	193	139

Source: Table 2.6 – author's own calculations.

In the late 1970s and early 1980s the UK apparel industry experienced a burst of productivity improvement which exceeded that achieved in UK manufacturing as a whole – see Table 2.6 in which sections B and C are of most interest in the present context. The periods 1978–81 and 1980–83 seem to have been particularly significant.

Previous commentators have identified the period 1954–1991 as one of significant productivity increase in the textile sector (Winterton & Barlow, 1996, p. 35), singling out as especially significant the years 1963–73 and 1978–87. This latter period matches that identified in Table 2.6. In a later publication (Winterton & Winterton, 1997, p. 27) identified the period between 1973 and 1993 as one in which productivity rose by 285% as opposed to an increase of only 61% in the previous decade. Irrespective of minor variations in isolated time periods it is clear that the industry experienced a surge of productivity growth from the late 1970s through the mid-1980s. This would conform with the findings of Harris & Trainer (1997) that productivity growth in the UK regions between 1968 and 1991 was highest after 1979 and that the peripheral regions (in which much of the apparel industry is located) did better in the 1980s than in any other decade.

As can be seen from Table 2.7, however, in terms of the relative performance of the sector over the long period the textile sector, widely defined, performed only moderately well. Productivity actually fell between 1990 and 1994 and again between 2000 and 2004. This is confirmed by the data in sections D and E in Table 2.6.

In terms of the apparel sector alone (as opposed to the textile sector widely defined) an alternative view of productivity might be obtained by combining the two series in Table 2.1. The result of this calculation is shown in Table 2.8 which tends to confirm that the late 1980s and early to mid-1990s were periods of rapid productivity growth. This series has the virtue of producing a figure for the apparel sector only. These were periods when total output was still stuck at 1978

Table 2.8 Productivity trends – an alternative view.

Year	Employment (A) (000s)	Productivity (B ÷ A)	Output (B) (as an index)
1978	203.5	0.53	108.8
1979	202.6	0.55	110.9
1980	178.5	0.56	99.9
1981	158.0	0.59	92.6
1982	150.0	0.62	93.4
1983	147.6	0.65	96.4
1984	158.6	0.69	102.3
1985	152.3	0.72	109.4
1986	148.9	0.74	109.7
1987	150.0	0.74	110.7
1988	149.7	0.73	109.0
1989	143.1	0.74	105.3
1990	129.5	0.82	106.2
1991	108.4	0.88	95.9
1992	101.7	0.97	98.5
1993	107.1	0.92	98.2
1994	103.1	0.99	102.7
1995	100.0	1.00	100.0
1996	97.3	1.05	102.1
1997	92.7	1.00	92.7
1998	85.7	0.97	82.9

levels. The fact that the greatest increases in productivity growth seemed to be occurring during periods of time when total output was *not* growing (or was even contracting) might be regarded as of some significance in that it could be argued that the recorded increases in output per head (productivity) owed less to any real improvement in technology and more to the fact that the relatively low (value) productivity functions were moving out of the UK leaving the relatively high value added jobs behind. Temple & Urga (1997), in their study of the competitiveness of the UK manufacturing sector, argue that: 'the evidence from imports does not suggest major improvements in the competitiveness of UK manufacturing'.

It should be noted that studies of the relative international productivity performance of the sector have normally found the UK industry to have performed rather poorly relative to other countries. Steadman & Wagner (1989, p. 41) in their comparison of the UK and German industries found that over a twenty-year period 'the value of net output produced per employee was greater in Germany than in Britain' and that, while the gap was narrowing, it reflected a real German advantage in quality which was related to their policy of producing smaller runs of higher quality products (see Chapter 7).

As will be seen in Chapter 3, the virtually unanimous conclusion from academic studies of employment change in the apparel and textiles sector in a range of periods and countries has been that the main cause of job loss was not import competition but productivity change. It would not appear plausible to argue the same point for the UK apparel sector in the period after 1985. This issue will be considered in greater detail, as indicated, in Chapter 3.

In summary, therefore, the picture which emerges from Table 2.6 in particular is of a steady rise in productivity (by UK standards) within the industry itself over the entire period from 1978 to 1998. Productivity rose significantly. Particularly large increases were recorded in the second half of the 1980s when output was still more or less at the 1978 level but employment was down by some 30 points or by some 80,000 (Appendix B).

Similarly, there were a few years in the 1990s (such as 1994 and 1996) when output rose towards the 1978 level but employment continued to fall so that productivity surged. As output itself dropped quite severely in the late 1990s productivity also fell especially after 2000. In terms of its relative productivity performance the textile sector widely defined enjoyed its best periods between 1978–83 and 1980–85. After 1985 the rate of increase in productivity within the sector fell badly behind that in UK manufacturing as a whole; became negative after 1990 and declined severely after 2000.

B. The sectoral division of the apparel industry

The industry can be sub-divided according to the type of garment manufactured. Table 2.9 is based on Winterton & Barlow (1996, p. 29) and is based on the old Standard Industrial Classification (1980). It can be seen that the Women's and Girls' Light Outerwear (4536) sector was historically the largest. In proportionate terms there have not been many significant changes over the period 1983–91. The largest sector has lost ground marginally while the two male

Table 2.9   Size of each sector (as percentage of whole).

	1983	1985	1988	1991
Weatherproof outerwear (4531)	5.8	5.8	6.8	6.5
Men's and boys' tailored outerwear (4532)	14.0	13.7	14.5	14.4
Women's and girls' tailored outerwear (4533)	13.7	10.6	11.8	12.3
Work clothing and men's and boys' jeans (4534)	8.2	8.6	9.1	9.3
Men's and boys' shirts, underwear, nightwear (4535)	9.1	10.6	11.5	12.9
Women's and girls' light outerwear, lingerie and infants' wear (4536)	37.5	37.4	35.7	32.8
Other dress industries (4538)	11.6	10.9	10.8	11.6

Source: Taplin (1996, p. 29).
Note: Figures are based on sales value.

related sectors (4534 and 4535) have made some small proportionate gain. Winterton & Barlow (1996, p. 28) relate these changes to sectoral differences in import penetration, stating that:

> 'the two sectors which are experiencing the highest rate of import penetration are the same sectors which appear to be shrinking as a proportion of the total industry, *viz*. sectors 4533 and 4536 in which according to figures reproduced by Winterton (1996, p. 27) the rate of import penetration rose by 89% and 75% respectively.'

At first sight this conclusion seems to clash with another statement by Winterton & Winterton (1997, p. 28) that:

> 'disaggregated statistics show that between 1973 and 1991, the women's sectors increased as a proportion of the total for clothing manufacture, while men's clothing came to account for a correspondingly smaller proportion of net output.'

The reason for the difference is, the present author suspects (apart from the slight variation in time period), that Table 2.9 is based on sales value while the latter statement is based on output data.

The latest available official statistics are presented in Table 2.10. These figures conform to SIC (1992) and are given in terms of employment, and value added. Unfortunately, the sub-sectors in the 1992 SIC do not match neatly to those in the 1980 SIC.

It is, therefore, extremely difficult to assess trends at a sub-sectoral level over time with any degree of confidence. Jones (2002) estimated that between 1991 and 1996 there had been a marginal fall in the importance of women's wear which, nevertheless, remained the major sector. The latest statistics (Table 2.10) are, unfortunately, not given in the same format.

Table 2.10   Sectoral divisions, 2003.

Sector	Employment		Gross Value Added	
	(000)	(%)	(£M)	(%)
Other wearing apparel and accessories (18.2)	63	98.4	1,477	98.1
Workwear (18.21)	7	10.9	152	10.0
Other outerwear (18.22)	24	37.5	722	47.9
Underwear (18.3)	9	14.1	222	14.7
Other wearing apparel and accessories NES (18.24)	23	35.9	381	25.2

Source: ONS (2004) Annual Business Inquiry available at http://statisics.gov.uk.
Notes: (1)   Percentages are of SIC 18.
(2)   Figures may not sum to 100%.
(3)   The figures for 18.21, 18.22 and 18.24 are parts of the figure for 18.2.

Table 2.11   Regional specialisation in the UK Apparel Industry
1851–1911 by location quotient.

Region	1851		1881		1911	
	M	F	M	F	M	F
London	1.6	1.8	1.5	1.6	2.2	1.8
S. East	0.7	1.0	0.8	0.9	0.7	0.8
S. Midlands	0.8	0.8	0.8	0.8	0.9	1.0
Eastern	0.8	1.0	0.7	1.0	0.7	1.1
S. West	0.9	1.2	1.0	1.3	0.9	1.2
W. Midlands	0.9	1.0	0.8	0.9	0.8	0.9
N. Midlands	1.0	1.0	0.9	1.0	0.7	0.9
N. West	1.0	0.9	0.9	0.9	0.9	1.0
Yorkshire	1.1	0.9	1.1	0.8	1.3	1.0
Northern	1.0	0.8	1.1	0.8	0.6	0.6
Wales	0.9	0.7	1.0	0.9	0.7	0.9
GB	1.0	1.0	1.0	1.0	1.0	1.0

Source: Godley, A. (1996) in I. Taplin & J. Winterton (eds) *Restructuring Within a Labour
Intensive Industry*, Avebury, Aldershot.

Notes: (1)   The location quotient is the density of apparel employment in a region divided
by that for England and Wales as a whole.
(2)   Therefore, figures over 1 indicate that the industry is prominent in a region.
(3)   M = male; F = female.

C. Regional distribution of the industry

The historical specialisation of the UK regions in the apparel industry is well
covered by Godley (1996). Table 2.11 shows the regional specialisation of
employment in 1851, 1881 and 1911. Godley (1996) argues that a greater insight
can be obtained by considering the role of urban centres and that, by 1911, four
such centres were of paramount importance – the East End of London, Leeds,
Manchester and Bristol. In Godley's view:

'the logic of growth also meant that once the relative position of firms and
regional centres had been established they were not going to alter, at least not
until the rather more dramatic changes of the 1960s and 1970s'.

The picture is brought more up to date in Table 2.12, which is derived from
Briscoe (1971, Table 20). This table suggests that by 1961 the three most important regions were London, Yorkshire and the North West.

The most recent comparable figures are for 1996 and are given in Table 2.13.
This table reveals one significant change in the regional distribution of apparel
manufacture in the UK – the rise in importance of the East and West Midlands.
This change is generally attributed to the re-emergence of the so-called ethnic
apparel industry. As Winterton (1997, p. 31) observes, substantial increases were:

Table 2.12 Regional distribution of employment in apparel, 1939–1961 (%).

Region	1939	1950	1961
London and South East	34	31	30
Eastern and Southern	7	7	8
S. West	4	4	3
Midlands	5	4	4
N. Midlands	5	6	7
E. and W. Ridings	16	13	14
N. West	20	20	19
North	2	5	6
Scotland	5	7	6
Wales	1	3	3

Source: Briscoe, L. (1971), *The Textile and Clothing Industry of the UK*, Table 20, Manchester University Press, Manchester.

Table 2.13 Regional employment 1971–1996 (in thousands).

	1981		1991		1996		2004	
S. East	49.0	(23.3)	22.6	(15.5)	22.0	(15.9)	18.2	(26.3)
E. Anglia	3.9	(1.9)	0.9	(0.6)	1.8	(1.3)	2.5	(3.7)
S. West	8.1	(3.8)	5.3	(3.7)	5.0	(3.6)	3.2	(4.6)
W. Midlands	11.9	(5.6)	12.7	(8.7)	13.0	(9.4)	5.2	(7.5)
E. Midlands	25.8	(12.2)	27.2	(18.6)	28.6	(20.7)	11.2	(16.2)
Yorkshire and Humberside	27.3	(13.0)	19.6	(13.4)	14.1	(10.2)	6.1	(8.8)
N. West	35.8	(17.0)	20.7	(14.2)	20.2	(14.6)	11.1	(16.1)
North	15.9	(7.6)	12.7	(8.7)	11.2	(8.1)	1.3	(3.2)
Wales	9.2	(4.4)	8.1	(5.5)	7.3	(5.3)	1.8	(2.6)
Scotland	23.6	(11.2)	16.3	(11.1)	15.0	(10.9)	5.2	(7.5)
GB	210.5		146.1		138.2		69.3	

Source: 1996 from *Labour Market Trends*, Nov 1997; earlier data from various editions of *Department of Employment Gazette*; 2004 data from UK Data Archive (University of Essex – I am grateful to Dr D. Tyler for providing these statistics).

Notes: (1) Figures in brackets represent percentages of the GB total.
(2) 2004 data not totally comparable to earlier data.

'concentrated in the East End of London, the East and West Midlands and West Yorkshire, where ethnic minorities are concentrated. The entrepreneurs from ethnic minorities . . . are able to exploit kinship ties and more extensive forms of gender subordination, employing women from the same or other ethnic minorities who form part of the underclass or secondary labour market. Small clothing enterprises . . . have been especially prominent . . . in the Asian communities of the West Midlands'.

These developments have been well documented by Ram (1994), for example. In effect, these companies have re-created areas of low (wage) cost activity within a relatively high labour cost country – they are exploiting a low order competitive advantage, in Porter's terms (see Chapter 1).

This phenomenon can be viewed from a number of perspectives. On the one hand the growth of this sector has prevented the total numbers employed in the UK from declining even more severely than they have. Many commentators, however, deplore the re-emergence of the old 'sweat shop', e.g. Winterton (1997) writes about this strategy as being one of wage depression and deskilling and of establishments being 'substantial through sweated labour'. He further argues (1997, p. 197) that 'wage depression based on ethnic minority exploitation is a feature of clothing in the UK, US and Germany because ethnic minority workers are concentrated in local labour markets in these countries'.

From a third point of view it is interesting to note that the growth of employment in the East and West Midlands which was commented upon by Jones (1996) has continued through to 1996. A 'shift share' or 'components of change' analysis of the variation in regional employment in the period 1971–1991 by Jones (1996, p. 67) suggested that in the case of the expanding regions of the East and West Midlands the biggest influences on the West Midlands pattern of regional change were locational factors captured by the so-called 'differential shift' (e.g. relative wages):

> 'over the twenty year period, only two regions succeeded in escaping the drain of jobs in the industry *viz* the East and West Midlands. In both the Differential Shift factor was dominant.'

It is a moot point as to whether or not this ethnic industry can survive and prosper in the next decade as trade liberalisation occurs, the potential female labour force aspires to wider opportunities and the impact of minimum wage legislation takes hold. The changes in the regional distribution of employment 1981–2004 are summarised in Table 2.13. It can be seen that the big 'winners' between 1981 and 1996 were the Midlands regions while the biggest 'losers' were the more traditional areas of the South East, Yorkshire and the North West.

The regional distribution of the industry can also be assessed in terms of the number of manufacturing groups. In terms of enterprises the most important regions (in 1997) were, by a wide margin, London, the North West and the Midlands regions (EMAP/MTI, 1998/9).

It is interesting to note that, in a study of changes in regional patterns of activity, Wren (1999) found that all UK regions became more specialised in the period 1971–1994 but that, somewhat paradoxically, industry has become less geographically concentrated over time, resulting in a convergence of regional structures towards a national norm. These trends were found to be strongest in the less well off regions (such as those in which textiles and apparel tend to be located) and to have been brought about by the decline of traditional manufacturing industries which had been encouraged by the availability of automatic but capital intensity related grants up to the end of the 1980s. They estimated that both the Regional Development and Regional Selective Assistance programme had exerted significant negative effects upon the textile and clothing sectors. In contrast, the employment related Regional Employment Premium had a strong positive impact upon employment in the sectors.

Unfortunately, the latest statistics (Table 2.13) are not entirely compatible with the earlier figures but they are robust enough to largely confirm the regional distribution as being concentrated in the South East, North West and the two Midland regions. The latter both exhibited a drop in numbers and percentage share of UK employment and were not, therefore, immune to the national decline in the industry.

D. The structure of the UK apparel industry

The aim of this section will be to utilise the S–C–P (structure–conduct–performance) model as a framework within which to describe the basic features of the UK apparel manufacturing sector. At each stage the implications of the structural features will be drawn out and the findings of research studies into each structural variable summarised.

(i) The size distribution of companies

The industry has traditionally been described as dominated by small firms. Singleton (1991, p. 209) argues that 'the industry has always been atomistic', quoting a figure from as far back as 1841 which shows that 73% of Lancashire cotton firms had under 200 employees.

The *UK Fashion Report* (EMAP/MTI, 1998/99) commented that:

> 'unlike many long established industries, the clothing industry shows few signs of "encroaching monopolism". Companies tend to be numerous and not very large'.

Research into the small firm sector by the Durham Business School (1999) revealed that the number of businesses in the footwear and clothing sector fell by 27% between 1988–1993. Although the sector was dominated by small firms it was not one of the biggest of the small firm sectors. Seventy-four per cent of the firms in the footwear and clothing sector had a turnover of under £250,000.

Briscoe (1971, p. 158) wrote that 'generally the average size of an establishment in the clothing industry is much smaller'. It is frequently argued that the small firms nature of the industry is one of the major factors which helps to explain the difficulties the industry encounters in such areas as raising finance, investment and human resource management. The sorts of problems faced by small firms have been well documented in the literature. This is one issue to which the positivist research philosophy can be applied: tests can be carried out to see if it is true that the small firm is over-represented in the apparel manufacturing sector. An extensive amount of statistical data is available on the size distribution of enterprises by industry and individual industries can be compared with the average for all manufacturing. This issue has been rigorously examined for the year 1991 by Jones (1993). In terms of cross-section data (at a fixed date) it was found that:

(a)   The apparel sector was not in any way unusual in terms of the prevalence of small units – in most industries most of the companies are small.

(b)   If, however, attention is focused on local units (premises) rather than ownership units then the apparel sector *does* show a marked bias towards smaller units, i.e. the percentage of the workforce employed in small premises is much higher than the average. Turnover data (as opposed to employment data) also revealed bias towards smaller operations. Gross and net output data (for 1990) showed that firms employing under 200 people were responsible for 40.1% of gross output and 40.3% of net output in the apparel sector as opposed to 23.1% and 24.7% in manufacturing as a whole.

Finally, Jones (1996) examined time series data over the period 1971 to 1991 in terms of both employment and turnover. He concluded that the trend in the apparel sector was the opposite to that experienced by manufacturing as a whole in that the latter witnessed a contraction in the relative importance of the larger size bands and an expansion in activity in the smaller ones. Paradoxically, therefore, the apparel sector was moving, very slowly, towards the norm, e.g. the percentage employed in the 1000+ band in the apparel sector in 1985 was 6% of the average, whereas in 1990 it was 21%. Statistics for 1996/1997 (Jones, 2002), while not in quite the same format as that of the earlier analysis, did nothing to significantly alter the conclusions drawn above, i.e. that in common with all industry, most enterprises in the apparel sector are small but that by comparison with the average, a greater proportion of employment (59.9% compared with 50.7%) was in an enterprise employing under 200 people and that, most significantly, in terms of gross output, a much higher proportion of activity (47.7% compared with 25.7%) was carried out in enterprises employing less than 100 people.

The latest statistics are summarised in Table 2.14. In terms of both enterprise and local unit analysis the distribution of units within the apparel industry by employment size band does still show a disproportionately high proportion of activity in the 5–99 size band –44% as opposed to the average of 25%. However, it can be seen that the percentage of enterprises in the lowest two size bands is actually lower than the average while the industry seems to be over-represented in the middle and higher size bands. In terms of employment size bands, again the percentage of enterprises and local units in the lowest size band in apparel is

Table 2.14   Basic size distribution analysis, 2003 (%).

	Apparel (SIC 18)	All manufacturing
Enterprise analysis		
Turnover band (£000)		
0–40	14.0	20.9
50–99	18.2	24.5
100–249	27.3	25.6
250–499	16.3	12.0
500–999	10.4	7.4
1,000–4,999	10.0	7.2
5,000+	3.7	2.4
Employment band		
0–4	54.4 (53.5)	74.1 (66.0)
5–9	18.7 (18.7)	13.5 (15.7)
10–19	13.3 (13.0)	6.7 (8.9)
20–49	9.6 (10.0)	3.4 (5.8)
50–99	2.2 (2.7)	1.1 (2.0)
100–249	1.8 (1.5)	0.6 (1.1)
250–499	0.2 (0.4)	0.2 (0.3)
500–999	0.1 (0.1)	0.1 (0.1)
1,000+	0.1 (–)	0.1 (0.4)

Source: ONS (2003) Size Distribution Analysis (BM PA1003).
Notes: (1) The analysis by employment bands can also be conducted at local
unit (factory) level. These results are shown in parentheses.
(2) The numbers show the percentage of enterprises and/or local units
in each size band.

much lower than the average. Therefore, it might be argued that the apparel industry as it has declined in size in the UK has become less unusual in terms of its size distribution. The extent to which this apparent change reduces the impact of the well-known problems of the small firms sector is problematical in the absence of further research. These problems have been extensively documented by such commentators as Bannock (1981); Storey (1994); Stokes (1995) and Barrow (1998).

In addition to all these problems it is pertinent to raise the question of the contribution made by the size distribution profile to the ability or inability of the sector to pull towards itself a large share of the value added in the textile pipeline.

If we take the economies of scale issue first, it is clear that output indicators are most relevant here. In this case, it is probably correct to argue that the clothing industry is different and is disadvantaged by the bias towards small producers (see Table 2.14). It must be recalled, however, that the evidence from Winterton (1996) suggested that the structure of the industry is changing over time towards more output being produced in larger units. The statistics presented in Table 2.14 support this argument so it could well be argued that the industry seems to be becoming less disadvantaged in this regard. In relation to arguments about the relative size of manufacturers and their (largely retail) customers, a different indicator would be more appropriate, such as a measurement based on the number of companies in the various size bands.

If the discussion is about financial strength, it is probably better to consider size bands in terms of turnover rather than employment. The fact that the size distribution of actual companies as revealed by the latest figures in the clothing industry is *not* significantly different from the all manufacturing norm appears to refute the proposition that special case status is required. It has to be said that this apparent change has not been reflected in any noticeable change in power relationships in the pipeline.

In terms of employment-related or human relations issues, things are a little clearer in that legislative changes, such as the introduction of a legal minimum wage, are more important than the statistical distribution of companies within the industry.

It is, therefore, not possible to offer a very simple, one sentence answer to the question posed at the beginning of this section. In simple terms, *most* sectors (as measured by the all manufacturing norm) are dominated by small firms. This is the norm, but, as has been seen, closer examination of the statistical evidence reveals a much more complex picture. It is worth noting that there have been significant changes in the clothing industry at the upper end of the size distribution.

(ii)   Cost structures and economies of scale

Economies of scale are said to exist when long-run average unit costs fall significantly with increased output and when, as a result, the minimum efficient size of operation is very large. In such industries the cost penalty suffered by operations below the optimum scale can be very large. Normally, the presence of significant scale economies is accompanied by heavy capital investment in fixed plant, a significant degree of automation and the repetitive production of highly standardised products. Studies of UK industry by Scherer (1975) and Pratten (1971) indicated that economies of scale were most important in such industries as brewing; paint; cigarettes; glass; steel; refrigerators; some types of yarn; oil; cement; detergent; and bread and brick production.

The manufacture of apparel is not characterised by the presence of significant economies of scale. As Singleton (1997, p. 144) observes, as a result of 'the lack of economies of scale in textiles and clothing, small and medium sized firms should be able to obtain a minimum efficient scale of production'.

The size distribution of companies in terms of the proportion of output produced in smaller units supports this argument in the sense that it is observed that small operations do exist and persist in the apparel industry. This line of argument was initially advanced by Stigler (1958). In brief, it argues that the observed size distribution of operations indicates which is the most efficient size – otherwise it would not survive. There are many objections to the use of this technique of analysis because survival can be the result of many other factors but Hay (1991, p. 51) concludes that 'it seems as though the technique is most applicable in competitive sectors'. Therefore, in the light of the weight of supporting evidence indicating such elements as low capital intensity and the shortness of production runs it is probably safe – and not too great a departure from the positive approach – to accept that the industry is not one in which small size is an unsurmountable handicap. The capital requirement needed to start up apparel production is not great as seen above in Table 2.4; e.g. capital employed per person in UK apparel manufacture is £703 compared to the average for the manufacturing sector of £3,633 and £8,460 in the chemical industry.

A second important feature of cost structures in the apparel sector is the very high degree of labour intensity which still characterises production. This feature of the industry can be illustrated in a variety of ways: the industry accounts for a much higher proportion of employment than it does of output; capital use per head is (as was seen above) extremely low; and, finally, turnover is produced using a relatively large amount of labour and a relatively small amount of capital (see Table 2.4). This continued labour intensity is the single most important feature of the apparel industry – it is this factor which is at the very core of many of the industry's current problems and as such it will be examined in greater detail in Chapter 4.

The most important single element in the cost structure of the apparel production process is fabric, which is normally held to account for around 40% of the total cost. In brief, it can be stated that the textile manufacturing companies – who are, therefore, the main element when supplier power is to be considered – tend to be much larger than apparel manufacturers.

(iii)   Barriers to new entry in the apparel industry

Entry barriers are features of the industrial landscape which prevent new producers entering the industry. The most important barriers identified in the literature include the existence of patents; the presence of important economies of scale; heavy initial capital investment requirements; and the existence of special skills or techniques which are not easily replicated. As has been seen above, capital requirements in the apparel industry are low; scale factors are relatively insignificant and, as was noted in Chapter 1, the technology is relatively simple. Therefore, entry barriers in the apparel manufacturing sector tend to be low. In the history of industrial economics it should be noted (Martin, 1993, p. 5) that 'the condition of entry was central to the S–C–P paradigm'. Therefore, the ease of entry into the sector is likely to be significant. Stead (1996, p. 5) argues that the role of 'entry barriers is important in that without them even the most complete monopoly is open to competition from new entrants'. The absence of significant entry barriers in apparel manufacturing would, therefore, be expected to produce relatively low profits in the sector.

(iv)   Vertical integration

A vertically integrated company is one which operates at more than one level of the pipeline illustrated in Fig. 1.1. If, for example, an apparel manufacturer moved into fabric manufacture it would be described as backward integration. If it moved into retailing it would be described as forward integration. Vertical integration has both advantages (such as co-ordination) and disadvantages (such as the absence of market discipline). There is no neat statistical measure available of the extent of vertical integration in UK industry. Clearly, vertically integrated companies have populated the textile–apparel pipeline – Courtaulds, Coats Viyella and the old Burtons organisation, for example. However, recent trends have been in the opposite direction with the large textile conglomerates breaking up into separate businesses – the best example being the emergence of Courtaulds Textiles in 1990. The majority of UK apparel manufacturers are not vertically integrated. This state of affairs seems to reflect the historical perspective in that Singleton (1997, p. 4) felt able to comment that even at the height of its powers the cotton industry exhibited few signs of integration even within the cotton sector. One caveat must be inserted at this point and that is the extent to which the traditional form of vertical integration (in which the integration was achieved by ownership) could be replaced by the relatively newer organisational concept of a managed supply chain. A supply chain is a group or network of legally independent companies which have agreed to work together to achieve some common objectives in the supply of a given product. This issue will be considered in more detail in Chapter 7. Finally, it is worth noting that vertical integration is somewhat more common in the apparel retailing sector. ICC (1998, p. 3) consider that, in their examination of the retail sector, 'vertical integration is a traditional characteristic of this sector' although current examples are, in the view of the present author, somewhat limited.

(v)   Research and technology

It has already been noted that the apparel manufacturing sector is not a strongly knowledge-based industry. This is confirmed by the evidence on expenditure on research (ONS, 1998) which shows that the textiles industry (including apparel) was responsible for only 0.3% of R&D expenditure in the UK in 1997. Pharmaceuticals, by way of contrast, was responsible for 22.5%. An earlier study by Jones (1989) was able to isolate the apparel industry and showed that, in 1986, it was responsible for only 0.1% of the total R&D expenditure in the UK. These issues will be considered in greater detail in Chapters 4 and 7. The point to be noted here is that researchers have concluded (Stead, 1996, p. 134) that 'the highest level of innovation is associated with oligopoly and four firm concentration ratios of about 50 per cent' whereas the five firm ratio in the apparel industry was, in 1992, only 20%, as is seen in section (vi) below.

The Sector Review (ONS, 1998) revealed that the apparel industry in the UK, in 1997, employed just 1000 scientists and spent £33 million on research (which represented 0.5% of the manufacturing total). Fifty per cent of the research in the industry was funded by overseas money. Clearly the amount of R&D carried out in any sector is affected by the technological opportunities available but, in addition, Stead (1996, p. 127) has shown that 74% of R&D is carried out by large firms employing over 10,000 people. In both respects the apparel sector is under-represented.

Most of the evidence suggests (Scherer, 1990, p. 660) that there is a

'threshold concept of the most favourable climate for rapid technological change. A bit of monopoly power in the form of structural concentration is conducive to innovation, particularly when advances in the relevant knowledge base occur slowly'

and that there is

'a modest positive influence for concentration especially in low opportunity industries'.

Therefore, the structure of the sector is not conducive to extensive R&D activity and the data confirm Singleton's (1997, p. 46) view that 'although R&D statistics are notoriously unreliable it is obvious that textiles and clothing are not knowledge intensive industries'.

One reason, accordingly, for the contraction of the sector might be lack of technological progress.

(vi)   The degree of buyer concentration

This is a measure of the extent to which the output of a sector is purchased by customers who represent a high proportion of the selling industry's total output. It is a significant feature of both the Five Forces Model and the S–C–P model and is often known as the degree of monopsony. The main customer of the apparel manufacturing sector is the retail sector. In the UK (see Chapter 10) apparel retailing is highly concentrated with a significant proportion of sales being concentrated in the hands of a small number of large retailers. The disparity in size between the largest UK apparel manufacturers and retailers is documented in Section E below. The importance of this fact is that as Hay (1991, p. 236) observes:

'many manufacturing sectors are concerned with intermediate products sold to a few buyers in another sector . . . major buyers will "shop around" . . . and thus put pressure on margins'.

Lustgarten (1975) found that buyer concentration ratios had a significant impact on profit margins. Hay (1991, p. 236) concluded that research studies on this issue 'indicate a significant, though not necessarily large, negative impact of buyer concentration on sellers' margins'.

It is generally recognised (Scherer, 1990, p. 517) that 'appreciable pockets of monopsony power can be found'. The power exercised by UK apparel retailers represents such a pocket and it would be surprising if they did not exercise this power to their own advantage within the pipeline, given the historical tendency towards adversarial relationships which has been noted in Chapter 1. As Dicken (1998, p. 294) observes, 'the production chain . . . is becoming increasingly transformed into a buyer-driven chain'. Gereffi (1999, p. 40) sees the apparel supply chain as 'a prototypical buyer driver commodity chain' as will be further considered in Chapter 12.

Cool's (1998, p. 921) study of the French manufacturing sector found that 'buyer power specifically strongly matters for seller profitability' and that 'buyer power had a much higher effect on seller profitability than supplier power'. Galbraith (1983, p. 248) had previously studied, using an American database, the impact of exploited power in the production chain and confirmed the hypotheses that 'power conditions between adjacent stages in the production chain are related to a firm's profitability'.

(vii)   The degree of seller concentration

This is the dimension of market structure which has received the greatest attention and which has, in a very real sense, been the major focus of research in industrial economics over the years. It is a measure of the degree of monopoly power exercised by the largest sellers in an industry and is associated at the national level with undesirable economic performance. The basic structural proposition is that high concentration produces high profits. As Chakravarty (1995, p. 1) observes, concentration has:

'been regarded as one of the significant dimensions of market structure because it is believed to have played an important role in determining market power and hence business behaviour and performance'.

A large number of measures of the degree of seller concentration exist but, in brief, it is normally assessed by using some form of the ratio of total industry output, sales or employment accounted for by a specified number of the largest sellers – i.e. the so-called concentration ratio. In the UK a five firm (employment) concentration ratio is available from the Census of Production. In 1992 the CR5 (net output) for the apparel sector was 20%, i.e. the top five firms accounted for only 20% of total output. In 2004 (based on turnover) it was 19.5%. It is clear that the apparel manufacturing industry remains fragmented. The degree of market power wielded by apparel manufacturers is, therefore, likely to be extremely low. The independent role of seller concentration in determining profits has turned out (from a huge volume of research in many countries) to be rather more complex than had been expected but its role does remain intact.

As Hay (1991, p. 260) concluded, half of the research studies: 'find a significant positive relationship' between profits and concentration. Scherer (1990, p. 410) stated that

> 'the classic testable hypothesis has been that . . . profit retention by firms in highly concentrated industries will tend to be significantly higher than in firms in . . . atomistically structured industries'

and that, while findings are mixed, a tentative conclusion that 'profitably is positively associated with a sellers' own market share' is justified.

Traditionally, as has been observed in Chapter 1, the apparel manufacturing industry has been regarded as atomistic (i.e. dominated by small firms with little market power). Scherer & Ross (1990, p. 77) produced, for example, detailed concentration data for the USA in the early 1980s which showed that sectors of the apparel sector were among the least concentrated of all industries.

(viii)   The degree of specialisation (or diversification)

The apparel manufacturing sector is extremely highly specialised (or demonstrates very little diversification); apparel manufacturers generally do not engage in other activities. The index of specialisation was 98% in 1987; 97% in 1991 and 93% in 1996 (ONS, 1996). Chakravarty (1995, p. 21) has noted that 'for a number of countries there is a clear indication of a rapid increase in diversification'. This has not been the case in the apparel sector which continues to have 'all its eggs in one basket'.

(ix)   The degree of import penetration

Finally, it is vital that the international dimension is brought into the centre of the analysis. As has been explained in Chapter 1, no serious analysis of the current state and future evolution of the UK apparel sector can be made which ignores this element. The degree of import penetration is the percentage of demand in a country which is supplied by imports rather than by domestic suppliers. As is demonstrated in Chapter 5, the degree of import penetration in the UK apparel market is now 92%. In terms of the model in Fig. 1.2, the role of imports can be brought in at a variety of points, e.g. as part of the consideration of the number of sellers in the field or as part of existing rivalry. The importance attributed here to the role of imports is justified by Hay's (1991, p. 236) statement that to

> 'the extent that imports and exports are important, domestic market structure will be an unreliable indicator of market power. An important extension of structure-performance studies, therefore, is the introduction of foreign trade, particularly for open economies where trade is sizeable in relation to industrial production. Imports represent the most immediate new entry threat in the domestic market . . .'

Some studies have tried to recalculate domestic concentration ratios by including imports in the measure of market size. The majority of these studies, such as Utton (1982), found that the inclusion of imports removed most of the measured changes in concentration which had been previously recorded. Accordingly, Hay (1991, p. 237) concludes that 'trade will make a significant difference to profitability'. Other studies have included trade variables in regression analysis and have usually found that import penetration reduces profitability. Hitiris (1978) found that in the UK penetration rates did significantly influence profit margins. Katics (1994), in a study of the USA, found that there was 'a sizeable effect of import competition on price-cost margins for the time period 1976–1986'. This was confirmed for the UK by Conyon (1991) who also found a positive relationship between the degree of seller concentration ((vii) above) and the level of profitability.

Therefore, given that concentration ratios in the apparel manufacturing sector were initially extremely low (indicating the presence of little market power), their modification to allow for the influence of an extremely high degree of import penetration must, by definition, reduce the ability of domestic producers to influence the market to something approaching zero.

E. The major players

The biggest UK-based apparel manufacturers in terms of sales are shown in Table 2.15. Clearly, such listings can quickly become dated but the table does serve to indicate who the major players in the UK industry are. It must be remembered that not all the actual manufacturing and processing takes place domestically. It is instructive to note that the turnover of the largest UK apparel retailer (Marks & Spencer) totalled £8,077.2 millions, i.e. 20 times more than the sales achieved by the biggest UK-based manufacturer. In fact, the top 17 retailers were all bigger than the biggest manufacturer in terms of turnover.

Table 2.15   The largest UK apparel manufacturers, 2003/2004.

Rank	Manufacturer	Turnover (£000)
1	Alexon Group plc	416,429
2	Courtaulds Textiles (Holdings) Ltd	349,019
3	Pentland Group plc	328,200
4	Burberry Ltd	311,999
5	Laura Ashley Holdings plc	283,500
6	Laura Ashley Ltd	267,449
7	Clematis Clothing Ltd	197,141
8	Alexon International Ltd	195,247
9	Castlecrafts Ltd	181,636
10	Remploy Ltd	160,545
11	Desmond and Sons Ltd	145,028
12	Bentwood Ltd	123,433
13	Austin Reed Group plc	111,899
14	Crystal Martin Int. Ltd	92,633
15	Baird Textile Holdings Ltd	91,000
16	S.R. Gent plc	75,553
17	Karen Millen Ltd	67,044
18	Castleblair Group Ltd	54,809
19	Velmore Holdings Ltd	53,289

Source: Fame Database.

The size of a company can obviously be measured in a variety of ways – sales, profits, assets and employees, for example. The top ten companies by those three measures are shown in Table 2.16. In terms of assets, the biggest UK-based apparel manufacturer was Pentland with assets of £385 million in 2004. The biggest retailer (M&S) had assets of £7,377 million. In terms of profitability the most successful UK-based apparel manufacturer was Burberry with £81,730,000. In comparison, the most successful retailer (in 2004) was Marks & Spencer with £674,300,000.

F.   The structure of the apparel sector and the current problems of the sector

The aim of this section is to evaluate the impact of the structure of the industry both upon its performance and its ability to cope with the problems it faces. The analysis must be seen in the context of general conclusions drawn upon the usefulness of the S–C–P model which can be captured by the view of Chakravarty (1995) that 'empirical studies report mixed results on the relationship between performance and structure' and Scherer (1990) that 'the competitive norm does seem to serve as a good approximation but it is hard to state in advance how much competition is needed to achieve desirable economic performance'.

Table 2.16   Ranking by turnover, assets and number of employees.

Manufacturer	Turnover	Assets	Employees
Alexon	1	4	2
Courtaulds	2	3	4
Pentland	3	1	9
Burberry	4	2	11
L. Ashley Holdings	5	6	5
L. Ashley Ltd	6	8	6
Clematis	7	7	14
Alexon International	8	5	3
Castlecrafts	9	9	21
Remploy	10	11	1
Desmonds	11	12	7
Bentwood	12	15	17
A. Reed Group	13	10	13
Crystal Martin	14	17	19

Source: as Table 2.16.

The main problem faced by the industry is, in brief, one of contraction and lack of influence and market power both within the pipeline and the wider economy. It has been argued above that in order to make sense of trends it will be useful to employ the model outlined in Fig. 1.5.

The industry revealed by the analysis (Section D) above is one which is almost uniquely *structurally disadvantaged* in its ability to deal with the problems it confronts. The following are the main structural features:

(1)   The industry is, according to some measures, still dominated by small firms, although the latest statistics do seem to suggest this view of the industry may need to be revised. Further research is needed in this area.

(2)   The degree of market power exercised by the industry, as indicated by the very low degree of seller concentration, is very low.

(3)   The industry is extremely labour intensive and is not knowledge based.

(4)   Scale economies are relatively unimportant.

(5)   There is little sign of diversification in the sector.

(6)   Barriers to entry appear to be low.

(7)   The degree of buyer concentration is abnormally high.

(8)   The degree of import penetration is very high.

The last two points are probably linked in that Gereffi (1999, p. 45) has argued that the retailer has switched from being the manufacturer's customer to becoming its competitor accounting for a rising share of apparel imports. These issues are more fully discussed in Chapter 12.

The main implication of these structural characteristics is that the industry would be relatively weak and lacking in market power. Profit margins, both in absolute terms, and relative to other sectors of the pipeline would be expected to be low. Paradoxically, the profile described above would lead to good public performance in the sense of providing wide choice and low prices to consumers, which expectation is largely confirmed by the analysis of the consumer market in Chapter 10.

These conclusions are confirmed by the application of the Five Forces Model which indicates that the ability of the apparel manufacturers to capture a share of the profit generated by the pipeline into which they fit is likely to be compromised by the fact that they have a low level of market power, squeezed as they are between larger and more powerful suppliers and buyers. The major source of power in the textile–apparel pipeline lies with the retailers. In Dicken's (1998, p. 294) words, 'demand is becoming increasingly dominated by the purchasing power of the major multiple retailing chains'.

As was shown in Section E above, the largest UK apparel retailer is some 20 times larger than the biggest manufacturer. Additionally, although the apparel sector is by far the biggest purchaser of fabric its atomistic structure further inhibits its ability to realise a large share of the value added generated by the conversion of fabric to garments. Therefore it could be predicted that apparel manufacturers would be less profitable than retailers and low in absolute terms.

Testing these predictions is difficult because of a lack of data. Some progress can be made, however. Data published by ICC and analysed by Jones (1989) showed that, in the mid-1980s, out of 27 broad industrial sectors, the textiles and footwear sector ranked tenth on the basis of profits as a percentage of capital employed, scoring exactly the industrial average. The profit : sales ratio was slightly below the average. At a more refined sub-sector level it was possible to identify the clothing industry in isolation from the rest of the textiles pipeline. In this case the apparel industry, in the mid-1980s, in terms of return on capital, came 35th out of 192 industries but, in terms of profit on sales, slumped to 58th. Unfortunately, the latest edition of the statistical source (ICC, 1997) no longer contains entries for the apparel sector. Official data on profitability do not include figures for individual industries. Kilduff (2005) noted that in the apparel industry in the USA margins were wafer thin at only 2.6%.

However, it has been noted above that the profitability of the apparel manufacturing sector is relatively low compared to apparel retailing. Therefore, while the data are less comprehensive than would be desired so that the profit expectations predicted cannot be easily confirmed or refuted, the balance of evidence – imperfect as it is – favours acceptance of the hypothesis that retailers will be more profitable than the manufacturers. It can be concluded that the task facing the industry – and by implication the firms within it – is a daunting one. The economic and structural environment within which actions have to be taken is extremely hostile. Success or failure is not, of course, entirely structurally determined. Strategic policy choices can make a difference even in the most adverse circumstances, as will be seen in Chapter 7.

There remains one factor to be considered – the importance of the international dimension. If attention is now focused less on the role of imports as a structural factor and is fixed instead on the role of the diamond framework (Fig. 1.5, top left corner) then the Porter Model's implications for the UK as a base for apparel manufacture do not appear strong. Few strengths remain in the supporting sectors in the UK; factor supply conditions (especially labour costs and research expenditure) promise little in the way of advantage; the impact of UK buyers in promoting excellence is somewhat problematical while the force of competition as a promoter of world-class performance has (somewhat perversely) probably been inhibited by the reliance of industry upon the support of major retailers promoting relatively long production runs.

These issues will be more fully explored in the next chapter, which reviews the evidence of global shift in the apparel industry. It can be noted at this point that given that the industry has remained labour intensive, it is logically consistent to argue that the (relatively) high cost of employing labour in the UK has been a major factor in the contraction of the industry within the UK. As will be shown in Chapter 3, many commentators point to international trade as *the* major factor behind the collapse of the industry in the UK. This view has been expressed forcibly by, for example, Winterton (1996, p. 26) who argued that 'the crisis in the UK clothing industry can be directly attributed to the increase in imports'.

It has been argued in Chapter 1 that in resolving questions of causation a positivist research philosophy should be adopted. In this case the argument that the decline of employment and output in the UK can be directly attributed to the rise in imports is not generally supported by the research (see Chapter 3, Section E). However, there are good reasons to discount this evidence as being based upon a research technique which is seriously flawed. It cannot, in the view of the present author, be seriously denied that the threat from low-cost sources of production created enormous pressures on UK-based producers (frequently exerted by the more powerful retailers) and was in Winterton's words (1997, p. 32) 'a major impulse promoting restructuring in response to successive crises' – crises which, as has been demonstrated above, the industry is almost uniquely disadvantaged to resolve. These pressures have been intensified in the early years of the new millennium as existing trade barriers were removed and UK retailers reduced their commitment to UK-based suppliers.

The reason for adopting what might seem to be an overly bleak and pessimistic view of the trends in employment and output in the sector is straightforward: if strategies are to be devised to deal with the problems, then realism is essential. Employing euphemisms or wishful thinking is unhelpful. The days when half a million people could be employed manufacturing garments in the UK are gone forever. There is little prospect that any UK government – whatever its political persuasion – is ever going to regard the industry as strategic (Jones, 2006). The pressures that have brought the industry to its current position seem unlikely to be reversed. Are there any serious commentators who would suggest that, for example, the labour-intensive nature of garment assembly is likely to be miraculously transformed, or that substantial protection against low wage based imports is likely to be re-introduced after 2005 or that the labour cost gap between the UK and developing countries is going to evaporate? In the absence of any of these events, the way forward must take place against a background very similar and equally as difficult as that which has transformed the global apparel sector over the last few decades. The challenges are formidable in the extreme and, in the main, of a global nature. Accordingly the next three chapters will deal with global and trade issues before attention is focused from Chapter 7 onwards on future strategic issues and developments.

References

Bannock, G. (1981) *The Economics of Small Firms*. Blackwell Publishers, Oxford.

Barrow, C. (1998) *The Essence of Small Business*. Prentice Hall Europe, London.

Briscoe, L. (1971) *The Textile and Clothing Industries of the UK*. Manchester University Press, Manchester.

Chakravarty, S.R. (1995) *Issues in Industrial Economics*. Avebury, Aldershot.

Conyon, M. & Machin, S. (1991) The Determination of Profit Margins in UK Manufacturing. *Journal of Industrial Economics*, **4**, 369–83.

Cool, K. & Henderson, J. (1998) Power and Profits in Supply Chains. *Strategic Management Journal*, **19**, 909–26.

Dicken, P. (1998) *Global Shift: Transforming the World Economy*. Paul Chapman, London.

Durham Business School (1999) *Small Business Trends 1994–98*. Durham Business School, Durham.

EMAP/MTI (1998/99) *The UK Fashion Report*. EMAP, London.

Galbraith, C. & Stiles, C. (1983) Firm Profitability and Relative Firm Power. *Strategic Management Journal*, **4**, 237–47.

Gereffi, G. (1999) International Trade and Industrial Upgrading in the Apparel Commodity Chain. *Journal of International Economics*, **48**, 37–70.

Godley, A. (1996) The Emergence of Mass Production in the UK Clothing Industry. In: *Restructuring Within a Labour Intensive Industry* (Eds I. Taplin & J. Winterton), pp. 8–25. Avebury, Aldershot.

Harris, R. & Trainer, M. (1997) Productivity Growth in the UK Regions. *Oxford Bulletin of Economics and Statistics*, **59**, 485–510.

Hay, D.A. & Morris, D.J. (1991) *Industrial Economics – Theory and Evidence*. Oxford University Press, Oxford.

Hitiris, T. (1978) Effective Protection and Economic Performance. *Economic Journal*, **88**, 107–20.

I.C.C. (1997) *UK Industrial Performance*. I.C.C. Business Publications, London.

I.C.C. (1998) *Clothing Manufacture.* I.C.C. Business Publications, Hampton, Middlesex.

Jones, R.M. (1989) Comparative Performance of the UK Clothing Industry. *Journal of Clothing Technology and Management*, **6**, 3–15.

Jones, R.M. (1993) The Clothing Industry: A Special Case. *Journal of Clothing Technology and Management*, **10**, 1–21.

Jones, R.M. (1996) Changes in Regional Employment in the UK Clothing Industry. In: *Restructuring in a Labour Intensive Industry* (Eds I. Taplin and J. Winterton), pp. 61–112. Avebury, Aldershot.

Jones, R.M. (2002) *The Apparel Industry.* Blackwell Science, Oxford.

Jones, R.M. (2006) *Editorial Journal of Fashion Maternity and Management*, **10.1**.

Katics, M. & Petersen, B. (1994) The Effect of Rising Import Competition on Market Power. *American Economic Review*, **88**, 107–20.

Kilduff, P. (2005) Patterns of Strategic Adjustment in the US Textile and Apparel Industries since 1979. *Journal of Fashion Marketing and Management*, **9.2**, 180–195.

Lustgarten, S.H. (1975) The Impact of Buyer Concentration in Manufacturing Industries. *Review of Economic Statistics*, **57**, 125–32.

Martin, S. (1993) *Advanced Industrial Economics.* Blackwell Publishers, Oxford.

ONS (1996) P.A. 1002 *Manufacturing – Summary Volume.* HMSO, London.

ONS (1998) *Sector Review.* HMSO, London.

ONS (2004) Annual Business Inquiry available from http://statistics.gov.uk

ONS (2005a) *Labour Market Trends*, June 2005. HMSO, London.

ONS (2005b) B.M. MIO International Trade by Industry available from http://statistics.gov.uk

Pratten, C.F. (1971) *Economics of Scale in Manufacturing Industry.* C.U.P., London.

Ram, M. (1994) *Managing to Survive.* Blackwell Publishers, Oxford.

Scheffer, M. (1992) *Trading Places.* University of Utrecht, Utrecht.

Scherer, F.M. (1975) *The Economics of a Multi Plant Operation.* Harvard University Press, Cambridge, MA.

Scherer, F.M. & Ross, D. (1990) *Industrial Market Structure and Economic Performance.* Houghton Miflin, Boston.

Singleton, J. (1991) *Lancashire on the Scrap Heap.* Oxford University Press, Oxford.

Singleton, J. (1997) *World Textile Industry.* Routledge, London.

Stead, R. (1996) *Industrial Economics.* McGraw Hill, London.

Steadman, H. & Wagner, K. (1989) Productivity, Machinery and Skills – Clothing Manufacturing in Britain and Germany. *Hollings Apparel Industry Review*, **6**, 3–43.

Stigler, G.J. (1958) The Economics of Scale. *Journal of Law and Economics*, **1**, 54–71.

Stokes, D. (1995) *Small Business Management.* DP Publications, London.

Storey, D. (1994) *Understanding the Small Business.* Routledge, London.

Temple, P. & Urga, G. (1997) The Competitiveness of UK Manufacturing: Evidence from Imports. *Oxford Economic Papers*, **49**, 207–26.

Utton, M. (1982) Domestic Competition and International Trade. *Oxford Economic Papers*, **34**, 479–97.

Winterton, J. & Winterton, R. (1997) Deregulation, Division and Decline. In: *Rethinking Global Production* (Eds I. Taplin & J. Winterton), pp. 18–41. Ashgate, Aldershot.

Winterton, R. & Barlow, A. (1996) Economic Restructuring of UK Clothing. In: *Restructuring Within a Labour Intensive Industry* (Eds I. Taplin & J. Winterton), pp. 25–61. Avebury, Aldershot.

Wren, C. & Taylor, J. (1999) Industrial Restructuring and Regional Policy. *Oxford Economic Papers*, **51**, 487–517.

Chapter 3
The Apparel Sector in the Global Economy

A. Global shift in manufacturing

It is important to start by affirming that the major centres of manufacturing activity remain within the developed world. Dicken (2003), for example, provides figures which demonstrate that (in 1996) the USA was still responsible for 25% of world manufacturing production followed by Japan with 20%; Germany with 12% and France and the UK with a combined share of 8.2% (see Table 3.1). However, one of the most significant developments in the world economy over the last three or four decades has been the shift in activity away from the older, developed economies towards the newer, developing countries. This trend has

Table 3.1 Sources of manufacturing production, 1996.

Country	Percentage of world total
United States	24.8
Japan	20.0
Germany	11.8
France	4.3
United Kingdom	3.9
Italy	2.3
Canada	1.7
Spain	1.4
Australia	1.0
Switzerland	1.0
South Korea	2.9
Brazil	4.1
China	2.7
Netherlands	0.8
Taiwan	1.1
Total	83.8

Source: Dicken, P. (2003) *Global Shift*, Sage, London.
Note: (1) The top four (all developed countries) were responsible for 60.9% of world manufacturing production.

Table 3.2   Growth of manufacturing production and exports (% of world total).

Country	Output		Exports	
	1963	1999	1963	1999
S. Korea	0.1	2.9	0.01	2.7
Taiwan	0.1	1.1	0.20	2.3
Hong Kong	0.1	0.2	0.80	3.2
Singapore	0.1	0.4	0.40	2.2
India	NA	0.5	0.80	0.7
Mexico	1.0	0.8	0.20	2.6

Source: Dicken, P. (2003) *Global Shift*, Sage, London.
Note: (1)   It is difficult to document the continuing changes in the pattern of global production into the new century because of gaps in the data for individual countries but European production fell by 44% between 1992 and 2001 according to UN statistics.

been comprehensively documented by Dicken (2003). This so-called 'global shift' can be illustrated by the following statistics from Dicken (2003):

(1)   The share of world production generated within the developed countries fell from 95% in 1953 to 80% in 1995, while the corresponding share produced in the developing countries rose from 5% to 20%.

(2)   The share of some 13 Newly Industrialised Countries (NIEs) rose from 11% between 1963 and 1987. The share of South Korea, for example, rose from 0.1% to 2.7% between 1963 and 1994.

(3)   In terms of world trade (as opposed to production) the changes, in proportionate terms, were even more dramatic. The growth rate of exports of manufactured products from the developed world between 1970–86 was, for example, only 13% p.a. as compared to 21% p.a. from East and South East Asia. The high growth rates achieved by some of the developing areas are demonstrated in Tables 3.2 and 3.3 together with the impact these

Table 3.3   Annual growth in apparel production, 1972–1994 (%).

	1972–1987	1980–1989	1990–1993
Developed countries	−7	−0.3	−3.7
Developing countries	+56	3.1	−1.5
Planned economies	+48	+2.0	—
First-generation NIE	N/A	+3.3	−5.0
Second-generation NIE	N/A	+3.6	+7.1

Source: Dicken, P. (1992) *Global Shift*, Paul Chapman, London, Table 8.4 and Dicken, P. (2003) *Global Shift*, Paul Chapman, London, Table 9.4.

differences in growth rates had on the world league table of exporters over a 30-year period. The majority of these movements were, in the words of Eenennaam (1996, p. 88) 'pursuing a low cost strategy'.

B. Global shift in apparel production

Dicken (2003, p. 39) pointed out that 'a key characteristic of NIEs' exports has been their selective nature' and that they do tend to be most heavily involved in industries which are particularly sensitive to global shift.

As has been noted in Chapter 1 the production of apparel has remained a labour-intensive operation, especially at the assembly (sewing) stage. Therefore, it follows logically that apparel production will be under particularly severe pressure to relocate to low-wage areas. As will be seen in Chapter 4, hourly labour costs in apparel assembly in, for example, China, stand at something like 3% of the UK level. It will not be surprising, therefore, to discover that global shift in apparel production has been particularly dramatic.

In addition, the textile and apparel sectors are frequently the first industries to be established as nations industrialise. As a result (Dickerson, 1995, p. 196) the 'developing countries' share of global apparel production more than tripled between 1953 and 1980, going from 8% to 25%'.

In Taplin's words (1997, p. 2) 'clothing production in the high wage economies is often regarded as a "sunset" industry' which has been, according to Kilduff (2006) exemplified in the 'shift in competitive advantage (in apparel) from higher income countries towards lower income nations over the period 1962–2003'.

Tables 3.3 and 3.4 illustrate the changes that took place in the geography of apparel production in the 30 years between 1965 and 1993. These changes have continued in that according to United Nations statistics (2001) European production of 14 categories of apparel fell by 44% between 1992 and 2001 and US production of six categories by 52%. These global shifts in production are inevitably reflected in declines in employment although changes in labour productivity influence the exact nature of the relationship between changes in production and movements in employment. This was particularly apparent in the case of the UK – see Table 3.5. The decline in employment in the developed countries has been quite spectacular. Dicken (2003, p. 311) observed that:

'the five leading EU countries . . . lost 700,000 jobs in clothing between 1970–1993. The early 1970s were a watershed for clothing employment in most of the leading industrialised countries. In the UK a total of 180,000 (disappeared) in clothing between 1970 and 1993. Almost 380,000 (jobs) disappeared in the clothing industry in the USA'.

Table 3.4 Growth of Apparel Production 1965–1985 (% per year).

Country	% growth
Germany	−7.1
UK	1.0
Netherlands	−5.7
USA	1.3
Turkey	4.1
Hong Kong	9.5
Singapore	8.7
South Korea	23.7
Malaysia	10.1
Egypt	11.0
Indonesia	10.4
Philippines	15.2

Source: Scheffer, M. (1992), *Trading Places*, University of Utrecht, p. 52.

Table 3.5 The influence of productivity increase on employment and production in the EU, 1984–1994.

Country	Influence of productivity increase
Germany	1.15
Denmark	0.99
Greece	1.50
Spain	1.70
France	0.80
Irish Republic	0.94
Italy	23.60
Portugal	0.24
UK	55.5
EU	1.33

Source: *1996 Annual of EU Textile Policy*.

Notes: (1) If the figure is 1.0 this means that the percentage changes in employment and production were the same e.g. both fell by 10% or both rose by 10%.

(2) If production and employment both fell then if employment fell more than production due to increases in productivity the figure is greater than 1. If employment fell less than production then productivity fell and the figure is less than 1.

(3) In the table both employment and production fell with the exception of Portugal where both rose but employment rose much more slowly than production indicating that production fell.

(4) All calculations by the author.

Table 3.6 Global shift in apparel production 1980–1990.

Country	Percentage change 1980–1990
USA	+1.6
Italy	−0.4
Germany	−2.0
France	−0.6
Japan	—
UK	+0.6
Spain	−0.2
Hong Kong	+1.3
India	+1.1
Brazil	+0.4
Mexico	+0.1

Source: Singleton, J. (1991) *The World Textile Industry*, Routledge, London, p. 15.

Notes: (1) Data converted to % change by author.
(2) The USA, Germany, France, Italy and the UK were still responsible for 54% of total production in 1990.

This process of what is somewhat euphemistically called 'restructuring' has continued unabated and it has been argued above (Chapter 1) that the late 1990s in fact represent a second watershed for the trend in employment in the apparel sector in the UK. The impact of global shift in apparel production is summarised in Tables 3.6 and 3.10.

It is important to note that the statistics normally used to illustrate global shift are often based on index numbers which show rates of change over time and convey no information about the size of the base from which those changes were calculated. A similar point is made by Young (1999) who argues that the generally accepted view of East Asian growth rates has been distorted by a failure to allow for the favourable (but maybe once and for all) impact of a rapid move out of agriculture, a vast increase in participation rates and a huge investment in education.

Therefore, the rapid growth of output and exports in areas starting from a small base need not and should not be necessarily equated with the total extinction of production or exports from the older, developed centres. Figures published by the United Nations for 1996–97 (see Table 3.7) suggested that the developing countries' share of world apparel exports by garment type ranged from 55% to 71%. Therefore, by definition, the share of exports still produced by the older, developed countries ranged from 45% to roughly 30% in the late 1990s. Statistics for 2002 (Table 3.8) show a somewhat different picture in that while the share of exports taken by the USA and Europe remains at around 30% the increased importance of China, Eastern Europe and Mexico is apparent. It is also clear from this table that the share of exports of apparel taken by many

Table 3.7   Developing countries' share of world apparel exports by garment type 1994/1995.

Men's outerwear (SITC842)	56.8%
Women's outerwear (SITC843)	55.0%
Underwear (SITC844)	71.2%
Outerwear knitted (SITC845)	57.0%
Underwear knitted (SITC846)	56.5%

Source: *UN Handbook of International Trade and Development Statistics 1996–97.*

Table 3.8   Share of world apparel exports, 2002 (%)

Country	SITC Division					Average all trade
	842	843	844	845	846	
USA	2.2	1.3	4.0	2.4	5.7	—
H. Kong	5.9	11.7	9.1	15.2	9.8	3.3
China	20.0	19.7	19.5	21.5	13.7	5.4
Europe	33.3	33.6	25.9	27.0	29.1	—
E. Europe	6.4	5.8	4.0	2.8	3.4	2.4
Asia	47.3	53.5	61.0	62.1	50.7	—
Pakistan	1.1	—	1.3	—	1.5	0.2
India	1.1	3.8	6.1	1.7	4.5	0.8
Turkey	2.3	3.9	2.6	4.2	6.0	0.6
Thailand	1.6	1.3	1.3	2.2	—	1.1
Indonesia	2.1	2.3	3.2	1.5	2.0	1.0
Mexico	5.9	4.0	1.6	0.3	4.6	2.6
Bangladesh	3.0	1.3	5.2	1.0	1.6	0.1
Morocco	1.9	1.7	1.0	0.8	1.3	0.1
Tunisia	3.5	1.4	0.9	—	1.0	0.1

Source: United Nations (2002) *International Trade Statistics Yearbook, Volume 2*, New York.
Note: (1)   It has to be noted that because of the evolution of global supply chains the exports from a country do not necessarily reflect ultimate ownership of the product.
Key: Men's outerwear – 842
Women's outerwear – 843
Underwear – 844
Outerwear knitted – 845
Underwear knitted – 846

developing copuntries is out of all proportion to their participation in world trade in general. There is no doubt that as Dicken (2003, p. 233) points out:

'global shifts in the textile and clothing industries exemplify many of the intractable issues facing today's world economy, particularly the trade tension between developed and developing countries'.

It should be noted that the experiences of the developing countries have not been uniform. Dicken (2003) argues that there has been a second global shift within that widely defined group of nations in that (between 1980 and 1993) the Philippines, Malaysia and Indonesia experienced explosive growth in apparel production, while the so-called first-generation NIEs such as Hong Kong and South Korea experienced only modest growth or even, as in the case of Taiwan, decline. Another shift within the developing world is taking place following the entry of China into the World Trade Organisation (WTO) in 2001 and the removal of quotas in 2005.

The result of this global shift over time has been to alter the composition of the league table of major apparel producers – as was seen in Table 3.6. The most notable features of this table are the rise in importance of Hong Kong, India and Korea, but also the remaining role of America, Italy, Germany, France and the UK. These five countries were still, in 1990, responsible for some 54% of world apparel production as opposed to 61% in 1980. However, it must be noted that these figures predate the rise of China as a centre of apparel production which is made apparent in the trade data below. The geography of world production can be studied (in volume terms) in United Nations Statistics (2001). The figures revealed some interesting changes between 1987 and 1996. World apparel production (in terms of pieces produced) seemingly rose by less than 1% in this period – almost exclusively because of the rapid growth in the production of underwear, as is seen in Jones (2002). In 1996 (Jones, 2002) the share of world production of apparel originating in the USA remained very high (on the assumption that the statistics were reliable) in that it appeared that in only four of fourteen categories of apparel did the Asian share of world production exceed the share produced in the USA. In the period 1996 to 2001 the statistics record a fall in world apparel production of almost 9% – see Table 3.9. This seems barely

Table 3.9 World apparel production in units.

	% of total 2001	% change	
		1987–1996	1996–2001
Men's and boys' jackets	1.6	+43	−24
Men's and boys' overcoats	0.2	−48	−4
Men's and boys' raincoats	0.2	−63	+28
Men's and boys' suits	0.7	−24	−25
Men's and boys' trousers	8.2	−13	−17
Women's and girls' blouses	10.7	−28	+5
Women's and girls' coats	0.7	−39	+1
Women's and girls' dresses	4.9	−18	−14
Women's and girls' raincoats	0.1	−20	−2
Women's and girls' skirts, etc.	14.6	−8	−9
Women's and girls' suits	0.9	−20	−30
Men's and boys' shirts	10.2	−16	−8
Men's and boys' underwear	18.0	+27	−30
Men's and girls' underwear	29.1	+17	−4
Total World Production (000 units)	5,701,787		−8.7

Source: UN Commodity Statistics Yearbook (2001).
Notes: (1) 1987–96 change from R.M. Jones (2002) *The Apparel Industry*. Blackwell Science, Oxford.
  (2) As noted in the text these figures exclude Mainland China and India.

Table 3.10   Shares of world production of apparel in volume terms 1990–2001 (%).

	1990			2001		
	USA	Asia	Europe	USA	Asia	Europe
M+B Jackets	14.1	46.5	32.9	NA	52.7	30.5
M+B Overcoats	5.3	24.7	68.2	12.3	8.6	76.0
M+B Raincoats	29.6	17.3	45.4	NA	48.2	24.4
M+B Suits	16.0	41.8	34.5	10.3	37.6	42.8
M+B Trousers	18.6	24.8	39.9	22.1	20.1	41.2
W+G Blouses	27.7	44.7	20.0	25.1	47.5	17.5
W+G Coats	NA	12.1	54.5	NA	29.8	47.9
W+G Dresses	50.8	13.3	23.9	50.3	26.6	16.0
W+G Raincoats	33.8	20.6	38.9	NA	5.4	21.5
W+G Skirts etc.	50.6	24.3	20.4	NA	9.2	25.6
W+G Suits	16.1	52.4	23.4	NA	28.6	42.0
M+B Shirts	14.4	36.1	28.8	NA	42.9	22.2
M+B Underwear	71.8	14.5	8.3	43.4	38.0	7.1
W+G Underwear	42.2	32.9	15.1	NA	18.8	12.4

Source: as Table 3.9.
Notes: (1) As is stated in the text the statistics exclude Mainland China.
　　　(2) M+B = Men's and boys'.
　　　(3) W+G = Women's and girls'.
　　　(4) The world total reported in 1990 was 6,508,918,000 garments while that in 2001 was 5,701,787,000.
　　　(5) NA = not available for 2001. The problem experienced here with the USA is not the same as that encountered with China in that in the case of the USA the problem is not a total lack of reporting of statistics but gaps for particular categories in certain years.

credible given that apparel prices have been falling and trade in volume terms rose by 18% over the same period. Table 3.10 shows the broad division of production between the USA, Asia and Europe by garment type (in volume terms) in 1990 and 2001. If the figures are taken at face value they show Asia as the major source of production in only four of the fourteen categories. In addition, the Asian share of world production rose in only seven categories. Unfortunately, as Jones (2002) pointed out there is a very severe problem with this statistical source in that it does not include any statistics for apparel production in Mainland China or for India. Private correspondence with the United Nations statisticians revealed that no figures for apparel production in Mainland China have been supplied since 1992. This problem was emphasised by Dickerson (1995, p. 197) but is easily lost sight of given that this series is virtually the only one available for studying these issues. Darnay's (1998) handbook of world manufacturing statistics also excludes China. Clearly this is a most unsatisfactory state of affairs given that qualitative and anecdotal evidence all points to the conclusion that Mainland China is both a major and increasingly important source of apparel production. The measures announced against Chinese apparel exports in 2005 (see Chapter 12) and the subsequent switch to sources in India attest to the importance of these countries as a production source. Trade statistics (which interestingly do incorporate China) suggest, as can be seen in Tables 3.8,

3.12 and 3.13, that China is responsible for about 20% of world apparel exports and India for 2–6%. Therefore, in relation to Tables 3.9 and 3.10 it is probable that the cause of the recorded reduction in world apparel production is the faithful recording of statistics by those developed countries in which production has fallen and the failure to record the increase in the two countries where it is believed production is expanding.

A large number of estimates of the level of apparel production in China can be found in the literature but they vary wildly from 2/3 billion to 12 billion pieces per year. Chen (2004) produces a figure of 7.6 billion items while Phillips (2004) puts the total at 12.2 billion. Liangjun (1999) had suggested that even in 1998 China produced 15 billion garments while Leung (1995, 2000) had suggested the figure was as low as 2/3 billion although he did state in correspondence with the author that statistics in China 'may not be precise' and that figures should only be used 'for reference and may not be 100% trustworthy'. If, for example, a total of 10 billion is added to the total reported in the UN statistics and all of that is allocated to Asia the share of world apparel output taken by Asia in 2001 rises form 26% to 73%!

If, initially, the UN statistics are accepted at face value the following conclusions would be justified:

(1) The USA was the main centre of production for only two garment categories in 2001.
(2) Asia was the main centre of production for five categories but had increased its share since 1990 in only four categories.
(3) Europe's share was, seemingly, the largest in seven categories – which conclusion does not fit well with the reported experiences of individual European nations.

It does seem that this is a spectacular example of the breakdown of the positivist approach advocated in Chapter 1 in that the statistics do not seem to be up to the task for which they are needed and that the deficiency identified will increase over time as production in China rises. Therefore, while it was possible in Jones (2002) to argue that, at least up to the mid-1990s, the developed world remained a significant producer of apparel, the more inclusive trade statistics and the experience of individual countries as recorded in their domestically produced production and employment statistics now suggest that this conclusion is unsustainable. The collapse of the industry in the UK has been documented in Chapters 1 and 2 above and has been repeated in a wide range of other developed nations, e.g. between 1980 and 2001 employment in the apparel industry in Germany fell from 250,000 to 61,000 while the number of enterprises fell from 3200 to 600 (Alder, 2004); in the Netherlands between 1995 and 2002 employment fell from 10,000 to 4,600 (Scheffer, 2004); in the USA apparel output fell by 50% between 1979 and 2002 while import penetration rose from 18% to 79%

(Kilduff, 2005). Nelson (2006) reports that in North Carolina some 37% of the companies and 53% of the jobs in the sector were lost between 1997 and 2003. It is simply not possible to reconcile these experiences with the UN production data. The decision was taken to include it here despite the concerns expressed because it is the main source of satistics and it may improve over time and to provide an example of the difficulties which can be encountered in adhering to a research philosophy in the face of real world problems.

The rise in importance of Mexico as a centre of apparel production since the formation of the North American Free Trade Area in 1994 is instructive in many ways. In the period 1990–1996 output of seven garment categories for which data was available rose by 132% (UN, 1996). Knight (1999) reported that output rose from 250 million pieces in 1992 to 380 million in 1996. Exports of clothing rose by 81% per year between 1991 and 1996. Khanna (1999) observed that Mexico had become, to the USA:

> 'the top supplier in terms of volume and for the first time it is also the leading supplier in value. Mexico is the USA's fastest growing supplier . . . In contrast, imports (into the USA) from China fell in both value and volume. Mexico's rapid growth will continue as Mexican and US firms take advantage of its special access to the US market under the North American Free Trade Area.'

Gereffi (1999) also argued that Mexico was becoming the most important supplier to the American market. However, more recent experience demonstrates the continuing nature of global shift in that after 2001 (when it joined the WTO) China regained its position as the main supplier to the American market with severe consequences for the industry in Mexico. Campaniaris (2005) shows that in the period 2000 to 2003 the Mexican apparel industry lost 175,000 jobs and 1,755 companies. The alleged damage done to the Mexican economy by low-cost competition (Hanson, 1999) may be being repeated. These events provide a potent illustration of the influence of trade barriers upon patterns of trade. This issue is discussed in more detail in Chapter 9.

C. The global pattern of consumption

As Dickerson (1995) points out, global apparel consumption is not easy to measure on a consistent basis across countries. Nevertheless, it is clear that consumer demand for textiles and clothing products varies greatly from country to country, irrespective of how consumption is measured (Dicken, 2003). Variations in fibre consumption per head by region are shown in Table 3.11. There is little doubt that the main cause of this variation is variation in income levels between countries. This relationship is well established in the literature (Jones, 1997; Norum, 1999), as is demonstrated by Fig. 3.1, for example.

Table 3.11   Fibre consumption per head (kilograms) and self-sufficiency
indices (%) 1993 and 2005 (forecast).

Area	Consumption per head (kilograms per head)		Self-sufficiency indices (%)	
	1993	2005*	1993	2005*
USA	29.0	32.5	76	66
EU (15)	16.7	21.5	65	47
Japan	21.3	26.0	66	52
Developed countries	16.4	21.7	72	61
China	5.3	6.4	136	150
South Asia	2.6	3.3	154	175
Developing countries	4.1	5.2	131	145

Source: Coker (1997), World Textile and Clothing Consumption: Forecasts to 2005, *Textile Outlook
International*, March 1997.
Notes: (1)   * Forecast.
      (2)   This is the latest global forecast available.

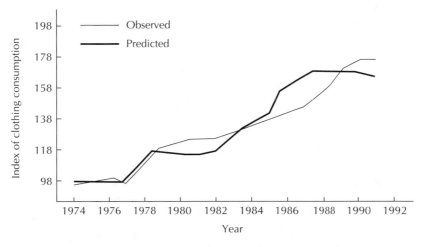

Fig. 3.1   The relationship between apparel consumption and income in the UK.
(Plot of observed *vs* predicted clothing consumption in the UK from 1974 to 1991.)
Reproduced from the *Journal of Fashion Marketing and Management*, 1997, 1, with
permission.

Traditionally the relationship between income per head and textile consumption is expressed by Fig. 3.2. Clearly, therefore, if forecasts of income
growth by country (or region) are available it should be possible to forecast
which areas are most likely to experience a growth in textiles and clothing
consumption. Forecasts for future world fibre consumption appear regularly in
Textile Outlook International, and Table 3.11 additionally summarises the forecast for the year 2005. The ratio between developed and developing countries
has barely changed over time – standing in 1995 at 4.9 (Coker, 1997). As would

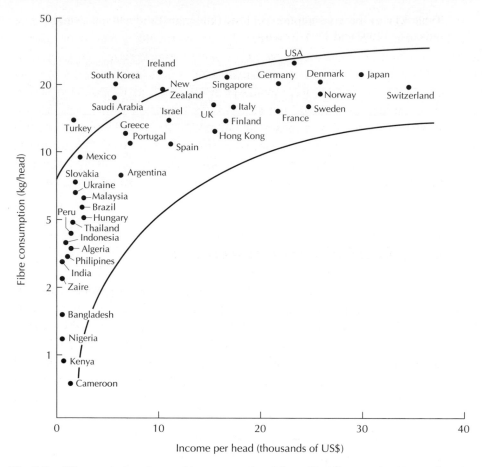

Fig. 3.2   Fibre consumption and income per head for selected countries. Reproduced with permission from *Textile Outlook International*, March 1997, p. 45.

be expected from the analysis of world production trends in Section B above, the developed countries have self-sufficiency indices of less than 100 while the developing countries have indices over 100 and export the surplus onto world markets – see Table 3.11. Increasingly the consumer markets in the developed countries are being supplied by imports. A detailed analysis of the role of emerging markets in the future evolution of the UK clothing industry is contained in Chapter 11.

It is received wisdom that the increase in the number of countries producing apparel has led to what Dickerson (1995, p. 143) describes as 'a global over-capacity' so that 'we can conclude that the global supply perhaps exceeds the global demand for the textile/apparel sector'. The deficiencies of the official statistics on apparel production have been noted above.

It has been proposed in Chapter 1 that our basic approach to issues should be one of logical empiricism. Unfortunately, there are no statistics on global apparel consumption which are cast in the same framework as that for global supply. Therefore, to a degree, this widely held assertion that global supply exceeds demand relies on other indicators, for example that apparel prices in developed markets have been falling and that new sources of supply are continually emerging. This view is so widespread that, in the absence of any hard contradictory data, it will be accepted as one of the main features of the environment within which future strategies have to be developed, despite the fact that the level of proof of this assertion falls somewhat below that which would be desirable in an ideal world.

D. The resultant evolution of trade patterns

It follows that if apparel production moves to areas of low wages but consumption is highest in areas characterised by high incomes then trade must result. Trade in textiles and clothing is conducted on a vast scale. Total world trade in apparel was valued at $201 billion in 2002 (WTO, 2003). Apparel trade dominates trade within the textile pipeline. Singleton (1997) calculated that textile and clothing products accounted for 9.3% of all world manufactured exports in 1993. Dickerson (1995) estimated that trade in apparel alone constituted, in 1992, some 5% of world trade in manufactured products. The WTO (2003) suggests a figure of 3.2% of all merchandise trade in 2002. Rates of growth of trade in textile and apparel products have fluctuated greatly over the last thirty years. The period of fastest growth appears to have been 1985–1990 at 18% per year (Khanna, 1999, p. 45) followed by a period of much slower growth between 1990 and 2000 (WTO, 2003).

Farnie (1997, p. 31) contends that the basis pattern of trade within the textile pipeline changed fundamentally after the mid-1950s. The main feature of this realignment was that:

> 'exports of clothing began to expand more rapidly than exports of textiles proper and increased nearly seven times as fast (1958–84) as exports of textiles'.

In 1987 world exports of clothing exceeded those of textiles for the first time.

The world's leading apparel exporters are shown in Tables 3.12 and 3.13. The main feature of this table is the spectacular increase in the importance of China as an exporting nation. In 1997 a small group of Asian suppliers (China, Hong Kong, South Korea and Taiwan) were the source of 33% of world apparel exports. Nevertheless, a group of developed countries comprising Italy, USA, Germany, France and the UK were still, in 1997, responsible for some 23% of world apparel exports but took in some 58% of world apparel imports. The

Table 3.12   Leading apparel exporters ($ billions).

	1963	1973	1990	1995	1997	2002
Italy	0.3	1.3	11.8	14.2	14.9	NA
Hong Kong	0.2	1.4	15.4	21.3	23.1	22.3
France	NA	NA	4.7	5.6	5.3	NA
Germany	0.2	0.9	7.9	7.5	7.3	NA
UK	0.1	0.4	3.0	4.6	5.3	NA
USA	0.1	0.3	2.6	6.7	8.7	6.0
Portugal	0.01	NA	3.5	3.8	3.3	NA
S. Korea	NA	0.8	7.9	5.0	4.2	3.7
Taiwan	0.01	0.7	4.0	3.3	3.4	2.2
China	NA	0.2	9.7	24.0	31.8	41.3
Turkey	NA	NA	3.3	6.1	6.7	8.1
Thailand	NA	NA	2.8	5.0	3.8	3.4
Indonesia	NA	NA	1.6	3.4	2.9	3.9
Netherlands	0.1	0.4	2.2	2.8	3.7	NA
Mexico	NA	NA	0.6	2.7	NA	7.8
Morocco	NA	NA	0.7	0.8	NA	2.4
Tunisia	NA	NA	1.1	2.3	2.3	2.7
Bangladesh	NA	NA	0.5	NA	NA	4.1
India	NA	NA	2.5	3.7	4.1	5.5
EU (15)	NA	NA	40.8	48.5	NA	50.5

Sources: 1963 and 1973, K. Dickerson (1995), *Textiles and Apparel in the Global Economy*, Prentice Hall, New Jersey. 1995 and 1997, *WTO Annual Report 1998*; and *Textile Outlook International* (1999), World Textile and Apparel Trade and Production Trends (March 1999); 2002 data from WTO (2003).

Notes: (1) NA = figure not given in the source indicated.
  (2) Although precise definitions of the sector were not given in all sources the fact that the generic source was common leads to confidence in the comparability of the data.
  (3) In the latest WTO report (2003) figures are not given for individual countries within the EU.
  (4) The figure for India is for 2001.

role of Italy is especially interesting and will be considered in more detail in Chapter 8.

Farnie (1997, p. 31) argues that Asia became the beneficiary of a 'revolution which could potentially have profited either hemisphere . . . because its labour was abundant, cheap and unregulated'. In the period 1980–94 exports of clothing from Asia: 'expanded at a rate 35% faster than those from the rest of the world'. The main markets were in western developed countries and it is no coincidence that this period saw, in the UK, both the explosion of apparel consumption and a surge of imports.

The leading apparel importing nations are shown in Table 3.14. This table contains few surprises in that the major importers are, as would be anticipated from the preceding analysis, the richer, more developed countries – in particular the USA and Germany, although the latter's share of world apparel imports has fallen dramatically between 1973 and 1997. China's exports of apparel grew by 326% in between 1990 and 2002.

Table 3.13 Leading apparel exports (1973–2002): percentages of world total.

Country	1973	1980	1992	1993	1995	1997	2002
Italy	10.7	11.3	7.5	8.9	8.9	8.4	NA
Hong Kong	11.6	11.5	12.3	7.0	6.0	5.3	4.1
France	8.5	5.7	3.2	3.4	3.6	3.0	NA
Germany	7.5	7.1	5.1	5.1	4.7	4.1	NA
UK	3.6	4.6	2.3	2.6	2.9	3.0	NA
USA	2.4	3.1	2.6	3.7	4.2	4.9	3.0
Portugal		1.6	2.4	3.1	2.3	1.9	NA
S. Korea	6.1	7.3	4.2	4.6	3.1	2.4	1.8
Taiwan	5.8	6.0	2.5	2.8	2.1	1.9	NA
China	1.6	4.0	10.2	13.9	15.2	18.0	20.6
Turkey	NA	0.3	2.6	3.3	3.9	3.82	4.0
Thailand	NA	0.7	2.3	3.1	2.9	2.1	1.7
Indonesia	NA	0.2	1.9	2.6	2.1	1.6	2.0
India	NA	1.5	1.9	2.7	2.6	2.5	2.8
Netherlands	NA	2.2	1.7	1.9	1.8	2.1	NA
EU	NA	42.0	NA	37.7	NA	24.1	25.1

Sources: 1973 and 1992 as Table 3.14.
　　　　1995, Dicken, P. (2003), *Global Shift*, Paul Chapman, London.
　　　　1993, Singleton, J. (1997), *World Textile Industry*, Routledge, London.
　　　　1997, WTO as Table 3.14; 2002 WTO (2003).
Notes:　(1)　Gaps in the table indicate data were not given in the named source.
　　　　(2)　For some countries the figure may be for a year near to the year indicated.

Table 3.14 Leading apparel importers 1973–2002 ($ billions).

	$ billions				Share of world apparel imports (%)	Share in country's total imports (%)
	1973	1990	1997	2002	2002	2002
USA	2.2	27.0	50.3	66.7	31.7	5.5
Germany	2.5	20.4	22.5	NA	NA	NA
Japan	0.6	8.7	16.7	17.6	8.4	5.2
HK/China	NA	6.9	15.0	15.6	0.8	7.5
UK	0.8	7.0	11.2	NA	NA	NA
France	0.6	8.4	10.8	NA	NA	NA
Netherlands	0.9	4.8	5.9	NA	NA	NA
Italy	0.2	2.6	5.3	NA	NA	NA
Bel-Lux	0.6	3.6	4.5	NA	NA	NA
Switzerland	0.5	3.4	3.4	3.4	1.6	4.1
Mexico	NA	0.6	3.4	4.0	1.9	2.1
Canada	0.3	2.4	3.0	4.0	1.9	1.8
Austria	0.2	2.4	2.9	NA	NA	NA
Spain	NA	1.6	2.8	NA	NA	NA
Sweden	0.4	2.5	2.1	NA	NA	NA
EU	NA	56.8	NA	84.9	40.3	3.5

Source: World Trade Organisation and K. Dickerson (1995), Table 7.10, p. 225, 2002 from WTO (2003).
Notes:　(1)　Most of these totals were re-exported.
　　　　(2)　The USA and EU took 72% of the worlds apparel imports in 2002.

Table 3.15   Trade balances in apparel, 2002 ($ millions).

USA	−60,699
EU	−34,430
Switzerland	−2,686
Poland	+1,105
Turkey	+7,774
Malaysia	+695
India	+5,442
Pakistan	+2,220
Philippines	+1,864
Indonesia	+3,914
Hong Kong	+6,697

Source: World Trade Organisation (2003) *Annual Report*.

Most developed countries exhibit large negative trade balances in the apparel sector (i.e. imports exceed exports) as can be seen from Table 3.15. In the case of the EU these deficits are particularly large with a small group of Asian suppliers. Dickerson (1995) estimated that, in 1992, the developed countries had a combined deficit on apparel trade of $62.4 billion, whereas the developing countries had a positive balance of $61.3 billion.

Dicken (2003) estimated that, in 1995, South Korea, Malaysia, Hong Kong and Taiwan alone had a combined surplus on apparel trade of some $198 billion. The UK runs a substantial and growing deficit on apparel trade which in 2003 reached some £7,885,193,000. The current UK trading situation is examined in detail in Chapter 5.

It is important to note that the developed countries tend to send their apparel exports to other developed countries (so-called intra-trade – see Chapter 4), while the developing countries generally direct apparel exports to the richer, developed countries. In 1996 (Dickerson, 1999) the developed countries purchased over 84% of world apparel exports, most of which (60%) came from developing areas (see Table 3.16). In 2002, according to WTO (2003) figures, intra-Western European trade in apparel amounted to $45.6 billion while Asian trade to

Table 3.16   Trade flows in the apparel sector, 1996 ($ billions).

Origin	Destination		World
	More developed	Less developed	
More developed	48.21	10.85	61.67
Less developed	81.91	9.07	94.11
World	137.22	19.98	163.32

Source: Dickerson, K. (1999) *Textiles and Apparel in the Global Economy*, Prentice Hall, New Jersey.

Table 3.17   Exports, of apparel by region in
$ billion and (%).

	1997	2002
Asia	78.9 (100)	89.9 (100)
To N. America	29.1 (36.9)	34.5 (38.4)
To W. Europe	19.4 (24.6)	20.9 (23.2)
To Asia	21.5 (27.2)	22.8 (25.4)
W. Europe	58.4 (100)	60.52 (100)
To W. Europe	44.2 (75.7)	45.6 (75.4)
To N. America	3.3 (5.7)	4.2 (6.9)
N. America	10.2 (100)	8.0 (100)
To Latin America	6.2 (60.8)	4.4 (54.7)
To W. Europe	0.7 (6.9)	0.4 (5.0)
To Asia	1.0 (9.8)	0.5 (6.7)

Source: as Table 3.15.

Table 3.18   Source of EU apparel
imports (2002).

Country of origin	% share
W. Europe	49.9
Asia	29.7
C. I E. Europe	11.5
N. America	0.5
Main suppliers	
EU	39.9
China	11.5
Turkey	7.8
Romania	4.1
Tunisia	3.2
	66.5
Other suppliers	
India	3.0
Morocco	2.9
Poland	1.9
Bangladesh	3.0
Indonesia	1.7

Source: World Trade Organisation (2003) as
      Table 3.17.

Western Europe amounted to only $22.8 billion (see Table 3.17). Sources of
EU clothing imports are shown for 2002 in Table 3.18 which emphasises the
intra-trade phenomenon.

By way of a broad generalisation, it can be stated that those countries in
which apparel production represents a significant proportion of the country's
economic activity tend to be countries which import relatively little apparel – as
can be seen from Table 3.19.

Table 3.19   Importance of apparel trade by country, 2002.

	% of total exports	% of total imports
EU	2.1	3.5
USA	0.9	5.5
Bangladesh	67.8	NA
China	12.7	0.5
India	12.4	0.1
Indonesia	6.9	0.1
Malaysia	2.1	0.2
Mexico	4.8	2.1
Morocco	30.4	NA
Pakistan	22.5	0.1
Poland	4.7	1.5
Romania	23.4	2.6
Switzerland	0.9	4.1
Thailand	4.9	0.2
Tunisia	39.5	5.6
Turkey	23.3	0.6
Macao	70.0	11.5
Mauritius	54.1	NA
Sri Lanka	49.5	NA
Philippines	7.2	0.1

Source: as Table 3.15.
Note: NA = not given.

One product of global shift will be that individually a number of the developing countries will account for a growing share of total world clothing exports as was seen in Table 3.12. This can be detailed for various categories of garments.

It can be seen from Table 3.20 that the Asian share of world apparel exports by category ranged from 47% to 68%. This table makes abundantly clear the

Table 3.20   Shares of world exports in 1995 and 2002 (in value terms as a percentage).

Category of apparel	1995				2002			
	USA	Europe	Asia	China	USA	Europe	Asia	China
842	4.7	31.9	47.2	18.4	2.2	33.0	47.3	20.2
843	—	33.5	51.8	15.6	1.3	33.6	53.5	19.7
844	6.2	20.1	63.3	16.5	4.0	25.9	61.1	19.5
845	—	34.1	54.3	11.7	2.4	27.0	62.1	21.5
846	7.0	30.0	50.4	11.9	5.7	29.1	50.7	13.7
847	5.3	45.3	44.8	12.1	5.5	32.5	55.7	19.5
848	4.2	21.1	68.0	22.1	2.9	25.1	67.5	32.5

Source: United Nations, *International Trade Statistics Year Book Vol. 2*, UN, New York.
Key: 842   Men's outerwear (not knitted).
       843   Women's outerwear (not knitted).
       844   Under garments (not knitted).
       845   Outerwear (knitted).
       846   Undergarments (knitted).
       847   Textile clothing accessories.
       848   Head gear.

increasingly important role of China in global apparel trade flows – confirming the post-1990 rise of China as an apparel producer previously alluded to above and reinforcing the need to obtain accurate data for production in that country.

E. Trade flows and employment in the developed countries

As has been seen above (Chapter 2), it is almost an article of faith that the main cause of loss of jobs in the textiles and apparel sectors in the developed countries has been the increase in imports (especially from low-cost areas) experienced by these countries. As Dicken expressed it (2003, p. 204) the:

> 'popular view and, indeed the political view, as expressed through such measures as the Multi-Fibre Arrangement, is that these job losses have been caused by the wholesale geographical shift of production to cheap labour locations in the Third World'.

There is an extensive literature detailing the results of research studies investigating that assertion. It is something of paradox that the results of the vast majority of these studies do not confirm the alleged relationship between imports and job loss. This research will now be reviewed in line with the research philosophy outlined in Chapter 1. The results of some of the major research investigations are summarised in Fig. 3.3. The so-called accounting procedure upon which these studies are based is summarised in Gibbs (1982) and Singleton (1991).

One of the best known of such studies is that conducted by Cline (1987) for the USA between 1962 and 1985. As Dicken (2003, p. 264) comments, a reading of these results leads to the conclusion that 'the effect of imports on employment change in textiles has been negligible compared with the effect of productivity growth'. Interestingly, from the point of view of the present text, the picture in clothing was far less clear cut. As can be seen from Fig. 3.3, during the period 1982–85, for example, the role of productivity change and trade was virtually identical.

In a similar study, Cable (1977) had produced data for the period 1970–75 in the UK, which indicated that in textiles (cotton fabrics) 4,700 jobs were lost due to productivity change as against 8,400 due to import penetration (of which 2,225 were lost due to low-cost competition). In the clothing sector the figures were 81,900 due to productivity increases, 30,800 due to import penetration and only 19,450 due to low cost competition. Silberston (1984) also found that between 1970–75, in the UK, the main cause of job loss in the cotton and man-made fibres sectors of the pipeline were productivity increases responsible for 10,898 and rising imports which accounted for 16,853 jobs lost. In a later study of the UK, Cable (1982) covered the period 1970–78. His conclusion was that 121,000 jobs were lost because of increased productivity against only 50,900 due

		Productivity	Imports	Exports	Demand
UK 1970–78[1]	T	−121,000	−50,900	—	+34,700
UK 1970–75[2]	C	−81,900	−30,800	—	+54,600
UK (Manchester) 1966–75[3]	C	−13,020	−8,497	—	—
UK 1970–75[4]	T	−10,898	−16,853	—	—
UK 1970–75[5]	C	−118,500	−52,500	—	+105,000
UK 1970–75[6]	C	−23.7%	−9.5%	—	+20.6%
UK 1970–75[7]	T	−17,213	−11,749	−26,658	−13,882
	T	−15,865	−13,329	−35,296	−24,569
	T	−463,400	−141,800	—	—
Germany 1962–75[8]	C	−160,000	−144,600	—	—
Germany 1980–89[5]	C	−39,800	−39,000	—	+7,500
W. Germany 1970–76[6]	C	−19%	−7.8%	—	+0.5%
Spain 1980–89[5]	C	−19,300	−14,400	—	+2,800
Netherlands 1980–89[6]	C	−3,500	−2,200	—	+800
Netherlands 1970–76[6]	C	−37.0	−38.3	—	+17.6
Italy 1980–89[5]	C	−18,400	+13,100	—	+5,100
Italy 1970–76[6]	C	−18.7%	+10.9%	—	+7.3%
France 1980–89[5]	C	−45,000	−22,300	—	+6,700
France 1970–76[6]	C	−18.7%	−2.2%	—	+8.0%
Belgium 1980–89[5]	C	+4,100	−7,300	—	−2,500
Belgium 1970–76[6]		−33.2%	−15.1%	—	+38.6%
USA[9] (in % terms)					
1962–67	T	−7.3	−0.4	+0.2	+9.1
1967–72	T	−3.9	−0.3	+0.1	+4.1
1972–77	T	−3.2	+0.2	+0.3	+1.4
1977–82	T	−2.7	−0.2	−0.1	−0.6
1982–85	T	−4.3	−0.7	−0.5	+3.3
1962–67	C	−2.1	−0.3	+0.04	+4.5
1967–72	C	−1.0	−0.6	+0.03	+1.6
1972–77	C	−3.1	−1.0	+0.02	+3.3
1977–82	C	−2.2	−1.0	+0.2	+1.9
1982–85	C	−3.8	−3.3	−0.4	+6.0

Sources: (1) Cable, V. (1982).
(2) Cable, V. (1977).
(3) Gibbs, D. (1982).
(4) Silberston, A. (1984) *The MFA and the UK Economy*, HMSO, London.
(5) Balasubramanyan, V. & Salisu, M. (1993).
(6) Arpan, J. & De La Torre, J. (1982) *The US Apparel Industry*, Georgia State University, Atlanta.
(7) Singleton, J. (1991).
(8) Keesing, D.B. & Wolf, M. (1980).
(9) Cline, W. (1987) *The Future of World Trade in Textiles and Apparel*, Institute for International Economics, Washington.

Note: T = textile studies; C = clothing studies.

Fig. 3.3   Job loss studies – a summary.

to increased imports. Gibbs (1982), studying the apparel industry in Manchester over the period 1966–75, likewise found that increases in productivity were responsible for almost twice as many job losses as was import competition and, furthermore, of those jobs lost which could be attributed to imports, only half could be blamed on imports from low cost areas. Therefore, UK studies were much more consistent in their findings that productivity changes were the main cause of job loss.

Singleton (1997, p. 124) argues that the period 1950–1970 needs to be split into three distinct periods and that (taking spinning and weaving together) the main factor accounting for decline in the period 1950–1955 was export failure. Loss due to imports is described as slight. In the second period, 1955–1960, rising imports became 'the major element in employment decline' but even then the loss due to rising imports was only marginally greater than that due to rising productivity.

Finally, during the 1960s, 'declining domestic demand for cloth and yarn took over as the primary contributory factor to the reduction in employment'. In relation to the primary textile sector, therefore, Singleton's conclusion, for the UK, was that (Singleton, 1991, p. 126):

> 'competition from the less developed countries was at its most devastating during the 1950s. During the 1960s and 1970s shifts in home demand . . . and productivity tended to be more important determinants of changes in employment in the cotton industry'.

Keesing (1980), reviewing evidence from the West German textile and clothing sectors between 1962 and 1975, concluded that just over three times as many jobs were lost in textiles due to rising productivity than were lost due to rising imports. In the clothing sector, however, the ratio was only just over one, i.e. the two factors were responsible for almost exactly the same volume of job losses but, as in the American case, the picture was less clear cut in clothing than in textiles.

Two more up-to-date studies of the UK have confirmed the emphasis placed on the role of productivity changes. Balasubramanyan (1993, p. 46) concluded that while both import penetration and productivity growth had led to substantial job losses, the growth 'in labour productivity . . . appears to have been the major factor in loss of jobs' between 1980 and 1989. Hine (1998, p. 1507), in a study of the period 1979–92 when nearly three million jobs were lost in the manufacturing sector, determined that 'the dominant factor has been productivity growth. Trade is seen as having only a minor role' while changes in efficiency resulting from increased penetration were seen as accounting for only 6.4% of the reduction in employment between 1981 and 1991 – although it was conceded (1998, p. 1510) that 'increased import penetration has stimulated an important defensive response'.

How can the results of this body of research be summed up? In relation to the apparel sector the picture is far less clear cut than it appears to be in the primary textile sector. For example, in Cline's study for 1982–85 and in Keesing's study for 1962–75 the two factors – productivity increases and rising imports – received almost equal weighting. Singleton, likewise, in the case of the primary textile sector, did not consistently rule out the role of import competition.

In Cable's research period productivity in the apparel sector did rise by some twenty points (at a rate slightly above the average – see Table 2.6 in Chapter 2) but in the same period, imports rose by a factor of six. In Balasubramanyan's later research period (1980–89) productivity did rise very rapidly in the early 1980s and by nearly thirty points over the whole period during which the rise in imports was roughly 300%.

This body of research has been reviewed in some detail because it bears so heavily on the conclusion that rising imports were the main cause of the industry's problems. However, it has now to be noted that the research technique used to produce these results (the so-called accounting or components of change technique) is seriously if not fatally flawed in that it assumes that the various factors which produce the observed change in employment are *totally unconnected*. This seems barely credible; it is difficult to believe that the impetus to the increase in productivity recorded in the UK apparel industry in the 1980s was not driven by the perceived need to compete with overseas competition. In addition, to the extent that import competition promotes low prices, this in turn could be expected to increase domestic demand. The problems with this research device have been summarised by Martin (1981) who concluded his examination of the accounting technique with the statement that it would 'attribute those employment losses only to the approximate cause, the rise in productivity growth, without recognising the causal influence of import competition' in promoting advances in productivity. Wragg (1978) also found that: 'industries take notice of potential competition and attempt to improve their performance'.

There is, at least, one alternative approach to this issue which has been pioneered by Choi (1985). This involves seeking associations between imports, consumption and production of apparel in particular countries. In a study of the USA (1978–82) it was found that for only three (out of 72) apparel categories did rising imports exceed the fall in production. In the case of the EEC (1978–81) there were nine cases of Multi Fibre Arrangement (MFA) supplies and production falling together; five cases in which MFA supplies rose; and three in which both imports and production fell together.

Choi (1985, p. 39), therefore, concluded that on the basis of this evidence:

> 'with a few exceptions, domestic production not only did not decline, but rose steadily faster from 1979–1981, even during periods when consumption and/or MFA developing country imports declined'.

Jones (1988a) studied the relationship between apparel imports, production and consumption in the UK between 1975 and 1985. This study was able to find virtually no evidence of an inverse relationship between levels of production and imports – except in the case of men's and boys' woven suits. The most normal scenario was for both production and imports to have increased together. This conclusion also held for a study of MFA imports between 1980 and 1985. Jones

(1988b) carried out further research on MFA products only for the period 1984–1987. The initial conclusion, using unlagged relationships, was that there was 'very little support for the argument that increases in imports are directly associated with decreases in production': out of 29 apparel categories studied, only nine displayed a negative relationship between imports and production (babies knitted undergarments; other knitted undergarments; woven shirts; knitted trousers; dresses; men's woven jackets; women's woven dressing gowns; skirts and men's woven suits). However, the introduction of time-lagged relationships (production being lagged on imports by one, two, three and four quarters to allow for imports to replace domestic production) did substantially alter the results in that (Jones, 1988b, p. 9) the total number of categories displaying a negative correlation between imports and production rose (from nine) to fifteen (or to 52% of the cases studied). In addition, the lagged data produced some spectacular reversals of the findings – especially in the case of jerseys, scarves and nightwear.

Martin (1981, p. 163) had concluded that it was important that studies of the causes of job loss should take account of the lagged effect of imports in production. To further complicate the issue it has to be noted that this period was one of both rapidly rising domestic consumption and of increasing rates of import penetration.

It is extremely difficult to produce a succinct and uncomplicated statement which captures the results of this body of research. The accounting procedure studies summarised in Figure 3.3 have to be studied given the importance they have assumed in the literature – in particular they have frequently been utilised in a political context to argue that trade restrictions are not needed given that imports cannot be shown to have been responsible for job losses.

As has been seen above, even this statement is only partially true in the case of apparel – as opposed to textiles. However, as has been suggested above, the present author believes the technique of analysis is so flawed that the results are unreliable – in which case it does not make much sense to rely on any of it! The collapse of employment in the apparel sector in the UK after 1998 cannot be ascribed either to rising productivity (which was falling) or to a lack of demand (see Chapters 2 and 10). The cause must, therefore, have been rising imports.

In the case of the UK, however, the increase in imports (in current prices) in most periods since 1975 has been extremely rapid. For example, over 120% between 1975 and 1980; over 215% between 1980 and 1990 (Jones, 1992). In the period 1985–1990 which was one of very rapid growth in consumption (by UK standards), the consumption of apparel in the UK rose by 60% in current terms or 26% in real terms. Over the same period imports rose by 97%. In the period 1980–90, apparel consumption rose by 153% in current price terms or 41% in real terms, but imports rose by 217%!

Additionally (see Chapter 5) import penetration rates have been rising remorselessly. In view of these facts and the results of the correlation studies reported above (Jones, 1988a) the only conclusion which appears tenable is that the impact of rising imports on the size of the apparel industry in the UK has been a negative one. It is probably not insignificant that the negative associations between imports and domestic production which were beginning to appear from the lagged data in the period 1984–87 were followed by falling output levels in the UK in the late 1980s and early 1990s (see Table 2.1).

References

Alder, U. (2004) Structural Change: the Dominant Feature in the Economic Development of the German Textile and Clothing Industries. *Journal of Fashion Marketing and Management*, **8.3**, 300–20.

Balasubramanyan, V. & Salisu, M. (1993) International Trade and Employment in the UK Textile Clothing Sector. *Applied Economics*, **25**, 1477–82.

Cable, V. (1977) British Protectionism and LDC Imports. *Overseas Development Institute Review*, **2**, 29–49.

Cable, V. (1982) Cheap Imports and Jobs. In: *Case Studies in Economic Development* (Ed. P. Maunder), pp. 53–83. Heinemann, London.

Campaniaris, C. (2005) Mexico: is the Bloom off the Rose? *Journal of Fashion Marketing and Management*, **9.1**, 5–7.

Chen, C. & Shih, H. (2004) The Impact of WTO Accession on the Chinese Garment Industry. *Journal of Fashion Marketing and Management*, **8.2**, 221–30.

Choi, Y.P. (1985) *The MFA in Theory and Practice*. Pinter, London.

Cline, W. (1987) *The Future of World Trade in Textiles and Apparel*. Institute for International Economics, Washington.

Coker, J. (1997) World Textile and Clothing Consumption Forecasts to 2005. *Textile Outlook International*, **70**, 35–77.

Darnay, A.J. (1998) *Manufacturing Worldwide*. Gale, New York.

Dicken, P. (1998) *Global Shift: Transforming the World Economy*. P. Chapman, London.

Dicken, P. (2003) *Global Shift: Transforming the World Economy*. Sage, London.

Dickerson, K. (1995) *Textiles and Apparel in the Global Economy*. Prentice Hall, New Jersey.

Dickerson, K. (1999) *Textiles and Apparel in the Global Economy*. Prentice Hall, New Jersey.

Eenennaam, E.V. & Brouthers, K.D. (1996) Global Relocation: High Hopes and Big Risks. *Long Range Planning*, **1**, 84–94.

Farnie, D.A. & Abe, T. (1997) The Asian Market for Cotton Manufacturers 1890–1997. *Journal of Modern Japanese Studies*, **19**, 44–83.

Farnie, D.A. & Jeremy, D.J. (1998) The Emergence of a New Paradigm in the Museums of the N. West. *Journal of Industrial History*, **1.1**, 107–22.

Gereffi, G. (1999) International Trade and Industrial Upgrading in the Apparel Commodity Chain. *Journal of International Economics*, **48**, 37–70.

Gibbs, D. (1982) Imports and Employment: The Case of the Manchester Clothing Industry. *Hollings Statistical Bulletin for the Clothing Industry*, **4.2**, 15–48.

Hanson, G.H. & Harrison, A. (1999) Trade Liberalisation and Wage Inequality in Mexico. *Industrial and Labour Relations Review*, **52**, 271–89.

Hine, R.C. & Wright, P.W. (1998) Trade With Low Wage Economies, Employment and Productivity in UK Manufacturing. *Economic Journal*, **108**, 1500–11.

Jones, R.M. (1988a) The Relationship Between Clothing Production, Consumption and Imports in the UK. *Hollings Apparel Industry Review*, **5.2**, 21–53.

Jones, R.M. (1988b) The Relationship Between Trade and Production in the UK Clothing Industry. *Hollings Apparel Industry Review*, **5.3**, 3–12.

Jones, R.M. (1992) Statistical Review. *Hollings Apparel Industry Review*, **9**, 53–96.

Jones, R.M. (2002) *The Apparel Industry*. Blackwell Science, Oxford.

Jones, R.M. & Robb, P. (1997) The Demand for Clothing in the UK and Sweden. *Journal of Fashion Marketing and Management*, **1.2**, 113–25.

Keesing, D.B. & Wolf, M. (1980) *Textile Quotas Against Developing Countries*. Trade Policy Research Centre, London.

Khanna, S.R. (1999) Trends in Textile and Clothing Imports. *Textile Outlook International*, **79**, 70–105.

Kilduff, P. (2005) Patterns of Strategic Adjustment in the US Textile and Apparel Industries since 1979. *Journal of Fashion Marketing and Management*, **9.2**, 180–95.

Kilduff, P. & Chi, T. (2006) Longitudinal Patterns of Competitive Advantages in the Textile Complex. *Journal of Fashion Marketing and Management* (forthcoming).

Knight, P. (1999) Profile of Mexican Textile and Clothing Industry. *Textile Outlook International*, **79**, 76–104.

Leung, P. (1995) Fifteen Years of Progress. *Textile Asia*, **26**, 67–8.

Leung, P. (2000) China – Output. *Textile Asia*, **31**, 58.

Liangjun, X. & Xiaoying, X. (1999) Apparel Production in China. *Japanese Textiles News*, 13–18.

Martin, J.P. & Evans, J.M. (1981) Notes on Measuring the Employment Displacement Effects of Trade by the Accounting Procedures. *Oxford Economic Papers*, 33, 154–64.

Nelson, N. & Karpona, E. (2006) Employment in the U.S. Textiles and Apparel Industries: a Comparison of Regional vs National Trends. *Journal of Fashion Marketing and Management* (forthcoming).

Norum, P. (1999) The Demand for Accessories, Footwear and Hosiery. *Journal of Fashion Marketing and Management*, **3.1**, 56–66.

Phillips, P. (2004) Textiles and Apparel in China: Preparing for Quota Free Markets. *Textile Outlook International*, **109**, 13–46.

Scheffer, M. & Duineveld, M. (2004) Final Demise or Regeneration: the Dutch Case. *Journal of Fashion Marketing and Management*, **8.3**, 340–50.

Silberston, A. (1984) *The MFA and the UK Economy*. HMSO, London.

Singleton, J. (1997) *Lancashire on the Scrap Heap*. Oxford University Press, Oxford.

Taplin, I. & Winterton, J. (1997) *Rethinking Global Production*. Ashgate, Aldershot.

United Nations (2001) *U.N. Commodity Statistics*. United Nations, New York.

United Nations (2002) *International Trade Statistics Yearbook, Vol 2*. New York.

World Trade Organisation (1996 and 2003) *Annual Report of the World Trade Organisation*.

Wragg, R. & Roberts, J. (1978) *Post War Trends in Employment, Production and Output*. Department of Employment, London.

Young, A. (1999) The Tyranny of Numbers: Confronting the Statistical Reality of the East Asian Growth Experience. *Quarterly Journal of Economics*, **110**, 641–80.

Chapter 4

The Role of Labour Costs and Theories of Development

A. *Labour costs in apparel production*

(i)   The labour intensive nature of production

The single most defining and unique feature of apparel production is its endur-ing labour intensity. The decreasing labour intensity of the manufacturing sector as a whole has long been recognised in the literature. Tulder and June (1988), for example, pointed out that, as a result of automation and subcontracting, the capital intensity of business has tended to steadily increase and the labour con-tent to steadily fall.

Ohmae (1985, p. 4) stated that:

> 'within the past decades, automation, robots, machine centres and numerical controls have increased productivity significantly in the broadest sense . . . Translated into quantitative terms, the labour cost context of traditional assembly operations has dropped from 25% to somewhere between 10% and 5% of the total cost of production'.

This has not happened in the case of apparel manufacture. In terms of the stages within the apparel manufacturing cell of Fig. 1.1 it can be concluded that inno-vations have largely been restricted to the pre-assembly stage, e.g. applications of microelectronic technology in pattern grading and marker making. According to Hoffman and Rush (1988) these advances reduced the grading process from four days to one hour and achieved considerable material savings at the cutting stage.

Singleton (1997, p. 85) , for example, recognised that:

> 'the design and preparatory processes in the clothing industry are amenable to the use of computer technology'

which confirmed the view of Taplin (1997, p. 2) that the application of new technology:

'has mainly been directed at the design and cutting stages, transported garments between machines, the overall monitoring and control of production
operations and ad hoc modifications to existing machinery'

while:

'make up or garment assembly has not been appropriate for the extensive
application of new technology . . .'

This is not to say that there have been no advances in sewing technology. Zeitlin
(1988) identifies three lines of innovation: (a) increased stitching speeds; (b)
developments of work aids; and (c) the emergence of automatic machines dedicated to special tasks, such as buttonholing.

In addition, as is noted in Chapter 7, a number of research programmes
have been carried out into the potential for increased automation of garment
assembly. Nevertheless, in spite of these efforts – and it has been noted that
apparel production is not regarded as a knowledge-based sector which spends
heavily on research – there is no sign of a revolutionary breakthrough which
shows any realistic prospect of achieving such widespread commercial acceptance and adoption as to lead to a dramatic decrease in the labour content in
apparel assembly.

The main reasons for this state of affairs are, first, technical ones relating to
the problems of automating processes utilising limp fabric and, secondly, economic in that plentiful supplies of cheap labour have been and continue to be
available. Zhou (1997a) concluded that 'a revolution in the sewing room which
would lead to a dramatic decrease in direct labour content in apparel assembly is
still awaited'.

A good illustration of the problems would be the extensive research programme funded by MITI in Japan which set the ambitious target (Singleton,
1997, p. 180) of creating 'a flexible automated system capable of producing two
thousand garments for a short production series' to be achieved over a nine-year
period with a budget of some thirteen billion yen. The results of the programme
were unveiled in 1991, and, according to Singleton (1997, p. 181), although complete automation has not been achieved 'the majority of technical operations,
such as picking up and moving fabric . . . have already been achieved'.

However, widespread commercial application of the results of this research
has not taken place. Anson (1997, p. 3) felt that it was reasonable to conclude
even at that late date that while a number of:

'islands of automation reduce the amount of labour needed for certain tasks
without compromising flexibility . . . the goal of true automation in garment
manufacture appears to be as far away as ever'.

Therefore, it remains the case that labour cost differentials between countries
remain the major factor which explains the gaining of market share by low cost

imports at the expense of apparel producers in the developed countries. The overall impact of the technological developments which have taken place at the assembly stage have been insufficient to wipe out the advantage of very low labour costs.

The fact that the percentage of total costs accounted for by labour charges has remained stubbornly high in apparel production can be confirmed by reference to many sources over the years, e.g. in 1971 the National Economic Development Office (NEDO, 1971) estimated the direct labour charge to be 20.5% of total costs. Khanna (1998) quotes 30% while Hoffman (1988) gave a figure between 20–40%. Therefore, it is logical to argue that so long as this remains the case, manufacturers will continue to seek out low labour cost locations. This has been confirmed, for example, by Scheffer (1994) who reported that for 75% of a sample of 165 apparel manufacturers in Europe, the most important factor in utilising foreign sources of production was the labour cost gap between countries. It is true that labour cost is not the *only* factor involved in the decision as to where to produce, but it is a crucial factor which cannot be over-stressed. The diamond framework outlined in Chapter 2, it will be recalled, had four major elements – the influence of labour cost enters via the element labelled 'Factor Conditions'.

Singleton (1997, p. 33) in his ambitious application of the Porter Model concluded that it was unlikely that other dimensions of the factor conditions element such as excellent management or improvements in the quality of labour, could ever 'offset the low wages enjoyed by developing countries'. Therefore, while recognising that the sourcing decision is a more complex question than simply locating the lowest figure in a table of labour cost statistics, the conclusion drawn by Scheffer (1994, p. 112) that the main driving force behind sourcing decisions is the differential cost of labour between countries can be accepted as a working hypothesis.

(ii)   The extent of labour cost variation

This labour cost differential is both substantial and enduring. As Taplin (1997, p. 11) concludes:

> 'the magnitude of the labour cost gap . . . between the high wage and low wage economies is so great that even taking other costs into account, clothing manufacturing costs in the UK . . . are 200% higher than in China'.

The most frequently encountered sources of data on labour and manufacturing costs by country are those produced either by Werner International or by Kurt Salmon Associates (KSA). Werner International has analysed international labour costs in textiles and apparel since 1968. Their cost comparisons for the primary textile sector (spinning and weaving) first appeared in 1968 and covered twelve countries. By the 1990s statistics covering almost 60 countries were available.

Figures for the apparel sector appeared much less frequently and ceased to be produced after 1998. Figures for the primary textile sector are available for 2004. Table 4.1 reproduces these figures with the UK ratio reworked by the

Table 4.1   Labour cost comparisons – apparel industry.

Country	Total Cost per hour (US$)			
	1998	1990/98 % change	Index 1998 UK = 100	2004 (Textiles)
Belgium	16.49	+28	152	30.42
Denmark	18.71	+17	172	NA
Germany	18.04	+150	166	27.69
Greece	6.55	+51	60	11.67
Spain	6.79	−4	63	14.06
France	13.03	+4	120	21.03
Irish Republic	8.72	+16	80	16.60
Italy	13.60	+9	125	19.76
Netherlands	14.71	0	136	NA
Austria	14.32	+44	132	24.55
Portugal	3.70	+61	34	6.87
Finland	13.96	−1	129	NA
Sweden	16.30	−8	150	NA
UK	**10.86**	**+35**	**100**	**20.17**
USA	10.12	+54	93	15.78
Canada	9.89	+13	91	18.61
Japan	13.56	+114	125	18.95
Poland	2.77	+454	26	3.80
Hungary	2.12	+130	20	NA
Czech Republic	1.65	−41	15	3.94
Romania	1.04	−40	10	NA
Turkey	1.84	+36	17	2.88
Morocco	1.86	+102	13	2.56
Egypt	0.68	+100	6	0.82
China	0.43	+65	4	0.48
India	0.39	+35	4	0.67
Indonesia	0.16	0	2	0.55
South Korea	2.69	+9	25	NA
Pakistan	0.24	−17	2	0.37
Bangladesh	0.30	NA	3	0.28
Taiwan	4.68	−10	43	7.58
Vietnam	0.22	NA	2	0.28
Sri Lanka	0.44	+83	4	0.46
Argentina	3.66	+242	34	2.86
Brazil	2.03	+105	19	2.83
Honduras	1.28	+167	12	NA

Source: Werner International – the author is grateful to the company for supplying these statistics.
Notes: (1)   The Werner figures for apparel are not available after 1998.
         (2)   The figures in the final column are for the textile sector.
         (3)   % changes and indices calculated by the author.
         (4)   1990 statistics were taken from Table 4.1 of the first edition of this book.

Table 4.2   Labour cost comparisons based on ILO data (US$ per hour).

Country	1981	1989
Netherlands	4.81	7.43
West Germany	4.62	7.86
Belgium	4.60	6.82
France	3.53	5.96 (1987)
UK	2.94 (1983)	4.98
Portugal	1.10	1.60 (1987)
Hong Kong	1.03	2.24

Source: Zhou, Q. (1997b) unpublished PhD dissertation and Zhou, G. (1995) 'Calculation of Labour Cost Variations', *Journal of Clothing Technology and Management*, 12.3, pp. 35–59.

present author. The two main features of the table are the absolute size of the gap and its enduring nature. It is intuitively unlikely that, in a labour-intensive industry, superior productivity or management could overcome the labour cost disadvantage incurred when, for example, costs in China are 4% of the UK figure.

Labour costs are clearly not the only factor involved in the sourcing decision – see Chapter 8. Furthermore, Taplin (1997) argued that there has not always been a close correlation between changes in relative labour costs and associated changes in the relative importance of counties as suppliers. Jones (2002a) showed that, in the period 1990–1996, while variations in UK apparel imports from China, India and Sri Lanka were in line with labour cost variations the experience of other suppliers was not in line with expectations. On the other hand, the recent explosion of apparel exports from China has again demonstrated the potential of very low cost sources to dominate world trade in apparel as was seen in Chapter 3.

In view of the doubts expressed by Werner International about the reliability of the figures for the apparel sector, Zhou (1995) approached the issue from a different direction using International Labour Office data for major industrial groups. The original cost data were standardised both for changes over time in working hours and for exchange rate fluctuations. The final results of the extensive series of calculations required to produce a meaningful comparative figure by country are shown in Table 4.2. Although the absolute levels of these figures vary greatly from the Werner figures the conclusions to be drawn from them do not substantially alter the implications for sourcing practice in that, first, a very large labour cost gap is confirmed; second, the gap was persistent over time; and, finally, relative country positions remained reasonably stable.

The loss of the apparel statistics after 1998 is clearly a problem in that the primary textile sector is more capital intensive but a comparison by the present author of apparel and textile statistics for a common year (1996) revealed a very close correlation between the two sets of numbers (+0.9936). Therefore, while the textile wages are higher than the apparel they may still provide a reasonable guide to the relative levels in each country.

Finally, in this section KSA data on costs by country in terms of total production costs per standard allowed minute of work time are examined. These figures take into account not only average labour costs but also productivity differences and overheads (KSA, 2005). The figures do not allow for transport or quota cost variations between locations. The statistics are given in Table 4.3. In the KSA material there is a very close correlation (based on 54 countries) between the simple labour cost statistics and sourcing costs (+0.9683) and between labour costs and standard minute costs (+0.9183), although the latter are not shown in Table 4.3. A ranking of countries according to the 1998 Werner data into low, medium and high costs when placed alongside four KSA cost measure (for 29 countries) showed that although 116 possible changes of classification were possible this happened in only 20% of the cases. Finally, a comparison of 24 countries for which both sets of figures were available revealed a correlation coefficient of +0.9765 on the basis of 1996 Werner data and 1999 KSA data (Jones, 2000). Therefore it can be argued that simple wage cost data do give a reasonably good guide to production cost variations between locations and that the ranking of countries according to their cost status is robust and consistent over a wide range of locations.

B. UK labour costs and minimum wage legislation

The last traces of control over minimum wages in the UK apparel sector were removed in 1993 when the TU Reform and Employment Rights Act abolished the old Wages Councils (Taplin, 1997). In 1999 a legally binding minimum wage was introduced at the rate of £3.60 per hour for workers aged over twenty-one. In October 2005 this rose to £5.05. It is a feature of legally determined minimum wages that they rise over time and usually at rates above inflation. Des Marteau (1997) showed that in America between 1990 and 1997 the minimum rate rose by 35.5% for example.

Wilson (1998, p. 257) estimated that the hourly rate in apparel manufacture in the UK before this date was £3.20. The most common form of payment system for machinists is a piece rate system so that this estimate was based on the existing 'fall back' wage of £125 per week for a 39 hour week. Many commentators argued that the new legislation would destroy jobs. In line with the research philosophy outlined in Chapter 1, it would be sensible to examine the evidence on the impact of minimum wage legislation. Economic theory predicts that the introduction of a legally enforceable wage above market rate destroys jobs (Hunter, 1969). Until the early 1980s the majority of studies did support a small

Table 4.3   Production costs by country (2003/4) – the apparel industry.

Country	Hourly labour costs (euros)	Index UK = 100	Productivity Index	Cost Index
Bangladesh	0.23	1.5	52	13
Belarus	0.62	4.1	45	27
Brazil	0.72	4.7	58	25
Bulgaria	0.68	4.5	45	37
Cambodia	0.18	1.2	40	14
China (Mainland)	0.28	1.8	50	12
Costa Rica	1.23	8.1	80	22
Croatia	2.90	19.1	65	40
Czech Republic	2.48	16.3	65	30
Dominican Republic	0.43	2.8	65	13
Egypt	0.63	4.2	52	24
El Salvador	1.03	6.8	70	24
Estonia	2.00	13.2	70	33
France	18.46	121.7	114	107
Germany	25.14	165.7	100	160
Greece	9.41	62.0	78	87
Guatamala	0.85	5.6	70	18
Honduras	0.85	5.6	75	17
Hong Kong	6.34	41.8	84	54
Hungary	2.24	14.8	70	40
India	0.24	1.6	45	18
Irish Republic	11.93	78.6	105	76
Israel	8.92	58.8	90	73
Italy	15.68	103.4	101	99
Jamaica	1.54	10.2	65	35
Japan	20.11	132.6	89	144
Latvia	1.68	11.1	65	23
Lithuania	2.01	13.2	75	32
Malaysia	0.88	5.8	74	17
Malta	5.03	33.2	90	48
Mauritius	0.91	6.0	55	35
Mexico	1.39	9.2	75	22
Moldova	0.34	2.2	40	29
Morocco	1.90	12.5	52	47
Nicaragua	0.43	2.8	65	13
Pakistan	0.18	1.2	50	12
Philippines	1.05	6.9	51	28
Poland	1.75	11.5	60	38
Portugal	5.20	34.2	75	57
Romania	0.85	5.6	60	31
Russia	1.14	7.5	55	38
Slovakia	1.47	9.7	55	39
Slovenia	4.18	27.6	80	48
South Korea	6.51	42.9	85	55
Spain	12.05	79.4	87	95
Sri Lanka	0.38	2.5	48	20
Taiwan	4.55	11.4	74	51
Thailand	1.24	8.2	59	28
Tunisia	4.55	11.4	74	51
Turkey	2.44	16.1	65	53
UK	**15.17**	**100**	**95**	**100**
USA	8.82	58.1	106	59
Uzbekistan	0.18	1.2	70	11
Vietnam	0.34	2.2	65	12

Source: Kurt Salmon Associates (2005) *Global Sourcing Reference* (7th Edition), Manchester.
        I am grateful to KSA for supplying a copy of this publication.
Notes: (1)   The productivity index is based on Germany.
           (2)   The Sourcing Cost index is based on the UK and on a 90 SAM, Medium-Sized Order.

but negative impact upon employment. However, more recent studies reached the opposite conclusion. A typical conclusion from this newer work is represented by Machin (1996), who wrote that 'our reading of the recent evidence is quite clear: the employment effect of minimum wages is rather minimal'.

Freeman (1994) concluded that 'if your previous view was that moderate increases in the (USA) minimum wage risk huge job losses, the new evidence should move you to a major re-think'. Similarly, a recent review of European evidence by Doladao (1996) concluded that the effects of minimum wages are exaggerated.

The best known piece of American research is that by Card (1995) in which he examined data from New Jersey and Texan fast-food restaurants. He found little or no evidence of the minimum wage affecting employment or an effect caused by rises in the minimum wage. The reaction in America to this research has been extreme with some commentators arguing that statistics which do not support the laws of supply and demand should be discounted as incorrect.

There have been a number of studies in the UK which have concentrated upon the impact of the Wages Council minimum. The majority of these studies also find little job destruction following from the fixing of minimum wage levels – and no evidence of job creation following their removal. Bell (1996) concluded that there was little evidence 'in support of the conclusion that the system of Wage Boards and Councils supported wages that were higher than in non-covered jobs' so that it would be logical to expect that if 'there are small wage effects then it is not surprising that there are small employment effects'.

A large exercise in model building carried out by Dickens (1994) studied twelve wages councils and concluded that a 'simple consideration of the raw data lends no support whatsoever' to the view that Wages Councils (setting minimum wages) had been bad for employment.

In another study Machin (1994) again concluded that

'consistent with the conclusions of several recent US studies, the findings suggest that the minimum wage had either no effect or a positive effect on employment'.

One UK study which reaches the opposite conclusion was published by Kauffman (1989) who estimated that a 10% rise in minimum wage reduced employment by 0.6%. Despite this, there is no doubt that the weight of evidence both in the UK and USA is that the introduction of or the raising of minimum wages cannot be shown to have destroyed jobs. The first report of the Low Pay Commission (1998, p. 253) concluded that the most 'recent data tends not to find such a relationship'.

It is interesting to note that the latest research (Economist, 2001) suggests that some accommodation is being reached between the two sides of what had been in the past a rather acrimonious debate. Card (2000) now seems to be arguing that the impact of the legislation has probably been neutral while Neumark (2000) has also placed less emphasis on the prediction of falling employment when minimum rates rise. Tulip (2000) has suggested that the main effect has been in the wider economy as opposed to within small groups of affected workers, e.g. wage inflation is increased via pressure on differentials which in turn generates higher general unemployment to reduce inflation.

On balance, therefore, the expectation must have been that, at the time of introduction, the expected consequence of the Legal Minimum Wage for the apparel industry would not be severe. Indeed, Jones (1999, p. 6) found that the initial reaction of a sample of UK apparel manufacturers was neither hostile to the concept nor to the £3.60 rate and concluded that 'the rate announcement would not be expected of itself to produce instant disaster of earth shattering proportions'. The gap between the wages paid in the lowest cost locations and those prevailing in the UK prior to 1999 was so large that it seemed unlikely at that time that the relatively small increase implied by the legislation could have much impact (see Table 4.1). However, the rate did proceed to rise steadily and at a rate above inflation so that by 2002 continuing research within the sample showed that initial confidence in their ability to compete with imports had totally evaporated with a rate of £5 seen as a crucial barrier to future survival (Jones, 2002b). The rate rose to £5.05 in October 2005 and is set to rise to £5.35 in 2006 (Blackman, 2005) while the TUC has called for a rate of £6 (Conway, 2004). The Low Pay Commission (2000) had concluded that the 'minimum wage had no significant adverse effects on the economy'.

In conclusion, therefore, while it cannot be categorically proven in the positivist mode that the impact of the minimum wage in the UK apparel sector was the main cause of the job losses observed in Chapter 1 it has to be remembered that, in relation to the rest of the manufacturing sector, the apparel industry is extremely labour intensive and open to ferocious competition from imports in a way which could not apply to, for example, the service sector or branches of local government. Therefore, any conclusions drawn for the whole economy may not apply to the apparel sector. It cannot be logical to regard job losses felt to be due to import competition as being entirely divorced from the labour cost gap between the developed and developing countries so that anything which pushes up rates in the former must be reflected in a widening gap, other things being equal. It is clear that Taplin's (1997) observation that the labour cost gaps 'largely explain why retailers and manufacturers have invested in sourcing abroad' represents an essential truth about apparel production. The UK industry has now embraced offshore production and the remaining issue is how this will be organised in the future and what role will be left for UK suppliers in these evolving global supply chain networks. This issue will be considered in Chapters 8 and 12.

C. Labour costs, global shift and theories of development

It could be objected, at this point, that placing so strong a focus on the role of labour costs in explaining the geographical dispersion of the clothing industry is, in effect, implicitly recognising the validity of theories such as absolute or comparative advantage which have been severely questioned by empirical studies. It might even be argued that a Marxist labour theory of value is being evoked.

While it is not possible to provide a comprehensive review of theories of trade and economic development in the context of this text it is important that this issue be addressed because there is a clear link between the labour-intensive nature of the apparel industry and the process of global shift. Theoretical models of development and of trade flows can, in the present context, be taken as synonymous given that trade flows can only originate from areas which have developed in certain directions.

As has been noted in Chapter 2, there has been a global shift of apparel production towards the low labour cost countries. The role and significance of the apparel sector in the economies of these developing countries is significant. Figures produced by Dickerson (1995, p. 216) indicated that, in 1992, textiles and apparel exports combined accounted for 67% of total exports from Bangladesh; 30% in the case of China and India; 77% in the case of Macao and 69% for Pakistan; 40% in the case of Turkey and 55% in the case of Sri Lanka. The comparable figure for the USA was 2.2%. Singleton (1997) estimated that the comparable figure for the UK and the Netherlands (in 1993) was just under 2%.

Table 4.4 shows the percentage of total exports of the named countries accounted for by apparel.

Apparel exports are, as would be expected, frequently an important contributor to the export effort of the developing countries. This fact is particularly noticeable in the case of Bangladesh, Cambodia and Sri Lanka and makes

Table 4.4   The contribution of apparel to exports (%).

Country	1995	2002
Bangladesh	52.7	67.8
Hong Kong	12.2	11.1
Turkey	28.3	23.3
Tunisia	42.4	39.5
Sri Lanka	46.3	49.5
Pakistan	20.1	22.5
Romania	17.2	23.4
India	13.0	12.4
Cambodia	NA	81.7

Source: World Trade Organisation (2003) International Trade Statistics, Geneva.
Note: (1)   The world average was 3.2% in both years.

changes to the world trade system particularly important for those countries (see Chapter 9).

Singleton (1997) has computed the so-called 'Revealed Competitive Advantage' (RCA) in apparel and textiles. This is defined as the share of apparel in the total exports of a country divided by apparel's share of the total exports of all products by all countries in the study. The 'best' countries had an RCA of +2 and included Morocco, Pakistan, the Philippines, Hong Kong, Columbia, Cyprus, Greece, India, Indonesia, South Korea, Thailand, Turkey and Uruguay. The 'worst' countries included the USA, UK, Germany, France, Canada, Japan, Sweden, Switzerland, Belgium, Norway, Australia, New Zealand, the Netherlands, Finland, Austria and Denmark – mainly high wage areas. It is interesting to note that Italy and Portugal appeared in the 'best' group with RCAs of +2. The position of these two EU members is unusual in that their experience frequently runs counter to that of the other members of the EU. These results were largely confirmed by a more up-to-date and much more comprehensive study by Kilduff (2006) who conducted a large-scale investigation into the trend in competitive advantage in the complete textile–apparel supply chain over the period 1962–2003 and found that, as expected, there was a shift in competitive advantage from higher income to lower income countries. This shift was – within the supply chain – most marked in the apparel sector. In the period after 1982 China, Turkey, India, Mexico, Malaysia, Indonesia and Thailand all grew strongly. Most developed countries lost ground although, in the EU, Spain performed better than would have been expected. The performance of the UK was the worst of all the EU countries. Somewhat paradoxically, however, the apparel section of the supply chain within the UK did better than the more capital-intensive parts which was counter to 'normal' experience in the developed countries. Potential lessons for the UK will be considered in Chapter 7, but it must be remembered that the concept of RCA indicates where products are best assembled or produced and that this is not the same concept as that employed by Porter when indicating which countries provide the best platform from which internationally competitive companies might best evolve.

A brief review of the theoretical models which have been advanced as explanations of the development process has been provided by Dickerson (1995), while a much more exhaustive report has been compiled by Perdikis (1998). There is no shortage of competing models ranging from the oldest models based on classical economic theory to the newest models of Porter (1998) and Rugman (1980). The classical models were damaged by empirical studies which revealed that trade patterns did not always accord with factor endowment in that capital-rich countries, for example, imported capital-intensive products. This is the so-called Leontief (1954) Paradox. The rise of intra-trade (Section D, below) also causes problems for such models. Life-cycle and sequential development models focus on observed imbalances in the geographical distribution of resources and the pattern of development countries seem to pass through. The so-called 'new international division of labour' theories concentrate upon the impact of wage differentials in global shift (Frobel, 1980) while the more modern theories of Rugman (1980), Dunning (1988) and Porter (1998) attribute a more central role to management strategies. Dunning argued that trade and various forms of international production should simply be seen as alternative forms of international involvement which is defined by Dunning (1998, p. 4) as:

> 'the extent to which its own economic entities service foreign markets with goods . . . irrespective of where the resources are located or used and the extent to which its own economic agents are supplied goods by foreign owned firms, irrespective of where the production is undertaken.'

Dunning's work seems to anticipate some of Porter's ideas (1998, p. 18) in that he argued that the way in which a firm decides to:

> 'organise its value adding activities (i.e. the extent to which it produced in-house along the value added chain rather than externalise its purchases) may well affect its capability in supplying the product . . . similarly, the choice of location may dramatically affect its global cost . . . and hence its ability to supply any particular market.'

The idea that the growth of intra-trade (especially on a regional basis) might be related to supply-side (as opposed to marketing) issues has also been stressed by a number of researchers and is associated with evolving supply chain relationships and subcontracting to low-cost areas as countries engage in upgrading their contribution to the supply chain, e.g. Hong Kong exporting apparel assembly to Mainland China. Gereffi (1999) argued that a growth in intra-Asian apparel trade could be observed in the 1990s – demonstrated by a rise in the proportion of total world apparel exports accounted for by intra-Asian trade from 4.3% in 1980 to 12.3% in 1996. He argued (1999, p. 63) that these trends in arrangements within the supply chain would lead inevitably to more intra-regional production and trade networks appearing in the apparel supply chain in Asia. In fact by 2002 this figure had dropped back to 11.3% (Table 3.17 allows this to be calculated).

It is necessary to take great care in interpreting statements about intra-trade, e.g. Gereffi's conclusion that between 1989 and 1996 Asian apparel exports to Western Europe fell as a proportion of the global total does *not* mean that exports of apparel from Asia to Western Europe fell in absolute terms because, of course, the global total was rising rapidly. In fact Asian exports of apparel to Western Europe rose from $6 billion in 1980 to $18 billion in 1996. It is true (see Table 3.17) that intra-Asian apparel trade continued to rise between 1997 and 2002 – from $21.5 billion to $22.8 billion – but as a proportion of all Asian apparel exports this represents a declining share whereas Asian exports to North America as a share were rising, for example.

The majority of intra-trade remains a developed region phenomenon despite the changing nature of supply chain relationships (which are fully reviewed in Chapter 12) as is clear from Table 3.17. This is confirmed by Dickerson (1999) despite her observation that between 1992 and 1996 intra-trade in apparel as a proportion of all apparel trade fell slightly. Dickerson's figures also confirm that intra-trade between the less developed countries was rather limited in relation to their total apparel exports – as is confirmed at least as far as Asia is concerned for the later period in Table 3.17 which reveals a fall from 27.2% to 25.4% between 1997 and 2002.

As will be seen in Chapter 5 some 66% of all UK apparel exports went to other member states of the EU in 2003. In addition some 25% of our imports also came from within the EU. This is typical intra-trade. The reasons for the growth of intra-trade are not fully understood but the role of quality differences is important as is seen below.

Dunning concluded that those companies to prosper will be those which succeed in creating so-called 'ownership' advantages (such as brands, patents or economies of scale) which strengthen their long-term competitive position and are also flexible enough to use a variety of systems to exploit these advantages including engaging in international activities and networks with other companies and locating activities anywhere in the world.

Rugman (1980) argued that a theory of internationalisation can explain the involvement of firms in the international arena by concentrating on the ability of multinational enterprises to retain technological advantage internally by engaging in direct foreign investment as opposed to other methods such as licensing or contracting – this will be apparent when emerging forms of global supply chains are discussed in Chapter 12.

Porter (1998) developed the 'Diamond Framework' reviewed in Chapter 1 to explain the alleged clustering of internationally successful companies within particular countries. It bears many relationships to the eclectic theory described above and incorporates both factor-related and strategic elements. The advantages of global operations (as a strategic option) also play a significant role in the Porter model, as will be described in Chapter 6.

It was determined in Chapter 1 that the 'Diamond Framework' would be utilised to inject an international dimension into the structural model of industrial performance. It can now be seen that this is but one of a number of competing models. Perdikis (1998) concluded his exhaustive study of alternative trade theories with the statement that:

'there is not at present a general theory in international trade. The existence of both inter- and intra-industry trade has complicated theoretical inquiry and the large number of factors that have been found to influence trade has rendered an empirical reconciliation impossible . . . Trade theory is clearly in disequilibrium'.

Therefore, given the unusually high proportion of total cost accounted for by labour costs in the clothing sector, it is appropriate and justifiable to place most emphasis on the special role of supply factors such as labour costs in this case. Kilduff (2006), after a large-scale analysis of trade patterns in the apparel sector, concluded that 'the pattern of export development generally reflects expectations regarding factor proportions theory and industry evolution models'. It could quite legitimately be argued that virtually all the models listed above would predict that the apparel manufacturing sector would migrate to the developing, low-cost countries. Therefore, it is felt to be a defensible position to adopt the Diamond Framework in subsequent analysis given that 'a consensus on an appropriate general trade model remains elusive' (Perdikis, 1998, p. 231).

D. Intra-industry trade

The concept of intra-industry or intra-trade has been alluded to above and it will be appropriate to deal with this concept in this chapter before a detailed examination of the UK apparel trade statistics is conducted in Chapter 5. Intra-trade is defined as (Begg, 1991, p. 538) 'trade in goods made within the same industry'. In brief, it refers to the fact that a high proportion of trade between countries consists of trade in 'identical' products, e.g. the UK both exports apparel to Germany and imports apparel from it, as will be seen in Chapter 5.

At a regional level it was seen in Chapter 3 that most apparel exports from developed countries go to other developed countries. Winterton (1996, p. 38) estimated that between 1980 and 1989 intra-EU trade as a proportion of all UK trade in apparel rose from 26.2% to 40.8%. On the basis of the data presented later in Tables 5.1 and 5.2 the corresponding figure for 1997 rose to 43% before falling back to 34% in 2003. Perdikis (1998, p. 149) estimates that in the mid-1980s, intra-trade accounted for about half of all world trade in manufactured goods. The existence of intra-trade poses great difficulties for models of trade and development which emphasise factor endowment as the basis for trade. Begg (1991, p. 589) suggests that the existence of intra-trade depends primarily upon the extent of branding within a generic product category and the impact of transport costs so that intra-trade is likely to be more prevalent between countries which are geographically adjacent to one another.

Caves (1981) concluded that 'there is much to applaud in intra-trade and little to deplore' in that it enriches consumer choice. In his view, intra-trade partly reflects the heterogeneity of the statistical categories used to generate trade statistics but he goes on to argue that its increased significance reflects the extent of product differentiation in the modern marketplace. Intra-trade will be encouraged where the produce represents a complex combination of many different features and if there are few economies of scale – both characteristics of the apparel market.

It has certainly always been recognised that (Perdikis, 1998, p. 172) product differentiation would play an important role in explaining intra-industry trade, although a variety of mechanisms have been proposed to activate this relationship. For example, it has been argued that consumers simply desire variety for its own sake or that they will try to purchase a favoured brand which comes closest to matching their ideal product. The first argument would produce a large number of producers and has been supported by the research. If the main difference between products was related to quality then some part of the variation could be related to factor endowment in that better quality products might be associated with capital-rich countries. Greenways (1999) identifies intra-trade due to quality differences as vertical, and found that this type of intra-trade was the most important in trading links between the UK and the EU.

Perdikis (1998, p. 173) concludes that most of the research supports the 'so-called country characteristics and institutional explanations of intra-industry trade'. The concept of intra-trade is not discussed by Porter, but does not pose as great a problem to the Diamond Framework as it does to other models because the Framework actively encourages companies to seek out opportunities to operate all elements (not just assembly) of the production value chain in a range of locations (countries) as a consequence of which it might first become more difficult to tell exactly where any given item was in fact made and, second, because it would become more probable that an interchange of basically identical (generic) products will occur between broadly similar countries. In the case of the relocation of basic, labour-intensive, assembly-type operations, on the other hand, intra-trade would not occur as often and trade would, in contrast, be reflected in flows from developing to developed areas.

References

Anson, R. (1997) E.U. Clothing Producers May Still Have a Bright Future. *Textile Outlook International*, **74**, 3–5.

Bell, D. & Wright, R. (1996) The Impact of Minimum Wages: Evidence from Wages Boards and Councils. *Economic Journal*, **106**, 650–58.

Begg, D., Fischer, S. & Dornbusch, R. (1991) *Economics*. McGraw Hill, London.

Blackman, O. (2005) *Daily Mirror*, 26.2.2005, p. 2.

Card, D. & Kreuger, A. (1995) *Myth and Measurement: The New Economics of the Minimum Wage*. Princeton University Press, Princeton.

Card, D. & Kreuger, A. (2000) Minimum Wages and Employment: a Reply. *American Economics Review*, **90**, 1397–1420.

Caves, R.E. (1981) Intra Industry Trade and Market Structure. *Oxford Economic Papers*, **33**, 203–21.

Conway, E. (2004) *Daily Telegraph*, 29.10.2004, p. 38.

Des Marteau, K. (1997) Industry Takes a Hit with Higher Minimum Wage. *Bobbin*, 44–46.

Dickens, R., Machin, S. & Manning, A. (1994) Minimum Wages and Employment. *International Journal of Manpower*, **15.2**, 8–25.

Dickerson, K. (1995) *Textiles and Apparel in the Global Economy*. Prentice Hall, New Jersey.

Dickerson, K. (1999) *Textiles and Apparel in the Global Economy*. Prentice Hall, New Jersey.

Doladao, J. (1996) Minimum Wages in Europe. *Economic Policy*, **23**, 317–73.

Dunning, J. (1988) *Explaining International Production*. Unwin Hyman, London.

Economist (2001) Economic Focus: debating the minimum wage, 3.2.2001, p. 107.

Freeman, R.B. (1994) Minimum Wages – Again. *International Journal of Manpower*, **15.2**, 1–25.

Frobel, F. (1980) *The New International Division of Labour*. Cambridge University Press, Cambridge.

Gereffi, G. (1999) International Trade and Industrial Upgrading in the Apparel Commodity Chain. *Journal of International Economics*, **48**, 37–70.

Greenways, D., Milner, C. & Elliott, R. (1999) UK Intra Industry Trade with the EU. *Oxford Bulletin of Economics and Statistics*, **61**, 343–65.

Hoffman, K. & Rush, H. (1988) *Micro Electronics and Clothing*. Praeger, New York.

Hunter, L.C. & Robertson, D.J. (1965) *Economics of Wages and Labour*. Macmillan, London.

Jones, R.M. (1999) The National Minimum Wage and the UK Clothing Industry. *Hollings Apparel Industry Review*, **3.1**, 4–6.

Jones, R.M. (2002) *The Apparel Industry*. Blackwell Science, Oxford.

Jones, R.M. & Hayes, S.G. (2002) The National Minimum Wage and the Clothing Industry in the UK. *Performance and Reward Conference Proceedings*, MMU, 11.4.2002.

Kauffman, A. (1989) Employment Effects of a Statutory Minima. *Economic Journal*, **99**, 1040–53.

Khanna, S.R. (1998) Trends in EU Textile and Clothing Imports. *Textiles Outlook International*, **78**, 77–108.

Kilduff, P. & Chi, T. (2006) Longitudinal Patterns of Competitive Advantage in the Textile Complex. *Journal of Fashion Marketing and Management* (forthcoming).

Kurt Salmon Associates (2005) *Global Sourcing Reference* (7th Edition), Manchester.

Leontief, W. (1954) Domestic Production and Foreign Trade. *Economica Internationale*, **7**, 9–45.

Low Pay Commission (1998) *First Report of Low Pay Commission*. TSO, Norwich.

Low Pay Commission (2000) *Second Report of Low Pay Commission*. TSO, Norwich.

Machin, S. & Manning, A. (1994) The Effects of Minimum Wages: Evidence from Wages Councils. *Industrial Relations Review*, **47.2**, 319–29.

Machin, S. & Manning, A. (1996) Employment and the Introduction of a Minimum Wage in Britain. *Economic Journal*, **106**, 637–76.

National Economic Development Office (1971) *Technology and the Garment Industry*. HMSO, London.

Neumark, D. & Waseher, W. (2000) Minimum Wages and Employment: Comment. *American Economic Review*, **90**, 1362–1395.

Ohmae, K. (1985) *Triad Power: The Coming Shape of Global Competition*. Free Press, New York.

Perdikis, N. & Kerr, R. (1998) *Trade Theories and Empirical Evidence.* Manchester University Press, Manchester.

Porter, M.E. (1998) *The Competitive Advantage of Nations.* Free Press, New York.

Rugman, A.M. (1980) A New Theory of the Multinational Enterprise. *Columbia Journal of World Business,* **15**, 23–29.

Scheffer, M. (1994) Internationalisation of Production by E.C. Textile and Clothing Manufacturers. *Textile Outlook International,* **74**, 101–23.

Singleton, J. (1997) *World Textile Industry.* Routledge, London.

Taplin, I. & Winterton, J. (1997) *Rethinking Global Production.* Avebury, Aldershot.

Tulder, R.V. & June, G. (1988) *European Multinationals in Core Technologies.* John Wiley, Chichester.

Tulip, P. (2000) *Do Minimum Wages Raise the NAIRU?* Federal Reserve Finance and Economic Discussion Group, Washington.

Wilson, J. (1998) The National Minimum Wage: The BCIA View. *Journal of Fashion Marketing and Management,* **2**, 204–209.

Winterton, R. & Barlow, A. (1996) Economic Restructuring of UK Clothing. In: *Restructuring in a Labour Intensive Industry* (Eds I. Taplin & J. Winterton), pp. 25–61. Avebury, Aldershot.

Zeitlin, J. (1988) The Clothing Industry in Transition. *Textile History,* **19**, 211–38.

Zhou, Q. (1995) Calculation of Labour Cost Variations. *Journal of Clothing Technology and Management,* **12**, 35–9.

Zhou, Q. (1997) *The Development of Global Companies within the UK Clothing Industry.* Unpublished MMU PhD dissertation, Manchester.

Chapter 5

The Facts: UK Apparel Trade – The Current Trade Position

A. Imports and exports

As will be explained below, the use of the overseas trade statistics to illuminate trends in the UK apparel sector is fraught with difficulties. Nevertheless, it is important that a clear and comprehensive picture of the trends is obtained because, as Winterton (1996, p. 58) observes:

> 'growth in international trade has had a dramatic impact on the UK clothing industry. Imports from developing and developed countries account for a large proportion of the domestic market and this is steadily increasing'

and because, furthermore, the trade situation is itself a powerful engine for strategic change on the part of UK-based manufacturers.

As is often the case when dealing with business statistics – and particularly when trying to establish trends over time – the facts are far more difficult to establish than would initially be expected. Industry definitions in official statistics, for example, frequently change and established sources either disappear or are modified. These problems are particularly severe in the case of statistics of the external trade of the UK, especially if a comparison is sought between pre- and post-1992 data. The completion of the Single European Market brought with it a very severe disruption of UK external trade statistics as trade with the other member states of the EU ceased to be regarded as 'foreign'.

In time, a new statistical series for trade between the UK and the other EU partners emerged, but this is based on VAT returns rather than customs data so is not directly comparable with the pre-Single European Market data. Unfortunately, when the series breaks, a seismic reversal of UK–EU trade balance occurs and it is difficult to know how to interpret this. In addition some data – such as the *Business Monitor* series on import penetration – has been discontinued. Further, the standard industrial classification system has been changed twice since 1980 and aligned to the PRODCOM system (see Appendix A for an explanation of these classification systems).

Finally, as will be seen later, the picture on import figures depends greatly on whether or not hosiery is included as part of the apparel sector. Therefore, as with all economic statistics, the 'facts' depend partly on definitions adopted. The basic data are to be found in HM Customs and Excise (2003) and is classified according to the SITC Division 84. However, the data on trade in 'clothing' also appear in a variety of other publications which often utilise marginally different definitions often based on the PRODCOM system which itself relates to SIC (1992). It is clearly a debatable point as to whether or not 'the clothing industry' should include or exclude leather, fur, footwear and hosiery. In addition, data can be in terms of value, volume or even weight.

The best starting-point is with Tables 5.1 and 5.2, which cover 1995 to 2003. This enables the basic trading position in apparel as defined by SITC Division 84 to be stated. The very close links to the EU market are immediately apparent. Nearly 70% of UK garment exports are destined for the EU member states. In addition, a further 10% go to other developed countries in Western Europe and North America. This pattern of trade between developed countries is entirely consistent with the global pattern described in Chapter 3. In Table 5.1 it is revealed that some 45% of UK apparel imports originate in developed areas (including Eastern Europe and Turkey which is classified as part of the rest of Europe – see Chapter 12) while some 55% come from the so-called developing world.

Table 5.1   UK apparel imports and arrivals (£000): SITC Division 84.

Source	1995	1997	1998	1999	2003	% 2003
EU	1,572,295	2,125,792	2,489,523	2,411,200	2,679,816	25.3
Rest of Europe	258,799	352,858	403,759	494,568	1,243,701	11.7
Eastern Europe	185,780	282,355	361,281	401,247	748,530	7.1
North America	104,087	154,456	136,009	130,130	119,431	1.1
Other Americas	19,231	23,831	18,387	21,898	23,684	0.2
Middle East and North Africa	347,991	477,279	501,113	600,128	653,208	6.2
Sub-Saharan Africa	142,597	183,123	175,740	178,391	178,288	1.7
Asia and Oceania	2,660,407	3,229,892	3,135,848	3,507,761	4,956,955	46.7
Total	5,291,186	6,829,587	7,221,660	7,745,323	10,603,614	

Source: HM Customs & Excise, Tariff and Statistics Office, Overseas Trade Statistics, UK Trade with EC and the World (ex BMMA 20), 2003.
This is now known as OTS (A).

Notes: (1) Imports are goods coming in from outside the EU while arrivals is the term used to describe goods coming from the EU member states. This distinction follows from the date of the start of the Single European Market.
(2) It is possible to obtain more up-to-date statistics in a variety of Government publications but these do not give the level of detail required.

Table 5.2 UK apparel exports and dispatches (£000): SITC Division 84.

Destination	1995	1997	1998	1999	2003	% 2003
EU	2,100,626	2,192,559	1,991,751	1,874,200	1,800,074	66.2
Other W. Europe	147,588	150,330	140,722	126,508	113,738	4.2
Eastern Europe	93,366	93,682	90,554	104,354	124,600	4.6
North America	135,260	185,256	181,526	156,980	154,140	5.7
Other Americas	15,709	13,269	13,141	9,849	6,567	0.3
Middle East and North Africa	208,517	289,743	331,329	284,270	272,922	10.0
Sub-Saharan Africa	23,294	24,479	18,137	16,268	14,229	0.5
Asia & Oceania	274,502	304,858	221,103	199,807	232,151	8.5
Total	2,998,892	3,254,176	2,988,259	2,772,236	2,718,421	

Source: HM Customs & Excise, Tariff & Statistics Office, Overseas Trade Statistics, UK Trade with EC and the
World (ex BMMA 20), 2003.
This is now known as OTS (A).
Note: Exports are goods sent to non-EU destinations. Dispatches are goods sent to other EU member states.

Table 5.3 Trade balances by region (£000).

Region	1995	1997	1998	1999	2003
EU	+528,331	+66,767	−497,772	−537,000	−879,742
Rest of Western Europe	−111,211	−202,528	−263,037	−368,060	−1,129,963
Eastern Europe	−92,414	−188,673	−270,727	−296,893	−623,930
N. America	+31,173	+30,800	+45,517	+26,850	+34,709
Other Americas	−3,522	−10,562	−5,246	−12,049	−17,117
Middle East and North Africa	−139,474	−187,536	−169,784	−315,858	−380,286
Sub-Saharan Africa	−119,303	−158,644	−157,603	−162,123	−164,059
Asia and Oceania	−2,385,905	−2,925,034	−2,914,745	−3,307,954	−4,724,804
Total	−2,292,294	−3,575,411	−4,233,401	−4,973,087	−7,885,193

Source: HM Customs & Excise, Tariff & Statistics Office, Overseas Trade Statistics, UK Trade with EC and the
World (ex BMMA 20), 2003.
Notes: (1) A negative figure indicates that imports exceed exports.
(2) The negative balance on apparel trade has more than tripled between 1995 and 2003.
(3) The negative balance for 2004 was − £7,881,000,000 (*Monthly Review of Trade Statistics*, 24.1.2005).
(4) In the UK statistics one billion is taken to be one thousand million, so the negative balance is £7.9 billion.

B. Trade balances

Table 5.3 shows the trade balances by area and in total and is derived from
Tables 5.1 and 5.2. These three tables illustrate the well-established trade deficit
in the clothing sector, i.e. that imports greatly exceed exports by an ever increasing amount. These figures are in value terms. Table 5.4 shows the trade balances
by main category of clothing. Trading balances with individual trading partners
(countries) are shown in Table 5.5(b). There are few surprises in these tables,

Table 5.4   Trade balances by garment type (£ millions).

	1997	2001	2003
Leather clothes	−84	−148	−103
Workwear	−4	−22	−35
Outerwear	−1,267	−2,612	−3,077
Underwear	−1,230	−2,111	−2,584
Other apparel	−158	−444	−505

Source: Business Monitor MQ10 (Third Quarter, 2004).

Notes: (1) MQ10 gives balances by category going back to 1970 but
earlier data are given by SIC (1980) and are, therefore, not
strictly comparable with later data (see Appendix A).
However, the data for 1970–1988, for example, reveal that
balances were usually negative for all garment categories with
the occasional exception of hats.

(2) Data on balances by sub-sections of SITC Division 84 can
also be obtained from BM OTS (A) [ex SMMA20].
Balances are normally negative with the exception of clothing
accessories.

other than, perhaps, the fact that in Table 5.3 the UK is shown to have a large positive apparel trade balance with the EU up to 1997 prior to a dramatic reversal in 1998 and 1999. The latter movement probably reflected the strength of the pound relative to the euro (Jones, 2001).

The apparel trade balance between the UK and the rest of the EU has undergone some dramatic changes since the formation of the Single European Market, at which time the basis upon which trade data within the EU were assessed diverged from that employed to measure trade with the rest of the world outside the EU. Table 5.6 contains the relevant data. It can be seen that prior to the opening of the Single European Market in 1992 the balance of trade in apparel was consistently negative, reaching some £250m in 1991. In 1997 this had been transformed into a surplus of some £67m, having reached £382m in 1996. This transformation was quite untypical of trade between the UK and the EU in general and has been reversed post 1998.

As Moore (1999, p. 41) observes, the general position is that the UK pays off most of her negative trade balance with the EU by what she earns from the rest of the world. Obviously, the composition of the EU has changed over time but this cannot explain the unusual reversal in apparel trade as it would have affected all trade. Furthermore, it can be seen from Table 5.7 that the balances in apparel trade with a number of individual member states have also been reversed since 1992. Given the latest figures showing a substantial decline in exports to the EU, the wisdom of concentrating so high a proportion of apparel exports on one market might be questioned.

The large and remorselessly rising negative global trade balance might initially be seen to be indicative of poor trade performance by the UK apparel industry, but this would be a misleading conclusion prior to 1998. It can be seen

Table 5.5(a)   UK apparel trade by country 1996–1999 (£000): STC Division 84.

Country	Exports				Imports			
	1996	1998	1999	2003	1996	1998	1999	2003
France	399,709	308,138	267,900	250,404	187,579	268,109	265,200	436,213
Belgium/Lux	134,485	118,685	106,700	66,133	166,119	233,116	262,200	329,494
Netherlands	188,000	121,255	100,500	81,494	178,510	445,422	304,400	210,244
Germany	455,539	416,367	369,400	380,017	290,455	373,448	400,400	370,637
Italy	108,063	104,081	77,500	110,753	426,408	520,326	442,400	583,915
Irish Republic	452,318	466,513	466,300	590,239	193,600	147,698	127,300	111,893
Denmark	80,537	59,728	51,900	39,764	29,821	41,821	40,400	40,289
Greece	62,461	43,452	40,900	46,421	56,819	53,307	73,500	96,213
Portugal	42,519	27,953	23,300	16,126	270,012	279,641	245,500	317,849
Spain	161,619	115,998	102,800	129,893	23,235	21,944	19,600	97,927
Sweden	105,913	78,128	59,400	49,647	12,045	15,630	15,100	16,392
Finland	42,366	31,859	30,800	20,622	6,268	8,366	7,100	5,746
Austria	49,566	27,035	23,700	18,562	58,229	70,436	66,800	63,003
Norway	46,974	39,160	33,316	21,551	2,344	3,059	2,840	1,662
Malta	14,039	13,589	13,403	10,060	21,612	23,692	29,637	31,507
Turkey	12,110	26,108	23,008	31,652	242,610	340,790	424,694	1,163,940
Poland	6,744	8,539	13,162	10,219	26,604	37,049	38,934	38,344
Romania	6,001	24,659	37,757	45,938	92,086	147,838	176,235	409,758
Morocco	92,754	147,754	128,728	93,447	157,635	232,059	287,699	305,524
Tunisia	3,304	6,883	9,978	27,440	20,109	30,149	33,193	79,850
Egypt	3,313	3,366	4,103	2,245	25,504	36,666	55,837	92,578
South Africa	8,363	4,902	3,691	3,253	31,217	32,747	34,564	37,944
USA	137,528	164,567	144,459	137,222	113,750	113,333	108,920	99,148
Cyprus	16,289	22,002	24,921	21,267	43,391	32,345	29,921	18,399
Israel	19,359	12,251	8,038	2,666	101,821	98,904	112,066	33,771
Pakistan	456	900	620	1,055	129,103	98,415	96,767	174,996
India	4,067	9,763	9,656	1,387	314,437	229,686	259,784	392,666
Bangladesh	253	348	368	372	219,385	196,010	199,335	449,227
Sri Lanka	2,599	4,308	5,626	2,046	166,454	209,596	256,937	316,062
Thailand	5,581	1,253	1,351	2,149	87,874	89,685	103,612	165,995
Vietnam	85	95	205	54	21,995	33,103	37,200	50,707
Indonesia	2,574	1,662	1,213	2,682	193,542	207,516	225,784	242,624
Malaysia	4,675	5,199	3,317	5,148	142,291	113,438	120,237	129,330
Singapore	26,257	13,686	10,310	13,949	52,324	63,388	78,532	101,380
Philippines	5,492	2,690	4,968	2,494	62,073	50,405	55,968	57,408
China	1,546	5,398	5,214	2,713	341,412	402,571	447,444	870,196
South Korea	28,174	6,961	14,429	35,834	62,753	83,008	112,537	93,971
Japan	134,477	100,699	82,607	81,981	15,524	15,866	15,921	14,861
Taiwan	8,635	9,106	7,470	8,573	73,514	86,089	88,038	56,963
Hong Kong	61,274	40,213	38,769	57,596	1,078,495	1,166,478	1,293,641	1,647,088
Macau	235	326	1,891	228	38,572	44,991	34,106	12,350

Source: HM Customs & Excise, Tariff and Statistics Office, Overseas Trade Statistics, UK Trade with EC and the World (ex BMMA 20).

Note: The figures for the Netherlands are influenced by that country's role as a world trade centre.

Table 5.5(b)   UK apparel trade balances by country 1996–1999 (£000).

Country	1996	1998	1999	2003
France	+212,130	+40,029	+2,700	−185,809
Belgium/Lux	−31,634	−114,431	−155,500	−263,361
Netherlands	+9,490	−324,167	−203,900	−128,750
Germany	+165,084	+42,919	−31,000	+9,380
Italy	−318,345	−416,245	−364,900	−473,162
Irish Republic	+258,718	+318,815	+33,900	+478,346
Denmark	+50,716	+17,907	+11,500	−525
Greece	+5,642	−9,855	−32,600	−49,792
Portugal	−227,493	−251,688	−222,200	−301,723
Spain	+138,384	+94,054	+83,200	+31,966
Sweden	+93,868	+62,498	+44,300	+33,255
Finland	+36,098	+23,493	+23,700	14,876
Austria	−23,968	−43,401	−43,100	−44,441
Norway	+44,630	+36,101	+30,476	+19,889
Malta	−7,573	−10,103	−16,234	−21,447
Turkey	−230,500	−314,682	−401,686	−1,132,288
Poland	−19,860	−28,510	−25,772	−28,125
Romania	−86,085	−123,179	−138,478	−363,820
Morocco	−64,881	−84,305	−158,971	−257,077
Tunisia	−16,805	−23,266	−23,215	−52,410
Egypt	−22,191	−33,300	−51,734	−90,333
South Africa	−24,395	−27,845	−30,873	−34,691
USA	+23,778	+51,234	+35,539	+38,074
Cyprus	−27,102	−12,343	−5,000	+2,868
Israel	−82,462	−86,653	−21,883	−31,105
Pakistan	−128,647	−97,425	−96,147	−173,941
India	−310,370	−219,923	−250,128	−391,279
Bangladesh	−219,132	−195,662	−198,967	−448,855
Sri Lanka	−163,855	−205,288	−251,311	−314,016
Thailand	−82,293	−88,432	−102,261	−163,846
Vietnam	−21,910	−33,008	−36,995	−50,653
Indonesia	−190,968	−205,854	−224,571	−239,942
Malaysia	−137,616	−108,239	−116,920	−124,182
Singapore	−26,067	−49,705	−68,222	−87,431
Philippines	−56,581	−47,715	−51,000	−54,914
China	−339,866	−397,173	−442,230	−867,483
South Korea	−34,579	−76,047	−98,108	−58,137
Japan	+118,953	+84,833	+66,686	+67,120
Taiwan	−64,861	−76,983	−80,568	−48,390
Hong Kong	−1,017,221	−1,126,265	−1,254,872	−1,589,492
Macau	−38,337	−44,965	−32,215	−12,122

Source: HM Customs & Excise, Tariff and Statistics Office, Overseas Trade Statistics, UK Trade with EC and the World (ex BMMA 20); 1999 figures for the EU are from OTS (2) and are provisional.

Note: (1) Data for the Netherlands are influenced by that country's role as a world trade centre.

Table 5.6 EU–UK trade balances (£ millions).

	1990	1996	1997	1998	1999	2003
Manufacturing total	−9,930	−4,622	−4,622	−5,582	−6,362	−22,272
All trade	−11,088	−4,073	−4,733	−6,250	−8,067	−21,966
Apparel	−547	+383	+67	−498	−537	−879

Sources: UK Overseas Trade Statistics (BMMA 20) – various issues.
Now known as OTS (A) – see Table 5.1.

Table 5.7 Apparel trade balances with EU member states (£000).

Member State	1991	1998	1999	2003
France	+37,565	+40,029	+23,700	−185,809
Belgium/Luxembourg	−4,011	−114,431	−155,500	−263,361
Netherlands	+3,652	−324,167	−203,900	−128,750
Germany	−75,954	+42,919	−31,000	+9,380
Italy	−193,045	−416,245	−364,900	−473,162
Irish Republic	+140,937	+318,815	+339,000	+478,346
Denmark	−9,178	+17,907	+11,500	−525
Greece	−34,757	−9,855	−32,600	−49,792
Portugal	−202,336	−251,688	−222,200	−301,723
Spain	+86,596	+94,054	+83,200	+31,966
Sweden	+95,540	+62,498	+44,300	+33,255
Finland	+5,464	+23,493	+23,700	+14,876
Austria	−30,121	−43,401	−43,100	−44,441

Sources: (1) 1991 data from Hollings Apparel Industry Review, Spring 1992, Table 39.
(2) 1999 data, OTS (2) December 1999.
Note: Trade statistics relating to the Netherlands may be influenced by that country's position as a major world trade centre.

Table 5.8 Growth of apparel exports – comparative performance (£m).

Year	Apparel	Manufacturers	All trade
1978	469	30,967	35,380
1990	1,154	90,230	103,735
1998	2,988	143,263	164,845
2003	2,377	168,567	188,602

Source: Business monitor MIO various editions.

from the data in Tables 5.8, 5.9 and 5.10 that the comparative export performance of the sector (measured in two ways here to cover the availability of data
over a long period) was quite respectable. In most time periods up to 1998 UK
apparel exports have grown at roughly the same rate as all UK exports or all UK
exports of manufactured goods; while in a number of time periods the performance of the sector has been superior to the average. Therefore, the negative trade

Table 5.9   Growth of apparel and footwear exports –
comparative performance (£m).

Year	Apparel and footwear	Manufacturers	All trade
1980	938	34,811	47,357
1987	1,628	61,006	79,760
1990	1,973	84,172	103,691
1996	3,929	140,865	168,041
1998	3,530	143,263	164,845
2003	3,123	156,329	187,846

Source: *Annual Abstract of Statistics* (various editions).

Table 5.10(a)   Comparative export growth (%).

Period	Apparel	Manufacturers	All trade
1978–1990	+146	+191	+193
1978–1997	+594	+372	+387
1990–1998	+159	+59	+59
1998–2003	−20	+18	+14

Source: Table 5.8.

Table 5.10(b)   Comparative export growth (%)
including footwear.

Period	Apparel*	Manufacturers	All trade
1980–1987	+74	+75	+68
1980–1996	+319	+305	+255
1987–1996	+141	+131	+111
1990–1998	+79	+70	+59
1998–2003	−13	+9	+14

* includes footwear.
Source: Table 5.9.

balance should not be seen (prior to 1998) as a failure of the sector to perform in world export markets – the problem lies in the extremely rapid rate of growth of apparel imports. This reflects the enormous increase which has taken place in consumption expenditure over time (see Chapter 10). Abbott (1996, p. 1124) has shown that consumption expenditure is 'the main determinant of UK imports'.

Another measure of trade performance frequently utilised is the export: import ratio. According to Winterton (1996, p. 32) a close examination of the data for the UK reveals that the ratio 'has begun to recover from the low point in 1989'. The average ratio (for all apparel) fell from 0.50 in 1983 to 0.41 in 1988 and then rose to 0.45 in 1991. The data in Tables 5.1 and 5.2 indicate the ratio rising to 0.48 in 1997 but then collapsing to 0.36 in 2003. The relatively strong export performance disappeared after 1998 when exports began to fall as can be seen in Tables 5.2, 5.9 and 5.10.

C. Penetration ratios

The concept of import penetration is well established in the literature as an indicator of performance. It is defined as the percentage of the UK market taken by imports. It is now possible (using the PRODCOM system) to obtain data for home production, imports and exports on a consistent basis. It is, therefore, easy to obtain a figure for the net UK supply (production – exports and imports) and to express imports as a percentage of that figure. This calculation is presented for 1993 and 2001 in Table 5.11. The figures are in value terms. It can be seen that the import penetration ratio has risen steadily from just under 60% to over 90% in eight years. It must be noted that this table is not strictly comparable with Tables 5.1 and 5.2 although the differences are marginal. According to Winterton (1996, p. 27) the comparative figure for import penetration in 1983 was just under 30%.

D. Main suppliers

Tables 5.12 to 5.14 list the main supplying countries for clothing entering the UK as imported products. These tables do not contain many surprises, given the previous discussion of global shifts and the value of labour costs in Chapter 4. However, there are a number of important suppliers who would not normally be thought of as possessing an obvious cost advantage over the UK and these are shown in Table 5.14.

Table 5.11 Import penetration 1993–2001 (value terms, £000).

	1993	2001	% change	Real price terms
UK sales	4,065,717	2,337,879	−42.5	−36.6
Exports	1,492,254	1,777,698	+19.3	+31.4
Imports	3,437,850	6,376,289	+85.5	+104.5
UK net supply	6,011,313	6,936,470	+15.4	+27.2
Import penetration in % terms	57.2	91.9	+60.7	+60.7

Source: R.M. Jones (2003) The UK clothing sector 1993–2001: hats, workwear and other wearing apparel and the final analysis. *Journal of Fashion Marketing and Management*, **7.4**, 1361–2026.

Notes: (1) These figures are not strictly comparable to those in Tables 5.1 and 5.2 due to marginal definitional differences.
(2) This time period does not show the fall in exports post 1998 simply because the comparison starts in 1993. This does not invalidate the conclusion that exports fell between 1998 and 2003.
(3) UK supply is UK sales plus imports minus exports.
(4) Import penetration is imports as a % of UK net supply.
(5) The final column uses a clothing price inflator.

Table 5.12   Apparel imports from Eastern European suppliers 1999–2003 (£000).

	1999	2003
Lithuania	39,154	91,582
Bulgaria	12,759	48,737
Ukraine	9,878	21,171
Czech Republic	17,566	48,774
Slovakia	10,994	11,762
Hungary	39,608	26,158
Romania	147,838	409,758
Poland	38,934	38,344
Latvia	8,268	11,433
Estonia	1,359	4,180
Slovenia	1,390	1,522
Total	327,747	713,391

Source: As Table 5.1.
Note: The share of UK apparel imports taken by the above rose from 4.3% in 1999 to 6.7% in 2003.

Table 5.13   The UK's leading low-cost suppliers, 1996 to 2003 (£000): SITC Division 84.

Country	1996	1998	1999	2003
Turkey	242,610	340,790	424,694	1,163,940
Hong Kong	1,078,495	1,166,478	1,293,641	1,647,088
Malaysia	142,291	113,438	120,237	129,330
Pakistan	129,103	98,415	96,767	174,996
India	314,437	229,686	259,784	392,666
Bangladesh	219,385	196,010	199,335	449,227
China	341,412	402,571	447,444	870,196
Indonesia	193,542	207,516	225,784	242,624
Israel	101,821	98,904	112,066	33,771
Mauritius	104,450	123,043	122,196	124,424
Singapore	52,324	63,388	78,532	101,380
South Korea	62,753	83,008	112,537	93,971
Taiwan	73,514	86,089	88,038	56,963
Thailand	87,874	89,685	103,612	165,995
Sri Lanka	166,454	209,596	256,937	316,062
Morocco	157,635	232,059	287,699	350,524
Romania	92,086	147,838	176,235	409,758
Portugal	270,012	279,641	245,500	317,849
Total	3,830,198	4,168,155	4,651,038	7,040,764

Source: Business Monitor MA20 Overseas Trade Statistics with the World. HMSO, London, various issues. Now known as OTS (A).
Note: The above suppliers were responsible for 61.8% of UK apparel imports in 1996; 57.7% in 1998; 60.0% in 1999 and 66.4% in 2003.

Table 5.14 Other sources of UK apparel imports, 1996 to 2003 (£000): SITC Division 84.

Country	1996	1998	1999	2003
USA	113,750	113,333	108,920	99,148
Germany	290,455	373,448	400,400	370,637
Italy	426,408	520,326	442,400	583,915
France	187,578	268,109	265,200	436,213
Netherlands	178,510	445,422	304,400	210,244
Irish Republic	193,600	147,698	127,300	111,893
(Portugal)	(270,012)	(279,641)	(245,500)	(317,849)
Total	1,660,313	2,147,977	1,894,120	2,129,899
Total excluding Portugal	1,390,301	1,868,336	1,648,620	1,812,050

Source: Business Monitor MA20 Overseas Trade Statistics with the World. HMSO, London. Now known as OTS (A).
Note: As percentage of total imports in 1996, 1998 and 1999 respectively, the above countries accounted for 26.8%, 29.7% and 24.5% with Portugal and 22.4%, 25.9% and 21.3% without Portugal. In 2003 the figures were 20.1% and 17.1%.

A group of Eastern European suppliers have increased their share of UK apparel imports from 4.3% to 6.7% over the period 1999 to 2003 – see Table 5.12. This represented a growth of 118% and may have been related to changes in EU trade controls on that region in 1998 – see Chapter 12. Bangladesh, India and Pakistan increased their share of imports from 7.2% to 9.6% over the same period. China's share rose from 5.8% to 8.2%.

E. Export markets and global reach

It has been noted above that the majority of UK clothing exports (direct exports from a UK base) go to the European countries – mainly to other EU members. This is, of course, in line with the normal pattern of developed country trade. However, as can be seen from Tables 5.15 and 5.16, the reliance upon EU

Table 5.15 The global reach of UK apparel exports (1996).

Exports to:	% of total		
	Division 84 (clothing)	All manufacturers	All trade
EU	69.8	56.2	56.9
Other Western Europe	4.5	4.7	4.4
Eastern Europe	3.2	2.7	2.8
North America	4.9	13.2	13.4
Asia and Oceania	9.2	13.8	12.9

Source: Jones, R.M. (1998), 'The Global Reach of the UK Clothing Industry',
Journal of Fashion Marketing & Management, **2**, pp. 137–53.

Table 5.16   Growth of trade with selected regions 1992–1996 (% change).

Region	Division 84 (clothing)	All manufacturers	All trade
EU	+64.5	−59.5	+56.9
Other Western Europe	−48.0	−9.3	−13.6
Eastern Europe	+166.8	+225.7	+175.2
North America	+44.4	+61.6	+60.6
Asia and Oceania	+103.5	+92.1	+85.8

Source: Jones, R.M. (1998) 'The Global Reach of the UK Clothing Industry', *Journal of Fashion Marketing and Management*, **2**, pp. 137–53.

markets is unusually high compared with the average figure for all UK manufactured exports. On the basis of these figures, the global credentials of the UK industry must be called into question. However, as will be argued below, it is possible that as the configuration of global production systems changes over time, the simple data on direct trade flows may become less reliable. In this case further analysis of UK outward investment flows in the apparel sector (Jones, 1998a) tended to confirm rather than challenge the picture presented by the trade data. It can be seen, for example, in Tables 5.17 and 5.18 that the global involvement of the apparel sector is not great. In most years, it is centred upon North America and/or Western Europe rather than the developing countries. The conclusion drawn, which remains valid, was that (Jones, 1998b, p. 245):

'the evidence from outward investment data seems on balance to indicate a limited global involvement; a true pattern of investment somewhat out of step

Table 5.17   Outward investment by the UK apparel industry (£ millions).

	£ millions
1994	10
1995	36
1996	−14
1997	−12
1998	−87
1999	−5
2000	30
2001	−23
2002	−3
2003	−6

Source: ONS – statistics supplied directly to the author for which he expresses his gratitude.

Notes: (1) A negative figure indicates a removal of investment.

(2) In 2000 the £30 million represented 0.02% of all UK outward investment.

Table 5.18   Inward investment in the UK apparel industry (£ millions).

	£ millions
1994	98
1995	−82
1996	67
1997	46
1998	24
1999	125
2000	212
2001	−9
2002	*
2003	309

Source: as Table 5.17.
Notes: (1) The 2003 figure represented 2.5% of all
                inward investment.
        (2) * figure not given due to risk of disclosure.

with the overall trend and a geographic distribution of investment which exhibits a substantial variation from the "average" UK pattern'.

F. UK apparel in the Eurozone

It has been demonstrated above that the EU market is extremely important to the UK apparel sector. In relation to the eleven members of the Eurozone some 58% of all UK clothing exports were destined (in 2003) for that region (Table 5.5(a)). The Eurozone has a population of 290 million with a total GDP of $6,000 billion and a per capita GDP of $20,000 based on 1997 figures published by Eurostat (Jones, 1999). Therefore, the issue of whether or not the UK joins the Eurozone by signing up to economic and monetary union could be of particular interest to the clothing sector over and above the general issues that membership of the EMU would pose for all businesses. If the euro is weak in relation to the pound while the UK is outside the Eurozone (as was the case in 1996–1999) then UK exports to that zone will become more expensive and, other things being equal, UK sales into the zone will fall (see Table 5.19). On these grounds and from the very narrow perspective of selling garments by direct export from the UK, being inside the Eurozone does therefore appear to be a desirable option in that it cannot make a lot of economic sense to be outside one's major market. The growth of negative balances can be seen from the data in Table 5.20, which largely confirms the theoretical expectations.

There can be virtually no doubt that membership of the Single European Market is a good thing for the apparel business. In the clothing sector a negative trade balance was turned into a positive one between the birth of the Single

Table 5.19   Changes in apparel trade with the Eurozone 1996–1999.

Country	Imports	Exports
Irish Republic	−34.2	+3.1
Finland	+13.3	−27.3
Portugal	−9.1	−45.2
Spain	−15.6	−36.4
France	+41.4	−32.9
Italy	+3.8	−28.3
Germany	+37.9	−40.9
Austria	+14.6	−52.2
Bel/Lux	+57.8	−20.7
Netherlands	+70.5	−46.5
Eurozone	+18.9	−22.9

Source: R.M. Jones (2001). Too many oeufs in one basket? *Journal of Fashion Marketing and Management*, Vol 5.2, 93–98.

Note: Over the same period UK apparel exports to the rest of the world fell by 15%. Imports in total rose by 25%. Therefore, it is clear that factors other than the relative value of the pound were at work, e.g. the decline in UK production and the strength of UK demand.

Table 5.20   UK apparel trade with the Eurozone 1996–2003: trade balances (£000).

	1996	1998	1999	2003
Irish Republic	+258,718	+318,815	+339,000	+478,346
Finland	+36,098	+23,493	+27,700	+14,876
Portugal	−277,493	−251,688	−222,200	−301,723
Spain	+138,384	+94,054	+83,200	+31,966
France	+212,130	+40,029	+2,700	−185,809
Italy	−318,345	−416,245	−364,900	−473,162
Germany	+165,084	+42,919	−31,000	+9,380
Austria	−8,663	−43,401	−43,100	−44,441
Bel/Lux	−31,634	−114,431	−155,500	−263,361
Netherlands	+9,490	−324,167	−203,900	−128,750
Total	+233,769	−630,622	−548,800	−862,678

Source: R.M. Jones (2001). Too many oeufs in one basket? *Journal of Fashion Marketing and Management*, Vol 5.2, 93–98.

Notes: (1)   A positive figure indicates that exports from the UK exceed imports to the UK.
(2)   The Eurozone took 62.2% of all UK apparel exports in 2003 as it did in 1996.
(3)   2003 figure from the same source as Table 5.1.

European Market and 1997 – provided that one believes the statistics and that we discount the possibility that the change in the way the statistics are drawn up which followed from the evolution of the Single European Market did not itself cause the transformation in the trade balance. Irrespective of that issue, the

Single European Market is an extremely large market which is geographically very close to the UK and it is doubtful if anyone would really question the value of membership of the free trade area by itself now. In addition, it is likely that the cultural gap between the UK and other members of the EU is relatively smaller in its impact upon fashion than, say, that between the UK and other markets in Asia or Eastern Europe.

The problem is that just because membership of the Single European Market is perceived to be beneficial, it does not automatically follow that membership of economic and monetary union will be – and it is important to be clear that it is not membership of the single currency that is at stake; it is membership of EMU, of which the single currency is just one feature – albeit the feature which is receiving the greatest prominence in the UK. Unfortunately, when we move the focus of attention away from the narrow interest of UK garment exports and onto the wider implications, not of the single currency, but of EMU, the picture becomes very uncertain. There is no consensus on the impact of joining EMU on the overall health of the UK economy or on the UK consumer. It is clear that EMU has the potential to affect business policy in such areas as pricing transparency; interest rates; job creation; trade; economic growth; macroeconomic policy; regional development; savings and investment; taxation levels; pension provision; and the centralisation of financial reserves. The uncertainty lies in determining exactly how it will affect these areas of activity.

In the textile sector (widely defined) a large proportion of trade activity is conducted in US dollars. Therefore, one crucial question will be the relationship between the euro and US dollar. The final factor to be taken into account is that the UK clothing and textile sectors do not exist in a vacuum – they will be affected by the general impact of EMU membership on the UK economy as well as the narrow, specific issues mentioned at the outset – and it is in these areas of impact that the greatest uncertainty lies. What is not in question is that following the final removal of MFA quotas in 2005 the liberalising ethos of EU textile policy will have an increasingly important impact on the UK apparel and textile sectors. This is discussed in Chapter 12 as we move beyond 2005, at which point tax harmonisation issues (such as VAT on children's clothing) and the removal of the final MFA quotas on sensitive items finally occur, EU issues will be increasingly important for the UK textile and apparel sectors.

G. Conclusions

The following observations seem to be justified:

(1) The negative balance and the rise in imports is to be expected given the discussion conducted in Chapter 3.

(2)   The 'problem' of rising imports cannot totally be laid at the door of low-cost producers – 37% of 2003 imports came from Western Europe.

(3)   UK clothing exports demonstrate a remarkable bias towards the EU.

(4)   Negative trade balances are to be seen in most trading areas and virtually all main garment categories.

(5)   A group of 18 low-cost suppliers are responsible for over 60% of UK clothing imports (Table 5.13). However, a range of suppliers who would not usually be thought of as possessing a cost advantage over the UK (rather the reverse) are also responsible for a significant proportion of UK clothing imports (see Table 5.14).

(6)   Import penetration exceeds 90%.

(7)   Eastern Europe and China have increased their share of UK apparel imports – this probably reflects changes to trading regulations.

(8)   A group of three suppliers (China, Hong Kong and Taiwan) provided 34.7% of UK apparel imports in 2003. If India and Bangladesh are added to the group their share rises to 42.7%.

These conclusions do, as it will be appreciated, depend upon the assumption that statistics of what might be called 'direct' trade (i.e. exports from a home base to a foreign market) do reflect the ability of one country to supply another with a product. There are, however, valid reasons for suspecting that the ability of the trade statistics to accurately represent this reality may be diminishing over time. As Singleton (1997) observes, 'the textile and apparel sector has many facets and these are constantly changing' and 'recent decades have witnessed an increase in the globalisation of the textile and apparel industries in so far as production units in several countries may co-operate in the production of a given item'.

Unfortunately, the form in which official trade statistics are organised does not change as quickly as do international production systems. The following situations are potentially important in assessing the relevance of the trade statistics which represent the physical transit of goods across national boundaries:

(1)   If a UK garment manufacturer subcontracts production to a non-UK location and brings the goods back into the UK for sale these show up as imports despite the fact that they represent (potential) income to the UK company – but, as has been seen, rising imports are usually taken to indicate deteriorating performance.

(2)   If these goods are then sold in Germany they show up simply as exports – there is no re-export data.

(3)   If the same manufacturer supplies a customer in Germany directly from the offshore production location, the sales would not show up anywhere in the official UK statistics – despite the fact that it represents income to the UK-based company.

(4) The representation – as to country of origin – of imports into the UK is also somewhat more complicated than might initially be anticipated. If, by way of illustration, a German-based garment manufacturer utilised a non-German production location (e.g. Taiwan) and transported the goods back to Germany prior to exporting them (from Germany) to the UK, then these items would show up as arrivals (imports) from Germany in the UK statistics. If, however, the same goods were transported through Germany (to the UK) under EU Transit before release into free circulation in the UK, they would be recorded as an import (into the UK) from Taiwan!

Therefore, the seemingly straightforward issue of the country of origin of UK clothing imports is complicated by the existence of global sourcing. In addition, to equate imports with 'decline' or 'poor performance' on behalf of the domestic industry is wrong. Therefore, it becomes increasingly difficult to be sure that statements about the relative contribution of low-cost sources to the overall negative trade balance and the implications of that negative balance are meaningful. Another way of approaching the issue might be to calculate the unit price of imports and exports – this might give further evidence of the role of low-cost imports in the evolution of the trade deficit.

In conclusion, while it must be recognised that there are questions surrounding the meaningfulness or otherwise of direct trade statistics as indicators of the strength or weakness of any specific industry, there is no escaping the fact that while these statistics exist, they will be used in analysis and it is important, therefore, that students of the industry have as full and complete a picture of the trading situation as revealed in these figures as is possible. In addition, research by Makhoul (1998) has shown that trade data (in their own terms) are becoming more accurate, hence the inclusion of the data here.

References

Abbott, A. & Seddighi, H.R. (1996) Aggregate Imports and Expenditure Components in the UK. *Applied Economics*, **28**, 1119–27.

HM Customs and Excise (2003) *Overseas Trade Statistics UK Trade with EC and the World (ex Business Monitor MA20)*. HMSO, London.

Jones, R.M. (1998a) The Global Reach of the UK Clothing Industry: Part I. *Journal of Fashion Marketing and Management*, **2**, 137–53.

Jones, R.M. (1998b) The Global Reach of the UK Clothing Industry: Part II. *Journal of Fashion Marketing and Management*, **2**, 240–57.

Jones, R.M. (1999) UK Clothing and the Eurozone. *Journal of Fashion Marketing and Management*, **3**, 205–7.

Jones, R.M. (2001) Too many oeufs in one basket? *Journal of Fashion Marketing and Management*, **5.2**, 93–98.

Makhoul, B. & Motterstrom, S. (1998) Explore the Accuracy of International Trade Statistics. *Applied Economics*, **30**, 1603–16.

Moore, L. (1999) *Britain's Trade and Economic Structure: The Impact of the EU.* Routledge, London.

Singleton, J. (1997) *World Textile Industry*. Routledge, London.

Winterton, R. & Barlow, A. (1996) Economic Restructuring of UK Clothing. In: *Restructuring Within a Labour Intensive Industry* (Eds I. Taplin & J. Winterton), pp. 25–61. Avebury, Aldershot.

Chapter 6
The Concept of Globalisation

A. Introduction

The words 'global' and 'globalisation' have assumed some significance in previous chapters. The concept of global shift has been described in Chapter 3 while the seeming lack of global export credentials displayed by the UK-based apparel manufacturing sector has been highlighted in Chapter 5. The idea that industry has become 'globalised' has received enormous attention both in academic circles and the popular press. In the words of Usunier (1993, p. 169) 'globalisation is a single word which has achieved great success'.

Unfortunately the words are frequently used in a variety of ways, often simply appearing to describe increased interconnectedness between nations or the fact that companies have customers or operatives in more than one country. Jay (2000, p. 130) in his survey of the history of economic growth observes that interconnectedness between nations can be traced back to the period between 1450 and 1750 when 'a fundamental shift began which eventually brought almost all areas of the world into a single network of continuous and transforming economic exchange' and confirms that, in the late eighteenth and early nineteenth centuries, the cotton textile industry was in the vanguard of the surge of tradable goods which followed the industrial revolution. As Dickerson (1995, p. 4) points out, the textile and apparel industries have been recognised as among the most dispersed of all industries. However, dispersion does not necessarily equate to globalisation, which refers to a rather special way of operating. As Douglas (1987, p. 19) pointed out:

> 'globalisation has become a key theme in every discussion of international marketing strategy. Proponents of the philosophy of "global" products . . . argue that in a world of growing internationalisation, the key to success is the development of global products and brands . . . a focus on the marketing of standardised products and brands world-wide'.

Jay (2000) confirms that the globalisation in the twentieth century which was caused by falling barriers to trade, investment and multinational operations and drawn by technological and informational revolutions, was a unique event.

The issue of globalisation can be tackled at a variety of levels, for example:

(1)   At a conceptual level – what does globalisation really mean?
(2)   At a strategic level – will only truly global companies (however defined) succeed in the future? The two main authors who have advocated the benefits of global strategies have been Ohmae (1994) and Porter (1998).
(3)   At a purely marketing level – has consumption been homogenised so that standard products can be sold everywhere, ignoring the role of national culture in determining demand? The main advocate of the globalised market has been Levitt (1983).
(4)   At an operational level – is it necessary for business practice to take account of cultural factors?

The first two issues will be considered in this chapter while issue three will be dealt with in Chapter 11 and the final issue in Chapter 8.

B. What is globalisation?

It will be useful at the outset to acknowledge that there is little argument that the degree of interconnectedness between nations and the extent of international operations conducted by businesses have both increased over time. The World Trade Organisation for example (WTO, 1998), records that trade growth has outstripped economic growth for 'at least 250 years except for a brief period from 1913 to 1950'; that foreign investment has risen by a factor of 17 between 1973 and 1996 and that trade by sea has risen by a factor of 10 between 1948 and 1993 while the unit costs of such transport have fallen by 70% over the last 10 years.

Usunier (1993, p. 177), although an opponent of the globalisation thesis, accepts that there 'is little doubt about the globalisation of competition' and that 'linkage between countries and therefore competition between companies continues to grow'. Competition is becoming more global or at least intra-country activity is increasing whether it be measured by trade flows, investment flows or people flows. The problem is that although the word globalisation can be used as a simile for internationalisation, it is also used by a variety of authors in a very much more specialised and unique way so that while, from one point of view, it would be perfectly feasible for internationalisation to proceed without globalisation, from another it would not.

The volume of world trade has risen sharply over the last 50 years both in general terms and, specifically, in textile and clothing, as was seen in Chapter 3. Parker (1998, p. 466) refers to a number of 'measures of globalisation' such as the percentage of a firm's sales derived overseas or the percentage of industry revenues derived from trade and provides data to illustrate that globalisation measured in these terms has increased over time. Parker (1998, p. 6) also stresses inter-connectedness by defining globalisation 'as increased permeability of traditional boundaries' between nations.

There is little doubt that competition has globalised in this sense of the word. It is, of course, open to debate as to whether or not the result of this expansion and liberalisation of trade has been wholly beneficial. The generally accepted model of the world trade system is that on a global scale and over the long run a system of unrestricted trade produces the best results (see Chapter 9) although this does not, of course, rule out the possibility that negative effects of trade upon specific groups will never occur. Kolodko (2003, p. 20) provides a list of countries where output per head actually fell.

In reality the way in which trade has evolved in the recent past has often had detrimental effects upon specific groups and regions. As Hopkins (2004) shows, the current wave of globalisation has missed out large parts of the world. Ferguson (2001) argues that globalisation post 1985 has led to widening income disparities between developed and developing countries. It is important, however, not to allow a recognition of these facts to be used to support an argument that global trade should be restricted. As Ferguson (2001, p. 24) says, 'globalisation is preferable to the alternative which is protectionism and institutionalised inefficiency'. This argument is supported by Stiglitz (2002, p. 214) in his far-reaching critique of the institutions of globalisation when he writes that abandoning globalisation is 'neither feasible nor desirable. . . . The problem is not with globalisation, but with how trade rules have been organised'. These arguments are particularly relevant to the apparel sector at a time when the rules which have governed world trade in textiles and apparel since 1974 are being abandoned. It is particularly important that these issues are considered from a sound theoretical base (as opposed to an emotional one) otherwise the farcical situation arises in which the very countries which argued against the introduction of quotas are now arguing against their removal! These issues are considered in detail in Chapter 9. As Kolodko (2003, p. 7) noted 'within the time span of a single generation the economies that take more active participation in globalisation managed to double their real income per head'.

A variety of terms are used in the literature to reflect the increased involvement of businesses in the international marketplace, e.g. multinational enterprise (MNE); international companies; transnational businesses and global companies. The latter term (and the associated concepts of the globalisation of a sector and global strategy) have come to refer to a rather special sort of player in world markets and to the emergence of a company with very special characteristics which have developed during a distinct process of evolution.

In order to avoid confusion it is useful to have a very clear idea of exactly what is meant by globalisation in this restricted sense, in particular because the process of becoming truly global implies significant changes in behaviour. In one sense it clearly does not matter what label is put upon an organisation as long as it is successful in gaining market share and generating profits – and this is really the point because some commentators argue that only truly global operators will survive in the future.

It can be recognised immediately that definitions which run in terms of mere dispersion of activities do not lead very effectively towards a definition of globalisation. Kefalas (1990) defines a multinational enterprise (MNE), for example, as a company which 'owns and manages businesses in two or more countries'. The proponents of globalisation make it clear that, in their view, an MNE is not a global company. Levitt (1983, p. 92) argued that:

> 'the multinational operates in a number of countries and adjusts its products and practices in each at high cost. The global company operates with resolute constancy at low relative cost – as if the entire world were a single entity because the world's needs and desires have been homogenised. This makes the multinational corporation obsolete and the global corporation absolute'.

A global company is identified by a range of features but two key benefits are those of the co-ordination and integration of activities across national boundaries which, it is argued, are becoming less and less meaningful over time. Parker (1998, p. 6) defines globalisation as 'the increased permeability of traditional boundaries' or 'the absence of borders and barriers between nations'. Usunier (1993, p. 195) describes a global strategy as one in which there is 'the configuration and co-ordination of activities . . . across national markets'. In this way a definition emerges which places less emphasis on physical presence in foreign countries and more emphasis on the way in which these markets are perceived and the way in which the company is organised to supply those markets. In the WTO's words (1998, p. 33) globalisation 'is a multi-faceted concept in so far as it describes both economic phenomena and their social, political and distributional consequences'.

Ohmae (1994) identifies five stages through which a company must move in order to become truly global. Two themes central to the evolutionary process described are that customers with similar levels of income and information will become very similar in their spending habits and that customers no longer care about the nationality of companies or where products are made.

The five stages are as follows:

(1) The export stage, in which all decisions are taken in the home base.
(2) The multi-local stage, in which branch offices are set up to take over responsibility for the marketing and sales functions.
(3) The relocation stage, in which the manufacturing base is relocated to the major markets. This requires a long-term commitment and the development of local people who can be allowed to make decisions without constant reference to headquarters.

(4)   The complete insiderisation stage, in which activities such as research and product development are transferred to other countries.

(5)   The truly global stage – at which final stage a number of key functions are pulled back to the centre, e.g. global branding. This is necessary to ensure that there is a common sense of corporate purpose and identity, and a common technology and operating philosophy must be adhered to.

A company would move from one stage to another if by so doing it would serve the customer more efficiently. Ohmae's contention is that increasingly it will become essential to move through the five stages. A company might, for example, move to stage three to overcome trade barriers or adverse currency fluctuations or because production in or near key markets is more cost-effective. A firm that has globalised to stage five would be rather special and would have all (or most) of the following features which can be distilled from the writings of the authors associated with the concept:

- It would make anywhere.
- It would sell everywhere.
- It would sell a homogeneous product and only move from this in extreme situations.
- It would be nationality-less.
- Its top management would be multicultural.
- It would cross-subsidise activities as between countries.
- It would see the main goal as being to maximise total returns by serving the customer best by whatever means were appropriate so that activities in all countries are integrated to this end.
- It would give a lot of freedom to the managers of operations away from head office.

The focus of the discussion up to this stage has been the 'company'. However, the term 'globalisation' is also often applied to the forces acting upon an entire sector or industry. Globalisation is seen as a process in which the entire world (for the supply of the products of the industry) comes to be regarded as one giant market. Regional or national variations in tastes can safely be ignored. This need not be taken to extremes in the sense that the existence of some variations are not admitted. Even Levitt (1983, p. 97), for example, concedes that we should not:

'advocate the systematic disregard of local or national differences, but a company's sensitivity to such differences does not require that it ignore the possibilities of doing things differently . . .'

The main focus of Levitt's (1983, p. 92) argument is that consumers everywhere want the same products so that the world is being driven towards 'a converging commonality . . . gone are the accustomed differences in national or regional products'. The term ethnocentric is sometimes used (Daniels, 1998) to describe a policy which assumes that what works at home will work everywhere so that differences between national markets can be safely ignored. A policy which focuses on the unique national differences between markets and, accordingly, seeks to produce unique products for each market is sometimes described as polycentric (Daniels, 1998, p. 103). This issue will be considered in greater depth in Chapter 11.

The driving force which is supposed to have produced this convergence of tastes is technology, which is seen as having had a number of effects, namely:

(1)   On communications – which according to Levitt (1983, p. 92) 'proletarises communications, transport and travel. It has made isolated places and impoverished people eager for modernity's allurements. Almost everyone, everywhere, wants all the things they have heard about, seen, or experienced via the new technologies'.

(2)   On technology in the sense of a more capital intensive process linked to economies of scale resulting in (Levitt, 1983, p. 92) 'the emergence of global markets for standardised products on a previously unimagined scale of magnitude. Corporations geared to this new reality benefit from enormous economies of scale'.

(3)   On technology in the sense that it enables the consumer to solve old problems in new ways – providing what people want out of life and making it easier to alleviate life's burdens at the lowest cost.

It has to be recognised that there is very little evidence – other than selected examples – to support this assertion. In the view of Douglas (1987, p. 21) what evidence there is 'suggests that the similarities in customer behaviour are restricted to a relatively limited number of target segments or product markets'. It is, therefore, important that the applicability of these ideas to the apparel sector is considered in some detail. It will be useful to make a basic distinction between 'culture-free' and 'culture-bound' products. The latter are products the demand for which is still affected by cultural influences so that global product standardisation will be relatively less feasible. Culture-free products are those which are equally acceptable across cultural boundaries – they represent the demand for cultural universalities. The majority of examples of the latter quoted in the literature are high technological products such as mobile phones, the Sony Walkman, medicinal drugs and communication products.

This view of the world has not gone unchallenged and contrary to the impression promoted by the advocates of globalisation, there is a substantial body of research evidence on a wide variety of issues related to the impact of cultural forces upon consumer demand. It is clear, therefore, that a dispersed industry is not the same thing as a globalised one because all the activity in a dispersed sector could be carried on entirely independently of all other activity. A globalised strategy or sector must be characterised by the presence of an integrated approach to supplying customers.

As Porter (1998, p. 54) says, the fact of being 'multinational does not imply a global strategy if the multinational has free standing subsidiaries which operate (more or less) independently in each nation'.

The term globalisation is best reserved for application to an industry for whose products the world is becoming a homogeneous marketplace and in which it is probable that only those companies which adopt a globally integrated approach to supplying the market will survive.

In the words of Stopford (1985), while

'there is no single force pushing for globalisation . . . a combination of technological developments (e.g. the micro-electronics revolution), cultural evolution (the homogenisation of tastes) and the breaking down of geographic and intra-industry barriers . . . means that the international business environment is being irrevocably changed'.

In such industries it is becoming increasingly true that globalisation as a strategy will be more appropriate.

A global strategy, therefore, represents a specific approach to international business. Porter (1998, p. 54), for example, defines global strategy by stating that firms

'compete with truly global strategies involving selling worldwide, sourcing components and materials worldwide and locating activities in many nations to take advantage of low cost factors'.

Furthermore, and this is a crucial point, the acceptance of a global strategy introduces an integrated approach to selling in world markets, recognising that performance in one market can influence ability to compete elsewhere.

A global strategy will be selected by a company if it is recognised that such an approach will enhance its competitive ability.

Porter (1998, p. 578) argues that the probability that this will become an imperative is increasing because:

'a firm cannot rely on its national circumstances to sustain its competitive advantage. A firm must select wisely, add to its advantages or offset its home base of disadvantages through activities in other nations. This is what a global strategy is about'.

If the industry is one in which the pressures of globalisation are extremely powerful, then it would be the case that adopting a global strategy is almost essential to success:

'A firm's competitive position in one nation significantly affects (and is affected by) its position in other nations. Rivals compete against each other on a truly worldwide basis, drawing on competitive advantages that grow out of the entire network of worldwide activities.'

In such an industry, firms who wish to succeed

'are compelled to compete internationally, in order to achieve or sustain competitive advantage in the most important segments. There may be segments in such industries which are domestic because of unique national needs, in which purely domestic firms can prosper'

but these will be the exception. The key factors in the existence of a truly global strategy are the existence of sales and production in all or most of the major markets and an integrated approach to the generation of competitive advantage. A global strategy is one in which competitive advantage is sought through stategies which are interdependent across national boundaries. Activities are co-ordinated and allocated to specific localities (which Porter calls configuration) with the aim of maximising the competitive advantage of the totality of the operation. Additionally, scale economies in the supply to world markets of a (more or less) homogeneous product which must be introduced in all major markets simultaneously plays a vital role.

A number of commentators argue that more and more industries are becoming global in character and that in these sectors, only companies operating global strategies will succeed. There are many differences between competing domestically and competing globally in that a whole new range of issues become important, such as quotas and exchange rate fluctuations. The main issue to be faced by companies is the possibility of gaining competitive advantage through competing globally. The advantages of a global operation (as compared to a purely domestic one) would include economies of scale; access to bigger markets; the spreading of risks; utilisation of optimum locations; early exposure to best practice; exploitation of Government assistance and the ability to cross-subsidise operations in different locations and to minimise tax payments by exploiting variations in tax regimes between countries.

Alternatively, will the company be threatened by other companies which are operating a global strategy? Therefore, it is important to understand the triggers to the globalisation of a sector, the sources of global advantage and the impediments to globalisation which might allow non-global strategies to be successful. It is important not to assume that global strategies are always appropriate and have been found to be most suitable, desirable or possible. In general terms, global strategies are always appropriate when the following conditions apply:

(1)   It is feasible to standardise the product.
(2)   Standardisation results in significant economies of scale being realised.

(3) Costs can be reduced and efficiency increased by locating different stages of the operation in different places.
(4) Cross-subsidisation of activities between global markets is useful.
(5) Operations need to be located in specific places to bypass trade barriers.
(6) Competitors are emerging with global strategies.

Triggers to the globalisation of a sector include the following:

(1) Convergence of tastes.
(2) Reductions in transport costs.
(3) Improvements in communications.
(4) Reduced government impediments.
(5) Technological changes leading to increased scale economies.
(6) Changes in the costs of factors of production.
(7) The emergence or recognition of common segments in many countries.
(8) Reductions in the cost of making product adaptations to national tastes.

On the other side of the coin are the impediments to globalisation which would include the following factors:

(1) Heavy transport or storage costs.
(2) Local product variation.
(3) Lack of world-wide demand.
(4) Local service importance.
(5) Government barriers which cannot be bypassed.

C. The application of the concept of globalisation to the apparel industry

These factors will not impinge on all sectors with equal force or to a common time scale and this is why it cannot be said that a global strategy is the optimum in all sectors at all times. The supporters of the 'globalisation' thesis would argue that the triggers are applying more universally, while the impediments are generally falling. It could be argued, therefore, that global strategies will increasingly play a part in the consideration of strategic options and the development of Sustainable Competitive Advantage. In an increasingly competitive world marketplace for apparel, all companies will have to recognise what the basis of their competitive advantage is to be. There will be a long list of these from lowest cost to highest quality, as will be seen in Chapter 7.

Globalisation itself might be seen as a means to competitive advantage because it would lead to lower costs, the ability to reap economies of scale and to cross-subsidise activities between markets. As has been seen, globalisation in the special sense in which it is used here is not the same as mere dispersion of activity, nor is the use of global sourcing by itself an indicator of the presence of global companies. There can be little dispute about the increasingly dispersed nature of apparel production, nor about increased use of offshore production. There is, however, more doubt about the incidence of globalisation in the apparel sector and of its appropriateness as a winning strategy.

It has been seen that the original works on the globalisation process stressed the influence of technology and the convergence of tastes between countries as promoting globalisation. A close reading of these works suggests that the influence of technology in the process can be subdivided into three areas:

(1)   Improved communications.
(2)   Economies of scale – which both demand and encourage a global approach.
(3)   The discovery of technologically new ways of satisfying old wants.

The first of these is common to all products, so that in practice three factors can be identified which are held to be pushing companies and industries inexorably down the path to globalisation, namely factors two and three from the above list, plus the alleged convergence of tastes. In brief, it is being argued that the pressure to globalisation will be greater if:

(1)   there are extensive scale economies;
(2)   there is a new solution to an old consumer desire;
(3)   consumer tastes have converged.

In the literature, the vast majority of examples given of products/markets which have been globalised are what can be called 'high tech' products, most of them in the electronics sector.

It is true that Levitt (1983) does argue that globalisation is not confined to such products and quotes the examples of Coca-Cola and Levi's in support of this point. Baden-Fuller (1991) also considers this issue when cautioning against taking arguments about globalisation of tastes too far when arguing that it is less clear that 'market-driven companies have as great a sense of urgency to expand globally as technologically driven ones'. Also, as has been seen in Chapter 4, Ohmae (1985) stresses the role of capitalisation in the development of the globalisation process, noting that the labour content of many operations has fallen from 25% to between 5% and 10% of total costs. This is not true in apparel manufacture.

Ohmae (1985) also places great emphasis upon the idea that industry has typically become a 'fixed cost' world. Therefore, the emphasis switches from boosting profits by finding ways to reduce marginal costs to maximising the marginal contribution towards fixed costs by increasing sales volume – which in turn implies a wide (global) market base.

In the case of the apparel industry it is normally accepted that economies of scale are relatively less important than in other sectors, and that capitalisation is still relatively low. It might also be argued (although this might be less widely accepted) that few apparel products represent new ways of doing things in a technical sense (this may be less true in textiles) unless you consider a new fashion to meet this point, and that cultural and national differences in dress are probably more entrenched than in other products.

Finally, while some of the authors in this area argue that global companies will almost by definition be relatively large (if only because of the resources required and the sophisticated management systems needed to run them) the apparel industry is well documented as a small firm sector. Therefore, it seems logical to conclude that in the apparel sector the imperative to adopt global as opposed to non-global strategies will also be relatively less strong. Jeans and trainers may be the exception to this point, because in the latter, there is an element of technological progress and both represent homogenised tastes. These ideas can be represented pictorially in a three-dimensional graph which is based upon Table 6.1 below and reproduced as Fig. 6.1. The y-axis represents the

Table 6.1   Globalisation by product.

Product	AXIS		
	X	Y	Z
A	8	7	9
B	8	4	6
C	3	3	3

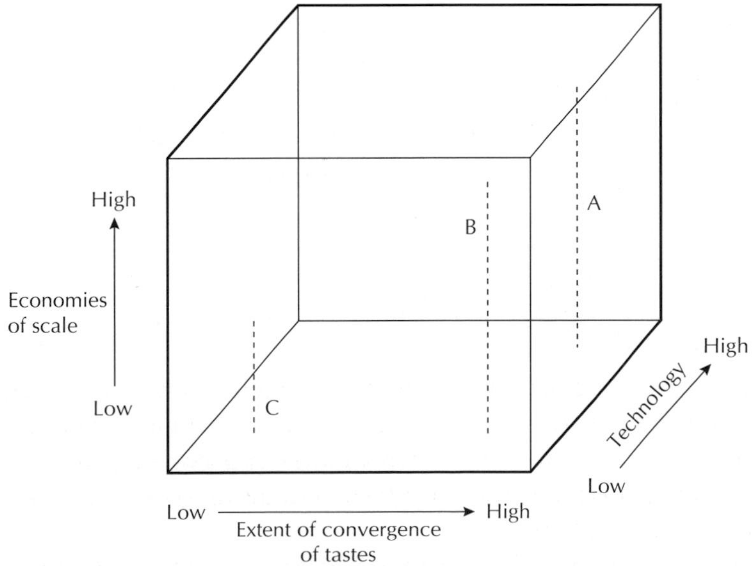

Fig. 6.1   The globalisation of markets.

importance of scale economies; the x-axis represents the degree of convergence of tastes; while the z-axis measures technological sophistication – all measured on a scale of 1 to 10.

Product A might represent an electronic product which is truly global, while Product C represents the other end of the scale, i.e. a product which does not reap scale economies, has a low technological content and for which a common worldwide taste has not evolved. Product B is in a midway position in that tastes are homogeneous to a degree, so that scale factors can progress and content, e.g. trainers with air bags. The question is, to what extent is most of the clothing sector nearer to B than to C in this model? A good recent example of a product with many global characteristics would be the Ford motor car, the Mondeo. Many of the so-called high level design and development functions in its development were carried out outside the home base of the parent company, production of various component parts is widely dispersed and the car was to be sold with few modifications in all major markets.

Economies of scale are vital to success and the success of the car in any of the major markets will have a significant impact on the fortunes of rival producers. Can examples of this sort be easily found in the apparel sector? If they cannot, it does not follow that apparel manufacturers are behaving illogically by not following the global model, because there is no single strategy which will be appropriate or optimal for all sectors at all times.

Unfortunately, economics and management science go through fashion trends no less frequently than garments and 'globalisation' as a strategy is 'in' at the moment – even when the word 'dispersed' might be more appropriate. Ghoshal and Nohira (1993) distinguish between two sets of environmental forces:

- Forces promoting global integration and forces.
- Forces producing a demand for national (local) responsiveness.

They then identify four types of trading environments which emerge as a result of the variable operating strengths of these two forces:

(1) A global environment in which the first force is strong and the second weak.
(2) A multinational environment in which the reverse is the case.
(3) A transnational environment in which both forces are strong.
(4) A placid international environment in which both forces are weak.

As a result of this analysis, the authors place textiles in the 'weak-weak' category. In terms of our analysis, we are suggesting that clothing production might fall into the category in which the forces promoting global integration may be relatively weak while those promoting local product diversity might be relatively strong.

In the rest of the paper, the authors identify a variety of organisational structures for the running of the companies which will be appropriate to each environment and considers whether or not those companies with a good match outperform those with a mismatch. The conclusion drawn was that 'companies require different organisational horses to manage superior performance in different environmental courses'.

Therefore, while it is possible to point to the advance of forces encouraging globalisation and the alleged retreat of those discouraging global development, it is not possible to point to any generally accepted body of evidence which demonstrates the unchallenged superiority of global strategies at all times in all sectors. For example, a paper by Baden-Fuller (1991) shows how changed economic conditions reduced the value of global strategies (which had previously been seen as crucial to success) in the European domestic appliance industry.

Critical in these changes were factors which have been highlighted above as of importance in the apparel industry, such as increased demand for unique national tastes expressed in words which could be applied to the clothing industry:

> 'The causes of such national differences are hard to determine. They seem deeply ingrained in cultural behaviour.'

The return on capital of global companies in this sector fell significantly from 1974 to 1985 to levels well below those returned by national producers. The authors concluded that while it was clear that 'early success of the Italian major appliance industry was based on a European strategy that exploited the international decision of labour', the market has since then fragmented and purely national strategies have regained their potency.

Another study by Mitchell (1992) concluded that both increasing and decreasing international presence are risky strategies. Yet a third recent study by Carr (1993), while accepting the findings of Baden-Fuller that national rather than global strategies may yet prove superior, points out that there are (at least) two other routes to international success, such as emphasis on technological superiority or customer service.

It would be prudent at this stage to be clear that, given the emphasis on the role of strategy, there is no body of research evidence which would support the argument that only companies which use the tools of strategic analysis always, at all times, in all places and sectors outperform those which do not act in such way.

Powell (1992) argues that the employment of strategic planning techniques may not in itself be the basis for sustainable competitive advantage as it is easily copied. It is fortuitous that one of the sectors examined was clothing and the conclusion drawn was that

> 'in the apparel industry, some findings reflect the fact that in addition to ongoing market instability (resulting primarily from its fashion orientation), this industry recently endured the competitive instability of intensified foreign competition'.

In view of the consequences for competition of the dismantling of the Multi Fibre Agreement described in Chapter 9, the present emphasis on strategy is probably justified.

In summary, therefore, at the conceptual level there are a number of inter-twined strands of thought. Porter (1998) has developed ideas about the selection of 'winning' strategies based on the identification of Sustainable Competitive Advantage. In some instances this winning strategy will be global; furthermore, it is likely that (in his view) there will be specific locations which favour winning strategies (the Porter Diamond) which means that activities must be dispersed and arranged on a global scale.

Levitt (1983) is more concerned with the convergence of tastes and the impact this has on the product adaptation strategy. Usunier (1993, p. 169) recognises the value of this perspective in accepting that globalisation 'means homogenisa-tion on a worldwide scale' but contends that while globalisation strategies exist, global marketing does not. This issue will be considered in more detail in Chapter 11.

Ohmae is also concerned with identifying a broad strategic concept which leads to the adoption of winning position. A key element in his model is that of the stateless company and a world in which the consumer cares little for the ori-gins of products.

However, he does not go as far as Levitt on the issue of homogenisation of consumer tastes, being satisfied to argue that it should be possible to develop a core model for the most important markets which could then – if this is abso-lutely necessary – be modified for the markets. There are, of course, common elements in the writings of the globalists: the emphasis placed on the diffusion of consumer information by new technology; the need to be customer-driven; the need to co-ordinate global activities so as to maximise benefit to the consumer, and the need to be willing to operate anywhere free of any ties to historical bases. The most important consideration is for each company to draw selectively upon these concepts in an appropriate manner given their own product, market and customer orientation. The aim of business is to win customers, gain market share and to make money while serving the customer better than rivals. In some cases this may require the adoption of a truly global strategy while in others it may not.

In conclusion, therefore, it can be stated that there is little doubt that globalisa-tion in the sense of an increased degree of interconnectedness between nations has taken place. It is far less obvious, however, that this means that only truly global companies and strategies will be appropriate in all sectors or that all markets have been globalised in the sense of becoming virtually culture-free. The evidence for the latter is far less clear cut than that for the former trend. These are not merely academic issues because the attitude taken to such practical matters as product standardisation, the homogenisation of advertising and promotional material and the types of managerial skills required will depend upon the attitude a company takes to these issues of globalisation.

The UK apparel industry does not, on the basis of available statistical indicators, display impressive global credentials in that, as was seen in Chapter 5, 66% of direct exports go to one trading block. In the last decade it is true that offshore production has been increasingly adopted by UK-based apparel suppliers and, as a result, global supply chains have become the norm (see Chapters 7 and 8). However, this does not equate to true globalisation. Historically, there has been very little outward investment by the UK apparel sector as was seen in Table 5.17. In the period 1995–2000 (OTS, 2005) outward investment was negative (which means investment was removed) in all but one year in which it represented only 0.02% of all outward investment. Inward investment ranged from −£82 millions to +£309 millions in 2003 which represented 2.5% of all inward investment for that year.

References

Baden-Fuller, C. & Stopford, J. (1991) Globalisation Frustrated: the Case of the White Goods Industry. *Strategic Management Journal*, **12**, 493–507.

Carr, C. (1993) Global, National and Resource Based Strategies. *Strategic Management Journal*, **14**, 551–66.

Daniels, J.D. & Radebough, L. (1998) *International Business*. Addison Wesley, Harlow.

Dickerson, K. (1995) *Textiles and Apparel in the Global Economy*. Prentice Hall, New Jersey.

Douglas, S.P. & Wind, Y. (1987) The Myth of Globalisation. *Columbia Journal of World Business*, **22**, 19–29.

Ferguson, N. (2001) The anarchists are wrong, but they ask the right questions. *Daily Telegraph*, 2.5.2001, p. 24.

Ghoshal, S. & Nohira, N. (1993) Horses For Courses. *Sloan Management Review*, **34**, 23–35.

Hopkins, A.G. (2004) *Globalisation in World History*. Pimlico, London.

Jay, P. (2000) *The Road to Riches*. Weidenfield and Nicholson, London.

Kefalas, A.G. (1990) *Global Business Strategy*. South Western Publishing Co., Cincinnati.

Kolodko, G.W. (Ed.) (2003) *Emerging Market Economics*. Ashgate, Aldershot.

Levitt, T. (1983) The Globalisation of Markets. *Harvard Business Review*, **LXI**, 92–103.

Mitchell, W., Shaver, J.M. & Yeung, B. (1992) Getting There in a Global Industry. *Strategic Management Journal*, **13**, 419–33.

Ohmae, K. (1985) *Triad Power: The Coming Shape of Global Competition*. Free Press, New York.

Ohmae, K. (1994) *The Borderless World*. Harper Collins, London.

OTS (2005) *MA4 Direct Investment*. I am grateful to the OTS for supplying statistics for the clothing industry as the figures were not available in the published document.

Parker, B. (1998) *Globalisation and Business Practice*. Sage, London.

Porter, M.E. (1998) *The Competitive Advantage of Nations*. Free Press, New York.

Powell, T.C. (1992) Strategic Planning as a Competitive Advantage. *Strategic Management Journal*, **13**, 553–8.

Stiglitz, J. (2002) *Globalisation and its Discontents*. Penguin, London.

Stopford, J. & Turner, L. (1985) *Britain and the Multinationals*. John Wiley, London.

Usunier, J.-C. (1993) *International Marketing – a Cultural Approach*. Prentice Hall, New York.

World Trade Organisation (1998) *WTO Annual Report*. WTO, Washington.

Chapter 7

The Response to Global Shift – Strategic Imperatives and the Diamond Framework

A. The background environment

The review of the evolution of the textile pipeline carried out above has produced the following conclusions about the role of apparel manufacturing in advanced economies and about the circumstances within which future development must occur:

(1) That the industry is not the dominant partner in a pipeline which has long been characterised by adversarial relationships.
(2) That the industry does not occupy a strategic role in the UK or any developed economy.
(3) That the structure of the industry is almost uniquely unfavourable to profit generation.
(4) That global shift has been inevitable given the labour-intensive nature of apparel production. There is global overproduction.
(5) That the possibility of relocation of production back to the developed world is virtually nil.
(6) That import penetration has risen strongly over the last decade and continues to rise.
(7) That the UK industry has entered a new period of severe contraction which is significantly different from that experienced over the last 20 years and probably irreversible.

The economic environment is, therefore, extremely hostile. Additionally, the early years of the twenty-first century will witness the removal of the system of managed trade which has operated since 1974, as the Multi Fibre Arrangement (see Chapter 9) is finally dismantled. Against this pessimistic scenario a number of positive signs can be discerned. For example, production in the developed regions does still remain a significant proportion of global totals while most of the world's major textile and apparel companies are based in developed countries. As Porter (1998, p. 37) points out, strategic choices are vital. As Singleton (1997, p. 97) comments, early studies of the sector's responses to crisis in the 1960s and 1970s clearly illustrated 'the importance of strategic decision making and shows how it relates to . . . elements of the diamond, such as perceptions about demand conditions and the choice of technology'. In order to achieve competitive advantage choices have to be made. These strategic competitive advantages can be created anywhere (not just in the home base) and at any stage of the process of converting inputs into profitable outputs – the so-called value chain. In particular, value advantage is not exclusively (or even primarily) created by or at the assembly stage of production. Therefore, the preoccupation with the sewing process in the apparel sector may not be particularly helpful – the difference in value added between a coat selling for £40 and one selling for £140 is almost certainly not the product of differences at the assembly stage. Singhal (2004) asserts that 61% of value added is created at the retail stage and only 19% at the assembly stage. There are clearly examples of relatively more successful apparel companies in developed countries. The question for the future is to identify those strategies which offer the best opportunity of success.

A starting point might be to identify (on *a priori* grounds) a list of potential strategies. Table 7.1 contains such a list. While recognising that there will be no single strategy that is universally appropriate it will be possible to indicate the probability of success of each strategy in a developed nation such as the UK. It has to be remembered that there is a world of difference between an economy's suitability for apparel assembly and as an environment which is liable to promote the evolution of winning strategies so that it becomes the home base of globally successful operators as is made clear in Fig. 7.1. If the company based in A had garments produced in B but returned to base prior to supplying market C then the export statistics would reveal A as having comparative advantage. However, if goods were sent to C direct from B then the latter would be revealed by trade data as possessing the advantage (Jones, 2001). Kilduff's (2006) major study of comparative advantage in the textile supply chain was reviewed on page 102.

B.   *Application of the Diamond Framework to the apparel sector*

It has to be remembered that the Diamond Framework is meant to identify countries within which clusters of internationally successful companies will develop. In Porter's words (Porter, 1998, p. 71) 'nations succeed in particular industries because their home environment is the most dynamic and the most challenging and stimulates . . . firms to upgrade and widen their advantages over time'. There are a number of issues which need to be clarified – first, that the emergence of an internationally successful cluster of firms in a particular

Table 7.1   Potential survival strategies.

Strategies	Issues
(1) Investment in high technology and labour replacement; technological restructuring.	Labour intensity. Low investment. Low knowledge-based content.
(2) Protectionism.	'Unfairness' of low cost competition; inevitability of global shift.
(3) Government subsidy and assistance.	Role of apparel sector in the economy; 'unfair' competition.
(4) Co-ordination in the textile pipeline; organisational restructuring.	Adversarial relationships.
(5) Manipulation of industrial structure; diversification.	Adverse industrial structure.
(6) Product differentiation; branding; moving up market; marketing strategies.	Low cost competition.
(7) Offshore production and OPT (geographic or spatial restructuring).	Labour costs.
(8) International strategies and globalisation (including relocation of production and the identification of new customers).	Costs. Demand.
(9) Restructuring of production of work organisation (team working; flexible manufacturing; local networks and external economies of scale).	Productivity. Flexibility.
(10) Process re-engineering; operational improvements; lean manufacturing and logistics.	Costs. Productivity.

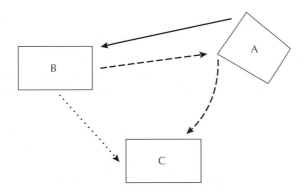

Key   A = Developed country base favoured by Diamond Framework.
      B = Low cost production centre.
      C = Market.

——————▶ Offshore production link.
– – – –▶ Goods flow via A.
·······▶ Direct supply to C.

Fig. 7.1   Revealed Competitive Advantage.

industry in a country does not necessarily mean that it will conduct most of its operations or employ most people in that country. Indeed it is a major element in the Diamond Framework that successful strategies will probably incorporate a global view of events. The home base is important because it is the place where key decisions are made but (Porter, 1998, p. 577) 'a global strategy supplements and solidifies the competitive advantage created at the home base'. The most successful companies (p. 578) 'amplified their home-based advantages and off-set home-based disadvantages through global strategies that tapped selectively into advantages available in other nations'. Secondly, in apparel production it may be the case, as Singleton (1997, p. 4) argues, that 'clustering may not be necessary for the initial attainment of competitive advantage which frequently stems from low labour costs'. This may be the case in respect of the growth of assembly activity in low cost countries but it is probably something of a misleading argument in relation to the evolution of truly successful global apparel companies in the sense that the possession of (temporarily) low labour costs is both probably a temporary (or low order) advantage and one which is only relevant to one element of the apparel production value chain. As Singleton (1997, p. 125) and Dickerson (1995) demonstrate, the majority of the world's top textile and clothing companies are either American, European or Japanese. The location of assembly production within the value chain is not, of itself, an indicator that a specific country is likely to be the home base for the most successful companies. In Porter's words (1998, p. 577) the 'most important sources of national advantage must be actively sought and exploited, unlike low factor costs obtainable simply by operating in a nation'. The geography of world production will be altered as companies seek to offset one specific home base disadvantage (high semi-skilled labour cost) as part of dispersing particular activities to 'whatever country enjoys advantages. There is no excuse for accepting basic factor disadvantages'.

With these thoughts in mind the next step will be to examine the Diamond Framework's application to identifying locations where the framework is favourable (or not) to the emergence of internationally successful apparel manufacturers – in which countries does it seem likely that the Diamond Framework will promote companies which select and develop winning strategies? The individual components of the Diamond Framework are examined below. It is clear that other factors could equally be examined – in Chapter 12 a Pentagon Framework is preferred.

(i)   Demand conditions

It has been demonstrated in Chapter 3 that the demand for apparel is a function of income and that, accordingly, the biggest markets are to be found in the developed countries. This may, of course, change over time, as is considered in

Chapter 11. At the present time the size of the domestic market confers clear advantages on companies in the developed world. The issue is, however, somewhat more complex than simply being one of the size of the market – the *quality* of demand expressed in that market can also be vital. While the UK measures up quite well in terms of market size it exhibits a number of other, less promising features. First, the proportion of total demand devoted to apparel consumption has been falling over the long run even though it is now stable (see Chapter 10). Second, in the sense that demand is expressed through the retail system the somewhat unique structure of apparel retailing in the UK with its historical emphasis on long production runs and safe design has probably not been entirely helpful (see Chapter 10). There is, in a real sense, a parallel here with the decline of the cotton textile industry in that virtually all commentators agree that over-concentration on long runs and low quality was a major contributory factor to the eventual decline of the sector. Choice of strategies *is* important. Although it is difficult (if not impossible) to assess factors like the sophistication of consumers within the positivist framework identified in Chapter 1, it is generally accepted that, in Singleton's word's (1997, p. 66) 'sophisticated tastes in the home market contribute to the international success of the Italian . . . clothing sector' and that 'the name of France as a centre for high fashion is a reputational asset'. On balance, therefore, demand conditions do not appear to be particularly favourable in the UK – in particular as an ageing population evolves in the next century. Owen (1999) argues that it was a particular element of the demand variable – lack of access to the EU market – which was primarily to blame for Britain's poor economic performance.

(ii)　Factor conditions

In considering factor conditions there is an obvious danger, in the present context, of concentrating exclusively on the supply and cost of semi-skilled labour. As has been seen in Chapter 4, the UK is a relatively high cost country in terms of Asian wage levels. Additionally, the problems of attracting labour into the industry have been well documented. Given that the labour cost gap is unlikely to disappear, that the probability of a major technological breakthrough to reduce labour content is virtually nil and that the possibility of offsetting the cost disadvantage via higher productivity is remote (Singleton, 1997, p. 33) this factor disadvantage will remain one that has to be overcome by relocation of activity. It is generally believed that the human factor is less mobile than non-human and that female, semi-skilled labour is among the least mobile of all factors. However, there are many other aspects of factor conditions which need to be considered, e.g. other categories of human labour, such as designers, entrepreneurial and managerial talent. Additionally, a range of non-human factors must be evaluated, e.g. capital; knowledge and information; and raw materials.

(iii)   Related industries

In Singleton's opinion (1997, p. 73) the most important supporting industries to the textile and clothing pipeline are 'the production of textile machinery . . . and chemicals (especially man-made fibres)'. In the case of apparel manufacturing the most important supporting industries are the primary textile industry itself, machinery and the design sector. As has been noted above (Chapter 1) the UK primary textile industry has suffered a severe decline over the years in addition to which the supporting relationship between the two sectors has been historically rather weak. The machinery industry has virtually disappeared in the UK. The major producers of electronic and computerised equipment for use in the design and preparatory process of apparel manufacture are French, German, Spanish, Canadian and American while the major producer of transport systems is Swedish. The leading manufacturers of sewing machines are American and Swiss. Singleton (1997, p. 79) shows that the UK was responsible for less than 3% of world exports of textile and leather machinery in 1993. The UK does, in contrast, have a good reputation for training and educating designers. Finally, the concept of external economies of scale can be mentioned in this context. This is the ability of an industry to draw competitive advantage from a geographical concentration of related activities – the best example of this in the apparel sector is to be found in Italy (see Section D). The UK has little advantage in these areas.

(iv)   Firm strategy

It has been noted in Chapter 1 that most commentators upon the decline of the cotton textile industry in the UK place some (if not all) of the blame upon a mistaken strategy, namely concentrating upon the wrong market and the wrong products. Clearly there are a range of global forces in the apparel sector which impact upon all the firms in the sector although not all firms react in the same way. Additionally, it is sometimes possible to identify 'favoured' responses within individual countries. Scheffer (1992, p. 193), for example, argued that it was possible to identify different strategies in the Netherlands, France, Belgium and the UK and that the industry in the UK made the wrong choices in concentrating on relatively long production runs organised in the traditional Taylorist system; in largely ignoring (for a long time) overseas sourcing options and, in effect, becoming trapped in 'the rigidity of the obsolete production system . . . which is geared to large retailers'. It does appear that very significant changes in strategic options are now being made by UK-based apparel manufacturers – frequently under pressure from the major retailers. Singleton (1997, p. 119) singles out Germany's enthusiasm for offshore processing. At this point, however, it will be important to observe that the role of international strategies is likely to be significant – in particular those strategies which go beyond direct exporting and incorporate elements of global sourcing and marketing. Singleton (1997, p. 22) concluded that irreversible decline 'can be avoided, it would seem, if firms in national economies are prepared to operate on an international level'. Historically it does not appear that the UK has been a particularly favourable environment in which to induce appropriate choices of strategy. These issues will be considered in more detail in Section D.

(v) Firm structure and rivalry

As has been seen in Chapter 2, the UK apparel sector is extremely atomistic in nature. Porter (1998) argues that strong domestic rivalry is a good thing in that it forces companies to become cost efficient and 'toughens them up' to face foreign competition. The possible conflict between this argument and the role of domestic rivalry in the Five Forces model has been noted in Chapter 1 and it seems to be true that, in the UK, while there are a large number of firms to provide rivalry, the way in which this has operated, particularly in relation to the retail customer, has been largely counterproductive. The pipeline is indisputably retail-driven. As Dicken (1998, p. 294) observes, the production chain 'is becoming transformed into a buyer-driven chain' and 'demand is becoming increasingly dominated by the purchasing policies of the major multiple retail chains'. The fragmented nature of the apparel industry has meant that firms do not have the market power to capture a significant (relative) proportion of the value added generated in the pipeline. In addition, the culture of individualism permeating the atomistic structure appears to have mitigated against the adoption of the sort of co-operative network strategy which has been so successful in Italy. As Porter (1998, p. 108) observes, nations will tend to succeed

> 'where the management practices and modes of organisation favoured by the national environment are well suited to the industries' sources of competitive advantage. Italian firms, for example, are world leaders in a range of *fragmented* industries . . . in which economies of scale are either modest or can be overcome through co-operation among *loosely affiliated* companies. Italian companies most often compete by employing focus strategies, avoiding standardised products and operating in small niches . . . and can adapt to market changes with breathtaking speed'.

In the UK, the fragmentation of the industry has manifested itself in quite a different fashion.

(vi) The role of Government

Finally, in this section, brief reference will be made to the role of Government. Government support for the textile and apparel sectors in the UK has been extremely limited and has largely been restricted to a mild form of protectionism via the Multi Fibre Arrangement. Most research suggests that levels of UK Government assistance to the various elements within the textile pipeline were at a relatively low level by international standards. Singleton (1997, p. 182) concluded that 'British policy in this area has been modest in comparison with the efforts of German and Italian regional authorities' while Zeitlin (1988) argued that 'central Government schemes aimed at promoting the restructuring of the clothing industry have largely been conspicuous by their absence'. Singleton (1997, p. 185) concurs observing that 'Government intervention (in mature economies) has generally been defensive and half-hearted in nature'. Somewhat paradoxically, it might appear, Porter (1998, p. 128) argues that this largely 'hands off' stance should be seen as beneficial rather than deplorable in that 'Government "help" that removes the pressures on firms to improve and upgrade is counterproductive'. Singleton (1997, p. 185) concludes his exhaustive investigation of the global textile industry by agreeing that direct Government intervention 'has rarely generated a competitive advantage in textiles'. It might, therefore, be more productive to seek the influence of Government upon the Diamond Framework in a somewhat more indirect manner – through its impact upon other elements of the Diamond in such areas as support for the education system, innovation, entrepreneurship, risk taking, investment in industry and research, and support for small business.

(vii)   Conclusion

The above analysis does not produce much in the way of comfort for seeing the UK as a potentially favourable environment for producing world class apparel manufacturing companies. Factor costs are, it is true, not high by developed country standards but are so in terms of comparison with the developing world. In addition, Porter (1998, p. 499) concludes that the UK's performance in education, investment in training and research is relatively poor. Owen (1999) placed far less emphasis on the impact of these two factors on Britain's comparative economic performance. Likewise, in relation to demand conditions, he concludes (p. 502) that while the UK was once 'on the cutting edge of world demand for both consumer and industrial goods', it is no longer the case. In addition, as successful clusters have weakened they have become 'increasingly poor buyers for other British industries' – the lack of 'support' offered to the UK's primary textile sector by the apparel sector being a case in point. Strategic decisions are also criticised by Porter (1998, p. 499) in that too often 'British manufacturers drifted towards competing on price with obsolete or low quality products and processes'. A number of successful, internationally competitive clusters of industries are identified – especially in the service sector – but the overall conclusion drawn (p. 494) is that 'Britain lacks comparative advantage in most areas of textiles and apparel'. Finally, it will be instructive to consider Singleton's (1997, p. 18) analysis of revealed comparative advantage (RCA) in the apparel sector. The measure is based on national export performance relative to the world average and is expressed numerically as the proportion of total national exports accounted for by apparel divided by the global proportion. Higher numbers would represent superior performance. Countries are ranked into three categories. The top rank (with RCA exceeding 2) includes a range of developing countries such as Hong Kong, Turkey, India, Indonesia, Tunisia, Thailand, Morocco, Pakistan and the Philippines which would be recognised as low cost producers. The lowest ranking group contains mainly developed countries such as Japan, the UK, the USA, Sweden, France, Germany and Spain. Italy and Portugal do appear in the first group but both – for different reasons – can be said to represent special cases in the developed world: Portugal because of its very low wages and Italy by virtue of its unique network of co-operative companies.

C. Consideration of alternative strategies

(i)   Investment in research and high technology solutions

As has been recorded in Chapter 2 capital investment per head in the apparel sector in the UK is extremely low. In addition, expenditure on R&D is also notoriously low. In 1986 the entire textiles, clothing and footwear sectors were responsible (Jones, 1988) for only 0.4% of all industrial R&D expenditure. In 1997 the figure had fallen to 0.3%. The Sector Review (ONS, 1999) reveals that the total number of scientists employed in the industry was only 1000. The lack of technological innovation in the sector is not a particularly UK feature, however. The inability of the industry to automate has been documented by many authors and cannot seriously be doubted. Briscoe (1971, p. 4) observed that a UN study had shown that 'for all countries the amount of equipment employed per person was lower for textiles and (author's emphasis) *very much lower for clothing*. This tends to favour production in countries which have a plentiful supply of labour relative to capital and where wages are relatively low'.

Little seems to have changed since that date in that Taplin (1997, p. 1) felt still able to record that there 'is a low level of technical innovation potential and those technical advances which have been made are only adopted by the most progressive enterprises' and proceeded to point out that the majority of the new technologies adopted have been 'mainly directed at the design and cutting stages, transport of garments between machines, the overall monitoring and control of production operations and *ad hoc* modifications to existing machines'. The most important (in terms of labour usage) area of assembly has remained largely immune to automation primarily because of the difficulty of automating a process using limp and varied fabric. In Winterton's words (1997, p. 1) the important element of 'garment assembly has not been appropriate for the extensive application of new technology in clothing for technical reasons'. The problems of automating the fabric handling process, for example, have been documented by Leung (1992) who concluded that the use 'of pick and place devices for handling limp fabric pieces has not been favoured by manufacturers because there is no universal . . . device which can be relied upon to handle a large range of fabric types'.

It is true that investigations into the possibility of automating the sewing process have been carried out. For example, in Japan in 1982, MITI set the objective of creating a flexible, automated garment production system (Taplin 1997, p. 180). The project was spread over nine years and spent almost 13 billion yen. In addition, between 1987 and 1991 700 million Ecu were allocated, by the EU, to the area of handling flexible materials under the BRITE (Basic Research in Industrial Technologies for Europe) banner. In the USA the Textile/Clothing Technological Corporation (TC^2) was set up in 1979.

In spite of these efforts it remains the case that large scale, commercial application of automated assembly remains elusive. Braithwaite (1991) concluded that 'full automation remains impossible'. It has to be concluded, therefore, that the assembly operation is likely to remain extremely labour-intensive. There is no evidence of widespread, commercial adoption of the technologies described above.

Winterton has also concluded (1997, p. 15) that there was little or no evidence that 'low technology clothing companies are less profitable than those which have invested in new equipment'. Tyler (1989) agrees that 'evidence that the technological route leads to increased efficiencies are inconclusive'. It is probable that the impetus towards the development of new technology has been severely retarded by the continued availability of extremely cheap labour around the globe.

Therefore, while it is always clearly desirable to utilise the most efficient technology available, it is probable that technological solutions will operate at best at the margin. The probability of technology ever significantly reducing the labour cost content of apparel manufacture to the degree that it can be seen as a viable strategy for achieving competitive advantage of itself is virtually zero. As De la Torre (1986, p. 222) observed, technological solutions were rare in that the 'difficulties inherent in automating the clothing assembly process and the fact that innovations could be easily adopted by any country may have contributed to the relatively low . . . commitment to R&D in the industry'. Consequently, while it could not logically be concluded that research must be abandoned, it seems obvious that by itself it could not solve the industry's problems. The final drawback of technological solutions is, of course, that they can be adopted anywhere and, as Hunter (1990, p. 148) astutely observed, the 'belief that the Far East cannot justify high technology because of low labour rates is simply not true'.

(ii)   Trade controls and protectionism

The textile and apparel sectors have a long history of trade controls. In this text attention will be focused on the post 1974 arrangements embodied in the Multi Fibre Arrangement (MFA). Earlier forms of trade control are summarised in Khanna (1991), Dickerson (1995) and Moore (1999) and have been used, in the UK, over a long period as Singleton (1997, p. 176), for example, records in 1959 'for electoral purposes, the Macmillan Government . . . imposed ceilings on imports of cotton cloth from Hong Kong, India and Pakistan, in what were euphemistically referred to as a "voluntary agreement" '. It is unlikely that trade controls will play as significant a role in the future as they have in the past.

The details of the removal of the MFA are considered in Chapter 9 but it can be noted at this point that interference in trade flows represents the main dimension of Government policy towards the textile and apparel sectors in the developed world since 1974. In the words of Zeitlin (1988, p. 228) the major 'form of state intervention in the industry over the past two decades has been the restriction of imports from low wage countries through participation in the MFA'.

From an economic standpoint trade barriers are normally viewed with distrust as leading to a non-optimal allocation of resources. The trend since the end of World War II – largely organised through GATT – has been to remove trade barriers on the assumption that an expansion of world trade brings general benefits (see Fig. 7.2). Trade barriers always carry with them a cost which ultimately has to be paid by the consumer and the tax payer. Porter, it will be no surprise to discover, also condemns all forms of subsidy and protection, writing (1998, p. 120) that 'Governments should only play a direct role in those areas where firms are unable to act (such as trade policy)' but, even then the 'Government "help" that removes the pressures on firms to improve and upgrade is counterproductive' and that Government policies should not preserve old advantages while simultaneously deterring the upgrading process. It is recognised that, because of the pressures of short term requirements in relation to employment, governments 'are prone to choose policies with easily perceived short term effects, such as subsidies, protection . . . such actions will dampen innovation and erode competitive advantage in the economy'. In particular there is pressure to provide (Porter, 1998, p. 625) 'protection from foreign rivals, usually justified by citing the "unfair" advantages they possess . . . Each of those tendencies . . . dooms a national industry in the long run'.

As will be seen in Chapter 9 the MFA was finally removed in 2005. The key concept underpinning EU textile and apparel policy is liberalisation. Therefore,

It is generally accepted that free trade in which each country specialises in producing only those items in which they have the *relatively* greatest superiority and obtain everything else by free trade produces the 'best' result for the *world as a whole* ('best' in the sense that resources are used most efficiently).

This is usually demonstrated by a numerical example such as the one below.

Production possibilities

	Countries	
Products	A	B
T	10	5
W	10	4

These figures are the units of resource required to produce one unit of W or one unit of T. Country B is therefore relatively superior in the production of W.

If both countries have 100 units of resource and devote 50 to T and 50 to W then a no trade scenario would be as follows:

No trade

Products	A	B	World production
T	5	10	15
W	5	$12\frac{1}{2}$	$17\frac{1}{2}$

If country A concentrates on product T in which it is the least disadvantaged we get:

	A	B	World total
T	10	$\boxed{5}$	15
W	0	$18\frac{3}{4}$	$18\frac{3}{4}$

B must produce 5 T to maintain the world total. This takes 25 units of resource (each 1 T takes 5 units). So B has 75 units of resource left to devote to producing W at a rate of 1 W taking up 4 units, i.e. it can produce $18\frac{3}{4}$ units of W. Therefore the world is better off by $18\frac{3}{4} - 17\frac{1}{2}$ units of W.

Fig. 7.2 The virtue of free trade. (*Source*: Daniels, J.D. and Radebough, L. (1998) *International Business*. Addison Wesley, Harlow.)

relying on protection is unlikely to constitute a viable strategy in the future. As Winterton concludes (1997, p. 11) the 'removal of the MFA . . . constitutes a liberalisation of clothing product markets which will act as an impulse, causing an acceleration of restructuring of garment manufacture in high wage economies'. Historically it is probable that, as De la Torre (1986, p. 224) concluded, the search for alternative strategies was hindered by the preference of the industry to 'obtain a strengthening and extension of import protection through a reviewed MFA'. It is instructive to note that Gruber (1998) concluded that 'the slow diffusion of innovation observed for the textile industry may be due to the high degree of protection granted to the sector'.

(iii)   Government assistance

In this section the provision of subsidy as opposed to the wider role of Government will be considered. As has been seen in Chapter 2, it is unlikely that apparel production will be seen as a strategically vital sector to the health of the economy in a developed country in which the total size of the manufacturing sector as a whole has fallen to some 20% of the total economic activity in the country. The level of Government assistance to the apparel manufacturing industry in the UK has never been large either in absolute terms or by international standards. Anson (1999) observed that in most Western, developed countries 'direct financial assistance to specific companies or specific sectors such as textiles and clothing has largely been eliminated'.

It is true that aid exists in other forms, such as via regional policies, but the apparel sector has not, historically, been a major beneficiary of such assistance. Jones (1990) studied the distribution of Regional Selective Assistance in the UK between 1977 and 1988 and found that share of such assistance attracted by the clothing sector ranged from 1.35% to 5.41% of the total aid distributed. As Singleton (1997, p. 165) observes, 'It is easy to understand the reasons for intervention in strategic industries. Engineering, electronics and aircraft industries may be deemed important for the preservation of national security. But textiles and clothing are not strategic industries.'

As was observed above, the industry has received (rightly or wrongly) very little in the way of subsidies – the main element of Government policy towards the sector having been, since 1974, a relatively mild form of protection.

In the UK it is true that there has been a number of specific schemes devoted towards the apparel and textile sectors such as the Wool Textile Scheme 1973–1979 and the Clothing Industry Development Scheme 1975–1977. These have been described by, for example, Miles (1976), De La Torre (1986) and Hardill (1987) but neither these schemes nor the £15 million aid package announced in June 2000 require Zeitlin's conclusion to be revised. The latter contrasts starkly with the assistance given to the car industry – £179 million to Nissan alone (Hope, 2005). The twelve-point plan (TCSG, 2000) was strong on exhortation and expressions of desirable actions but contained little in the way of substance although it has been more enthusiastically received by some (Horrocks, 2001).

Most commentators on the textile and clothing sectors have concluded that direct Government intervention has been rare even on a global basis. Singleton (1997, p. 185) concluded his survey of the global textile industry by stating that in 'mature economies, Government intervention has been generally defensive and half-hearted in nature. Direct intervention has rarely generated a competitive advantage in textiles although it had strongly negative results in post independence India, for example'. The same author (1997, p. 170) argued that Government policies were rarely if ever a critical factor in the expansion of the industry in Asia and that 'market forces would have ensured similar outcomes'. Different developed countries have followed different paths and varying timetables as will be seen in Section D.

(iv)   Organisational restructuring and the manipulation of industrial structure

It might be argued that if pipeline organisational and structural deficiencies have been identified it should, in theory, be possible to devise strategies which mitigate the worst effects of the observed weaknesses.

Historically, the biggest weakness in the textile–apparel pipeline has been (as was recorded in Chapter 1) the adversarial nature of the relationship between the various elements within the pipeline. There is very little published evidence on the existence of non-adversarial relationships within the apparel sector. Groves (1997, p. 20) studied the nature of relationships in a small sample of UK apparel manufacturers and found that in a range of performance indicators 'partnerships appear to achieve higher scores on average, thus implying a potential trend towards better performance'. In addition, in the UK, the DTI and other interested parties, established in 1995 the so-called Apparel and Textile Challenge which aims to develop more effective supply chain partnerships in the sector. Smith (1999, p. 6) argued that while it was recognised that the nature of supply partnerships had to change, there was 'still resistance to change'. It is clear, however, from evidence published relating to other industrial sectors that partnership relationships can be made to work and do generate benefits. Whether or not it is now, in the UK, too late to 'save' the textile–apparel pipeline via this route is open to question.

In relation to the issue of the existence of a number of unfortunate structural characteristics (such as a low level of seller concentration) it is true that modern students of industrial economics place increasing stress on the ability of companies to manipulate structure actively, i.e. to seek feedback from conduct to structure. Hay (1991), for example, refers to the crucial distinction between 'active' and 'passive' firms. Unfortunately, it is difficult to envisage the apparel sector behaving in a very active manner to correct structural deficiencies because of its extremely atomistic nature.

(v)   Marketing strategies

This group of strategies, which incorporates branding, niche marketing and related policies seems more promising. Many commentators have contrasted the failure of UK policy which concentrated on long runs of relatively standardised products with the more successful policy adopted in Italy of securing strong positions in niche markets. Such policies would also have the virtue of, in effect, partially correcting the observed structural feature (Chapter 10) that the industry, somewhat surprisingly, spends relatively little on advertising and promotion. In addition, from the point of view of the UK it would have the added benefit of playing to one of the national strengths identified for the UK within the Diamond Framework – the strength of the UK's advertising industry (Porter, 1998, p. 494). The main problem from the viewpoint of the UK apparel manufacturer is that this activity tends to be undertaken by the retailers. Nevertheless, a good case can be made for incorporating new approaches to marketing in future strategies.

(vi)   Changes in work organisation

The traditional form of work organisation in the apparel sector is usually defined as Fordist or Taylorist. In essence this means that the production system is characterised by a high degree of division of labour and de-skilling and a low degree of self organisation as is expressed in the progressive bundle system in the apparel sector. An alternative view is represented by (Winterton, 1997, p. 15) who argues that 'changes in labour processes, reflected in the . . . autonomy afforded to individuals and the division of labour between different categories of works' are epitomised by team working or modular manufacturing. A variety of terms exist in the literature to describe this concept, e.g. modular manufacturing; cellular manufacturing; flexible manufacturing and flexible work groups. The latter has been defined by Hill (1992) as 'a management concept involving a team of apparel associates' working with minimum supervision and deploying multiple skilled operatives paid as a team, while NEDO (1991, p. 10) defined a modular system as 'a contained, manageable work unit . . . performing a measurable task in which operations are interchangeable and incentives are based on group output'.

It is possible that some commentators would prefer to maintain a distinction between the concepts of modular manufacturing and team working on the grounds that the latter enjoy more autonomy but this distinction is not crucial in the context of the present discussion. Flexible manufacturing systems have as much to do with people and organisation as with new equipment, requiring (Bentham, 1998, p. 384) 'a significant cultural change . . . and a move away from piecework systems, flow line production and heavy management presence'.

This does not mean that the technological input can be completely ignored (Tyler, 1989), e.g. semi-automatic machines may be incorporated into the modular groups as is exemplified by unit production system technology (transfer systems which deliver one item to work stations) while the ability to repair faulty equipment rapidly assumes even greater importance than within more traditional production systems. The key concept is, in essence, to try and retain the cost benefits of mass production while supplying markets which increasingly demand lower volumes, more variety and more responsive customer service. The main component of a flexible manufacturing system would include team working; multi-skilled operators; continuous training; delegated authority; minimum supervision; team responsibility for quality and team payment systems. The expected benefits include lower stocks and work in process; improved motivation; lower absenteeism; reduced inspection costs; fewer rejects; better quality and quicker throughput.

Hunter (1990, p. 157) who defined the modular plant as one 'made up of many product centres in each of which the complete garment is made by small groups of workers responsible for all operations' estimated that, according to some research, the introduction of modular systems could raise the return on capital by anything from 10–20%.

Flexible manufacturing is often seen as a component of the Quick Response and Lean Manufacturing philosophies which will be described in the next section. As Carr (1994) observes, 'at the heart of lean production is team working'. Alder (1997, p. 146), describing the recent evolution of the German apparel sector, comments that Germany is fortunate in having a pool of skilled labour with exceptionally good vocational qualifications which facilitate the adoption of team working in that element of production retained domestically. There is, therefore, little doubt that modular systems can produce benefits in appropriate conditions as described, for example, by Bentham (1998).

Lowson (1999, p. 103) produces a comparison of the time taken by traditional progressive bundle systems and team/modular systems which suggest that production turnaround times can be reduced from weeks to minutes. However, their introduction appears to have been limited in scope in the UK industry. NEDO (1991) concluded their study of modular systems with the observation that they were neither cheap nor instant solutions to the industry's problems but that there was sufficient evidence that they can produce substantial benefits if top management is sufficiently committed. However, the report estimated that, in the USA, only 5% of companies and 1% of factories were utilising such systems.

(vii)   Quick response, logistical and supply chain management solutions

The major threat to apparel production in developed countries has come (see Chapter 3) from regions enjoying the benefit of extremely low wages. Most (but, significantly, not all) of these areas are relatively distant from the major apparel markets. Proximity to the market was, accordingly, seen as representing an advantage to domestic producers who could supply customers more quickly than distant producers and secure a price premium for this service. Strategies embodying this principle have evolved under a variety of titles such as quick response, logistics and supply chain management, lean manufacturing, time compression strategies and agile supply chains.

These initiatives, while not all exactly the same, have substantial elements of commonality. Lowson (1999, p. 26), for example, recognises these terms as essentially 'euphemisms for the same basic group of theories'. As Forza (2000) observes, the sector is increasingly perceiving time as a crucial variable within competition. Hunter (1990, p. 1) argued that the industry could improve its competitive ability simply by making changes in management style which reflected the fact 'that textile manufacture, garment making and retailing are not separate businesses, but must operate as parts of an integrated consumer responsive supply system'. The essential elements of a quick response strategy were then identified as the integration of all parts of the supply chain; the utilisation of rapid data transfer and total quality management to reduce stocks and waste, and the sharing of information so that the supply chain can be collapsed.

It will be recalled from Chapter 1 that, in the traditional supply chain, the times at which decisions have to be taken within the chain and the quality of information available at those times produces enormous problems and potential for waste. Hunter (1990) estimated that, in the traditional supply system, out of 66 weeks lead time only 11 weeks were allocated to the processing element of the chain and of this only 1% was used for actual processing activity. Sewing time was usually measured in minutes. The vast proportion of the 66 weeks was taken up by storage. He estimated (1990, p. 31) that losses resulting from the inefficiencies of this system amounted to 25% of total retail sales value.

A Quick Response (QR) strategy is defined by Hunter (1990) as 'an operational philosophy and a set of procedures aimed at maximising the profitability in the apparel pipeline' and by Kincade (1993, p. 23) as 'a state of responsiveness in which a manufacturer seeks to provide a product to a customer in the precise quantity, quality and time frame required. In doing so lead times and expenditures for labour, materials and inventory are minimised; flexibility is emphasised in order to meet the changing requirements of a competitive market place', while Lowson (1999, p. 27) stresses its capacity to 'make demand driven decisions at the last possible moment . . . Quick Response places an emphasis upon flexibility and production velocity [and] encompasses a strategy, structure, culture and set of operational procedures aimed at integrating enterprises in a mutual network'. This definition has the advantage of stressing the link with both flexible manufacturing (considered in the previous section) and with supply chain management.

The net effect of adopting this strategy is to reduce lead times and costs thereby improving competitiveness and performance. Tamilla (2000) reports The Limited as achieving 60 days and Gap 42 days. It is clear that there must be a close relationship between quick response, with its concern over relationships within the supply chain, and the concept of supply chain management. The latter is usually defined in terms of managing a network of legally independent but co-operative enterprises so as to reduce waste and time in the chain. Lowson (1999, p. 33) considers that 'Supply Chain Management describes the management of the entire chain of activity from raw material supply to final consumer in order to minimise the time taken to perform each activity, eliminate waste and offer an optimal response' and, accordingly, sees logistics as a sub-set of supply chain management. In effect a supply chain 'embraces all the activities associated with moving the goods from the raw materials stage to end use so that supply chain management can be considered to represent the task of ensuring that all of these activities run smoothly in collaboration with one another'. Logistics is frequently defined in similar terms. Cooper (1994, p. 2), for example, argued that 'logistics is now widely used and understood throughout the business world, and refers essentially to the management of supply chains in commerce and industry' while Quayle (1997) sees logistics as 'the process which seeks to provide for the management and co-ordination of all activities within the supply chain from sourcing and acquisitions, through production . . . to the customer. The goal of logistics is the creation of competitive advantage through the simultaneous achievement of high customer service levels and value for money'.

It can be seen from the above discussion that one of the major aims of quick response, logistics and supply chain management is to remove waste and time from the system. This brings us into contact with two other related concepts of time-based competition and lean manufacturing. Stalk (1990) observed that 'many executives believe that competitive advantage is best achieved by providing the best value for the lowest cost . . . Providing the most value for the lowest cost in the least amount of time is the new pattern for corporate success'.

The traditional view of the manufacturing process saw a dichotomy between long production runs of standardised products at low cost on the one hand and short runs of high quality, diversified products produced at relatively high unit costs, on the other. In a very real sense the objective of time-based competition is to capture the best of both worlds by having low cost, short production runs of high quality, differentiated products. This argument is captured diagramatically, for example, by Spanner (1993) and is further advocated by Lowson (1999, p. 32) when he argues the case for a new approach to production 'based on the use of information technology and customised, short-run manufacturing' which will reverse the principles of mass production which were based on reaping low costs over long runs but increasingly are found to be at odds with the demands of an ever more capricious market place.

The concept of time-based competition is closely connected to that of flexible manufacturing which was described above, in that the latter is seen as one element in the sequence of organisational, managerial and technical changes required to implement a time-based strategy. The main objective of all the above is to develop the so-called seamless supply chain in which waste, time and non-value adding activities have all been removed or minimised. Hines (1997) identified seven types of waste – overproduction, waiting, transportation, inappropriate processing, surplus stock, unnecessary motion and defects – while Towill (1996) identified seven types of cost (but not value) adding activities – counting things, inspecting things, finding and chasing things, storing items, and re-working items.

The aim is to remove all wasted time as far as is possible. The key, it is argued, to achieving this result lies in co-ordinated supply chain management which will remove the waste by better co-ordination, forecasting and sharing of data and will remove cost adding activities by increasing co-operation and trust within the supply chain.

The main elements within the quick response or seamless supply chain would include a reduction of demand forecasting errors; superior and all embracing sharing of more rapidly transmitted data; a substantial reduction in defects and inspection; a reduction of stock held at all stages in the supply chain; the introduction of new working practices such as modular manufacturing; some technological changes especially in relation to information transfer; the reduction of both internal and external transport times to a minimum; and the evolution of partnership as opposed to adversarial relationships within the supply chain. The major benefits anticipated from the introduction of these changes would be less end of season mark downs; greater productivity; fewer faults; reduced inspection costs; better quality; less forecasting risks; quicker response times and improved customer service, all of which should theoretically be transformed into lower costs and higher profits.

Technological change does have a role to play in the implementation of QR strategy. New (1993) and Scott (1991), for example, showed that throughpull times could be reduced from 35 to 12 days in the case of underwear manufacture, simply by changing the fabric dyeing process. Forza (2000) also demonstrated that the textile delivery time for a product using fibre dyeing was 120 days (of which 30 was 'waiting time') but that the time allowed for actual garment manufacture was only 15 days and that even in this figure the proportion of time spent on real value added activity was very small. The introduction of CAD and Computer Controlled Cutting are examples of technological changes at the apparel manufacturing stage. In Forza's (2000) estimation, however, while some technical and work organisational changes are implied, the most important changes required relate to changing prevailing managerial attitudes and entrenched business cultures. It will be recalled from Chapter 1 that the history of co-operative behaviour within the textile supply chain has not been a good one. As Hunter (1990, p. 19) commented, each 'sector in the supply system has traditionally regarded itself as a separate business with its own strategies', noting that real interest in QR strategies only dates from the mid 1980s and even at the end of the 1990s (Forza, 2000, p. 141) most experts believe it will be a major task to overcome 'long standing sectorial traditions and cultural barriers'.

Traditionally it was argued (Forza, 1993) that the key to improving supply chain performance should be sought in improved demand forecasting. Hunter (1990) showed that forecasting errors fell dramatically as lead times were reduced. Inaccurate demand forecasting requires (Forza, 2000) retail margins to be high. An alternative solution would be to move away from forecast-driven/inventory-based chains towards demand-driven/replenishment-based chains. In essence this is what so-called agile chains are about and an extensive literature base has grown up advocating the virtues of such responsive systems (Harrison, 1999; Christopher, 2000; Lowson, 2001). Specifically the agile chain (Christopher, 2004) is characterised by fast replenishment of stock driven by capture of point-of-sale data and reliance on network-based chains which are virtual in the sense that every member has immediate access to all information. Clearly there can be no possible objection to any system which provides less cost and waste and which offers greater flexibility and shorter lead times. There can be no excuse for not adopting any proven best practice. This is particularly true when understanding of the fashion process is limited (see Chapter 10). The problem of data transmission within the supply chain is less severe (in a technical sense) and has been revolutionised by Electronic Data Interchange (EDI) which can be defined as (Riddle, 1999, p. 133) 'the transmission of data in structured formats between firms who normally do business with each other'. Hunter (1990, p. 70) argued that the importance of data transmission to QR 'cannot be overemphasised' but it must be recognised, as Forza (2000) points out, that EDI by itself cannot produce QR because saving a few days within the context of a 4–8 month cycle will never be very significant.

There is little doubt that the retail sector has been the driving force behind the implementation of QR strategy. As Riddle (1999, p. 134) observed, major retailers 'are using their buying power to require manufacturers to implement EDI . . . Consequently QR is becoming a competitive necessity for apparel producers, rather than a source of competitive advantage'. Abernathy (1999) also highlighted the influence of lean retailing in forcing apparel manufacturers to reduce lead times arguing that (1999, p. 3) 'direct labour content is not the primary issue. The companies which have adopted new information systems and management functions . . . are the ones with the strongest performance . . .'. This raises the question of who has gained the most, within the supply chain, from the benefits associated with the adoption of QR strategies.

A large number of reports based both on simulations and trials have quantified these benefits. These are summarised in Hunter (1990) and report substantial gains amounting to (1990, p. 91) some $12.5 billion for the USA in

1985 of which $8.2 billion was captured by the retail sector. Trials in three partnerships produced (1990, p. 113) results which 'were almost unbelievably good' in that the three retailers involved experienced improved margins of between 30% and 82%. Another study by Arthur Anderson and Co. in 1989 reported (Hunter, 1990, p. 141) a 'yield of $9.6 billion in improved performance for the apparel retailing industry as a whole'. Forza (1993) gives examples of QR gains amounting to a 31% increase in sales and a 30% reduction in stocks together with a 50% reduction in forecasting errors in American textile supply chains. It is noticeable in the literature that the enthusiasm for QR is rooted in the retail sector and that gains to that sector usually outweigh gains to the other cells in the pipeline. This has generated a degree of scepticism on the part of certain commentators as to the real benefit of QR to the apparel manufacturer. Taplin (1995, p. 10), for example, argues that vastly increased buying power of major retailers 'forced manufacturers to develop complementary skills to match these buyer-driven changes' and that (1995, p. 12) many senior managers in the apparel sector see QR both 'as a necessary evil of the cost of doing business and one that is being forced upon them by retailers' and as a way 'to increase retailer value added at the expense of the manufacturers'.

This is, of course, not quite what is implied by true partnership sourcing. There are, for the UK, a number of small pieces of evidence which lend some support to Taplin's thesis. For example, Jones (1997, 2002) found that the level of stocks held by UK apparel manufacturers was very high compared with the manufacturing average while Groves (1997) found that the evidence for improved performance in non-adversarial relationships in the textile pipeline was extremely mixed.

A review of the literature suggests that there is a long way to go before the objectives of QR can be achieved and that the greatest amount of work remaining is between the textile and garment manufacturing elements of the chain. Riddle (1999) for example, found that most applications of EDI had taken place between manufacturers and retailers. Forza (2000, p. 142) identified the lack of involvement of fabric producers at the garment design stage as a residual weakness in the supply chain so that (p. 145) the reduction 'in textile supply lead time is the most critical intervention' remaining.

The potential for QR strategies to reduce the rush offshore has proven limited. Lowson (1999, p. 113) concluded that the adoption of QR systems was still 'piecemeal and incomplete' and that, in respect of the argument that QR would counteract the cost advantage of offshore production 'the jury is still out' because offshore suppliers have themselves responded well to the use of QR philosophies. Somewhat unexpectedly Levy (1996, p. 96) considered that although it was normal for international supply chains to be characterised by longer lead times 'the reduction in defects . . . associated with lean production can stabilise the supply chain' so that while 'lean production may be more difficult and expensive in the international context . . . it may still be worthwhile'. Supporters of the concept of the agile supply chain still argue (Christopher, 2004) that linking this idea to that of hidden costs offers a prospect of retaining production in high cost locations if only sourcing managers would do their sums correctly. As has been stated above it is not credible that, after decades of sourcing experience, managers are still ignorant of the true costs involved. In addition the argument that flexibility and offshore production are totally incompatible is flawed. A number of offshore locations are not that far away from the major markets and many experts have identified one of China's strengths as the flexibility of its supply chains. Finally, many of the companies frequently quoted in the literature, such as The Limited and Gap, do make extensive use of offshore sourcing – it is not an 'either–or' scenario. As Kilduff (2005, p. 183) notes, 'US apparel companies have sought lower cost manufacturing arrangements while establishing . . . more responsive supply chains' and that the anticipated benefits of retaining a domestic competitive advantage via supply chain improvements have not been realised. Birnbaum (2004, p. 21) noted that 'lead times for imports of . . . trousers from Mexico are longer than those from China. This is despite Mexico's proximity to the USA'.

   Holmes (1995) found that, in a survey of UK companies, while 80% reported that supply chain management issues had increased in importance, concern with purely national chains had fallen to only 20% of the sample. The same author in an earlier study of small and medium-sized apparel manufacturers in South Wales (Lowson, 1999) found that there was very little implementation of QR techniques and little evidence of partnership relationships in the supply chain. He argued that the firms needed (Lowson, 1998, p. 41) to 'challenge the traditional sourcing decisions of the retailers'. In view of the analysis carried out in Chapter 2 this would seem to represent a somewhat unrealistic scenario.

(viii)   Spatial restructuring and international strategies

A number of individual elements can be grouped under these two headings, e.g. offshore production or sourcing strategies; the use of Outward Processed Trade; exporting; direct overseas investment; joint ventures; globalisation strategies and the exploitation of new or emerging markets. As will be explored in the remainder of the book this group of strategies almost certainly represents the only way forward for the UK apparel manufacturing industry. There are two main reasons for drawing this conclusion. First, there is some evidence that industries which went down this route have been relatively more successful than those which did not (see section D below) and, second, that all the alternative strategies, while holding out some limited expectation of gain in certain areas of the industry, appear to be inadequate to sustain domestic production in (relatively) high labour cost regions. *These policies therefore come to the fore almost by default* and will be examined in detail in Chapters 8, 9 and 11 given that they have achieved such an important role in the evolution of strategies for the future.

All the strategies reviewed above can make, in particular circumstances, a positive contribution to increasing efficiency and reducing costs and, thereby, enhancing international competitiveness. However, it is now clear that participation in global supply chains has become an essential element for survival. Therefore, the issue of global supply chain management has become increasingly important over time and has given rise to an enormous literature base.

D. The existence of national strategies

It is, of course, true that, in the absence of nationalisation, strategies are made by companies and not by Governments. However, it is clear from a review of the literature that the recent history of the apparel sector in the developed countries does reveal fairly distinctive intra-country variation in strategic imperatives. It is not possible in the context of the present text to give a comprehensive description of the evolution of policy in a wide range of countries but it is both possible and instructive to highlight the different emphasis placed upon the strategies identified above in a selection of countries where this appears to have impacted upon performance. More detailed descriptions of national strategies can be found in De La Torre (1986) and Singleton (1997).

In the UK the history of Government involvement with the textile and apparel sectors is a very long one dating (De La Torre, 1986) from the adoption of the Cotton Spinning Act of 1936. A summary of early interventions can be found in Miles (1968). De La Torre (1986, p. 219) also contends that the UK and Italy were the two European countries in which job support schemes in apparel were the most developed although this relative position must not be taken as an indicator of extensive subsidy in absolute terms. Furthermore, it cannot be taken as an indicator that any consistent or long term strategy existed. As Singleton (1997, p. 182) observed 'British post-war policy on textiles has been rather inconsistent'. Throughout the 1950s and 1960s most UK Governments, according to De La Torre (1986, p. 217) 'paid little attention to their clothing industries'. This history of public intervention prior to 1970 was largely 'confined to Government support for industrial development programmes of a general nature and to the orderly marketing arrangements negotiated since 1955 to limit imports'. Largely as a result of its enduring labour intensity the UK apparel sector was the main beneficiary of an emergency measure – the Temporary Employment Subsidy – in the 1970s: by the middle of 1978 (De La Torre, 1986) half of the applications received had come from the textile and clothing sector. This seems, however, to have been the exception rather than the rule in that the same author (1986, p. 117) concluded that the use made by the sector of general and regional subsidy schemes was rather poor.

Jones (1990) studied the take-up of Selective Financial Assistance by the apparel sector in the UK between 1977 and 1988 and found that apparel manufacturers received between 1.3% and 5.4% of total assistance granted. In general terms the deployment of regional incentives in the UK in relation to the apparel sector was (Singleton, 1997, p. 182) 'modest in comparison with the efforts of German and Italian regional authorities'. Therefore, while Government support did exist, it did not in practice amount to extensive support for the sector. There was a specific Clothing Industry Scheme between 1975 and 1977 but, in Zeitlin's words (1988, p. 228) 'central Government Schemes aimed at promoting the restructuring of the industry have largely been conspicuous by their absence'.

Local authorities, on the other hand, have supported a number of resource and fashion centres in Glasgow, London, and Nottingham, for example, and in 1986 the Local Action for Textile and Clothing group was formed. The impact of these initiatives, however, has been extremely limited. The main strategic response to the emergence of low cost competition was, first, 'the restriction of imports from low wage countries through participation in the MFA' (Zeitlin, 1988, p. 228) and, second, as Owen (1999, p. 57) argues 'to restructure industry through mergers and takeovers. This proved to be a mistake'.

This view is echoed by Toyne (1984, p. 153) who concluded that the 'lack lustre performance of the British textile industry . . . during the 1960s and 1970s can be traced to the strategic option initially selected and the method used for its implementation: development of an undifferentiated strategy concentrating on standard . . . fabrics while protected from low cost imports', and is further echoed by Scheffer (1992, p. 193) who concluded that while apparel manufacturers in the Netherlands, for example, concentrated on the development of offshore sourcing the 'crisis in the UK can . . . to some extent be put down to the rigidity of the obsolete production system it upholds which is geared to large retailers'.

The third element in the strategy was the emergence of large multiple retailers who supported the domestic industry via the purchase of relatively standardised long production runs of garments. The 1960s witnessed a series of mergers designed to bring about greater co-operation within the pipeline and to ensure economies of scale. Details of the merger movement in the textile sector can be found in Owen (1999), Singleton (1997) and Winterton who wrote (1996, p. 55) that the 'relationship between retailers, clothing manufacturers and textile companies are crucial to understanding the changes in the organisation of garment making. Between 1950 and 1975 increased concentration of the distributive trades brought long and consistent production runs in clothing'. This movement was not confined to the textile sector but was characterised by the formation of the Industrial Reorganisation Corporation in 1966. As Owen

(1999, p. 76) relates, this grand design started to unravel in the 1970s and by the late 1980s and 1990s demergers were in vogue as exemplified by the flotation of Courtaulds Textiles in 1989/1990. In Owen's words (1999, p. 76) the entire strategy 'was based on a misreading of the market . . . Instead of a growing demand for standard, mass produced fabrics, European consumers wanted more differentiated, more colourful and more stylish fabrics. This called for flexibility . . . and quick response to changing fashions'.

Entirely the same arguments could be applied with even more force to the apparel market. In relation to UK experience a number of authors, notably Winterton (1996, 1997), offer a somewhat pessimistic view of the extent to which responses designed to retain domestic employment represent a retreat into working practices and forms of work organisation which are, in various dimensions, undesirable. They argue that deregulation of labour markets in the USA and the UK (exemplified by the removal of Wages Councils in 1993) have promoted a replication, particularly in inner city areas, of conditions normally found in the low wage, developing economies.

Winterton (1997, p. 36) writes that because small firms have limited access to capital, 'competitiveness was sustained through sweated labour' and 'the replication of the employment conditions of the NICs'.

Other European countries adopted different responses to the common challenge. It is generally argued in the literature (Toyne, 1984, p. 127) that the German Government was the least protectionist. Germany and the Netherlands followed a policy of niche marketing and the heavy utilisation of offshore production. This is confirmed by Alder (1997, p. 133) who wrote that 'more and more German firms have looked to overseas production to achieve cost competitiveness' together with a focus on fashion-orientated production domestically. The ratio of Outward Process Trader (OPT) work to total turnover in Germany rose from 4% in 1970 to nearly 30% in 1995 (Alder, 1997, p. 146). In the Netherlands (Scheffer, 1992) overseas production already accounted for 61% of output in 1983, rising to 73% in 1992. The same author records that, in Germany, the proportion of total output produced domestically fell to about 30% in the early 1990s. French garment manufacturers, like the British, resisted the movement of production to low cost centres for a long time and, in parallel, relied upon the introduction of new technology to maintain competitiveness. In Toyne's words (1984, p. 124) this was not particularly successful and the desperate situation of much of the industry in France is recorded by Hetzel (1998).

The situation in Italy is somewhat unique as was seen in Chapter 3. Belussi (1997) argues that the competitive power of the Italian industry rests on 'mature product specialisation' and (1997, p. 81) a high degree of systematic integration exploding geographic or external economies of scale. Nolan (1997, p. 275) similarly argues that supply chain collaboration is the main reason for the success of the Italian apparel industry in which 'vertically integrated companies were replaced by co-operative small scale production units'. The concept of the Italian regional district with its network of collaborating micro-firms 'combining design flair, product quality and flexible specialisation' has, in Scheffer's words (1992) become a model for European clothing production. There is little doubt that (Nolan, 1977, p. 280) the 'strategic network business system appears to match the needs of the business environment, allowing flexibility, responsiveness and control of quality to co-exist in a most efficient way'. A thorough description and analysis of the concept of the Italian industrial district is provided by Pyke (1990).

These districts are defined (Pyke, 1990, p. 2) as 'geographically defined productive systems, characterised by a large number of firms that are involved at various stages, and in various ways, in the production of a homogeneous product. A significant feature is that a very high proportion of these firms are . . . very small'. Typically the firms are characterised by the flexible specialisation mode of production. In the context of the textile sector the best known examples would be Prato and Carpi-Modena. A detailed study of these industrial districts, however, reveals quite a degree of heterogeneity between them and (Amin, 1990, p. 213) it is by no means obvious that 'blanket solutions based upon the experiences of particular areas' will travel successfully to other localities in other countries. In particular, it is clear that (Pyke, 1990, p. 2) the success of the Italian districts is not purely an economic phenomenon but is also a reflection of 'broader social and institutional aspects'. This opinion was confirmed by the work of Digiovanna (1996, p. 373) who also emphasised the great diversity of industrial districts, stressing that 'the success of industrial districts . . . depends on the institutionalised social compromises which exist in the region'. It is probably not insignificant that (Brusco, 1990, p. 142) many of the Italian districts 'are located in regions . . . dominated by the Communist Party'.

Rabellotti (1998) highlighted the differences between supplier/buyer relationships in the Italian and Mexican footwear sectors, for example, demonstrating that while co-operative relationships were common in the former they were not in the latter. Therefore, it is clear that the concept of the industrial districts is far more complex than is often alleged and that the possibilities of duplicating their success in other societies is far from a foregone conclusion. It must not be forgotten that the industry, in earlier years, received massive amounts of state aid and that, in De La Torre's words (1986, p. 209) within Western Europe 'only Italy . . . was actively involved (prior to 1970) in trying to salvage a number of important textile and clothing companies for political reasons'. One indirect effect of this policy was to retain a skilled workforce in place. In addition, as Scheffer (1992) makes clear even in Italy, from the late 1980s, a movement to overseas production was beginning to gather pace.

The situation in Portugal is likewise idiosyncratic in that it historically enjoys labour costs closer to Asian than European levels. Historically, therefore (Ussman,

1999, p. 85), the 'main basis of Portugal's competitive advantage has been low wages'. This appears, by 2005, to have become unsustainable and Portugal's experience, therefore, does not contain many lessons for other developed countries.

Finally, the experience of the apparel sector in the USA must be noted, given (Chapter 3) the remaining importance of that country as a manufacturing sector. Dickerson (1995) documents in detail the breadth of responses made by the domestic industry to low cost competition but records (1995, p. 290) that many US firms are 'participating increasingly in offshore production of their garments'. This is confirmed by Taplin (1999, p. 364) who noted that the 'highly competitive nature of the industry has forced many domestic apparel manufacturers to move production facilities to lower cost locations outside the US'. The special position of Mexico after 1994 has already been noted in Chapter 3 and Taplin (1999, p. 365) records that Mexico, by 1998, was 'fast replacing China as the principal source of imported apparel'. The US industry has made extensive use of the so-called 9802 (ex-807) production facility which is similar to the OPT system described in Chapter 8. Taplin (1999) identifies Mexico, the Dominican Republic and Honduras as the main beneficiaries of this arrangement. The extent to which American companies have increasingly participated in foreign assembly is reflected, according to Dickerson (1995, p. 309) in the increasingly soft line taken against imports by the domestic trade association. She concluded that (1995, p. 311) world wide 'sourcing is basic to many US firms and offshore assembly . . . is one of the most common strategies'. A second response to foreign, low cost competition has been identified by Taplin (1999), namely, in certain regions of the USA a resort to illegal and exploitative working practices.

It can be seen therefore, that the responses of a range of developed countries to the challenge of low cost competition exhibit both similarities and differences. The range of strategies employed – investment incentives; employment subsidies; decommissioning incentives; technological incentives; inducements to mergers; regional incentives – can be found in most countries at some point in time. Historically most countries appear to have had some enthusiasm for trying to preserve the sector but this policy was eventually found to be both very expensive and incapable of stemming the tide of global forces. In the mid 1970s more and more reliance was placed – in most countries – upon the mild form of protection afforded by the MFA. A number of countries effectively abandoned domestic production more quickly than others, notably Germany and the Netherlands. Taplin (1997, p. 198) concluded his extensive survey of national policies by stating that 'the differences between the patterns of restructuring of clothing in high wage economies are more of degree and emphasis than of fundamental principle'.

This is clearly correct in the sense that it is possible to identify similar elements of policy in most countries – even if adopted at different points in time – but it probably understates the somewhat unique reliance within the UK upon a strategy based on long production runs coupled with a relatively belated acceptance of the necessary role of offshore production. Most developed countries' producers have now swung around to reliance upon offshore production as a major element in their production strategies.

Is there any evidence that different strategies were more or less successful in meeting the challenge posed by low cost competition? Clearly there is no point in examining employment data as strategies which focused on offshore production would by definition have the effect of reducing domestic employment and, as was shown in Table 3.5, employment fell in most European countries. One indicator which might offer guidance would be success in world markets as indicated by shares of world trade, as both OPT and 9802 production is recorded, if subsequently sold abroad, as an export and would, therefore, affect the share of world trade captured by a country.

This approach would be in line with the advice of Porter (1998, p. 7) that 'the ability to compete successfully against foreign rivals' be regarded as a key indicator of success. In a European context the relative fortunes of the UK, France, Germany and the Netherlands might be instructive – the first two being more reliant upon domestic strategies while the latter two pioneered the movement offshore. The data in Table 3.13 are somewhat inconclusive. For example, over the long period 1980–97 all lost share of world exports with the exception of the Netherlands. Germany's loss was greater in proportionate terms than that of the UK. France performed most badly. Support for the offshore option is, therefore, somewhat qualified. In the period 1980–93 the evidence is rather more in favour of the offshore solution in that the losses (proportionately) experienced by Germany and the Netherlands were much smaller than those experienced by the UK and France. In the latest period 1993–97 the Netherlands gained share while the UK and Germany suffered a broadly similar proportionate loss. This could reflect the increasing amount of offshore activity taking place in the UK sector following the opening, for example, of OPT in 1991. Italy's performance was superior to that of the UK, France and Germany but not as good as that achieved by the Netherlands although (Table 3.13) Italy, the Netherlands and somewhat paradoxically, the UK did well, in terms of the value of apparel exports. In the final analysis both the EU and the USA have consistently lost domestic production and employment to import competition as has been seen in Chapter 3 so it could be argued that none of the above policies was particularly successful in the long run. As IFM (2004) concluded, over 'the last decades the EU textile/clothing industry has gradually lost much of its proactive power'. The attempts in 2005 to restrict imports from China were mainly driven by the Southern members of the EU which suggests that their strategies which had been successful in the past were finally failing also. Italy and Portugal have both suffered crises of various proportions and for varying reasons. The exception in 2005 seems to be Spain.

Therefore, the evidence is no more than partially supportive of the hypothesis that the UK apparel industry would have been better served by an earlier adoption of offshore production on a large scale, although Alder (1997, p. 147) does claim that 'compared with the clothing industries of other EU member states Germany's clothing industry has shown a relatively good performance' and that, at least in the 1970s and 1980s the industry's profitability was above that of most other industries. Nevertheless, it is clear that by the end of the 1990s, the pressure upon UK apparel manufacturers to embrace offshore production had reached irresistible levels. Accordingly in the next two chapters the major issues associated with utilisation of production facilities outside the home base will be examined.

References

Abernathy, F.H., Dunlop, J.T., Hammond, J.H. & Weil, D. (1999) *A Stitch in Time: Learn Retailing and the Transformation of Manufacturing.* OUP, Oxford.

Alder, U. & Brutenacher, M. (1997) Production Organisation and Technological Change. In: *Rethinking Global Production* (Eds I. Taplin & J. Winterton), pp. 131–56. Avebury, Aldershot.

Amin, A. & Robins, K. (1990) Industrial Districts and Regional Development. In: *Industrial Districts and Inter Firm Co-operation in Italy* (Eds F. Pyke, G. Becaltini & W. Sengenburger), pp. 185–220. International Institute for Labour Statistics, Geneva.

Anson, R. (1999) Who Wants Free Trade in Textiles and Apparel? *Textile Outlook International*, **83**, 3–5.

Belussi, F. (1997) Dwarfs and Giants. In: *Rethinking Global Production* (Eds I. Taplin & J. Winterton), pp. 77–131. Avebury, Aldershot.

Bentham, L. (1998) Eversure Textiles – Team Working. *Journal of Fashion Marketing and Management*, **2**, 383–5.

Birnbaum, D. (2004) The Rise and Fall of the Garment Industry in Mexico and the Caribbean Basin. *Textile Outlook International*, **112**, 12–26.

Braithwaite, A. (1991) Hands Off Clothing Production. *Textile Asia*, **22**, 50–53.

Briscoe, L. (1971) *The Textile and Clothing Industries of the UK.* Manchester University Press, Manchester.

Brusco, S. (1990) The Idea of Industrial Districts. In: *Industrial Districts and Inter Firm Co-operation in Italy* (Eds F. Pyke, G. Becaltini & W. Sengenburger), pp. 10–20. IILS, Geneva.

Carr, F. (1994) Introducing Team Working. *Industrial Relations Journal*, **25**, 199–209.

Chistopher, M. (2000) The Agile Supply Chain: Competing in Volatile Markets. *Industrial Marketing Management*, **29.1**, 37–44.

Christopher, M., Lowson, R.H. & Peck, H. (2004) Creating Agile Supply Chains in the Fashion Industry. *International Journal of Retail and Distribution Management*, **32.8**, 367–76.

Cooper, J. (1994) *Logistics and Distribution Planning*. Kogan Page, London.

De La Torre, J. (1986) *Clothing Industry Adjustments in Developed Countries*. Macmillan, Basingstoke.

Dicken, P. (1998) *Global Shift: Transforming the World Economy*. Paul Chapman, London.

Dickerson, K. (1995) *Textiles and Apparel in the Global Economy*. Prentice Hall, New Jersey.

Digiovanna, S. (1996) Industrial Districts and Regional Economic Development. *Regional Studies*, **30**, 373–86.

Forza, C., Vinelli, A. & Filippini, R. (1993) Telecommunication Services for Quick Response in the Textile–Apparel Industry. *Proceedings of International Symposium in Logistics, University of Nottingham*.

Forza, C. & Vinelli, A. (2000) Time Compression in Production and Distribution Within the Textile–Apparel Chain. *Integrated Manufacturing Systems*, **11**, 138–46.

Groves, G. & Valsmakis, V. (1997) Supplier–Customer Relationships: Do Partnerships Perform Better? *Journal of Fashion Marketing and Management*, **1**, 9–26.

Gruber, H. (1998) Diffusion of Innovation. *Applied Economics*, **30**, 77–85.

Hardill, I. (1987) *The Regional Implications of Restructuring the Wool Textile Industry*. Gower, Aldershot.

Harrison, A., Christopher, M. & van Hoek, R. (1999) *Creating the Agile Supply Chain*. Institute of Logistics and Transport, London.

Hay, D. & Morris, D. (1991) *Industrial Economics – Theory and Evidence*. Oxford University Press, Oxford.

Hetzel, P. (1998) The Current State of the Clothing Industry and Market in France. *Journal of Fashion Marketing and Management*, **2.4**, 386–91.

Hill, E. (1992) Flexible Manufacturing Systems. *Bobbin*, **33**, 70–80.

Hines, P. & Rich, N. (1997) The Seven Value Stream Mapping Tools. *International Journal of Operations and Production Management*, **17**, 44–60.

Holmes, G. (1995) *Supply Chain Management*. E.I.U., London.

Hope, C. (2005) Nissan invests to build new car in Britain. *Daily Telegraph*, 2.2.05, p. 34.

Horrocks, R. (2001) The UK Textile Sector: Has the Time Arrived for Real National and Regional Strategies? *Journal of Fashion Marketing and Management*, **5.4**, 269–75.

Hunter, A. (1990) *Quick Response in Apparel Manufacture*. Textile Institute, Manchester.

IFM (2004) *Study on the Implications of the 2005 Trade Liberalisation in the Textile and Clothing Sector*. Institut Français de la Mode, Paris.

Jones, R.M. (1988) Research and Development Expenditure in the UK Clothing Industry. *Hollings Apparel Marketing and Management*, **5**, 97–101.

Jones, R.M. (1990) Regional Selective Assistance to the Clothing Industry. *Journal of Clothing Technology and Management*, **7**, 27–46.

Jones, R.M. (1997) Stock Changes in UK Manufacturing with Particular Reference to the Clothing Manufacturing Sector. *Journal of Fashion Marketing and Management*, **1**, 200–207.

Jones, R.M. (2001) Porter's Clusters, Industrial Districts and Local Economic Development. *Journal of Fashion Marketing and Management*, **5.3**, 181–7.

Jones, R.M. (2002) Not Quite a Seamless Supply Chain. *Journal of Fashion Marketing and Management*, **6.4**.

Khanna, S.R. (1991) *International Trade in Textiles*. Sage, London.

Kilduff, P. (2005) Problems of strategic adjustment in the U.S. textile and apparel industries since 1979. *Journal of Fashion Marketing and Management*, **9.2**, 180–95.

Kilduff, P. & Chi, T. (2006) Longitudinal Patterns of Comparative Advantage in the Textile Complex. *Journal of Fashion Marketing and Management* (forthcoming).

Kincade, D. & Cassil, N. (1993) Company Demographics as an Influence on Adoption of QR. *Clothing and Textiles Research Journal*, **11**, 22–30.

Leung, S. (1992) Evaluation of Two Pick and Place Devices used on Clothing Materials. *Journal of Clothing Technology and Management*, **9**, 29–49.

Levy, D. (1996) Lean Production in International Supply Chains. *Sloan Management Review*, **38**, 94–103.

Lowson, B., King, R. & Hunter, A. (1999) *Quick Response – Managing the Supply Chain to Meet Consumer Demand*. John Wiley, Chichester.

Lowson, R.H. (1998) *QR for Small and Medium Sized Enterprises*. Textile Institute, Manchester.

Lowson, R.H. (2001) Retail sourcing strategies: are they cost effective? *International Journal of Logistics*, **4.3**, 271–96.

Miles, C. (1968) *Lancashire Textiles*. Cambridge University Press, Cambridge.

Moore, L. (1999) *Britain's Trade and Economic Structure: the Importance of the EU*. Routledge, London.

New, C. (1993) The Use of Throughput Efficiency as a Key Performance Measure. *International Journal of Logistics Management*, **4**, 95–103.

Nolan, T. & Condotta, B. (1997) Closes Knit Relationships Hold the Key to Italian Fashion Industry Success. *Journal of Fashion Marketing and Management*, **1**, 274–83.

ONS (1999) *Sector Review*. ONS, London.

Owen, G. (1999) *From Empire to Europe*. Harper Collins, London.

Porter, M. (1998) *The Competitive Advantage of Nations*. Free Press, New York.

Pylze, F., Becaltini, G. & Sengenburger, W. (1990) *Industrial Districts and Inter Firm Cooperation in Italy*. IILS, Geneva.

Quayle, M.R. (1997) *Logistics: An Integrated Approach*. Tudor Business Publications, Seven Oaks.

Rabellotti, R. (1998) Collective Effectiveness in the Italian and Mexican Footwear Industry. *Small Business Economics*, **10**, 243–62.

Riddle, E., Bradford, D., Thomas, J. & Kincade, C. (1999) The Role of EDI in Quick Response. *Journal of Fashion Marketing and Management*, **3**, 133–47.

Scheffer, M. (1992) *Trading Places*. University of Utrecht, Utrech.

Scott, C. & Westbrook, R. (1991) New Strategic Tools for Supply Chain Management. *Institute of Physical Distribution and Logistics Management*, **21**, 23–37.

Singhal, A., Sood, S. & Singh, V. (2004) Creating and Preserving Value in the Textile and Apparel Supply Chain. *Textile Outlook International*, **109**, 135–56.

Singleton, J. (1997) *World Textile Industry*. Routledge, London.

Smith, D. (1999) Suppliers Need to Focus on Design and Flexibility. *Drapers Record*, 10.4.99, p. 6.

Spanner, G.E. (1993) Time Based Theories. *Long Range Planning*, **26**, 90–101.

Stalk, G. & Hout, T. (1990) *Competing Against Time*. Free Press, New York.

Tamilla, R. (2000) What is the Importance of Logistics to Marketing Management? *Third International Meeting for Research in Logistics, Canada*.

Taplin, I. (1995) Changes in Buyer–Supplier Relationships. *Journal of Cleaning Technology and Management*, **12**, 1–19.

Taplin, I. (1999) Continuity and Change in the US Apparel Industry. *Journal of Fashion Marketing and Management*, **3**, 360–69.

Taplin, I. & Winterton, J. (1997) Restructuring Clothing. In: *Rethinking Global Production* (Eds I. Taplin & J. Winterton), pp. 1–18. Avebury, Aldershot.

TCSG (2000) *A National Strategy for the UK Textile and Clothing Industry*. HMSO, London.

Towill, D. (1996) Time Compression and Supply Chain Management. *Supply Chain Management*, **1**, 1–11.

Toyne, B. (1984) *The Global Textile Industry*. Allen and Unwin, London.

Tyler, D. (1989) Managing for Production Flexibility in the Clothing Industry. *Textile Outlook International*, **24**, 63–84.

Ussman, A.M. (1999) The Portuguese Clothing Industry and Market Trends. *Journal of Fashion Marketing and Management*, **3**, 85–90.

Winterton, R. & Barlow, A. (1996) Economic Restructuring of UK Clothing. In: *Restructuring in a Labour Intensive Industry* (Eds I. Taplin & J. Winterton), pp. 25–61. Avebury, Aldershot.

Winterton, J. & Winterton, R. (1997) Deregulation, Division and Decline. In: *Rethinking Global Production* (Eds I. Taplin & J. Winterton), pp. 18–41. Avebury, Aldershot.

Zeitlin, J. (1988) The Clothing Industry in Transition. *Textile History*, **19**, 211–38.

Chapter 8
Issues in Offshore Production Strategies

A. Introduction

It has been argued in the preceding chapter that a review of the evolution of the apparel industry reveals three dominant trends – first, as Taplin (1996, p. 4) puts it, 'Economic logic would suggest that clothing manufacture is increasingly an inappropriate industry for a high wage economy'; second, that some 30 years ago the industry in the UK responded to burgeoning foreign competition by following a strategy of consolidation of production into large units producing long runs for major retailers while at the same time sheltering behind the mild protective barrier afforded (to a greater or lesser degree) by the Multi Fibre Arrangement (Winterton, 1996, p. 25); and third, that this policy has become increasingly vulnerable to changes in the market place to the point where it is hardly viable. With the benefit of hindsight, that this should have proven to be the case is, perhaps, hardly surprising. It is more surprising that the logical inconsistencies in this strategy have taken so long to develop to breaking point. The reasons for advancing this view would be that it was not obviously sensible to aim for economies of scale in an industry such as apparel manufacture in which the minimum economic size of unit seems to be small and in which the application of new technologies has been so (relatively) slow; that the concentration on relatively long runs of 'safe' products was not, given the way the consumer market evolved, appropriate although whether or not this could have been foreseen is another question; that following EU entry the strategy was liable to be undermined by the liberal trading tendencies of that institution; and that improvements in global logistics were bound to facilitate global sourcing.

It was becoming clear by the early 1990s that the policy of (relative to other developed countries) eschewing offshore production was becoming unsustainable. This was recognised by Anson (1993b, p. 12) who wrote that the 'use of Outward Processed Trade on the continent contrasts sharply with UK practice; where a policy of local sourcing by some of the major retailers has until recently provided a reasonably secure . . . market for the UK clothing industry's products' but that the time had arrived when producers should contemplate how they were going to adapt to new circumstances. The same author (Anson, 1993a) concluded that 'competitive pressures . . . will force European clothing manufacturers to undertake more outsourcing to take advantage of lower labour costs' and that 'the principle for trading pay for job security is difficult to defend in Western Europe in the 1990s. Besides, it serves merely to postpone the inevitable'.

It will be the theme of this chapter that the argument over the role of offshore production in future strategies is effectively over and has been decided in favour of the offshore option. As Moore (1999, p. 280) observed, the majority of the largest UK-based apparel manufacturers have announced plans to increase the proportion of their output produced offshore. In following this trend the industry would not be ploughing a new path – the same trend has been evolving in many other sectors. Edwards (1984) conducted a major survey of offshore manufacture and concluded that costs achieved were normally 20–30% lower than the UK despite lower productivity, but that transport costs rose. The questions today are: what form will offshore production take, where will it be located and who will perform the range of operations within the supply chain?

The word 'sourcing' is often used to describe, as Newberry (1993, p. 105) puts it, 'a conscious decision on the part of a manufacturer or retailer to obtain merchandise from other countries'. However, the term is not always used consistently: Blyth (1996, p. 112), for example, describes 'sourcing as an alternative to own manufacture' which could, obviously, take place within the base country. Furthermore, in a more general sense the word 'outsourcing' is often used simply to describe the decision to subcontract part of an operation (e.g. physical distribution) to a third-party specialist. Therefore, in this text the decision to utilise capacity in a country which is not the country in which the head office of a company is based will be termed 'offshore production'. This chapter will start from the point of view that an increase in offshore production is now inevitable and will explore a number of key issues raised by this trend. The main impetus towards an increased use of offshore locations is the labour cost gap between countries which has been dealt with in Chapter 4.

B. Operational issues

(i)   Types of offshore production

If the decision has been taken to abandon autochthonous production in favour of production in another country there exists a wide range of alternative forms of organisation to implement this change, see for example, Dickerson (1995, p. 294) who lists eight sourcing options. These would include:

(1)   Outward Processed Trade arrangements (OPTs).
(2)   Simple contractual arrangements with a supplier in another country into which category can be included CMT (Cut, Make, Trim) arrangements.
(3)   Joint ventures – in which two companies join together in the formation of a new company.
(4)   Direct investment in capacity in another country – usually termed FDI or Foreign Direct Investment.
(5)   If the market is also in the second country licensing arrangements can be used. In this case the product is produced offshore by another company under licence granted by the originator.

These alternatives have individually both strengths and weaknesses and their appropriateness in specific instances must be judged on a case-by-case basis – there is no single 'best' option universally. OPT arrangements are discussed in more detail in Section C(i) below. The advantage of contractual arrangements lies in their flexibility while the main disadvantage is a potential lack of control. Joint ventures have experienced a growth in popularity and have the virtues of spreading the risk and of promoting cultural awareness via the involvement of (normally) a local partner. The main danger is of unintended technological transfer and the training of a potential competitor. A similar danger arises with licensing arrangements.

(ii)   Manufactured cost variations and the concept of hidden costs

In Dunning's (1988) words 'enterprises will engage in foreign production when-ever they perceive it is in their best interests to combine partially transferable factors with at least some mobile factor endowments in other countries'. The extent of the labour cost gap has been explored in Chapter 4. This gap will be reflected in the final cost of manufacture in alternative locations and, as was seen in Chapter 4, there is quite a close correlation between labour costs and manufacturing costs. Tables 8.1 and 8.2 illustrate the gains to be realised from offshore production in the apparel sector.

Hunter (1990, p. 37) reports Boston Consulting Group estimates which suggested that the expected advantage of offshore operations (in terms of gross margins) fell by 1–4% after allowing for hidden costs.

The concept of 'hidden costs' has been invoked by a variety of commentators to suggest that the advantages of offshore production are in part an illusion – the result, in effect, of an inadequate comparison of the real costs. Blyth (1996) lists items such as co-ordination costs and the costs of maintaining offices overseas. A report on the French textile sector (Clautier, 1993) included extra financial and documentation costs, such as those associated with international financial instruments. Other costs could include export taxes, additional warehousing,

Table 8.1   Cost comparisons by location (1993).

Country	Shirts + Suits
UK	100
Hong Kong	82
Portugal	77
Tunisia	62
Malaysia	59
E. Europe	50

Source: Newberry, M. (1993) A Balanced Sourcing Strategy for the UK Market, *Textile Outlook International*, **49**, 105–121.

Note: Figures converted to an index based on UK by the author.

Table 8.2   Manufacturing cost variations: jersey knit sweatshirt.

	Landed cost (£)
UK	13.00
Hong Kong	8.40
Indonesia	7.46
Korea	9.01
Morocco	8.20

Source: Blyth, R. (1996) Sourcing Clothing Production. In: *Restructuring in a Labour Intensive Industry* (Eds I. Taplin & J. Winterton), pp. 112–42. Avebury, Aldershot.

Notes: (1)   Data are for 1993.
(2)   UK figure is for own factory.

transport and insurance charges and the costs of maintaining extra buffer stocks. Finally, there is the risk factor – that the product will fail to arrive on time and to specification.

It is argued that if these costs are properly taken into consideration the cost advantage of the low labour cost locations is greatly reduced. Hergeth (2000) argues, from the results of a survey of 28 smaller American companies, that the biggest deficiencies of locational cost comparisons were related to misallocation of overhead charges specifically associated with offshore operations, such as the extra costs of mobile quality inspectors so that such costs 'are hidden because they are assigned to the wrong product or to a general time period and no specific product at all'. The problem with this argument is that it is a fact that most overhead costs are not scientifically allocated and that if, for example, a company has moved to a position in which, say, some 70% of output is produced offshore then allocating these costs as overhead over the entire output will not produce a result which is substantially invalid. The present author believes that

Table 8.3   Sourcing costs ($ per piece).

	Far East	Mexico
Price (FOB)	8.00	8.00
Duty	1.34	0.54*
Risk/Letter of Credit (5%)	0.40	—
Agents' commission	0.40	0.50**
Transport	0.50	0.40
Landed duty paid price	10.64	8.99

Source: J. Kwok and R.M. Jones (1998) High Kicking Chorus Line.
          Journal of Fashion Marketing and Management, **2**, 177–94.
Notes: * At NAFTA lower duty paid rate.
          ** No agent's fee but there is an inspection cost.

it is difficult to sustain the argument in the face of the seemingly remorseless rise in the use of various forms of offshore production. This would imply that vast numbers of decision makers are continually taking the wrong decision either out of stupidity or a failure to appreciate the realities of global costing. This seems a somewhat farfetched notion. A more plausible explanation would be that some sort of risk assessment exercise is being undertaken in that the probability of securing the main benefit of offshore production – cheap labour – is seen as one, while the probability of something going wrong to an extent which outweighs the labour cost saving is perceived as much less than one. Table 8.3 which is based on Kwok (1998) clearly indicates that competent management can easily take some of these factors into account in drawing up a comparison of landed costs from various sources (see also the figures on page 311).

It is unlikely that the concept of hidden costs can ever be invoked to support a relocation of the assembly operation back to high cost centres (Jones, 2002). In addition there may be hidden costs in developed countries in the increasing 'red tape' burden (Evans-Pritchard, 2001; Gribben, 2004).

(iii)   Switching costs

The global pattern of cost advantage is constantly changing. Locations which were once the cheapest (particularly in terms of labour costs) lose that competitive advantage as they become more developed. Locations may become disadvantaged by political instability, the imposition of trade barriers or by exchange rate fluctuations. It is unlikely, therefore, that the decision on where to produce or source can be taken once and the resultant pattern of activity remains fixed for all time. However it has to be recognised that constantly shifting the location of activity in pursuit, for example, of the lowest priced labour will incur so-called 'switching' costs. These are reviewed by Blyth (1996) and include start-up costs, learning costs, reputational costs and cost of failure when dealing with a new partner. Blyth concluded that it would be sensible, on the basis of experience, to expect that 'it is not until at least the third year of cooperation that the full benefits and mutual respect . . . in the sourcing arrangement begin to form'.

In line with the research/philosophy outlined in Chapter 1 it would clearly be desirable to obtain a test of the hypothesis that a policy of chasing low labour costs by constantly switching production leads to superior (or inferior) long run performance. Unfortunately no such evidence seems to be available for the apparel sector but at a time when the value of developing sound buyer–supplier relationships is increasingly recognised, running all over the world looking for cheap labour does not appear to represent an efficient strategy. The danger is that one would end up as a sort of economic refugee and a buyer on the run with very little influence. As Eenennaam (1996, p. 91) observed, relocation 'is an expensive proposition . . . if the relocated activity is not successful and increases costs even further . . . The important thing is to identify those value chain activities which are mobile and to identify locations where a comparative advantage exists for these activities'.

(iv)   Choice of offshore location

In the apparel sector any company based in a developed country would have an extremely wide range of options which would provide the benefit of lower labour costs. This list has to be screened and a choice made. A variety of techniques exist to assist in this decision-making process and it is normally argued that a choice of location would normally precede the choice of supplier. A list of the major factors to be taken into account would include the following:

 (1)   Labour costs.
 (2)   Labour supply.
 (3)   Material costs and availability.
 (4)   Training costs.
 (5)   Local labour laws.
 (6)   Communications.
 (7)   Political stability.
 (8)   Ownership possibilities.
 (9)   Local government aid packages.
(10)   Local tax and profit regulations.
(11)   Market access.
(12)   Cultural compatibility.
(13)   Exchange rate risks.

It is unlikely that any one location will be the 'best' under all headings – some trade-offs will probably have to be made. Various devices are suggested to assist in the selection process. A relatively simple example is the selection grid illustrated in Fig. 8.1. This can contain as many variables as is desired and each must be weighed in order of particular importance to the company making the

Factor	Weight	Score		
		Country A	Country B	Country C
Labour cost	0.5	3 (1.5)	2 (1.0)	1 (0.5)
Labour supply	0.3	1 (0.3)	3 (0.9)	2 (0.6)
Stability	0.2	2 (0.4)	1 (0.2)	3 (0.6)
Final score		2.2	2.1	1.7

Notes: (1) Weights are subjective but must total to 1.0.
       (2) Best score = 3.
       (3) ( ) = weight × score.
       (4) Final score = total of ( ).

Fig. 8.1   Country selection grid.

decision. Each country is then given a score under each variable. The main problem is that many of the variables – such as political risk – are hard to measure in an objective sense. However, it is possible to obtain country rankings which offer expert opinion on a wide range of factors as can be seen from Table 8.4.

Table 8.4   Country ratings – non-financial data.

Country	Political stability	Cultural barriers	Transport	Communication	Raw material	Shipping time (days)
Bangladesh	5	5	2	2	4	18/2
Cambodia	4	2	1	1	4	24/2
China	7	5	3	6	5	24/2
Czech Republic	8	8	7	6	5	3–4 (truck)
Egypt	5	4	3	4	2	16/2
Hong Kong	7	9	10	9	9	24/1
Hungary	8	8	7	8	5	3–4 (truck)
India	7	7	3	4	6	18/1
Indonesia	4	6	4	5	6	25/2
Mauritius	9	8	8	9	6	20/2
Morocco	6	4	4	7	5	14 (3 truck)
Pakistan	5	6	3	7	6	18/2
Poland	8	8	6	8	5	3–5 (truck)
Sri Lanka	6	7	3	4	5	18/2
Taiwan	7	7	8	9	8	22/1
Tunisia	6	4	4	5	6	14 (3 truck)
Turkey	7	7	5	7	8	4–6 (truck)

Source: KSA (1999) *Sorting Your Sourcing: the Fifth Cost Comparison Study*. KSA, Manchester.
Notes: (1) In the final column the first figure is for transportation by ship; the second is for air unless otherwise stated.
       (2) High numbers indicate good performance.
       (3) A similar table can be found in KSA (2005) and in IFM (2004) Tables 29 and 30.

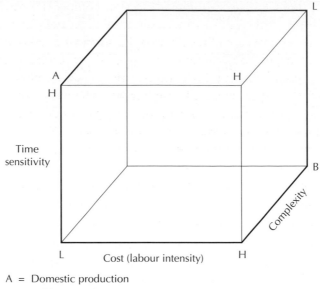

A = Domestic production
B = Offshore production
H = High
L = Low

Fig. 8.2   Offshore *vs* domestic selection.

(v)   *Which products to produce offshore?*

The conventional wisdom is that suitability for offshore production depends primarily on two factors: (a) the sewing time involved and (b) the complexity of the product. Blyth (1996, p. 139) concludes that the 'advantage of sourcing is greatest therefore when the garment . . . involves high amounts of labour time'. Additionally, it can be argued that time-sensitive products would be less suited to offshore production. This view is captured by Fig. 8.2 which suggests that product A with low labour intensity, high time sensitivity and high complexity would be produced at home. Lead times for production in various regions fluctuate markedly as can be seen from Table 8.4. Therefore, a three-way relationship can be envisaged as illustrated in Fig. 8.2. Walwyn (1997, p. 255) reflects this viewpoint when he states that the choice of sourcing location will 'be based on an assessment of product and service characteristics', namely price, responsiveness and quality. The attempt to accommodate the varying demands of the marketplace and production facilities is sometimes known as balanced sourcing which will be described in the next section.

(vi)   *The concept of balanced sourcing*

Kotabe (1992) defines balanced sourcing as the 'management of the interfaces among Research and Development, Manufacturing and Marketing on a global basis . . . such that the firm can exploit its own competitive advantages and the comparative advantages of various countries'. This definition captures the essence of Porter's (1998) use of the Diamond Framework described in Chapter 1 and highlights the main reason for the use of offshore production to offset the disadvantages (predominantly high wages) inherent in developed economies. Newberry (1993) defines balanced sourcing as 'balancing fabric availability against cost; and balancing the merchandise buying mix between product development and product replenishment to maintain stocks'. Kwok (1998) demonstrated how one Californian apparel manufacturer implemented a balanced sourcing policy in a variety of regions to maintain and develop a competitive position in the American women's wear market across the five product divisions which comprise the company. Products requiring quick response tend to be made in Mexico while those for whom the main driver is price tend to be sourced in the Far East.

(vii)   The basis of the transaction

There are a range of internationally recognised definitions which describe the division of responsibility as between buyers and sellers (see Fig. 8.3). Locke (1996) recommends using ex-works or DDP. It is clearly important that all quotations are made in the same format. A further complication, which is likely to increase in importance as international production spreads, is that of international transfer pricing between units of the same organisation located in different countries. Domestic transfer pricing is in itself a complex issue and is covered in most standard economics textbooks (Pappas, 1993). However, the addition of the international dimension significantly complicated the issue as differential rates of taxation have to be taken into account. Elliott (2000, p. 220) concluded a survey of transfer pricing in the global sector with the warning that 'international transfer pricing is set to become a major concern [as] compliance costs and the threat of audit . . . increase'.

---

(1)   Ex-works: the seller places goods for collection by buyer at the time and place specified. Buyer loads.

(2)   FAS (Free Alongside Ship): seller places goods alongside vessel. The buyer is responsible for everything else.

(3)   FOB (Free On Board): the seller moves the product onto the ship and clears it for export.

(4)   C + F (Cost and Freight): the seller is responsible for all costs and freight to a named port of destination.

(5)   CIF (Cost, Insurance, Freight): as above but the seller also pays for insurance.

(6)   DDP (Delivered Duty Paid): the seller bears all the costs and delivers the product duty paid to a specified destination.

Fig. 8.3   Terms of sale.

(viii)   Methods of payment

A variety of financial instruments have been developed to facilitate payments related to international transactions. The most commonly encountered are the Letter of Credit and the Bill of Exchange. A letter of credit is defined as a written undertaking by a bank (by prior agreement with a client) to honour a withdrawal by a third party (the seller). It is usually at the request of the buyer but is in favour of the seller. The bank promises to pay money out of the account of the buyer into the account of the seller after certain documents have been received, i.e. the bank allows the seller to withdraw from the buyer's account the agreed sum. A bill of exchange is drawn by the seller (the drawer) on the buyer (the drawee) who signs it. It obliges the buyer to pay the seller an agreed sum upon fulfilment of certain conditions. The buyer accepts a liability when he or she signs it. It is a request for payment and carries with it a risk that the buyer will not be able to make the payment at the time specified, but with a Letter of Credit, the buyer's bank is obligated to accept an instruction to pay money out to the seller, i.e. the bank is in effect guaranteeing that payment will be made. Locke (1996) contends that technological change means that there are now superior alternatives to the above, such as wire transfers.

(ix)   Information flows and quality control

In an age of ever improving systems of electronic data transmission it is increasingly probable that problems associated with ensuring an efficient flow of data within a global supply chain will diminish over time. Cooper (1994) observes that improvements in the information network enables control over global supply chains to be exerted in ways which would have seemed inconceivable a few years ago. It is clear that the dispersion of production was initially cost-driven but (Popp, 2000, p. 141) argues that 'reflection makes it clear that it will impact in a complex way on a wide range of business functions' and that, among these, the impact on quality procedures has been relatively poorly researched. Thus the increasingly international nature of apparel supply chains controlled by companies based in developed countries is not only a matter of relocating assembly operations but is becoming part of (or initiates) a more complex process of change in company structure, evolution and the process of inter-company relationships.

Popp's research (2000) concentrates upon the concept of information costs as expounded by Casson (1997) who argues that 'as technological progress drives down communication costs over long distances, so institutions adapt by increasing the geographical scope of their activities'. Therefore distant and diversified operation of the supply chain is facilitated by developments in information technology and electronic communications.

However, these problems have not been entirely removed. Chen (2005), for example, suggests that communication problems and associated loss of understanding remain significant problems in supply chain involving UK and Chinese partners. It has also emerged from the review of potential strategies carried out in Chapter 7 that improving logistical and supply chain management capability has emerged as a significant factor. Internationally configured supply chains are, by definition, more complex than domestic ones and, therefore, the internationalisation of the apparel industry exemplified by the increased use of offshore production introduces contradictory pressures which have to be resolved by the development of appropriate institutional structures and practices.

The area of quality control is a particularly good example of this point. Quality can be a critical element in competition and there is a significant body of research (Ouchi, 1981; Jacobson, 1987; Wong, 1988) which highlights the role of quality in securing and retaining customers. The word 'quality' can have a range of meanings. The British Standards Institute (1987) defines quality as the 'totality of features and characteristics of a product or service that bear on its ability to satisfy stated or implied needs'. Garvin (1988) identifies five concepts of quality: (a) the transcendent view which equates quality to excellence; (b) the product-based view which assumes that quality is measurable in an objective sense; (c) a user-based view which relates to fit to consumer preference; (d) a value-based view which refers to excellence at an affordable price and, finally, (e) the conformance view which defines quality as conformance to a specification. It is the latter viewpoint which is normally utilised in studies of supply chain performance.

Popp (2000, p. 142) argues that 'the location within the supply chain, in geographical and institution terms, of responsibility for assessing quality may constitute a significant difference between supply chains'. Clearly the ability of competing supply chains to manage the information flows associated with quality control could form the basis of a competitive advantage. Popp's initial research indicated that quality issues had played an important role in the evolution of all the supply chains examined despite the diversity of markets served. Supply chains which, for example, concentrated on chasing low price and ignoring information issues appeared to risk encountering severe quality problems. The early conclusion drawn from the research was that (Popp, 2000, p. 160) while a wide range of strategies had emerged to deal with global supply chain issues, prominent amongst them has been the 'assignment of responsibility for monitoring quality to third parties, most often located in the source country and sharing national or at least cultural and linguistic affiliations with that country'.

More important issues	New issues
Distance barriers	Trade barriers
Logistics	Exchange rates
Communication barriers	Language issues
Lead times	Postponement
Co-ordination issues	Cultural issues and conflicts
Multiple production sites	Multiple markets
Diversity in supply and demand conditions	Political issues
Stock levels	Duties
Multiple freight modes	Subsidies
Quality control	Break bulk and multiple consolidation options
Information flows	
Extended transit time	

Note: Most of the terms will either be self-explanatory or will relate to issues discussed in the text. The following may require some explanation: 'break bulk and multiple consolidation' refers to the fact that there is a wide range of choice available in gathering products together from suppliers and then breaking them up into smaller lots.

Fig. 8.4   Domestic *vs* global supply chains.

(x)   *Global versus domestic logistics*

Global supply chains tend, almost by definition, to be longer and more complex than domestic ones. In the opinion of Bowersox (1996, p. 126) while 'domestic logistics focuses on performing value-added services in a relatively controlled environment . . . Global logistics operations must accommodate all domestic requirements and also deal with the increased uncertainties' of the international trading environment. The issues which are either only present in global supply chains or which are of greater importance in them are summarised in Fig. 8.4. Locke (1996, p. 128) considers that the issues are not as big an impediment as they might appear and that the optimum solution is to subcontract the task to a specialist logistics provider because 'there are a lot of organisations . . . to co-ordinate a lot of these steps at a cost most people accept as reasonable'. The major questions of the impact of trade barriers and exchange rate fluctuations are considered in Chapter 9.

Cooper (1994) has produced an extremely useful taxonomy which assists in identifying the extent to which global logistics will be important elements in a company's operations. He divides companies into five so-called clusters: (a) invaders, (b) settlers, (c) cloners, (d) barons and (e) outreachers. Invaders enter a foreign market with the aim of supplying it using external sources of supply. Therefore, their demand is mainly for inbound logistics. Settlers, in contrast, utilise local suppliers and, as a consequence have little demand for either inbound or outbound logistics. Cloners tend to duplicate production operations within each market they supply and have limited needs for global logistics. Barons concentrate both sourcing and production in one place and consequently have a high level of demand for both inbound and outbound logistical services. Finally, outreachers concentrate production in one location but sell globally and have a high demand for both types of global logistics.

The concept of logistics reach is also of use in determining the locational flexibility of the various elements of the supply chain and this is related to the physical characteristics of the product, such as weight and bulk. The term 'value density' is used to relate the value of an item to its weight and volume. If an item is said to have a high value density it can be transported over long distances, e.g. a watch. If it has a low value density, production and use tends to be localised. Therefore, the logistics reach (the propensity to move the item) is positively related to value density – if value density is high then logistics reach will be great.

One implication of this concept within the textile apparel supply chain would be that activity is likely to be pulled more towards the fabric production centres than towards the final market as it is probable that garments have a higher logistics reach than basic fabric. The essence of this issue is nicely illustrated by Taplin's (1995, p. 3) observation that other than 'items with a high weight to labour ratio the majority of items could be more inexpensively manufactured overseas'.

Finally, global supply chains afford the opportunity to engage in what is known as 'postponement' of activities. This refers to the existence of opportunities to delay carrying out certain activities within the value chain so as to delay the point at which a product becomes irretrievably dedicated to a specific customer, e.g. belts could be added to trousers when the product reaches the final market so as to save weight during transport; pressing can likewise be postponed; and differential packaging can be carried out in the final market place. Cooper (1994) considers that opportunities for postponement are related to the answers obtained to three simple questions: (a) is the brand global?; (b) is the product formulation global? and (c) are the peripherals (such as packaging) common to all markets? If, for example, all three questions can be answered in the affirmative then the most appropriate logistics strategy would be a concentrated one with fully centralised (in one location) production and distribution – with a correspondingly high demand for both inbound and outbound logistics and little or no postponement. If the answer to the second and third questions was, by way of contrast, negative then deferred assembly would be indicated and postponement increased.

(xi)   Vendor selection and the issue of ethical sourcing

The identification of an overseas supplier is clearly a major decision which will determine whether or not a supply chain will function efficiently. Popp (2000) has produced a number of case studies which clearly indicate the impact of mistakes in this area. A number of devices exist to assist in the selection process many of which are similar to the grid illustrated in Fig. 8.1 although in this case the selection factors would incorporate elements crucial to supplier choice such as price, quality and dependability. Locke (1996) suggests that country selection should precede supplier selection and that subsequently a short list of potential suppliers should be drawn up on the basis of an ex-works price quotation from which landed costs can be calculated. This is defined as (1996, p. 203) 'the total cost to buy the products, bring them to your receiving point and finance the inventory required both in your stock room and in the shipping pipeline'.

It does not follow that the supplier with the lowest landed cost will inevitably be selected. A number of other factors must be taken into account, e.g. exchange rate risks, trade barriers, premium freight requirements, political risks and so on.

An issue which has received increased attention is the reputation suppliers and/or locations enjoy for adhering to recognised standards of employment conditions. This issue is generally referred to as that of ethical sourcing. Ethical sourcing can be defined as the utilisation of offshore sourcing locations and suppliers in compliance with a set of pre-determined standards of employment conditions including such factors as wage levels, working time, age restrictions and hygiene and welfare conditions. Ethical consumption can be defined (Cran, 2003, p. 290) as 'the conscious and deliberate choice to make certain consumption decisions due to personal and moral belief'.

The question of ethical sourcing has attracted a lot of attention in the developed countries. In the UK, for example, the Ethical Trading Initiative sets out to encourage retailers to establish best practice. A number of charities have also become involved such as 'Labour behind the Label' in the UK and the National Labour Committee in the USA. In addition, a large number of companies such as New Look, Debenhams, Gap, Levis, Reebok, Nike, IKEA and Liz Clairbourne have developed ethical sourcing policy statements (Parker, 1998, p. 355). The company which made the most positive move towards monitoring suppliers was C&A which, in 1996, launched an independent auditing unit. This, in the UK, was not rewarded by customer loyalty.

These issues are extensively covered by Ross (1997) and Jarnow (1997) and it clearly is theoretically possible for a concern over ethical sourcing practices to be developed as part of a company's competitive advantage provided that consumers are willing to take this into account. This issue is part of a wider question concerning the relationship between product origin, brand name and consumer perception of quality and value. As Usunier (1993, p. 249) states, there 'is an important relation between images of products and the symbols diffused by this materiality'. In order for consumers to reject apparel made under unacceptable working conditions they must first be able to identify accurately which countries have poor practices; second, they must be able to recognise the country of origin of the garment or the brand and to be able to distinguish between country of manufacture and country of brand origin; and, third, they must be willing to pay extra for products made under better and (usually) more expensive conditions although Adams (2002) argues that wages are only responsible for 0.5–1.0% of the final selling price of a garment.

Clearly it is possible to manipulate 'made in' labels and brand names and to exploit positive associations related to country images as part of the marketing mix. There is a mass of research evidence – summarised by Usunier (1993) – to support the argument that consumers do associate country of origin with product attributes but that they do so in rather complex ways and not in isolation of other product characteristics such as price. Lumpkin (1985), for example, found that consumer perceptions of the risks associated with products from various sources varied according to product type. Similarly, a number of studies of ethnocentric consumerism (the desire to buy own nationality products) suggest that this is also related to product type so that while Usunier (1993, p. 254) can conclude that it 'has been persistently demonstrated that in most developed countries domestic products generally enjoy a more favourable evaluation than foreign-made products' this has clearly not happened in the apparel sector in that import penetration rates in most developed countries are extremely high and rising.

The important commercial questions from the point of view of an apparel manufacturer or retailer planning to switch production away from a domestic base to an offshore one are: first, will the country of origin have to be stated on the garment and, if so, is there any danger that consumers will associate specific locations with poor quality? Second, is there a danger that relocation will affect the price consumers are willing to pay? And third, is there any real danger that revelations about poor employment practices in certain low cost countries will result in consumer boycotts of products from those areas? These are questions upon which research evidence can be consulted.

With regard to the first question, it is not a legal requirement within the EU that the country of origin (which would normally be defined in law as the place in which the last significant manufacturing process was carried out) be identified on the garment, although in practice it often will be. It could be an offence to use a logo or brand name that was liable to mislead the consumer as to the country of origin.

There is evidence in Usunier (1993) that relocation of production has damaged the sales of certain products (usually relatively high technology items) in the USA and that brand names can convey country and quality associations. Seaton (1999) in a study of automobile values, found that moving production from mainland USA to Mexico resulted in a 12% fall in the value of the product. This confirms early research by Johansson (1986) who demonstrated that the status and quality images of American cars fell when production was moved to low labour cost countries: he estimated the price premium for made in the USA vehicles to be around 30%. A similar result was found by Jaffe (1989) in relation to electronic products.

In relation to the third question there is a limited amount of evidence that consumers do identify certain countries with low quality apparel production. Lea-Greenwood (1999) found that consumers were able to articulate beliefs about inter-country variations in standards of working practices but the evidence for concern being translated into an unwillingness to purchase was extremely flimsy, e.g. only 55% of the sample stated they would pay more for goods produced under superior working conditions. Dickson (1999) also found that, in an American study, even 'in the most altruistic apparel purchase situation consumers . . . place more importance on quality criteria than they do on social issues' in that 57% of the respondents said they would only buy from socially responsible businesses if they really liked the product while 39% said they did not usually check where the product was made if it suited their needs. A series of reports in 2005 (Stern, 2005; Tyler, 2005) reinforced the view that price and quality issues far outweighed any ethical considerations in purchase decisions. This confirmed the findings of Carrigan (2001), Auger (2003) and Shaw (2004), leading to the inevitable conclusion that while there is concern about these issues there remains a big attitudinal–behavioural gap. Zolka (1997) found that brand-conscious men were more sensitive to ethical issues than other men while women were more concerned with these issues than men. The problem for retailers and manufacturers is further compounded by the observation (Creyer, 1997, p. 429) that ethical behaviour 'may be a multidimensional concept – different ethical corporate acts could result in different consumer responses'.

Therefore, while it may be the case that (Wong, 2000, p. 72) ethical consumerism 'is predicted to become a significant trend in the future' and that there 'is a growing awareness of human rights and environmental issues in the textiles and apparel industry' the actual amount of hard evidence of consumer action which damages sales is somewhat limited.

The issue is further complicated by the necessity to distinguish – in a world increasingly characterised by global supply chains – between the influence of country of manufacture and that of country of brand origin. The research evidence is relatively clear on this issue in that, for example, Min Han (1988) found that the sourcing country had more influence than the brand name. Iyer (1997) investigated the difference between country of brand origin and actual country of manufacture on consumer perceptions of quality and value and also found that there was 'a strong effect of country of manufacture . . . in all product categories' but that 'the relative salience of country of manufacture and country of brand origin varies according to whether the product is a non-technical fashion product or a low technology technical product'. Somewhat counter-intuitively they found that country of manufacture was more important for fashion products. Knight (1999) likewise found that consumer preferences were more likely to be influenced by the country of manufacture than by the company's country of origin. Lim (2001), in contrast, found that consumers could more readily identify the cultural origin of brands than their country of origin.

In a world characterised by the presence of increasingly dispersed supply choices it could be argued that the very concept of 'made in' is losing any real meaning in that it is unlikely that all the components or all the processes are carried out in one place. But it does appear from the evidence that country of manufacture is significantly more important than country of brand origin in determining consumer perceptions. Therefore while it may be true that as Wong (2000, p. 79) puts it, increasingly 'companies are being held accountable for the policies and practices in this entire supply chain' it does somewhat surprisingly seem to be the case that the country of actual manufacture is more important than the country of origin of the brand, i.e. than the reputation of the company perceived to be the leader of the supply chain. Verschoor (1998, p. 1515) studied those companies from the top 5000 in the USA which claimed commitment to ethical behaviour in their annual reports and found that there was a 'statistically significant linkage between a management commitment to strong controls that emphasise ethical and socially responsible behaviour . . . and favourable corporate financial performance' although it is not clear how (or if) companies were standardised for variations in other significant variables.

It is not easy to arrive at a simple statement of the operational implications of the research. Clearly it is important that companies protect their good name but equally it would – on the basis of the available evidence – not be sensible to reject the offshore production option because of concerns over consumer perception of the product. The market remains price-driven and origin issues cannot be divorced from other factors in the consumer decision-making process. The trade figures clearly indicate that apparel consumers in developed countries have few problems with the purchase of apparel made in a wide variety of non-domestic locations. It should also be observed that as Basu (1998) concluded, if the labour market is somewhat primitive and rigid, which is very likely in very poor countries, then a ban can worsen the condition of the workforce. A recent report by Dessy (2005) also concluded that banning child labour without tackling the root causes of poverty would make things worse rather than better.

This conclusion was also reached in later research by the same author Basu (2000) who, in an investigation into the link between the use of child labour and the existence of a minimum wage, concluded that 'the suggestion of using minimum wage legislation in developing countries as a form of international labour standard has the risk of exacerbating the problem of child labour'.

A thorough review of labour issues arising from globalisation is provided by Parker (1998, Chapter 6). As is stated in Chapter 9, the standpoint taken in this text is that, as a general rule, more and freer trade is to be preferred to restricted and reduced trade. Frankel (1999, p. 379), for example, concluded that 'trade has a qualitatively large and robust . . . positive effect on income' while Lee (1997) observes that while there is some consensus about the universal observance of core ILO standards there remain substantial differences of opinion about such issues as how to deal with problems caused by job destruction if such standards are applied.

(xii)   Remaining problems with offshore strategies

It would be difficult to find any commentator on the apparel industry who did not regard the debate over the efficiency of offshore production as settled. It is true that organising a supply chain which is spread over several countries will be more complex than organising a purely domestic chain but most of the disadvantages are declining or becoming more soluble over time. For example, transport costs fell steadily from 1920 to 1990 (McRae, 2002) although the rapid growth of China has caused an increase after 2002 (Bootle, 2004); global communications are improving; and revolutions in information technology enhance the ability of companies to co-ordinate geographically dispersed activities. However, if companies increasingly engage in globally dispersed production chains a number of issues will assume greater importance in the future. Two such issues are the differences between domestic and global logistics and the question of ethical sourcing dealt with above. A third will be covered in this section.

The impact of culture on global business has been examined at length by Parker (1998), Flaherty (1996) and Locke (1996). The main impetus for offshore production remains the comparatively low wages. The vast majority of the countries with very low labour costs are countries which exhibit significant religious, linguistic and cultural differences from the UK. Ignorance of these differences can have severe negative impacts upon the efficiency of offshore operations so that there is a danger that, in Parker's words (1998, p. 175), differences 'in cultural dimensions often are expressed in business behaviours that become the source of culture clash'. Locke (1996) identifies two main areas of cultural impact on business transactions: values (how people think) and behaviour (how people act).

The most important issues in the first area are attitudes to inequality and power which may affect the status of the customer; attitudes to uncertainty avoidance which may generate masses of regulations and a lack of flexibility; attitudes to traditional as against new forms of behaviour; attitudes to individualism; gender relationships which may make it impossible for women to conduct business; the need for harmony and concern over guilt, shame and face. In relation to behavioural issues some of the most important dimensions of inter-cultural activity seem to be the style of communication adopted; the relative inability of some cultures to say 'no'; the extent of the distinction between personal and business relationships; attitudes to time and the concept of urgency; attitudes to physical closeness and touching; and, finally, variations in the rules for conflict resolution and the existence of so-called 'escape hatches' which prevent disputes from getting out of control.

Parker (1998, p. 210) considers that it is vital that managers 'increase their cultural sensitivity' and, as international activity increases, adopt a 'broad, non-parochial view of the company'. Managers' operating across cultural boundaries will require certain skills and attributes such as the ability to work with people from diverse backgrounds; the ability to read and be sensitive to cultural signs and to avoid cultural mistakes. Parker (1998) draws a picture of divergent business practices in the USA, Asia and Europe, for example, contrasting the emphasis on individualism in the USA with the group or collectivist theme dominant in Asia. Pitta (1999) points out that even a simple word such as 'yes' has different meanings across cultures – in China, for instance, it means I'm listening, not that I agree. It cannot even necessarily be assumed that all countries in a region will be culturally homogeneous. Parker (1998) draws distinctions between Japanese and Chinese values and between prevailing practices in Southern and Northern Europe, for example. There is quite a lot of research evidence on the existence of national cultural values. Hofstede (1984) identified four dimensions of national culture (individualism; power distance; uncertainty avoidance and gender issues) while Trompenaars (1994) isolated five variables (universalism; individualism; emotional displays; concepts of time; the importance of personal space and meritocracy). A ranking of countries according to a number of these variables is presented by Parker (1998, p. 172) so it is partially feasible for companies entering new countries or regions to prepare to deal with these issues and to avoid costly problems and failures. In the context of the apparel industry it may be significant for Western manufacturers utilising offshore facilities in Asia that Kwan (1996) found that even Hong Kong-based companies utilising production facilities in China discovered that cultural problems were surprisingly severe.

(xiii)   Quick response and offshore production

In Chapter 7, potential survival strategies were reviewed and the concept of 'quick response' was introduced. At first sight it might appear that the concepts of quick response and offshore (i.e. distant) production are mutually exclusive. However, it is important to note that the benefits to be derived from a quick response system achieved through integrated supply chain management do not entirely depend on the reduction of physical distribution costs, i.e. the achievement of a quick response result does not rest entirely upon quick physical transportation of product. Therefore, while it is true (as was seen in section x) that global supply chains are usually longer and more complex than domestic ones, they do not necessarily invalidate the benefits of quick response. Companies and countries have made great strides in reducing the wastes in global systems so that (Levy, 1996) lean production may still be feasible within internationally dispersed systems. Many low cost locations are relatively near to the UK market, for example.

C. *The future development of offshore production and the role of buying offices*

(i)   *The extent of offshore production*

It has been argued above that the increased use of offshore production by the UK apparel industry is inevitable. This conclusion is based upon analysis of the extent and persistence of the labour cost gap (Chapter 4); an assessment of the probability that the labour cost content within total production costs will fall; and a series of announcements in the trade press concerning the increased use of offshore sources by major UK companies. For example, Coats Viyella announced in the year 2000 that they were moving production overseas and were advertising for staff willing to move to Sri Lanka while Tait (2000) reported that since 1979 'CV and Courtaulds have both eliminated more than 10,000 positions each, and Dewhirst more than 2000 because of overseas sourcing policies . . . All have increased their capacity abroad (in Morocco, Sri Lanka, Indonesia, China etc.) and, it has been said, now employ more abroad than they do in the UK'. Marks & Spencer announced (Tait, 2000, p. 20) that it would be sourcing 70% of all its apparel from lower cost countries by 2002.

There is no neat statistical source, however, which indicates the use of offshore production by UK apparel manufacturers but there are data on one specific form of offshore production known as Outward Processed Trade (OPT). This is a special form of offshore production which allows EU garment manufacturers to export fabric to low labour cost locations so that the assembly process can be carried out at low cost. Garments can be re-imported back into the EU at reduced duty payable only on the 'value added' component. In Europe OPT regulations can (Zhou, 1997) be traced back to the 1970s but were not formally rationalised until 1982. OPT is largely limited by quantitative restrictions and a regime of prior authorisation. In the case of some Eastern Bloc countries, securing prior authorisation ensures duty-free entry into the EU. In 1994 these special arrangements were made available to the Czech Republic, Hungary, Poland, Romania, the Slovakian Republic and Bulgaria. Therefore, the proposed enlargement of the EU to include a number of these low cost producers will not have a significant impact on imports from these areas. The fabric should be EU-sourced and companies should also produce similar items within the EU.

Table 8.5 The growth of OPT in the UK 1991–1999.

Year	Quantity (pieces)
1991	608,539
1992	1,569,568
1993	5,417,145
1994	11,509,370
1995	13,975,862
1999	215,595,000

Source: DTI Import Licensing Branch.
Notes: (1) These figures are the maximum totals available.
(2) The author could not agree the 1999 figure with staff at the DTI who insisted the total was 77 million, not 215 million (see Table 8.6).
(3) OPT use in 2005 is limited to a few countries in which quotas remain. Therefore this table cannot be updated due to disclosure risks.

It is generally accepted (Anson, 1996) that the biggest users of OPT arrangements have been Germany and the Netherlands, e.g. Scheffer estimated that German OPT activity accounted for 56% of all OPT imports into the EU in 1995. In 1988 (Zhou, 1997) it was estimated that OPT accounted for about 17% of the volume and 24% of the value of EU apparel imports. In 1995 (Anson, 1996) it was calculated that EU imports from OPT activities in Eastern Europe rose from 65,000 tons in 1990 to 180,500 tons in 1995 so as to represent some 70% of all EU apparel imports from that region. In 1996 it was estimated (OETH, 1997) that OPT activity accounted for 9.3% of all EU clothing exports – ranging from 20% in Germany to 2.4% in the UK. In the case of the UK the first OPT quotas were opened as late as 1990 but no prior authorisations were issued until 1991 (see Table 8.5).

The relatively late introduction of OPT arrangements into the strategies of UK-based apparel manufacturers reflects the evolution of policy towards the industry in the UK which is reviewed in Chapter 5. Specifically, it most probably was a product of the relatively low level of labour costs in the UK and the policy of relying on the support of a number of larger retailers to purchase domestically produced products.

The figures in Table 8.6 confirm the growth of these arrangements in a spectacular fashion. If 1991 is taken as a base year the 1999 figure represents an increase by a factor of 354 in just eight years! In addition, the use of OPT by UK companies grew to span the whole range of garments whereas, in 1991, 70% was accounted for by trousers. In 1999 the major UK OPT locations were Belarus (15%); Bosnia-Herzegovina/Croatia (21%); China (9%); Pakistan (7%); India and Sri Lanka (5%) and the Ukraine (23%) (see Table 8.6). OPT-produced garments show up as imports in the UK trade statistics. If they are subsequently

Table 8.6   OPT locations 1999.

Year	Quantity (pieces)
Belarus	33,332,000
Boznia-Heregovina/Croatia	44,141,000
China	18,811,000
India	9,561,000
Indonesia	2,515,000
Macao	959,000
Malaysia	1,270,000
Pakistan	15,340,000
Philippines	1,064,000
Singapore	695,000
Sri Lanka	10,188,000
Thailand	2,158,000
Ukraine	50,138,000
Vietnam	11,504,000
Yugoslavia	13,919,000
Total	215,595,000

Source: As Table 8.5.

sold outside the UK they are treated as exports in the normal way and appear in the export figures. This is also true of the USA (Taplin, 1995). Therefore, while OPT use may reduce UK employment it can also influence favourably the share of world markets taken by UK-based producers (see Chapter 7).

To the extent that OPT activity increases it most probably represents replacement of domestic activity. As IFM (2004, p. 42) concluded, the development of OPT has 'not avoided the drastic restructuring . . . in countries that had already shifted to OPT . . .'. If domestic producers move an activities offshore the need for OPT obviously disappears – which may explain its decline after 2001 in the UK. In the USA practices similar to OPT are carried out under the so-called 9802 system (Dickerson, 1995, p. 170) which, although not limited to the Caribbean region, is heavily concentrated in that area.

(ii)   The role of buying offices

As the trend towards sourcing products offshore gathers pace, the role of the offshore buying office in co-ordinating and managing the activities of the increasingly global supply chain will be enhanced. Humphrey (1996) defines the role of a buying office as being to 'liaise with the manufacturer on the importing company's behalf and [to be] responsible for ensuring that the goods meet the quality specifications, delivery dates and prices agreed in the contract'. Clearly the offshore buying office has to fit within the overall configuration of the textiles–apparel supply chain structure and it is by no means certain that their role will remain limited to that specified in the quotation above. The functions carried out by the offshore buying office could expand to include vendor selection, fabric sourcing, quality control and monitoring of ethical manufacturing standards and logistics management, for example. Locke (1996) considers buying offices to represent an excellent solution to the difficulties introduced by distance, culture, currency fluctuations and geographic distance (see Chapter 12 for further discussion of this issue).

(iii)   The strategic role of offshore production

The historical impetus to the utilisation of offshore production has normally been the desire to obtain low cost labour. A more modern approach would be to accept Samli's (1998, p. 185) argument that 'global sourcing is likely to become a major part of the strategic plan' as opposed to representing opportunistic sourcing to produce short-term cost savings. In the words of Walwyn (1995, p. 3), sourcing then becomes 'a vital element in a product supply strategy that will respond to the demand for value. The extent to which sourcing is used and the locations chosen will reflect product type, price level and volume to allow for a fully competitive performance' so that the idea that sourcing is simply used to lower cost is progressively abandoned in favour of recognising its strategic and dynamic role in creating consumers and price points which can be achieved.

The decision to adopt a global sourcing perspective will also influence the sorts of problems a company encounters with exchange rate and trade barriers issues. In Walwyn's (1995, p. 6) words it is becoming increasingly clear that the 'real winners will be those who apply the principles and practices of fulfilling consumer demand on a global basis'. The issues raised by exchange rate fluctuations and trade barriers will be considered in the next chapter while those related to identifying consumers in the global marketplace will be covered in Chapter 11.

References

Adams, R. (2002) Retail Profit and Sweatshops: a Global Dilemma. *Journal of Retailing and Consumer Services*, **9**, 147–53.

Anson, R. (1993a) Why Global Sourcing May Be the Only Way Forward. *Manufacturing Clothier*, **74**, 13–14.

Anson, R. (1993b) Outward Processing: The Future for UK Clothing? *Manufacturing Clothier*, **75**, 12–13.

Anson, R. (2006) Gearing Globally. *Knitting International*, September 2006, 8–10.

Auger, P. (2003) What Will Consumers Pay for Social Product-features? *Journal of Business Ethics*, **42**, 281–304.

Basu, K. & Van, P.H. (1998) The Economics of Child Labour. *American Economic Review*, **88**, 412–27.

Basu, K. (2000) The Intriguing Relationship Between Child Labour and the Minimum Wage. *Economic Journal*, **110**, 50–62.

Blyth, R. (1996) Sourcing Clothing Production. In: *Restructuring in a Labour Intensive Industry* (Eds I. Taplin & J. Winterton), pp. 112–42. Avebury, Aldershot.

Bootle, R. (2004) Is inflation dead? *Sunday Telegraph*, 29.2.04.

Bowersox, D.J. (1996) *Logistics Management – The Integrated Supply Chain Process*. McGraw Hill, London.

B.S.I. (1987) *Handbook of Quality Assurance* (3rd Revision), London.

Carrigan, M. & Attalla, A. (2001) The Myth of the Ethical Consumer. *Journal of Consumer Marketing*, **18.7**, 560–77.

Casson, M. (1997) *Information and Organisation: a New Perspective on the Theory*. Clarendon Press, Oxford.

Chen, Z. (2005) Quality Management in International Clothing Supply Chains. Unpublished PhD, Manchester, MMU.

Clautier, D. (1993) Garment Sourcing Options for EC Markets. *Textile Outlook International*, **47**, 91–120.

Cooper, J. (1994) *Logistics and Distribution Planning*. Kogan Page, London.

Cran, A. & Malten, D. (2003) *Business Ethics: A European Perspective*. OUP, Oxford.

Creyer, E. & Ross, W. (1997) The Influence of Firm Behaviour on Purchase Intentions. *Journal of Consumer Marketing*, **14**, 421–33.

Dessy, S. & Callage, S. (2005) A Theory of the Worst Forms of Child Labour. *Economic Journal* as reported in Harrison, D. *Sunday Telegraph* 30.1.05, 8.

Dickerson, K. (1995) *Textiles and Apparel in the Global Economy*. Prentice Hall, New Jersey.

Dickson, M. (1999) U.S. Consumers' Knowledge and Concern with Apparel Sweatshops. *Journal of Fashion Marketing and Management*, **3**, 44–55.

Dunning, J. (1988) *Explaining International Production*. Unwin Hyman, London.

Edwards, A. (1984) *How To Make Offshore Manufacturing Pay*. EUI, London.

Eenennaam, E.V. & Brouthers, K.D. (1996) Global Relocation – High Hopes and Big Risks. *Long Range Planning*, **1**, 84–94.

Elliott, J. & Emmanuel, C. (2000) International Transfer Pricing. *European Management Journal*, **18**, 216–21.

Evans-Pritchard, A. & Sparrow, A. (2001) Britain leads E.U. – in red-tape stakes. *Daily Telegraph*, 20.11.01.

Flaherty, M. (1996) *Global Operations Management*. McGraw Hill, New York.

Frankel, J. & Romer, D. (1999) Does Trade Cause Growth? *American Economic Review*, **89**, 379–400.

Garvin, D.A. (1988) *Managing Quality: The Strategic and Competitive Edge*. Free Press, New York.

Gribben, R. (2004) Companies brace for red-tape day. *Daily Telegraph*, 30.10.04.

Hergeth, H. (2000) *Invisible Costs of Offshore Production*. Proceedings of Annual Conference. Textile Institute, Manchester.

Hofstede, G. (1984) *Culture's Consequences*. Sage, San Francisco.

Humphrey, A. (1996) *International Trade Procedures for the Clothing and Textiles Industry: A guide to procedures and documentation involved in importing, exporting and offshore production*. MMU Press, Manchester.

Hunter, A. (1990) *Quick Response in the Apparel Industry*. Textile Institute, Manchester.

IFM (2004) *Implications of the 2005 Trade Liberalisation in the Textiles and Clothing Sector*. Institut Français de la Mode, Paris.

Iyer, G. & Kalita, J. (1997) The Impact of Country of Origin and Country of Manufacture on Consumer Perception of Quality and Value. *Journal of Global Marketing*, **11**, 17–29.

Jacobson, R. & Aacker, D. (1987) The Strategic Role of Product Quality. *Journal of Marketing*, **51**, 31–44.

Jaffe, E. & Nebenzahl, I. (1989) Global Promotion of Country Image. In: *Dynamics of International Business* (Ed. R. Luostarinen), pp. 358–85. European International Business Association, Helsinki.

Jarnow, J. & Dickerson, K. (1997) *Inside the Fashion Business*. Prentice Hall, New York.

Johansson, J. & Nebenzahl, I. (1986) Multinational Production: Effect on Brand Value. *Journal of International Business*, **17**, 101–26.

Jones, R.M. (2003) Hidden Costs – Only Surface Deep? *Journal of Fashion Marketing and Management*, **7.1**, 7–11.

Knight, G. (1999) Consumer Preference for Foreign and Domestic Products. *Journal of Consumer Marketing*, **16**, 151–63.

Kotabe, M. (1992) *Global Sourcing Strategies*. Quarum Books, New York.

Kurt Salmon Associates (1999) *Sorting Your Sourcing*. KSA, Manchester.

Kurt Salmon Associates (2005) *Global Sourcing Reference* (7th edn). KSA, Manchester.

Kwan, C. (1996) The Use of Offshore Production by the HK Clothing Industry. *Journal of Fashion Marketing and Management*, **1**, 71–83.

Kwok, J. & Jones, R.M. (1998) High Kicking Chorus Line. *Journal of Fashion Marketing and Management*, **2**, 177–94.

Lea-Greenwood, G. & Morton, V. (1999) Ethical Sourcing – 2. *Journal of Fashion Marketing and Management*, **3**, 96–8.

Lee, E. (1997) Globalisation and Labour Standards. *International Labour Review*, **136**, 173–90.

Levy, D. (1996) Lean Production in an International Supply Chain. *Sloan Management Review*, **38**, 94–103.

Lim, K. & O'Cass, A. (2001) Consumer Brand Classifications: an Assessment of Culture-of-origin vs Country-of-origin. *Journal of Product and Brand Management*, **10.2**, 120–36.

Locke, R. (1996) *Global Supply Chain Management*. Irwin, London.

Lumpkin, J., Crawford, J. & Kim, G. (1985) Perceived Risk as Factor in Buying Foreign Clothes. *International Journal of Advertising*, **4**, 157–71.

McCrae, H. (2002) Mobiles build up a head of steam. *Independent on Sunday*, 5.5.02.

Min Han & Terpstra, V. (1988) Country of Origin in Effects. *Journal of International Business Studies*, **5**, 68–74.

Moore, L. (1999) *Britain's Trade and Economic Structure: The Impact of the EU*. Routledge, London.

Newberry, M. (1993) A Balanced Sourcing Strategy for the UK Market. *Textile Outlook International*, **49**, 105–21.

OETH (1997) *The EU Textile and Clothing Sector*. OETH, Brussels.

Ouchi, W.G. (1981) *Theory Z*. Addison-Wesley, London.

Pappas, J.L. & Hirschley, M. (1993) *Managerial Economics*. Dryden Press, London.

Parker, B. (1998) *Globalisation and Business Practice*. Sage Publications, London.

Pitta, D.A. (1999) Ethical Issues Across Cultures. *Journal of Consumer Marketing*, **16**, 240–57.

Popp, A., Ruckman, J.-Y. & Rowe, H. (2000) Quality in International Clothing Supply Chains. *Journal of Fashion Marketing and Management*, **4**, 140–62.

Porter, M. (1998) *The Competitive Advantage of Nations*. Free Press, New York.

Ross, A. (1997) *No Sweat Fashion*. Verso, London.

Samli, A.C., Browning, J.M. & Busbia, C. (1998) The Status of Global Sourcing as a Critical Tool of Strategic Planning. *Journal of Business Research*, **43**, 177–82.

Seaton, F.B. & Laskey, H.A. (1999) Effects of Production Location on Perceived Automobile Values. *Journal of Global Marketing*, **13**, 71–87.

Shaw, D. & Tomalilo, D. (2004) *Understanding the Ethical Issues in Fashion*. In: *International Retail Marketing* (Ed. M. Bruce). Butterworth-Heinemann, Oxford.

Stern, S. (2005) Lend an ear to your customers. *Daily Telegraph*, 3.2.05.

Tait, N. (2000) M & S Shifts Supplier Base. *Bobbin*, **41**, 20–26.

Taplin, I. (1995) Changes in Buyer Supplier Relationships – Evidence from the USA. *Journal of Clothing Technology and Management*, **12**, 1–19.

Taplin, I. (1996) Introduction. In: *Restructuring in a Labour Intensive Industry* (Eds I. Taplin & J. Winterton), pp. 1–8. Avebury, Aldershot.

Trompenaars, A. (1994) *Riding the Wave of Culture*. Irwin, Burr Ridge, Illinois.

Tyler, R. (2005) Shoppers push 'do goody' issues down priority list. *Daily Telegraph*, 27.1.05.

Usunier, J.-C. (1993) *International Marketing – A Cultural Approach*. Prentice Hall, New York.

Verschoor, C. (1998) The Link between a Corporation's Financial Performance and its Commitment to Ethics. *Journal of Business Ethics*, **17**, 1509–16.

Walwyn, S. (1995) A Vision of Sourcing. *Journal of Clothing Technology and Management* (*Special Edition*).

Walwyn, S. (1997) A Vision of Sourcing for a Global Market. *Journal of Fashion Marketing and Management*, **1**, 251–59.

Winterton, R.W. & Barlow, A. (1996) Economic Restructuring of UK Clothing. In: *Restructuring in a Labour Intensive Industry* (Eds I. Taplin & J. Winterton), pp. 25–61. Avebury, Aldershot.

Wong, E. & Taylor, G. (2000) An Investigation of Ethical Sourcing Practices: Levi Strauss & Co. *Journal of Fashion Marketing and Management*, **4**, 71–9.

Wong, V. (1988) The Quality of British Marketing. *Journal of Marketing Research*, **12**, 60–67.

Zhou, Q. (1997) *The Development of Global Companies within the UK Clothing Industry*. Unpublished PhD thesis, Manchester.

Zolka, L., Downes, M. & Paul, K. (1997) Measuring Consumer Sensitivity to Corporate Social Performance. *Journal of Global Marketing*, **11**, 29–46.

Chapter 9

The Role of Trade Barriers and Exchange Rate Fluctuations in the Global Apparel Market

A. *Trade barriers and the Multi Fibre Arrangement*

(i) *Trade barriers – the historical picture*

Trade in textiles and clothing has been constrained or managed by a variety of restrictive devices for many years. Summaries of earlier arrangements can be found in Khanna (1991), Dickerson (1995) and Moore (1999), but after 1974 the main regulatory framework was the Multi Fibre Arrangement or MFA. This derogation from the normal rules governing world trade established a complex system of quotas which restricted the growth of exports from a selected number of low cost producers into the developed markets. The theoretical effects of a quota are illustrated in Fig. 9.1 and discussed later in this chapter. The domestic demand and supply curves are Dd and Sd. In a free market supply is represented by the horizontal line PW WP. Price is PW and supply reaches from O to Qd (8 units). Domestic output is from O to Qs (2 units). Therefore imports must be OQd minus OQs or 6 units. If a quota restraint of 4 units is introduced (shown as the space between Qs and Qs*) then the new supply curve is shown by ACNSq. Price rises to PQ and the protected domestic industry increases output to Q^1s (3 units). The total market shrinks to the distance between O and Q^1d (7 units) of which 4 are supplied by imports. The most important impact on UK trade statistics would be to restrain the increase in UK imports from the MFA suppliers. However, to the extent that the MFA enhanced the ability of domestic producers to survive, there would be a protective effect upon continued production and employment in the UK.

On a global scale the main effects of the quota system on the observed trade pattern would be to slow down the total volume of trade flowing from those countries covered by quota arrangements; to divert trade towards countries with a favoured status, e.g. Turkey; to freeze trade patterns within existing patterns as indicated by quota availability; and to impose costs upon consumers in the importing countries.

In the following discussion it will be assumed that the statement that free trade is preferable to restricted trade is accepted. The theoretical case for the advantages of free trade is rehearsed in many texts such as Begg (1991, pp. 587–590). A brief summary of the case is contained in Begg's Figure 7.4 and is reflected, for example, in the conclusion drawn by Frankel (1999) that 'trade has a quantitatively large and positive effect on income'. Therefore, from this global standpoint it can be stated that the imposition of the MFA had to be regarded as a retrograde step and its removal as a positive step. It is, of course, quite compatible with this viewpoint that individual groups of people in specific industries and locations could be damaged by free trade as patterns of competitive advantage shift over time – that, in effect, was the *raison d'être* of the MFA in the first place.

In addition to the existence of this complex system of quantitative trade controls the apparel sector is further protected by a relatively high tariff structure. A tariff is a tax on imports. Singleton (1997, p. 179) presents data for 1962–87 which show that tariffs on apparel in the EU were in 1987 double the average on all manufactured goods, having started at a point of equality in 1962. Dickerson (1995, p. 501) argues that tariffs on apparel in the USA were over five times greater than the average.

Given the demise of this system of managed trade in the year 2005 it is not felt appropriate in this context to embark upon a detailed description of the MFA itself. Readers wishing to obtain such details are referred to the following sources: Khanna (1991), Anson (1994) or Dickerson (1995).

In brief, the MFA was a quota-based system of trade control in which products were assigned category numbers and originally grouped into one of five groups – Group 1 products being the most sensitive. Initially the agreement was expected to last four years from 1974 to 1978 but was renewed several times until MFA IV emerged in 1986.

Each quota was assigned a growth rate and, until the formation of the Single European Market, imports covered by the MFA were shared between the EU member states under the so-called 'burden sharing' arrangement. The MFA could be modified during its life to take account of unanticipated disruptive trade movements by a variety of instruments such as the 'basket extractor mechanism'. The introduction of the MFA meant that (Khanna, 1991, p. 21) the 'liberal and non-discriminatory rules of international trade enshrined in the GATT were never applied to the field of textiles and apparel'.

The main focus of attention at the present time must be the identification of the threats and opportunities posed by the re-integration of textiles and apparel trade into the liberal and non-discriminatory system of rules governing world trade as enshrined in the GATT/WTO. The start of this process was signalled by the emergence of the Agreement on Textiles and Clothing (ATC) from the Uruguay Round of GATT negotiations concluded at the end of 1993.

(ii)   The level of protection provided by the MFA

The existence of the MFA has generated a great deal of passionate debate over the years. Opponents have, in particular, been keen to condemn the arrangement which was described by Khanna (1991, p. 24) as 'designed to manage trade to the advantage of countries that were fast losing international competitiveness . . .'.

It is, therefore, a little surprising that the amount and quality of evidence which measures objectively how protective it actually was is somewhat limited. An effectively protected product can be defined as one which could not be sup-plied by non-domestic sources at a time when growth in domestic demand was outstripping the capability of the domestic industry to meet that demand and when non-domestic production was available. In this case import penetration would not rise despite the existence of excess demand and prices would rise relatively sharply. As Moore (1999, p. 267) expresses it, quotas 'are only effective in so far as they reduce imports below the level they would be in their absence. Clearly this is somewhat difficult to ascertain'.

The majority of tests of the effectiveness of the MFA and/or the level of protection present in the UK or globally have not been cast in these terms. The alleged impact of the MFA is usually demonstrated by statistics such as those reproduced in Table 9.1. MFA III is taken as evidence of a protective effect. The level of protection within individual countries is often measured by data such as the level of imports per head of the population or in proportion to national income (Anson, 1994). Prior to the formation of the Single European Market it was possible to compare the share of imports taken by each member state with the share indicated by the so-called 'burden sharing formula' (Anson, 1994). On all these measures, the UK appears to have been relatively well protected.

Table 9.1   The MFA and levels of protection.

A.	EEC (12) Imports from (as %):	1973	1981	1986
	Developed countries	35.3	27.6	27.8
	Developing countries	49.6	60.4	58.5
B.	Average import penetration (%) from developing countries			
	MFA I	34.9		
	MFA II	36.4		

Source: based on R. Anson and P. Simpson, (1988) *World Textile Trade and Production Trends* (EIU Special Report, No. 118).

However, on the basis of the test of a protected product outlined above, rather a different picture emerges in that in the period 1973–82 (roughly the life cycle of the first two MFAs) import penetration of the UK market rose from 11% to 35% (ONS, 1994, p. 231) during which period apparel consumption in real terms (at 1980 prices) rose by 23% but UK output (see Table 2.1) rose only very slowly. Moore (1999, p. 269) observes that, in the period 1978 to 1988, 'in spite of restriction by MFA quotas import penetration in the clothing industry rose from 25% in 1978 to 39% in 1988' and it has continued to rise ever since. Between 1975 and 1983 imports of apparel to the UK (in real terms) rose by 105% while consumption rose by 40%. It was shown in Chapter 5 that import penetration has now reached 92%.

On the other side of the argument it can be demonstrated that the number of products and suppliers subject to restraint did rise over time and that (Dickerson, 1995, p. 349) 'The impact of quota control can also be seen in individual cases such as the 25% reduction of USA imports of newly restrained fibres between 1986–1988'.

Estimates of the proportion of trade under restraint vary greatly but Dickerson (1995, p. 347) estimates that, in 1994, 65% of USA textile and apparel imports were covered by restraints and that, globally, 35% of apparel trade was free of restraint, while only 40% was covered by the MFA. Evans (1995) reported that the MFA covered some 35% of world trade in apparel. Secondly, and linked to this fact, there have always been a number of major suppliers not subject to restraint so that in practice one of the major effects of the MFA has been trade diversion rather than trade destruction. Therefore, while the MFA did restrict imports from the controlled countries, there were so many other sources of cheap imports that trade supply increased from those sources so that the overall level of import penetration was able to rise. Khanna (1994, p. 22) confirms that EU imports from the preferential countries showed 'sharp increase under MFA III, e.g. Turkey, Morocco, Tunisia, Egypt, Malta and Cyprus'.

It is significant that Wolf (1984), while being mainly concerned to stress the costs of protection and confirming that the MFA did 'appear to achieve what is intended, namely a curb on the growth of imports from restricted suppliers', pointed out that growth rates into the EU (1976–81) were much higher for the smaller countries and that this allowed developing countries as a whole to increase their share of both EU and USA markets. Wolf's conclusion was (1984, p. 194) that 'purchases are likely to be diverted towards the most competitive unrestricted producer'.

Moore (1999, p. 269) argues that trade diversion is indicated by the fall in Hong Kong's share of the UK market and the associated rise in the proportion taken by other less developed countries from 21% to 29% over the same period (1974–1987).

In conclusion, therefore, the most likely explanation of the apparent paradox is that a substantial proportion of trade remained unrestricted, which mitigated the impact of the MFA and allowed penetration of the so-called protected markets to rise substantially. Spinanger (1996) shows that the proportion of developed country imports emanating from 'new' suppliers rose sharply over time, which could support the above hypotheses. In so far as trade was diverted to the second best suppliers, this production was relatively costly, so that the existence of costs of protection was not necessarily incompatible with the existence of rather mild levels of protection. This issue will be considered in the next section.

(iii)   The costs of protection

If it is accepted that free trade generates the maximum global benefit then it follows that restrictions upon trade must represent a sub-optimal situation, i.e. all forms of protection involve costs as well as benefits. These costs normally fall upon the consumer and can be demonstrated by reference to Fig. 9.1.

The basic concept involved in any calculation of the cost of protection is that of consumer surplus. This is defined as the difference between what the consumer actually pays to consume a given volume of a product and what they would have paid if they had been charged a different price for each unit. This is represented by the area beneath the demand curve or the area ZGJ in Fig. 9.1. This falls to ZFL with the quota. The loss is, therefore, LFGJ. Some of this lost surplus is captured by producers or the Government and some of it is simply dissipated by the inefficiencies introduced by protection. The former is usually called the cost of protection while the latter is known as the 'dead weight loss' of protection. In Fig. 9.1 the cost to consumers is represented by LFHJ. EFHI is transferred as quota rent to producers or agents while ECJL represents extra revenue to producers from higher prices and revenue to domestic producers. This, it will be clear, leaves the two areas ECI and FGH which have simply evaporated into thin air. These represent the 'dead weight loss', i.e. a loss to the global economy introduced by inefficiency. The former represents the relative inefficiency of the (increased) local production under protection while the latter represents loss of consumer surplus brought about by the fall in consumption from Qd to Q^1d. On the other side of the coin it can be seen that the domestic industry has expanded from Qs to Q^1s under the protection offered by the quota.

The output generated by the local industry also rises from OQs × PW to OQ^1s × PQ. The gain is shown by LECJ some of which obviously represents wages earned by workers whose jobs would have been lost in the absence of protection. Therefore, the gain to the labour force from the protection is some proportion of LECJ. Given that the whole of LECJ is much smaller than the costs of

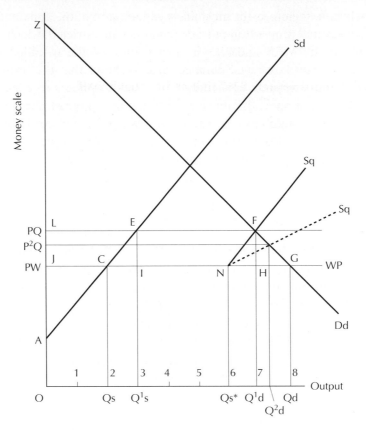

Fig. 9.1   The impact of a quota.

protection represented by LFHJ it is easy to see why opposition to trade restrictions grows. Theoretically LECJ could only equal LFHJ if Sd and Dd were *extremely* inelastic. The estimates of the size of these benefits relative to the costs will be considered below.

A large number of calculations have been made of the cost to the consumer consequent upon the protection of the textile and clothing sectors in, for example, Sweden, UK, USA and notably, Canada. These studies are summarised in Dickerson (1995) and Wolf (1984). Somewhat surprisingly there have been far fewer detailed estimates of the actual level of protection afforded to the sectors, although clearly there is an implication that the two things are positively related, i.e. a high level of effective protection must, by definition, lead to more cost than a low one. Unfortunately, in this case there does seem to be a mismatch between estimates (such as they are) of the degree of protection and the estimate of the costs of protection which have been given great prominence in the battle to remove the MFA.

The results of the estimates of the costs of protection are summarised in Table 9.2. In addition, Singleton (1997, p. 179) quotes a global figure for both

Table 9.2 The costs of protection – the apparel sector.

Costs of protection		
Country	Year	Cost ($ million)
USA	1984	8,500–12,000
USA	1984	18,000
USA	1984	13,000
Canada	1984	923–1,462
Australia	1980	235*
EU	1997	12 billion Ecu

Dead weight loss		
Country	Year	Cost ($ million)
Canada	1979	92
Canada	1984	73–356
EU	1980	1,409
USA	1980	1,509

Source: Dickerson, K. (1995), Tables 14.3 and 14.4.
Notes: (1) * In dollars per household.
(2) Dead weight loss is defined above as the loss of consumer surplus brought about by inefficient production plus the reduction in overall consumption.
(3) EU 1997 in IFM (2004).

textiles and clothing of $15 billion. In the case of the UK, Silberston (1984) put the cost to consumers at some £500 million and in a later study (Silberston, 1989) estimated that the MFA had added 5% to UK apparel prices. Trela (1990) argued that the global gain from the elimination of restraints would be $23 billion.

One of the best known studies was that by Jenkins (1982) for Canada. The total loss to the Canadian consumer was estimated to be $107.5 million, of which 38% was due to the existence of quotas; 43% to inefficient use of resources and 19% due to the enforced reduction of consumption following the effect of price increases generated by the protective devices.

As has been seen from Fig. 9.1 there will also be some 'winners' in that some jobs were saved – as has been stated above some proportion of the area LECJ represents wages paid to employees who would otherwise most probably have lost their jobs. Unfortunately, the number of employees in the sector in most developed countries was by the mid to late 1980s very small relative to the number of consumers, so it was very difficult to envisage circumstances in which their gain (part of LECJ) could go anywhere near matching the loss to consumer represented by LFHJ. The result is that all the studies of the costs and benefits of protection concluded that the former substantially outweighed the latter. Cable

(1982, p. 235), for example, quotes an estimate for the late 1970s of dead weight losses of seven times the benefits, concluding that the gain from the removal of restrictions far exceeds 'any plausible estimate of the employment costs'. Jenkins (1982), in his study of the Canadian economy, estimated that the gain to domestic producers from protection was approximately $267 million or roughly half the cost to consumers.

In an attempt to calculate both the dynamic and macro-economic impacts of protection of textiles in the UK, Cable (1982) used the Cambridge Growth Model to simulate the impact of restraints. The results did not support the protective argument and that although 'the assumptions made (in the model) are somewhat favourable to a protectionist outcome . . . it is . . . all the more significant that the textiles case gives a generally negative result.'

It was also shown that the tariff equivalent level of protection required simply to hold the degree of import penetration at a steady level in the case of apparel in the UK in 1990 would have been extremely high at 55%. This is twice as high as the estimated (Evans, 1995) level of MFA quotas and provides further support to the contention made above that the actual overall level of protection afforded to the sector was, in fact, rather low. There is, therefore, a second paradox to be resolved: why should the estimates of the cost of the MFA be so high and so aggressively promoted if the actual protective impact on trade flows and prices was, as has been suggested above, rather weak?

A number of explanations may be put forward to reconcile this apparent conflict. First, it has to be recalled that the proportion of trade under MFA restriction has generally been relatively low – many unrestricted, low cost suppliers to the EU could be located such as Bangladesh, for example. The effect of the existence of uncontrolled low cost producers on the outcome can be illustrated inserting a new supply curve Sq^2 in Fig. 9.1. This represents the behaviour of preferential suppliers: their existence has the effect of increasing the elasticity of the supply curve and mitigating the price increase caused by quota controls so that prices rise only to P^2Q rather than to PQ. The market now only shrinks to Q^2d, not to Q^1d. Gereffi (1999, p. 51) argues that the most important factor shaping the pattern (not the volume) of apparel imports into the USA was the MFA and concluded that although 'the clear intent . . . was to protect developed country firms from a flood of low cost imports . . . the result was exactly the opposite' because suppliers were forced to upgrade and buyers forced to find new sources.

In the free trade situation the total market was 8 of which imports supplied 6 and domestic producers 2. In the quota-controlled situation imports fell to 4 and domestic output rose to 3. However, if preferred, low-cost suppliers exist then imports under control stay at 4, domestic production rises (less) to 2.5 and the preferred sources supply 0.5. The loss to the consumer is much reduced as prices rise less and consumption falls less than under the previous scenario.

Second, the methodology whereby the cost estimates were reached could be suspect. While it is always true that the inability of economists to conduct controlled experiments raises difficulties in conducting statistical tests, it seems, to the present author, that in the particular context under discussion this is not a major issue. The studies used a variety of standard econometric devices and often employed quite sophisticated economic models. It is true that if, for example, estimates of demand and supply elasticities were changed this produced rather large swings in the cost estimates. It has to be accepted that the cost figures were produced by extremely thorough and respected methodologies. Therefore, the main explanation for the apparent paradox probably lies in the actual size of the cost estimates relative to the absolute size of the economies involved, e.g. in the case of the UK (in the mid-1980s) the Silberston figure represented some 0.17% of GDP and 0.25% of total consumer expenditure.

In the final analysis, the argument that the costs of protection were unjustifiable carried the day. In De La Torre's (1986, p. 220) words, 'the job preservation strategy proved to be extremely costly and ineffective in maintaining employment'.

The political will to maintain the MFA was slowly eroded. In particular, a survey of the literature suggests that the EU's view gradually swung from the protective to the liberal. Khanna (1991, p. 128) described the EU's position in 1981 prior to MFA III 'as the most protectionist of all' but by 1986 he described their stance as 'liberal'. The lack of political support for the sector is not surprising given the increasingly marginal contribution it makes to the economy, as outlined in Chapter 1. Moore (1999, p. 217) contrasts the view taken on the cost of the MFA with that taken on the Common Agricultural Policy in the EU which is estimated to cost £134 per person per year in the UK (roughly £6 billion per year) despite which 'consumer pressure groups do not appear to have exerted much influence; the population at large seems scarcely aware of how high food prices are compared with international prices'.

In the case of the USA also, Khanna (1994) pointed out that the textile lobby weakened significantly in its political impact between 1986 and 1994. In addition, the developed countries producers were increasingly turning (other than in the UK) to the exploitation of offshore production as a method of regaining some competitive advantage so that the existence of quotas became seen as more of a hindrance than a benefit. In Anson's (1992, p. 13) words:

'a few firms in the West are glad to see the back of MFA. And even some of its supporters now question its value . . . at a time when technology needs to grab all the opportunities it can for keeping costs under control . . . [another] argument against retention [of the MFA] has emerged as the industry has become more international. To maximise their competitiveness, more and more companies in the UK are chasing an optimal mix of own manufacturing and buying in . . . MFA quotas can get in the way . . .'

As late as 1986, De La Torre (1986, p. 136) could write that the official EC view was that 'a return to free trade . . . remains a very unlikely eventuality' and yet, for the reasons explained above, by the start of the Uruguay Round in 1986 this item was at the top of the agenda.

(iv)   The phase-out arrangements

The Uruguay Round was eventually concluded in Geneva on 15 December 1993. The Final Act of the Round (ATC, 1995) was signed in May 1995. The Agreement (of December) sets out (GATT, 1994) 'provisions to be applied by members during a transition period for the integration of the textiles and clothing sector into the GATT 1994' (Article 1, para 1).

This is a logical result of the Punta Del Este agreement that 'negotiations in the area of textiles and clothing shall aim to formulate modalities that would permit the eventual integration of this sector into GATT'.

The Agreement sets out the steps by which the MFA is to be phased out, thus re-integrating textiles and clothing into the GATT system over a period of ten years. The system of bilateral quota control of trade flows will be terminated. In addition, textile exporting countries are required to reduce their own barriers to imports from other countries. As soon as the Agreement was ratified each signatory:

> 'shall integrate into GATT 1994 16% of the total volume of imports in 1990 of products with Annex (which defines the products covered by the Agreement) in terms of HS (Harmonised Commodity Description and Coding System) lines or categories' (Article 2, para 6).

The text of the Agreement does not specify which products must be freed from quota control in this way, implying that each country can select which products to free provided that, in total, the categories selected total at least 16% of the volume of imports in 1990.

The rest of the products have to be integrated into GATT (i.e. have quotas removed) in three further stages:

(1)   on the first day of the 37th month that the Agreement is in effect 'products which, in 1990, accounted for not less than 17% of the total volume of 1990 imports' (Article 2, para 8A);

(2)   on the first day of the 85th month that this Agreement is in effect, products which, in 1990 'accounted for not less than 18% of the total volume of 1990 imports' (Article 2, para 8B);

(3)   on the first day of the 121st month 'the textiles and clothing sector shall stand integrated into GATT 1994, all restrictions . . . having been eliminated' (Article 2, para 8C), i.e. the last 49% will be removed from quota.

These percentages and timing are minimum requirements and the Agreement does allow an earlier removal of controls if countries desire this. It will be realised that the percentages given above through the above stages sum to 51% of volume of 1990 trade and that, by themselves, these removals from control cannot take us to the total elimination of controls – particularly as it is probable that the volume of trade has grown since 1990 in most cases. At each stage of the removal of restraints it is clear that some products (a declining number) remain under quota control. The base levels for these controls will be the levels obtained the day before the final signing of the Agreement (May 1995). During the first stage of quota removal (i.e. in the first 36 months):

> 'the level of each restriction (i.e. size of quota . . . in force for the twelve month period prior to its entry into force (i.e. prior to final agreement) shall be increased annually by not less than the growth rate established for their respective restrictions, increased by 16%' (Article 2, para 13).

Thus, if a remaining quota was, under the existing arrangements, due to rise by (say) 2% annually, it would now rise by 2.32% annually, i.e. 2% plus 16% of 2%. Finally, along the same lines a similar adjustment to growth rates will be made in stages 2 (37th to 84th month) and 3 (85th month to 120th month) in that annual growth rates of quota on those products remaining under quota control will be increased by 25% and 27% respectively. In our example, therefore, the (now) 2.32% would grow to 2.9% and 3.68 p.a. respectively.

Nordas (2004) estimates that, in the case of the EU, the accumulated quota growth over the ten years was 18% which could have rendered many non-binding. Khanna (2004) likewise argued that quotas often grew to a level where they ceased to be restrictive. Quotas remained binding on China.

It is further stated that flexibility provisions of 'swing, carry over and carry forward applicable to all qualitative restrictions in force . . . shall be the same as those provided for in bilateral agreements' prior to the final signing of the Agreement (Article 2, para 16).

The Agreement also makes provision for the termination of quantitative restrictions which may have been developed outside the MFA. Most countries using the MFA have examples of such restriction, e.g. UK and China. It is stated that:

> 'within sixty days following the entry into force of this Agreement, members maintained restrictions on textile and clothing (other than restrictions maintained under the MFA – whether consistent with GATT 94 or not, shall (a) notify them in detail to the Textiles Monitoring Body or (b) provide to the TAB notifications with respect to them which have been submitted to a . . . other Multilateral Trade Organisation' (Article 3, para 1).

All these restrictions must either be:

(1)   'brought into conformity with the GATT 94 within one year . . .' or
(2)   'phased out progressively according to a programme to be presented (within) six months' (Article 3, para 2).

The text of the Agreement then moves on to deal with items such as falsification of the country of origin which importing countries (such as the UK) have always considered to be a flaw in the MFA system. The Agreement states that:

'circumvention by trans-shipment, re-routing, false declaration concerning . . . place of origin . . . frustrates the implementation of this Agreement to integrate the textiles and clothing sector into the GATT 1994. Accordingly, members should establish the necessary level provisions . . . to address and take action against circumvention'. (Article 5, para 1)

If a mutually satisfactory solution cannot be found, the matter can then (para 2) be referred to the TAB for 'recommendations'. In Article 4, para 4, it states that if such actions can be proven, various steps can be taken against the guilty party, e.g. denial of market entry and introduction of restraints against all countries involved.

Article 6 deals with transitional safeguards (during the transition period) for importers, i.e. things which could be done during the phasing-out period 'to protect' sectors which are suffering severe problems as imports rise. This is covered in Article 6, para 2, by the statement that safeguard action may be taken if:

'it is demonstrated that a particular product into its territory in such increased quantities as to cause serious damage or actual threat there of, to the domestic industry producing . . . directly competitive products'.

It must be noted, however, that a member state would have to prove that the damage was caused only by the increased imports and not by other factors, such as technological change or changes in consumer preferences.

Finally, the vexed question of reciprocal access to the domestic markets of the exporting countries is dealt with in Article 7. The Agreement states that all members must take such action as is necessary to:

(1)   achieve improved access to markets for textile and clothing products;
(2)   ensure the application of policies relating to fair trade in textiles and clothing.

Many Western commentators believe the reciprocity clause is weak, and argue that it should have been specifically linked to the quota phase-out programme.

The final sentence of the text states that after the ten-year period, textiles and clothing will be integrated into GATT and that there 'shall be no extension'. It is clear then that plans must be made for a new trading environment free of quota restraints, i.e. strategies need to be reconsidered; even if it is agreed (as was suggested above) that the real level of protection was somewhat low, no one has argued that there was no protective effect. As Anson (1996, p. 6) stated, integration has a finality about it.

A note of dissent is voiced by Spinanger (1996, p. 91) who argued that because a large percentage of trade (49%) remained under quota until the very last day of the agreement 'there is a potential danger that this embodies the seeds of a new round of protectionism' although there does not seem to be any evidence to support this conclusion.

This is confirmed by Majumdar (1996, p. 35) who notes that 'once a product category has been integrated importing countries are not permitted to reintroduce quotas restricting imports of that product.'

Although it is true that tariffs remain relatively high, this would not seem to constitute a basis for any optimism that some form of protection will be reintroduced simply because, since 1974, this has been the rule. It is somewhat surprising, therefore, to find that Barton (2000) in a survey of practitioners found that there was a general feeling that 'something will be done' to replace the MFA. This confirmed the findings of an earlier survey by Jones (1997) which uncovered a similar situation in the north-west of England in that 31% of respondents had never heard of the MFA, while 92% had no specific plans in place to deal with the consequences of the re-integration process. It is recognised that both surveys were small, but the state of affairs revealed compared unfavourably with the responses obtained to similar enquiries in, for example, Hong Kong, as revealed by Moon (1999, p. 164) who found that most companies had anticipated the removed of the MFA in making future plans and concluded that the view of the Hong Kong industry was that:

> 'the demise of the MFA will, inevitably, change the current disposition of the global textile and clothing trade, which, in turn, provides opportunities and challenges for the MFA exporting members. There is little question that those clothing manufacturers striving for future success should re-examine their marketing approaches in order to fit in with the new trading arena.'

The remarkably flexible mindset of the Hong Kong industry is further revealed by Au (1999) in his review of the overseas investment policies of the Hong Kong industry over time which, he concludes, 'represents a *continual* pursuit for advantageous overseas locations both in terms of quota availability or market access and lower production costs.' Ignorance of the changing nature of the trading environment and/or faith that 'something will be done' hardly appears a responsible response by comparison.

While the phasing out of the MFA was the major change taking place in formal trade arrangements affecting apparel trade, it was not the only one. The EU had, for example, already signed agreements of association with most of the countries of Central and Eastern Europe in anticipation (EU, 1998) 'of their eventual accession to the EU. Textile quotas on imports from these countries are already high and will be *abolished completely in the next few years* so rarely present an obstacle to trade.'

Therefore, the entry of such countries into the EU did not pose a threat but did throw up some complex issues. These CEE countries (Czech Republic, Estonia, Hungary, Lithuania, Latvia, Poland, Slovenia, Slovakia, Bulgaria and Romania) all have large apparel industries with a share of manufacturing employment ranging from 3% to 24% against the EU average of 7.6% and employing around one million people. Somewhat paradoxically their entry into the EU at the time when the latter is liberalising trading arrangements for apparel produces a situation where (IFM, 2004, p. 367) 'they will suffer from liberalisation as their present preferential access to the EU will be eroded in comparison to Asia' with Poland and Hungary identified as being at the greatest risk.

The future nature of Turkey's relationship to the EU is clearly vital given the size and competitiveness of its apparel industry. There has been free access to the EU for imports from Turkey since 1996 via a customs union and in 2005 accession talks began although these are not expected to produce a conclusion in the immediate future.

The entire thrust of current EU textile policy is one of liberalisation. The *official* view (EU, 1998) is that this will not be the most important factor affecting the competitive position of the EU textile/apparel sector because it is estimated that only 30% of textile trade by value is affected by liberalisation policy. The present author would argue that this official view is not obviously shared by expert commentators such as Khanna (1994) or Majumdar (1996, p. 31) who argued that:

> 'the phase out will have a significant impact on the pattern of extra-EU trade and sourcing over the next nine years. It will also have major impact on the evolution of the EU's textile policy'.

The present author would also contend that – in so far as they were aware of the situation – this was not the view of UK industrialists, although he would accept that some of the surveys of opinion have been small. For example, Barton (2000) found that the removal of the MFA was felt to be the most important factor influencing future company strategy.

(v)   The phase-out process in the UK

The phase-out process is now complete and proceeded largely according to plan although most developed countries retained control over the most sensitive items until the very last minute. In the words of the WTO (1998, p. 23):

'the integration of clothing and textiles under the Agreement on Textiles and Clothing has continued with the second stage underway from 1 January 1998. In the first two stages a total of 33% of members' textiles and clothing imports was brought under GATT 1994 rules; where the integrated products were subject to quota these were removed. The third stage of the integrative process . . . reaching 51% of imports by volume, will begin on 1 January 2002. Growth rates of the remaining quotas have also been increased at the beginning of each of the first two stages.'

In Stage 1 of the phase-out the majority of the products freed from quota were non-sensitive items – see Fig. 9.2. In Stage 2 the UK phased out quotas on 23 categories of which eight were under restraint and most were in the non-sensitive groups – see Fig. 9.3. Therefore, the impact likely to have been felt is liable to

Knitted ties
Men's knitted suits
Other ties
Wadding
Coated fabrics
Metabolised yarns
Jute yarn
Woven jute fabrics
Jute sacks and bags

Fig. 9.2   MFA phase-out – UK – stage 1.

Woven handkerchiefs
Synthetic yarn
Corded/combed wool
Carpets
Narrow woven fabrics
Knitted fabrics
Knitted accessories
Synthetic tights
Swimwear
Knitted ensembles
Woven workwear
Woven ski suits
Woven scarves
Corsets
Woven gloves
Woven socks
Tents
Non-woven fabric
Laminated fabric
Mattresses
Camping goods
Staple fibres

Fig. 9.3   MFA phase-out – UK – stage 2.

have been small, which might offer a partial explanation for the calm with which UK companies were, seemingly, viewing the process. In Stage 3 (2002), of course, the phase-out had by definition to bite into more sensitive categories. As Anson (1993) put it:

> 'while the products liberated from quota so far were never really restricted in the first place, the next phase of quota integration after 2002 is likely to see the liberalisation of real quotas.'

It has also to be re-affirmed that, as was seen above, the most spectacular growth of imports into the UK in recent years has come from countries not under MFA restraint, such as Turkey and the CEEC countries with which the EU has negotiated preferential agreements. As Nordas (2004, p. 26) observed, the 'EU has less restrictive quotas than the US/Canada . . . It has also provided a number of countries with tariff and quota-free market access . . .'.

Quotas are (since 1993) set on an EU-wide basis. Quota removal is organised by the Article 113 Textile Committee which operates on the principle of qualified majority voting. The UK has ten votes out of 87, therefore, in principle, it is possible for a particular member state to determine which products are phased out and/or the balance between garments and textiles if it can carry sufficient votes.

(vi)   The general impact of the MFA

This was not difficult to predict. Standard economic theory as outlined in Figure 9.1 predicts that the removal of quotas would be followed by a rise in imports and a decline in domestic production in the face of falling prices. In addition, two major studies produced by the WTO and the EU both came to the same conclusion. The latter (IFM, 2004) also summarised previous studies into the impact of trade liberalisation on domestic employment and trade patterns. In all cases (ranging from Australia, Norway and Sweden to studies of the immediate impact of China's accession to the WTO) the result was a massive surge in imports from low cost centres and a severe fall in domestic production. For example, in the USA China's share of apparel imports rose from 8% in 2001 to 10% in 2002; in the EU 11 categories were liberalised between 2001 and 2002 and in all cases EU production fell sharply as import prices fell. China was the main beneficiary. Australia dismantled quotas in 1992/1993 and in the period 1991–2001 apparel imports grew by 22% while domestic production fell by 23%. Again, China benefited the most and now accounts for 72% of Australian apparel imports. Walkenhort (2003) forecast a substantial reallocation of resources away from the developed countries. In addition, most studies foresaw large welfare gains to consumers following quota removal. For example, Glisman (2000) estimated that each family in the EU would gain 270 Ecu per year via failing prices; Fouquin (2002) confirmed this result for developed countries but also found significant losses for many developing countries with the exception of China; Yang (1997) calculated a global gain of $75 billion; in the USA USITC (2002) estimated that almost all the gain from the removal of protection came in textiles and apparel; Van Schoppenthau (2002) studied the impact of liberalisation in Germany and concluded that apparel manufacture had the most to fear but that most companies had already adjusted to the new regime.

The WTO study by Nordas (2004) concluded that import penetration would rise in the EU and that the biggest winners would be China and India stating that (Nordas, 2004, p. 28) both 'would almost double their market share and China will be the single biggest exporter'. He also observed that in the 11 countries which had integrated all categories in one move, imports had risen sharply. In the same vein the EU study (IFM, 2004, p. 370) concluded that the 'industry will face severe restructuring in the coming years' and that this conclusion (2004, p. 367) could also be extended to the accession countries. Interestingly, the report concluded that (2004, p. 54) there was not 'any correlation between industrial performance and protection intensity' and that it was 'especially for clothing products that there is no correlation between global performance and degree of protection'. The report's main conclusion was to confirm (2004, p. 272) that 'the main change will consist in a substantial increase in imports from China'. There was, therefore, no excuse at all for the farcical events of July 2005 when the EU imposed safeguard quotas on China resulting in masses of garments being blocked at the ports and then claiming that this could not have been foreseen (Jones, 2006).

What conclusions can be drawn now that the MFA has been removed? First, it did not prevent a massive rise in import penetration in the UK – probably because of the existence of uncontrolled or preferred suppliers; second, a major effect was trade diversion as opposed to trade restriction; third, it follows that the main effects of the removal of the MFA will be a further rise in imports and further trade diversion as retailers switch from operating in a quota holders' market to a buyers' market; fourth, China's entry into the WTO was at least as important an event as the phasing-out of the MFA itself; fifth, while there are other forms of restraint which can be applied (such as tariffs, rules of origin and anti-dumping measures), their use will not constitiute a return to an MFA-like regime in the future.

UK experience has to be seen in the context of EU trade policy on textiles and apparel. As stated above, the whole philosophy of EU policy is one of ongoing liberalisation. The EU is committed to global liberalisation governed by WTO rules and there is no evidence that the latter would ever contemplate the re-establishment of a system of control along the lines of the MFA. The EU had MFA bilateral agreements with some 26 WTO members and its policy has always been based on distinguishing between various types of countries such as, for example:

(1)   Preferential access countries, such as Tunisia and Morocco.
(2)   Lomé Convention (Cotonou Agreement) members, such as Mauritius.
(3)   The Least Developed Countries, such as Bangladesh.
(4)   EFTA members.
(5)   OECD members.
(6)   Autonomous regimes, such as North Korea.
(7)   Central and Eastern European countries.
(8)   WTO member countries.
(9)   China and Taiwan (now in WTO).

In brief, categories 6–9 were restricted although there are also some tariffs applied to OECD members (Majumdar, 1996). In addition, restraints on Central and Eastern countries were weak and eventually removed. Moore (1999, p. 279) confirms that 'in comparison with the MFA developing countries the CEEC countries receive preferential treatment'. In practice, duties and quotas on goods from the CEECs would have been virtually phased out by the end of 2002 prior to their accession to the EU.

In principle there are no formal quotas on imports from Turkey which, in 1994, was the EU's biggest supplier of clothing in value terms (Majumdar, 1996, p. 46). Morocco and Tunisia were the third and fourth major suppliers. An EU–Mexico Trade Agreement was concluded in 2002 which covers trade in textiles/apparel in both directions under which Mexican goods enter the EU duty-free.

The view taken of this process of liberalisation obviously depends upon the views of various interest groups. Coster (1996, p. 131) reports the sharply diverging views expressed by importers who were 'at pains to defend their textile and clothing industries' and those of the exporters who 'expressed their disappointment at the delaying tactics of the main importing regions'. The categories of apparel remaining under restraint included the sensitive items which, by definition, would have to be used to meet the obligations under the agreement.

The general picture seems to be that most product categories represent rather small proportions of the total remaining under protection and that the percentage of trade represented by restricted trade is generally less than 50%.

The process of phasing out restrictions was well under way by 2002 and the ability of importers to restrict this process to non-sensitive items was a thing of the past. In addition China's entry into the WTO in late 2001 had momentous consequences as it made removal of controls on Chinese apparel exports inevitable. It is possible to exert some control until 2008 and – with even more difficulty – until 2014. The short-term measures introduced by the EU and the USA in July 2005 do not call for any reconsideration of the conclusions drawn above about the advent of liberalised trade. Such restraints and safeguard measures were always possible under the terms of China's access to the WTO. In the case of the EU, quotas were introduced on ten categories to run until the end of 2007. In these categories the increase in imports during 2005 ranged from +51% to +534%. In the USA, imports of major categories of apparel doubled in one month. In the year 2004–2005 Chinese exports of cotton trousers, for example, rose by + 1300%. These issues will be discussed again in Chapter 12.

(vii)   The impact of quota removal on company strategies

It is clearly the case that the actual impact (as opposed to the theoretical) of the removal of a trade barrier will greatly depend on how effective the barrier was in restraining trade. This is a vexed question in that some experts argue that the MFA was effective – Scheffer (1992), for example, argued that this was the case between 1976 and 1986 – while others point to the fact that many quotas were never fully utilised as evidence that they did not 'bite' and were correspondingly ineffective (Curran, 1995). This argument is even further complicated by the contention of Khanna (1991) that quotas could, in fact, still be effective at restraining exports from the low cost countries even when quotas were not fully taken up because administrative inefficiencies often resulted in potential exports being unable to take up spare quota. The majority view seems to be that, with the exception of MFA I, the system did act to slow down the growth of exports from some low cost producers into the developed countries and it must be assumed that liberalised trade flows will be greater than those which took place under the system of managed trade. Zeitlin (1988) concluded that the UK engaged in a 'mild form of protection after 1974' but it must be recognised that the MFA produced significant trade diversion as opposed to sample trade reduction. This reduced the real level of protection as did product diversification into non-controlled items.

Anson (1994), for example, concluded that there was no doubt that 'import penetration in the West would have been higher without the MFA' while Winterton (1996, p. 38) likewise argued that the MFA 'has affected some protection to the UK clothing industry'. Therefore, it must be assumed – especially in those instances where quota utilisation is very high – that imports into the UK will rise as the MFA is progressively removed. UK-based producers will face ever more severe competition from low cost sources with consequent effects on output and employment.

In addition to exposing Western producers to more competition, it is probable that further trade diversion effects can be anticipated. As Khanna (1994) observed, the agreement 'will have a major impact on the pattern of world clothing and textile trade'. Companies sourcing offshore will be more able to optimise their production locations. The impact of trade liberalisation will vary as between interest groups. The view of Evans (1995) is that the big winners will be the consumers in developed countries while the major losers will be domestic producers in high wage locations. The main beneficiaries are expected to be

China and India as trade patterns flow back to cost-related locations. There may be a second type of trade diversion if, for example, the USA takes a tougher line against China than the EU. This will be considered in Chapter 12.

The impact of quota removal on a domestic industry might be indicated by the experience of countries which have gone through this experience such as Australia and Sweden. Van Acker (1997) studied the Australian example and concluded that, following the announcement in 1987 of a plan to phase out protection, employment and production had steadily declined while import penetration climbed remorselessly. Jones (1990, p. 36) found that, in the case of Sweden, 'deregulation . . . increased competition between suppliers' and prices fell. Sung (1994) found that after three years of free trade in Sweden, imports from China had doubled.

The great unknown is the future of China. As Khanna (1994) expressed it, quotas are likely 'to remain on China, which is not a GATT member, but if its application for membership is successful, China unrestricted by quota could end up supplying 60–80% of Europe's and the USA's import volume'. China's entry into the WTO in 2001 was probably as significant an event as the phasing out of the MFA.

B. The role of exchange rate fluctuations

(i) Introduction – the theory

One of the major differences between domestic and international business trans-actions is the impact of exchange rate fluctuations on income, costs and profits. An exchange rate is the number of units of one currency which can be exchanged for a second, e.g. if £1 buys $1.80 then the rate is 1:1.8. If the rate changes so that £1 buys more of the second currency (e.g. £1 buys $2) then the pound is rising in value (and the dollar is by definition falling). Alternative terms for rising are strengthening or appreciating while a falling currency can also be said to be weakening or depreciating. A model of exchange rate fluctuation is given in Appendix C. Therefore, a rising pound against the dollar makes UK exports to the USA (or anywhere else using the dollar) dearer, so that they should fall while simultaneously making imports from the USA into the UK cheaper. A falling pound has the opposite effect. Prices of products sourced offshore therefore depend partly on the local cost and partly on the cost of purchasing the currency required to pay for them. Exchange rate fluctuations can, therefore, be expected to influence trade flows including those which represent sourcing decisions. Since 1973 most major currencies have been free to move against each other. The sterling exchange rate is shown in Table 9.3 and the rate against the Euro and the dollar in Table 9.4.

Table 9.3   Sterling exchange rate (1990 = 100).

Year	
1975	129.6
1978	107.2
1982	123.3
1984	111.4
1987	99.3
1998	103.9
2000	107.5
2003	100.2
2004	104.1

Source: *Economic Trends* (2004) Annual Supplement, Table 5.1 and 2005.

Table 9.4   Sterling exchange rate against the US$ and the Euro.

Year	$ per £	Euros per £
1945	4.0	—
1950	2.8	—
1965	2.8	—
1970	2.4	—
1975	2.2	1.7
1985	1.3	1.7
1990	1.8	1.4
1998	1.7	1.5
2001	1.4	1.6
2003	1.6	1.4
2004	1.8	1.5

Source: *Economic Trends* (2004) Annual Supplement, Table 5.1 and 2005.
Notes: (1)   The period 1945 to 2001 represented a falling £ against the $.
(2)   1996–2002 showed a strong £ against the Euro but after that the Euro gained in strength and the £ weakened.

Anson and Simpson (1988) pointed out that the value of the dollar is particularly important to the evolution of trade flows in the textile and apparel sector because the 'currencies of most of the Far Eastern producers are linked to it'. Scheffer (1992) likewise observed that some 75% of EU textile imports and 50% of exports are traded in dollars. The £ : $ rate is shown in Table 9.4.

Therefore, it is clear that the observed pattern of UK apparel trade and sourcing owes some part of its evolution to fluctuations in exchange rates. The pound was in effect devalued when the UK left the Exchange Rate Mechanism in 1992, but has subsequently enjoyed (or endured) a period of relative strength after 1995 although it weakened against the dollar between 2000 and 2002 before rising again in 2004 (Bootle, 2004).

Sterling was one of the strongest currencies in the period 1995–1999 during which period it rose by over 20% (Table 9.3). It is important, however, to note that in the same period the dollar rose by 15% so that, while the pound has gained substantially against, for example, other major European currencies, it did not do so against the dollar (Table 9.4). This is important because a large proportion of trade in textile and apparel products is conducted in dollars and because of the impact a weak pound relative to the dollar has on labour cost comparisons (Jones, 2002). The Euro gained against the US dollar as the latter weakened after 2002.

As Moore (1999) observes, the UK's interest in exchange rate stability 'is as much with the rest of the world as with the EU'. As Segall (2000) noted, the pound was at a six-year low against the US dollar in May 2000. It is vital that the trend in the currency is not used as an irrational explanation for all economic problems. When C&A announced the closure of its UK operations, for example, the unions involved stated that this demonstrated that the strong pound was hurting all sectors of the UK economy – but C&A was not exporting from the UK and sourced centrally from the Eurozone so, if anything, the strong pound should have helped the company, not damaged it!

(ii)   The impact of exchange rate fluctuations

The major problem introduced by exchange rate fluctuations is the passage of time and the uncertainty this introduces. If fluctuations could be perfectly anticipated many of the problems would disappear. It is true that a number of forecasting systems have been developed but none has proven to be sufficiently reliable or accurate as to remove the element of uncertainty completely.

Exchange rate fluctuations can impact on a variety of business decisions and activities, for example:

(1)   Exporting.
(2)   Sourcing (or purchasing of inputs).
(3)   Raising finance and investment decisions.
(4)   Payment practices.

As was noted in Chapter 1, the UK apparel industry exports some 40% of its UK produced output. Therefore, the potential for exchange rate fluctuations to impact the prosperity of the sector is large. A strong pound makes exports from the UK into areas against which the pound is strong more expensive and, depending upon the elasticity of demand, will cause demand to fall. An issue of current importance is that of the relationship between the pound and the euro. As Jones (1999, p. 205) pointed out, some 62% of the UK apparel exports go into the Eurozone. If the pound is strong against the Euro then this task becomes more difficult. The potential impact of the weakness of the euro against

Country A quotes	$10,000
Country B quotes	60,000 francs
Country C quotes	30,000 D-marks
Exchange rates are	£1 = 2$
	£1 = 10 francs
	£1 = 4 D-marks
Rates change to	£1 = 1$
	£1 = 15 francs
	£1 = 3 D-marks

Fig. 9.4   Sourcing costs and exchange rate fluctuations.

the pound is illustrated by the case of Toyota's sourcing policy. In 2000 it was reported that Toyota was increasing Eurozone sourcing at the expense of UK suppliers. Clearly, if the pound buys more euros then the cost to a UK buyer of supplies denominated in euros would fall over time. Toyota planned to force UK suppliers to trade in euros rather than the pound. In relation to the model set out later in Fig. 9.5 it must be noted that decisions need to be reversed because Toyota as the buyer was trying to protect its income.

It has been argued in Chapter 7 that offshore production or sourcing will become increasingly important in the future. Sourcing decisions can be influenced by changes in exchange rates in a variety of ways. Most importantly the basic choice of the cheapest supplying source can be affected. Figure 9.4 contains a simplified example of the issue. If it is assumed that the choice depends entirely on price then supplier A would be chosen on the basis of the rates prevailing today when the decision is taken (the so-called 'spot' rates). Payment has to be made at some time in the future at which point the rates in the bottom section of the table prevail and these would be called 'forward' rates. Clearly supplier B should have been selected.

Fluctuations in local rates against the currency used to settle accounts – which is frequently the US dollar – can also mitigate the impact of local inflation on costs. Table 9.5 illustrates this position in that it demonstrates how depreciation of domestic currencies in the Far East against the UK dollar could have the effect of maintaining competitiveness. In 1980–91, for example, although wages in China grew by 200% in local currency they only rose by 70% in dollar terms. In the same period costs in Indonesia, while rising by 89% in local terms, actually fell in dollar terms. A brief summary of the impact of exchange fluctuations on the textile complex appears in Dickerson (1995, p. 215).

Investment decisions can also be affected by fluctuations in exchange rates. It can become very attractive for a company based in a strong currency zone to build capacity in a country with a weak currency if construction costs are paid in the local currency because the strong currency will buy vast quantities of the weak currency. The decision on where to raise finance can also be influenced by

Table 9.5   Exchange rates and inflation.

	Percentage change 1982–1992	
	Exchange rate	Local inflation
Turkey	−237	+290
Philippines	−34	+37

Source: *Textile Outlook International*, September 1993, p. 118.

the relative strengths of different currencies. For example, the real cost of borrowing dollars in an overseas financial market is influenced not only by the rate of interest payable, but by the relationship between the dollar and the local currency if that is to be used for repayment. If the dollar is falling over time against the repayment currency, the cost of repayments would be rising each year.

The research evidence does not always confirm the predictions of the model in Appendix C. Clautier (1993), for example, indicates a very poor relationship between apparel trade flows between the EU and low cost suppliers and the strength of the dollar. Curran (1995) studied apparel trade flows between the UK and a variety of EU members (prior to the introduction of the euro). This research revealed that the theoretical implications of exchange rate fluctuations on apparel trade flows were only partially validated by the evidence. In the case of UK–German trade, for example, the pound was falling against the Deutschmark between 1985 and 1989, but UK apparel imports from Germany rose. The data on trade with the Eurozone (Chapter 5) does, for the most part, reveal the expected relationships as has been shown by Jones (2001). This would be further supported by, for example, Khanna (1991) who commented that the rise in exports from India to Europe in 1987 was partly caused by the fall in the value of the rupee against the US dollar and most European currencies. Gereffi (1999) likewise argued that a major cause of the sharp fall in Taiwan and South Korea's apparel exports in the late 1980s was the appreciation of their currencies against the US dollar.

There may be a number of reasons for the existence of conflicting data: non-price variables may be important, for example, or effects may be lagged in time in a complex manner. It is likely that small and short-lived fluctuations can be ignored as is argued by Blyth (1996, p. 125) who contends that the evidence in the textile sector suggests that 'most fluctuations within one year make no difference to sourcing decisions' but 'year to year fluctuations can change the basis for the number of items which should be sourced or not and where they should be sourced'.

Finally, it must be noted that because much textile/apparel trade is conducted in US dollars it would be the case that any rise in the value of the pound against the dollar (or any weakness of the dollar against the pound) would magnify the advantages of offshore production as against domestic production. The fact that the Chinese currency is fixed in terms of the dollar is very significant. As Bootle (2005) points out, while the dollar was falling against other major currencies it was not moving against the Chinese currency at all, making Chinese exports even more price competitive. However, as Kaletsky (2005) points out, China's wages are so low that even a massive revaluation would be of little help to labour-intensive industries in the USA and Europe.

(iii)   The management of exchange rate issues

The basic aim of managing exchange rate risk is to protect company income and profits from the negative impact of exchange rate fluctuations and to ensure that income and profits are at least equal to what they would have been had operations been entirely domestic. There are two main types of exchange rate risk:

(1)   'Transaction risk' refers to the possibility that the amount of receivables and payables invoice values from foreign transactions may change over time as rates fluctuate.
(2)   'Translation risk' is the term used to describe events which cause the value of the balance sheet to change as rates fluctuate.

Companies which are open to these risks are said to be 'exposed' to exchange rate risks. This can be a particular problem if a company's liabilities are more exposed than its assets. In particular, the worst scenario is that liabilities (spending) are in a hard/strong currency which is expensive to purchase in the (weak) domestic currency while income is in a weak currency which then translates into relatively small amounts of (strong) domestic currency – therefore, having a cost base in a hard currency and an income base in a weak one is a very unfortunate event.

It can be stated by way of a broad generalisation that offshore sourcing primarily directed by the search for low labour costs will result in the local costs normally being in weak currencies – but the problem may be that payment has to be made in a relative strong currency, such as the dollar.

One of the basic issues which will be faced is whether or not to follow a lead or lag policy. If a transaction is conducted earlier than is contractually necessary then it is called a lead policy and *vice versa*. In this context there is a basic difference between domestic and international strategies in that if a buyer owes money to a supplier in a hard or rising currency it pays to lead and settle early. This is the opposite of normal business policy in a purely domestic situation, such as if a UK buyer has to pay $200 to an American supplier and the dollar is rising (and the pound falling) from $1 = 56p to $1 = 71p (or from £1 = 1.79 to £1 = 1.41) then early payment would cost £112 while delayed payment would cost £143. If the UK company had to collect money owed to it in a foreign currency which is falling against the pound it would be vital to collect as early as possible. Thus, if $300 is to be collected in three months during which time the £:$ rate changes from £1:$1 to £1:$2 then collecting now would convert to £300 but collection in three months would generate only £150.

A related issue is the choice of currency in which the transaction will be conducted. The currency used to set the purchase price is known as the pricing currency. The currency in which the account is actually settled is known as the payment currency. If a buyer allows the price to be set in the seller's currency then the buyer is taking on the risk. If, for example, the buyer is in the UK and agrees to buy an item whose price is set at 5,000,000 yen at £1:85Y and the rate changes to £1:75Y (the pound is weakening) then the UK buyer would have to find £66,667 to purchase the currency rather than £58,824 and the extra cost to the buyer would be £7,843. The supplier still, of course, would receive 5,000,000 yen so has assumed no risk. If the transaction had been in pounds (say, to pay £58,824) all the risk would have shifted to the seller who would have received only 4,411,800 yen instead of 5,000,000 yen. If the bill were in yen and the pound rose, both supplier and purchaser would be all right. Why would the buyer accept the risk of paying in yen? According to Locke (1996) the reason could only be to receive a price discount.

Mathur (1982) has laid down some ground rules for setting the billing currency. These are reproduced as Fig. 9.5. It must be remembered that the aim in this case is to protect the income of the seller. The seller wishes to gain as much of his own currency as possible so that if a UK seller with a German customer expresses the invoice in D-marks when the D-mark is rising, then the D-mark received will convert into more pounds as time passes.

A number of financial instruments exist which permit the risks identified above to be minimised. The majority of text books recommend some form of hedging. In brief this shifts the risk to a bank upon payment of a fee. The simplest kind of hedging is known as forward hedging. If an exporter makes a £10,000 sale payable in the *customer's* currency in 30 days' time and the rate of exchange moved from £1:$1.50 now to £1:$1.40 over the period the seller would receive only $14,000 not the expected $15,000. This risk can be transferred, for a fee, to a bank by agreeing to sell to the bank £10,000 in 30 days at an agreed forward rate of £1:$1.50. The exporter thus receives the expected $15,000 less the

	Seller in →	Hard currency	Soft currency
Buyer in ↓	Hard currency	Invoice in buyer's currency	Invoice in buyer's currency
	Soft currency	Invoice in seller's currency	Neutral

Source: Based upon Mathur, I. (1982), Managing Foreign Exchange Risk Profitability, *Columbia Journal of World Business*.

Note: If the buyer is in a hard currency while the seller is in a soft currency, the invoice should be in the buyer's currency, and so on.

Fig. 9.5   Currency of settlement decisions.

fee. The bank will make equal and offsetting contracts to sell the same amount of currency it has agreed to buy in this transaction.

Locke (1996) argues against the use of hedging practices, favouring instead the use of currency options. This is the right to buy or sell (without obligation) a specified currency at a negotiated rate on a particular day. It is not a contract so that if its use appears questionable it can simply be allowed to expire. If, for example, a UK company is required to pay 50 million yen in six months when the spot rate is £1:85Y it is possible to purchase (for a set price) an option to buy in six months at the current rate. If the rate in fact changes to £1:80Y (i.e. the pound weakens) the option to obtain 85 yen to the £ would be exercised. If the pound rose the option would be allowed to expire.

Locke (1996) demonstrates that the relative costs of managing exchange rate risk by a variety of techniques change if the buyer's currency is rising. In this case buying at spot price when needed is the cheapest option. If the buyer's currency is weak then this, in contrast, would be the worst choice and either an option or a forward purchase would be preferable. The problem is, of course, that there is no way of predicting with certainty which way the currency values will move. If the company is risk averse then options are cheaper than forwards if the buyer's currency rises.

Glaum (1990) argues that the management of exchange rate risks should be seen as a long-term strategic issue rather than as a short-term tactical problem and that the tools to exercise this management should include the choice of products to be made, the sources of manufacture and purchase of inputs, and the selection of markets into which to sell. Again the problem is that this might introduce heavy 'switching costs' (see Chapter 8).

References

Anson, R. (1992) Outward Processing: the Future for the UK Clothing. *Manufacturing Clothier*, **73**, 12–13.

Anson, R. (1993) Why Global Sourcing May be the Only Way Forward. *Manufacturing Clothier*, **74**, 13–14.

Anson, R. (1994) The MFA and Implications for Marketing Towards 2000. *Journal of Clothing Technology and Management*, **11**, 1–39.

Anson, R. (1996) Liberalisation or Procrastination. *Textile Outlook International*, **67**, 3–6.

Anson, R. & Simpson, P. (1988) *World Trade and Production Trends*. Economist Intelligence Unit, London.

ATC (1995) *The Agreement in Textiles and Clothing*. GATT, Geneva.

Au, K. & Yeung, K. (1999) Productivity Shift for Hong Kong Clothing Industry. *Journal of Fashion Marketing and Management*, **3**, 166–79.

Barton, K. (2000) *GATT '94 Implications for Sourcing*. MMU dissertation, Manchester.

Begg, D., Fischer, S. & Dornbusch, R. (1991) *Economics*. McGraw Hill, London.

Blyth, R. (1996) Sourcing Clothing Production. In: *Restructuring in a Labour Intensive Industry* (Eds I. Taplin & J. Winterton), pp. 112–42. Avebury, Aldershot.

Bootle, R. (2004) Preparing for a very weak dollar. *Sunday Telegraph*, 21.11.04.

Bootle, R. (2005) The inscrutable problem of China. *Sunday Telegraph*, 6.02.05.

Cable, V. (1982) *Protectionism and Industrial Decline*. Hodder and Stoughton, London.

Clautier, D. (1993) Garment Sourcing Options for EC Markets. *Textile Outlook International*, **47**, 91–120.

Coster, J. (1996) The Liberalisation of World Trade – The Views of Exporting and Importing Countries. *Textile Outlook International*, **66**, 131–58.

Curran, L. (1995) *An Evaluation of Fashion in the SEM and its Implications for the Sourcing of Clothing*. Unpublished PhD dissertation, MMU, Manchester.

De La Torre, J. (1986) *Clothing Industry Adjustment in Developed Countries*. Macmillan, Basingstoke.

Dickerson, K. (1995) *Textiles and Apparel in the Global Economy*. Prentice Hall, New Jersey.

EU (1998) *EU Textile Annual*. EU, Brussels.

Evans, P. & Walsh, J. (1995) *EU Guide to World Trade under the WTO*. Trade Policy Research Centre, London.

Fouquin, M. (2002) *Globalisation and Regionalisation: the Case of the Textile and Clothing Industries*. French Ministry of Industry, Paris.

Frankel, J. & Romer, D. (1999) Does Trade Cause Growth? *American Economic Review*, **89**, 379–400.

GATT (1994) *The Final Act (Uruguay Round) of Multilateral Trade Negotiations*. GATT, Geneva.

Gereffi, G. (1999) International Trade and Industrial Upgrading in the Apparel Commodity Chain. *Journal of International Economics*, **48**, 37–70.

Glaum, M. (1990) Strategic Management of Exchange Rate Risks. *Long Range Planning*, **23**, 65–73.

Glisman, H. & Spinange, D. (2000) *The Cost of EU Trade Protection in Textiles and Clothing*. Institute for World Economics, Kiel.

Harrison, G.W., Rutherford, T.F. & Tarr, D.G. (1997) Quantifying the Uruguay Round. *Economic Journal*, **107**, 1405–29.

Helm, T. & Jones, G. (1999) Enlargement – We Won't Join the Club. *Daily Telegraph*, 11.12.99, p. 12.

IFM (2004) *Study on the Implications of the 2005 Trade Liberalisation in the Textile and Clothing Sector*. Institut Français de la Mode, Paris. Available at www.europa.eu.int/comm/enterprise/textile

Jenkins, G. (1982) *Costs and Consequences of the New Protectionism*. North-South Institute, Ottawa.

Jones, R.M. (1990) The Swedish Clothing Industry: A Case Study of Import Penetration. *Hollings Apparel Industry Review*, **9**, 27–67.

Jones, R.M. (1997) Mainly for Academics. *Journal of Fashion Marketing and Management*, **1**, 198–203.

Jones, R.M. (1999) UK Clothing and the EuroZone. *Journal of Fashion Marketing and Management*, **3**, 205–7.

Jones, R.M. (2001) Too Many Oeufs in One Basket? *Journal of Fashion Marketing and Management*, **5.2**, 93–98.

Jones, R.M. (2003) Hidden Costs – Only Skin Deep? *Journal of Fashion Marketing and Management*, **7.1**, 7–11.

Jones, R.M. (2006) *Journal of Fashion Marketing*, **10.1**, Editorial (forthcoming).

Kaletsky, A. (2005) Europe and USA must beware of the five tigers. *The Times*, 12.04.05, p. 46.

Khanna, S.R. (1991) *International Trade in Textiles*. Sage, London.

Khanna, S.R. (1994) The New GATT Agreement. *Textile Outlook International*, **52**, 10–37.

Khanna, S.R. (2004) Trends in EU Textile and Clothing Imports. *Textile Outlook International*, **112**, 49–108.

Locke, R. (1996) *Global Supply Chain Management*. Irwin, London.

Majumdar, M. (1996) The MFA Phase Out and EU Clothing Sourcing. *Textile Outlook International*, **63**, 31–61.

Mathur, I. (1982) Managing Exchange Risk Profitability. *Columbia Journal of World Business*, **17**, 1–25.

Moon, K.L., Leung, C., Chong, M. & Yeung, K. (1999) MFA in Transition. *Journal of Fashion Marketing and Management*, **3**, 157–66.

Moore, L. (1999) *Britain's Trade and Economic Structure: The Impact of the EU*. Routledge, London.

Nordas, H.K. (2004) *The Global Textile and Clothing Industry Post the ATC*. WTO (Paper 5), Geneva.

ONS (1994) *Annual Abstract of Statistics*. HMSO, London.

Scheffer, M. (1992) *Trading Places*. University of Utrecht, Utrecht.

Segall, A. (2000) Sterling at a six year low. *Daily Telegraph*, 19.5.2000, p. 35.

Silberston, A. (1984) *The MFA and the UK Economy*. HMSO, London.

Silberston, A. (1989) *The Future of the MFA*. HMSO, London.

Singleton, J. (1997) *World Textile Industry*. Routledge, London.

Spinanger, D. (1996) Is There Life After Death? *Journal of the Federation of Asian Professional Textiles Associations*, **3**, 82–92.

Sung, K. (1994) Editorial. *Textile Asia*, October 1994, 6–7.

Trela, I. & Whalley, J. (1990) Global Effects of Developed Country Trade Restrictions in Textile and Apparel. *Economic Journal*, **100**, 1190–205.

USITC (2002) *The Economic Effect of Significant United States Import Restrictions*. United States International Trade Commission (3rd update).

Van Acker, E. (1997) Trade Liberalisation and Its Impact on the Australian Clothing and Footwear Industries. *Journal of Fashion Marketing and Management*, **2**, 9–21.

Van Schoppenthau, P. & Brenton, P. (2002) *The Implications of ATC-Liberalisation on the German Textile Industry*, available at www.eppa.com.

Walkenhort, P. (2003) *Liberalising Trade in Textiles and Clothing: a survey of quantitative studies*. OECD Trade Directory.

Winterton, R. & Barlow, A. (1996) Economic Restructuring of UK Clothing. In: *Restructuring in a Labour Intensive Industry* (Eds I. Taplin & J. Winterton), pp. 25–61. Avebury, Aldershot.

Wolf, M. (1984) *Costs of Protecting Jobs in Textiles and Clothing*. Trade Policy Research Centre, London.

WTO (1998) *Annual Report*. WTO, Washington.

Yang, Y., Martin, W. & Yanagishima, K. (1997) Evaluating the Benefits of Abolishing the MFA. In: *Global Trade Analysis* (Ed. T. Hertel). CUP, Cambridge.

Zeitlin, J. (1988) The Clothing Industry in Transition. *Textile History*, **19**, 211–38.

Chapter 10

The Economics of the UK Apparel Market

A. *Introduction*

The main focus of this book is the apparel manufacturing sector of the textile pipeline. The justification for the inclusion of a chapter on the fourth cell in the pipeline – the apparel market – is twofold. First, the pipeline is, as has been demonstrated, retail-driven and, second, some 80% of the output of apparel produced in the UK is retained for sale in the domestic market. The major aim of this chapter is to consider the role of economic factors in determining the size and structure of that market. However, it would be foolish and counterproductive to pretend that an understanding of the apparel marketplace can be achieved by reference to economic factors alone. In fact it is unlikely that the market for any consumer goods could be explained in this way. As Chisnall (1985, p. 16) puts it, the complexity of 'modern patterns of consumption demands sophisticated understanding; explanations based solely on economic theory are clearly inadequate. The other social sciences – psychology, sociology and anthropology – can provide extra valuable knowledge of buying behaviour'.

Many commentators argue that social and psychological factors are relatively more important in apparel markets than in others and that the apparel market is, in some sense, unique. This concern manifests itself in a variety of ways. The role of design provides a good illustration of this issue. Good design is clearly vastly important as a marketing feature in many product areas, in particular in those areas where product differentiation is the main route to competitive advantage, e.g. the Apple iMac computer. The subtle difference between these markets and the apparel market is that design or 'fashion' in the latter is frequently elevated to the role of an art form almost for its own sake. In addition, for largely historical reasons in the UK, design has been taught in art schools rather than marketing departments.

The danger this produces is that apparel designers and apparel marketing specialists tend to come from radically different academic and philosophical cultures. This problem is compounded by the further difficulty that, as Sproles

(1981, p. 123) observed during his study of the fashion cycle, there is a 'pervasive obstacle to scientific analysis', in that 'the fashion industry has a mystique . . . that fashion is not susceptible to science . . .'. Therefore, in order to provide a comprehensive review of contributions from a range of disciplines towards an understanding of market trends it is frequently necessary to move away from the positivist research tradition identified in Chapter 1.

It is, by way of an illustration, quite common to come across statements such as 'the fashion market is becoming more fragmented' or 'the speed of fashion change is increasing' without such statements being supported by objective, empirical data. This is not to argue that alternative research methods are wrong but it is important to recognise that they are different and that these differences do generate very real problems in model building and testing particularly when (see Section D) an attempt is made to combine two research philosophies in one model. The interface between competing research paradigms can often be an uncomfortable space to occupy.

Finally, it will be recalled that an early decision was taken to adopt the word 'apparel' rather than the word 'fashion'. In the context of this chapter it will be occasionally necessary to abandon this convention and revert to the use of the word 'fashion' in order to obviate the necessity to employ a cumbersome phrase to describe a change in style, design or colour in the marketplace.

The apparel market can be examined from a variety of perspectives:

(1) The size and rate of growth of the market.
(2) The structure of the market.
(3) The process of consumer decision making expressed in the marketplace.
(4) The speed of change in demand for various products. This might be closely linked to the issue of size of the market if, as is likely in the case of apparel, most purchases do not represent replacement of worn out goods, i.e. it is 'wants driven' not 'needs driven'.
(5) The concept of the fashion cycle defined as the time elapsing from the introduction of a new fashion to its replacement.
(6) The direction of, and mechanism whereby, new styles flow through society. This can be defined as the process of fashion change which has been defined by Davies (1992, p. 103) as a 'complex system of influences and interactions among people, institutions and organisations which animates the cycle'.

The decision to concentrate on economic issues has been taken mainly because this reflects the focus of the text, but also in the belief that while economics can provide a good base from which to study the first two issues listed above, it has very little useful to contribute to an examination of issues (4)–(6). Issue (3) is extensively covered in general marketing texts such as Chisnall (1985) and Schiffman (1994) while a brief summary in the context of the apparel sector can be found in Easey (1995).

Table 10.1   Expenditure on clothing in the UK 1900–1983 (in £ millions).

	At 1938 prices	At 1980 prices
1900	342	3,170
1924	366	—
1930	401	3,708
1935	425	—
1938	439	4,060
1939	447	—
1945	229	2,688
1948	432	—
1950	479	4,468
1955	491	4,698
1960		5,719
1965		6,555
1970		7,436
1978		8,350
1980		9,863
1983		11,683

Sources: (1) Sigsworth, E.M. (1990) *Montague Burton – The Tailor of Taste*. MUP, Manchester.
(2) Mitchell, B. & Deane, P. (1962) *Abstract of Historical Statistics 1900–1983*. Cambridge University Press, Cambridge.
(3) *Economist* (1985) *Economic Statistics 1900–1983*.

B. The evolution of the UK apparel market

(i)   Market size

The long-term trend in consumer expenditure on apparel in the UK is shown in Table 10.1. It can be seen that the market grew very little between 1906 and 1938 – by only 28% in real terms. Rationing was introduced in 1941 and removed in 1948 so that by 1950 the market had recovered to its pre-war size. The emergence of an apparel market of the order of magnitude which was commonplace in the late 1990s can be traced not to the 1960s but to the period 1975–1990 during which period the market grew from 40–70% of its 1999 size in value terms. The so-called youth market of the 1960s represented only some 30% of today's apparel market which has exploded despite the fact that the population has been ageing rapidly since the early 1970s. The explanation would appear to lie entirely in the increasing wealth of the community and the incredible value for money represented by apparel in a period of steady inflation. As TMS (1996, p. 1) concluded, 'the boom conditions of the late 1980s, supported by high earnings and personal disposable income, drove consumer expenditure to almost unheard of growth rates'. The most recent figures on expenditure in the UK by broad product category are shown in Table 10.2.

Table 10.2 Consumer expenditure: changes in the pattern of expenditure 1997–2003 (£ million at current prices and % of total).

	1997		2003	
	£ million	%	£ million	%
Food	53,832	10.7	63,493	9.3
Alcohol and tobacco	21,420	4.3	27,330	4.0
Clothing and footwear	30,901	6.1	41,255	6.1
Clothing only	26,500	5.3	35,579	5.2
Housing	90,214	17.9	125,554	18.4
Transport	75,458	15.0	98,388	14.4
Health	7,566	1.5	12,050	1.8
Communication	10,014	2.0	15,446	2.3
Recreation and culture	59,971	11.9	83,315	12.2
Education	7,440	1.5	9,649	1.4
Restaurants and hotels	56,960	11.3	80,800	11.9
Miscellaneous services	59,171	11.8	84,655	12.4
Total	502,469		681,769	

Source: Consumer Trends at www.statistics.gov.uk various editions.
Notes: (1) Categories do not sum to total.
(2) Do not double-count clothing.

These reveal some quite encouraging trends in that the growth of expenditure on apparel has been quite impressive, e.g. between 1990 and 1998 it rose by 47% as against a 16% rise in total expenditure in real terms. It can also be seen (from Tables 10.2 and 10.3) that the proportion of expenditure devoted to apparel pur-

Table 10.3 Consumer expenditure: changes in the pattern of expenditure 1964–2004 (£ millions and % of total) at 2001 prices.

	1964	1984	1994	2004	
	%	%	%	£ millions	%
Food and drink	17.1	12.3	10.7	63,873	9.4
Alcohol and tobacco	11.3	7.2	5.0	26,312	3.9
Clothing and footwear	3.8	4.2	4.8	47,236	6.9
Clothing only	3.0	3.4	4.0	41,208	6.0
Housing	25.9	24.2	21.0	118,160	17.3
Household goods and services	5.3	4.9	5.5	40,503	5.0
Health	2.1	2.1	2.0	11,356	1.7
Transport	11.5	15.3	14.7	97,422	14.3
Communications	0.5	1.0	1.4	15,985	2.3
Recreation and culture	4.3	6.8	8.9	90,603	13.3
Education	1.4	1.4	1.6	9,565	1.4
Restaurants and hotels	14.0	13.6	12.7	78,280	11.5
Miscellaneous services	9.3	10.3	13.1	81,898	12.0
Total domestic expenditure	100	100	100	681,193	100

Source: *Consumer Trends* (3rd Quarter, 2004).

chases has risen in real terms during the period 1964 to 2004. This is important because the accepted wisdom is that (*Retail Intelligence*, 1999) the trend has been steadily downward: in 1960 the proportion was just over 10% whereas at the end of the 1990s it had stabilised at around 6%. Unfortunately, the conclusion is sensitive to the basis of measurement – the long-term decline shows up most clearly if measurements are conducted in current price terms, e.g. it fell from 9.7% in 1960 to 5.9% in 1990 (ONS, 1999b) and from 7.7% in 1976 to 5.9% in 1995 (Curwen, 1997). In real terms, however, a different picture emerges: between 1980 and 1990 the percentage rose from 6.1% to 6.4% at 1985 prices (ONS, 1999b) and in 1990 prices, from 5.3% in 1971 to 6.9% in 1995 (ONS, 1997, p. 108). As can be seen from Table 10.3, the percentage is rising in terms of 2001 prices. Therefore, the picture is far from bleak and should not be overlooked because while, as will be seen below, the rise in expenditure on apparel has clearly been driven by the (almost) uninterrupted rise in incomes, it does not follow automatically that the proportion of expenditure devoted to all product groups will rise as affluence and expenditure rises.

As *Social Trends* (ONS, 1997, p. 108) observes, total expenditure in the UK 'increased by 77% in real terms between 1971 and 1995 [but] the pattern of spending changed considerably . . . reflecting both changes in quantities purchased and the relative prices of the different categories of goods and services . . . The proportion spent on food has fallen by a third since 1971; that spent on alcohol fell by a quarter . . . In contrast the proportion spent on recreation, entertainment and education rose by nearly two-thirds over the same period'. *Social Trends* (2000) recorded that in 1998/9 for the first time spending on leisure goods and services was the biggest item of household expenditure.

There is obviously competition for the consumers' purse and over time new products will be brought to the market, some of which will be successful and absorb consumer spending – the most spectacular recent example being the mobile phone. Changes in the pattern of expenditure as between product groups will be brought about by a variety of factors such as changes in the relative real cost of products; demographic changes and more complex social and cultural change. These issues will be considered in Section C below.

The enormous increase in expenditure on apparel can be explained by reference to the growth in consumption and real incomes over the period and is usually expressed in the concept of the aggregate consumption function (Begg, 1991, p. 372) which reveals 'the level of consumption desired at each level of personal disposable income'. There is a very strong relationship between consumption and income which seems to hold not only at the aggregate level but also (see Section B (ii) below) for various product categories. Therefore, by far the most 'salient influence on consumption . . . is probably current income' (Artis, 1992).

Consumption as a proportion of national wealth grew from 60% in 1980 to 64% in 1995 while between 1971 and 1996 real consumption rose by 80%

Table 10.4   Changes in key variables 1950–1998.

Period	% change in real consumption	% change in expenditure on clothing	% change in real incomes (at 1995 prices)
1950–1955	+11.5	+5.1	+13.2
1955–1960	+14.0	+21.8	+19.1
1960–1965	+13.4	+14.8	+17.0
1965–1970	+10.6	+13.5	+10.5
1970–1975	+13.7	+12.4	+16.5
1975–1980	+9.9	+18.2	+12.5
1980–1985	+11.4	+25.3	+8.9
1985–1990	+25.5	+20.4	+23.0
1990–1995	+5.5	+28.2	+12.7
1995–1998	+11.4	+11.9	+6.1
1998–2003	+17.3	+55.7	+19.2

Source: *Economic Trends 2004 (Annual Supplement)* (ONS, 2004), Calculations made by the author.
Notes: (1) The index of real income for 2003 was 103.6 – see Table 10.13.
(2) The 1998–2003 figures are at 2001 prices.

(Curwen, 1997). This is not to deny that, in the period under consideration, many important social changes occurred and these will be considered below (Section C). It can be seen from Table 10.4 that the periods of most rapid growth in expenditure on clothing corresponded to periods of very rapid growth in income and consumption.

These figures confirm the rapid expansion of the market (in real terms) in the period 1980–1990 and the role of changes in real incomes in promoting expenditure on apparel. As is made clear below, the trend in real incomes in the UK has been steadily upwards over a long period – as Curwen (1997) concludes, 'personal income has risen continuously since 1979'. It is a statistical fact that consumption is very closely related to income – a relationship which is expressed by economists in the concept of the consumption function (Begg, 1991) as was noted above. Therefore, the UK apparel market is likely to remain attractive to both domestic and foreign suppliers by virtue of its size. Women's wear accounts for some 56% of the market.

According to latest research (Mintel, 2000) men care little, in the UK, about their appearance. The report revealed that only 2% of men bought the latest fashions while just one in 14 were shopaholics compared with one in five women. A quarter of all men in the survey said they were 'anti-shopping'. This view is confirmed by Moore (2000) who concluded that it was 'apparent that the British (male) fashion customer is much less confident than his European counterparts' and is 'characterised by a sense of alienation . . . as they search for fashion clothing'.

In the period 1992–1998 expenditure upon women's wear rose from 3.2% to 3.7% of all consumer expenditure despite the fact that women as a proportion of the population fell marginally over the period (ONS, 1999c). The size of various

Table 10.5   Size of apparel market by
segment in the UK, 2000 (£ million and %).

	£ million	%
Women's wear	17,424	58.5
Outerwear	11,848	39.7
Outsize	3,176	10.7
Underwear	2,095	7.0
Men's wear	6,798	22.8
Outerwear	5,846	19.6
Underwear	679	2.3
Children's wear	55,858	18.7

Source: Mintel (2002) Clothing Retailing in Europe.
Note: Categories do not total to 100%.

sub-sectors of the market is indicated in Table 10.5. The pessimistic sentiments expressed in 1998 about the future size of the UK apparel market have not been confirmed by events and future growth is expected to be steady if not spectacular. Trends in prices will be examined in the next section and it is the case that the market is extremely competitive, as witnessed by the decision of C&A to leave the marketplace in spring 2000.

(ii)   Price trends

It was demonstrated in Chapter 5 that a very high, and rising, proportion of the UK market is supplied by imports. In addition, the market is extremely price competitive. These two facts are almost certainly connected in that there is extensive literature which confirms the power of import competition to influence prices. Katics (1994, p. 277) concluded a study of the effect of rising imports in the USA with the statement that 'our estimates indicate a sizeable effect of import competition on price cost margins for the . . . period 1976–86'. Conyan (1991) also found that high degrees of import penetration were positively associated with lower margins. In the words of *Retail Intelligence* (1999, p. 37) 'one virtual constant remains and that is price deflation', estimating that between 1994 and 1999 men's wear prices fell by 3%; women's wear by 9% and children's wear by 2% at a time when the average price change was +15.6%. Prices remain under severe pressure as can be seen from Table 10.6.

This pressure in turn promotes the search for lower cost, offshore locations. Competition is fierce, resulting in extensive discounting and a wide choice for the consumer.

These competitive pressures are also reflected in the retail sales figures. It can be seen from Table 10.6 that volume figures normally run far ahead of value figures. *Retail Intelligence* (1999, p. 29) concludes that the sales figures do not necessarily 'suggest an upturn in the sector's fortunes as retailers are having to

Table 10.6   Price and retail sales trends.

(a)   Price trends (1987 = 100)

	Clothing and footwear	All items
1990	115.0	126.1
1995	120.6	149.1
1996	119.7	152.7
1997	120.6	157.5
1998	119.9	162.9
2000	112.3	170.3
2001	107.5	173.3
2002	102.4	176.2
2003	100.8	181.3

(b)   Retail sales (2000 = 100)

	Volume		Current price value	
	CTF	All items	CTF	All items
1997	88.1	89.9	93.4	89.9
1998	88.8	92.5	93.8	93.4
1999	92.9	95.7	96.0	96.5
2000	100	100	100	100
2001	109.4	106.1	105.8	105.1
2002	121.0	112.7	112.4	111.1
2003	128.9	116.6	118.3	114.0
2004	139.0	123.6	124.5	119.2

Sources: (a)   Consumer Trends (2nd Quarter, 1999 and 3rd Quarter, 2004).
         (b)   Retail Sales (Business Monitor SDM 28).
         (c)   CTF = Clothing, textiles and footwear.

make some substantial markdowns in order to generate this volume growth' as was seen in the price trend data.

Although it has been demonstrated above that the main factor behind the explosion in expenditure on apparel has been the virtually uninterrupted rise in real incomes experienced in the UK, it has also to be recognised that the very slow rate of increase of apparel prices has reinforced this trend by representing exceptional value for money in real terms. Jones (1994) showed that the apparel price index, over the period 1974–1991, had collapsed to 50% of the average (see Table 10.7). In fact inflation is a comparatively modern phenomenon and Newman (1995) shows that the purchasing power of the pound which fell by only 44% in the period 1900–1939 fell by 80% in the period 1960 to 1980. If 1985 is taken as the base year it can be shown (ONS, 1999b) that the purchasing power of the pound fell by a factor of 200 between 1950 and 1998 and by 42% between 1985 and 1998. Apparel prices rose very little during these times of rapid inflation and therefore represented extremely good value to the consumer. This reflects the general fact that inflationary pressures are not constant across

Table 10.7   Apparel prices relative to the
Average Price Index (1974 = 100).

Year	Jan 1974 = 100	Ratio[1]
1974	100	100
1975	126	94
1976	139	86
1977	157	86
1978	171	87
1979	187	84
1980	205	79
1981	208	71
1982	210	66
1983	215	65
1984	215	61
1985	223	60
1986	229	59
1987	233	58
1988	250	59
1989	254	56
1990	266	53
1991	275	51

[1] The ratio is given by $\dfrac{\text{Apparel Price Index}}{\text{RPI}} \times 100$

Source: Jones, R.M. (1994) 'The Demand for Clothing
in the UK 1974–1991', *The Journal of Clothing
Technology and Management*, **11**, 85–114.

all product groups, e.g. (Manning, 1999) shows that between 1965 and 1999 bread prices fell by 16% while beer prices rose by a factor of 19.

Unfortunately most of the studies of consumer prices do not refer to apparel. The ONS, contacted by the author, commented that we 'do not release information relating to the average prices of individual goods . . . other than those in the food category'. (It is not immediately obvious why trends in apparel prices should be regarded as sensitive!)

Robinson (1999) conducted a study of the relative change in apparel prices and the average wage in the UK between 1974 and 1988 for a range of garments based on data from the Littlewoods catalogue. This data source was selected for the convenience of providing a single source over a long time period. Table 10.8, based on Robinson's data, confirms the exceptionally good value for money enjoyed by apparel consumers in the UK. By way of a generalisation this study suggested that the time worked to earn a selection of garments had fallen by a factor of between two and three. In a comparison of price movements between 1971 and 1996 it was estimated (ONS, 1997) that the time required to earn the motor vehicle excise licence also fell by a factor of two whereas the working time needed to earn a pint of beer had hardly changed.

Table 10.8   Time worked to purchase apparel in minutes.

Garment type	1974	1979	1984	1989	1994	1998
Blouse	338	144	116	140	131	146
Skirt	297	144	136	280	139	138
Suit	1,559	1,032	851	668	624	588
Shirt (male)	332	104	128	143	69	88
Collar T-shirt	223	116	99	133	62	76

Source: Robinson, N. (1999) *A Study of Working Time and Apparel Purchases*, unpublished MMU Research Paper. This research was funded by the Hollings Faculty Short Research Project Fund.

This downward trend in the value of working time required to purchase apparel is further confirmed, for GB, by the International Metal Workers Federation (1998) in their study of the wages of various groups of workers in the metal industry between 1982 and 1995. A motor vehicle worker, for example, had to work for 25 hours to purchase a suit in 1982 but for only 18 hours in 1995. This may help account for the stabilisation in the proportion of expenditure devoted to apparel which was noted above although it is clear that as the range of consumer goods and services (such as electronic products) available to the consumer expands over time the struggle to maintain the proportion of expenditure devoted to purchases of apparel will continue. In this context, it may be significant that the apparel industry spends a surprisingly small amount of money on advertising and a survey of the top 100 UK advertisers in 1998 (Bainbridge, 1999) revealed that there was not a single apparel manufacturer or retailer in the list. In 1998, in the UK, the top brand advertisement in the apparel sector was (EMAP/MTI 1998/9) Levi Dockers spending £1.4 millions which amounted to 1.3% of what the top advertiser spent (£105 million). In 1997, for example, BT (British Telecom) spent more on advertising than the entire UK apparel sector. In 1997 the sector of the apparel industry which advertised most heavily was jeans and this sector *as a whole* spent 25% of the amount spent by *one* motor vehicle manufacturer, Ford.

Finally, it can be noted that Waterson (1999) has produced a calculation of the advertising:sales ratios for a variety of products. High ratios indicate intensive advertising activity. With the exception of the aforementioned jeans, most types of apparel scored in the region of 0.1 to 0.2 whereas the heavy spending product groups (such as toys, cereals, aspirins and deodorants) scored between 8.0 and 11.0. It is recognised that advertising is only one element in the promotions mix and that apparel products benefit from, for example, exposure in magazine articles and from in-store promotions and point-of-sale displays. It has already been recorded above that the share of consumer expenditure devoted to apparel has remained stable in the recent past and this could be taken as justification for the low level of advertising expenditure noted above. It is, nevertheless, somewhat striking that an image-driven product such as apparel should spend such relatively small amounts on a major element of the promotional mix and it will be interesting to see if this does, over time, impact unfavourably on apparel spending, in particular as new products, such as electronic communications, come on stream. *Social Trends* (2000) noted that spending on TV and audio equipment rose by a factor of four between the late 1960s and 1999, for example. These trends are confirmed by Table 10.3.

(iii)   Retail structure and the future of apparel retailing in the UK

Existing structure

The UK retail market for apparel is highly concentrated. Easey (1995, p. 152) estimated that some 30% of apparel sales in 1990 were controlled by the top four retail groups. De Silva (2000) concluded that 'when taking account of cumulative inflation for the period (1992–6) there was in fact a real decrease in sales by smaller businesses of 11.1%. The share of total sales taken by larger businesses . . . increased by 3.7% to 83.2% of the total'. *Retail Intelligence* (1999) estimated that 72.5% of UK apparel sales went through larger retailers in 1998. The position is similar in the USA where (Gereffi, 1999) the top give retailers controlled 68% of all apparel sales in 1995.

It was noted in Chapter 1 that the textile–apparel supply chain is retailer-led. The importance of this cannot be overstressed. As Murphy (1999, p. 379) puts it, 'the most significant trend in retailing has been the shift in power between the suppliers to the retail trade. Up until the mid-1960s manufacturers held a powerful position in distribution channels as they were the source of almost all product innovations and new product developments' but changes began to take place as retailers sourced from a greater variety of manufacturers and geographical locations. In De Silva's estimation (2000, p. 166) the existing structure of the retail sector is best described as 'one where concentration prevails . . . larger retailers are increasingly controlling the supply chain, gaining relative bargaining power at the expense of manufacturers'. Zuhone (1995), in a study based on the theory of power-dependency, found that there was a marked imbalance of power 'with retailers having greater power than manufacturers in key decision making areas' and that this was likely to continue in the future.

In McGoldrick's opinion (1990, p. 4) the main reasons behind this trend have been the abolition of Retail Price Maintenance in 1964, the increase in the relative size of the retailers (see Chapter 2) and the rise in the importance of retail brands. This factor was also stressed by De Silva (2000) who noted that the retailers 'do not rely on the innovation of the supplier in creating new lines'. In terms of the Five Forces Model it has been suggested (in Chapter 2) that, in the UK, the dominance of the supply chain by large retailers seeking relatively long

Table 10.9   Retail market shares (%).

Type of outlet	All clothing and footwear (1998)	Clothing (2004)
Variety chains	19.6	
Department stores	8.6	12.4
Multiples	23.7	—
Independents	11.2	—
Discounters	3.9	—
Mail order	9.4	8.8
Supermarkets	2.7	5.4
Clothing specialists	—	66.1
Sports shops	—	4.3
Textile specialists	—	2.0
Others	—	1.0

Sources: 1998 figures from The UK Fashion Report (EMAP/MTI 1998/1999);
2004 figures from The Clothing Market in the UK (Mintel, 2005).

and 'safe' production runs resulted in the degree of sophistication of the buyer to the manufacturer being relatively low and, in the long run, counterproductive to the ability of UK-based manufacturers to develop winning strategies on a global basis.

The current division of the UK apparel market between the various distribution channels is summarised in Table 10.9. The dominant role of multiples and variety chains is clear. Department stores have suffered a slow but steady decline between 1988 and 1993 (Williams, 1997) but have enjoyed a minor renaissance since the mid-1990s, prompted perhaps by the ageing of the population. The share of the market taken by mail order has been static – at about 10% – for some time although this may, in the future, be influenced by the rise in electronic shopping. As for the independents, most commentators, such as the UK Fashion Report (EMAP/MTI 1998/9, p. 13), contend that 'clothing retailing is heading for a shakeout and . . . the future for most independents is bleak'. The major UK apparel retailers are identified in Table 10.10. The most important recent trends have been the rise of the so-called 'discounters' such as Matalan.

As Murphy (1998) concluded, the current UK apparel retailing industry shows indicators of both a transformation and being in a state of flux. The future importance of a number of previously dominant retail groups seems to be in doubt while the challenge of new shopping modes looms on the horizon.

However, it is clearly possible – if ever more difficult – to achieve success as has been shown by the performance of companies such as Gap, New Look and Matalan who have demonstrated what can be achieved by adopting a differentiation strategy. There seems little doubt that the retailers will remain dominant in the supply chain and that increasingly they will look to offshore sources of supply. The biggest single change has been the rise of the so-called 'discounters'

Table 10.10   Largest UK apparel retailers.

No.	Company		Turnover (£m)
1	Marks & Spencer plc	(quoted)	8,077.2
2	GUS plc	(quoted)	7,146.0
3	John Lewis Partnership plc		4,246.1
4	Next plc	(quoted)	2,202.6
5	Arcadia Group Ltd		2,019.4
6	Littlewoods Ltd		1,844.6
7	Debenhams Retail plc		1,810.2
8	Matalan plc	(quoted)	1,021.5
9	House of Fraser	(quoted)	963.5
10	JJB Sports Ltd	(quoted)	934.3
11	BHS Stores Ltd		882.2
12	New Look Group plc	(quoted)	643.4
13	Primark Stores Ltd		488.4

Source: FAME database.
Note: (1)   I am grateful to Michael Jeffrey for producing these figures.

or low price retailers, such as Primark. In addition, as Mintel (2002) notes, the 'grocers have grown their market share since the 1990s'.

The role of the retail buyer

The concentration of retail power described above has elevated the role of the retail buyer to a position of great importance. There have been few recent studies of the precise nature of the apparel retail buying process. As Sternquist (1989) noted, 'the literature about retail buyers' behaviour is sparse'. In more general terms, most standard marketing texts contain sections on the differences between the personal and organisational buyer which recognise the complexities of the latter. Chisnall (1985, p. 183), for example, summarises the distinction by recognising that organisational buying is 'complex, in that it deals with suppliers often far more sophisticated in nature than most consumer products; the process of buying is seldom settled entirely by one person's decision; scale of purchase is mostly substantial and the repercussions of purchasing a specific product . . . may be profoundly felt . . .'.

   In the words of McGoldrick (1990, p. 188), buying 'represents the translation of a retailer's strategic positioning statement into the overall assortment and the specific products to support that statement. The retail buyer holds a pivotal role in the implementation of a retail strategy . . .'. McGoldrick (1990, p. 190) argues, first, that there is some evidence that successful buying does translate into good overall company performance and, second, that the buying function has become increasingly centralised. Fairham (1990) also found that buyer performance and experience affected profits.

One of the specific studies of the role of the buyer in the apparel industry was carried out by Harris (1991) who compared the attitudes of apparel buyers in the USA, Canada and Western Europe. The study largely confirmed both the changes in global sourcing highlighted in Chapter 3 and revealed some interesting variations in buying practices between the three regions studied. European buyers exhibited greater enthusiasm for non-domestic sourcing and expected it to increase, and price was given as the dominant reason for a change to non-domestic sourcing which is in line with the importance placed on labour costs in Chapter 4.

Interestingly, Canadian buyers gave quotas as a reason for decreasing imports from major offshore suppliers, which may support the view expressed in Chapter 9 that the main effect of the MFA was trade diversion. Quick response, somewhat surprisingly, was not recognised as a major factor in the buying decision. Hong Kong dominated the private label field as the source of first choice whereas in the case of high priced products Italy ranked as the number one source in designer labels. In terms of rating the factors which would be considered in selecting a source country, a conflict emerged between (Harris, 1991, p. 93) the 'declared principle of seeking quality of product and service and the apparent practice of buying on the basis of price. It could be assumed that, while quality and service are what buyers believe they are seeking, price is the determining factor'. This again justifies both the emphasis placed on labour costs and the conclusion drawn that offshore sourcing is bound to increase.

Finally, there were substantial differences in the sources of information utilised by buyers in identifying potential suppliers; in Canada sales agents were dominant whereas in Europe, international domestic trade shows were the preferred source. In the USA, buying offices were three times more important than any other source of information. The study by Sternquist (1989) had also found that quality was the main factor given for purchasing foreign products and noted that retail buyers did not perceive sourcing offshore to be risky. De Silva (2000) found in a survey of 102 UK apparel buyers that there was not 'a general, all encompassing way of describing how buyers make decisions' but that they typically functioned within a group and frequently enjoyed considerable autonomy although when making sourcing decisions they typically had to liaise with others for approval on issues of a budgetary nature. The majority of apparel buyers were female and there was a clear trend towards the employment of more graduates.

It may be significant – in relation to the future of the apparel industry in the UK – that the performance of buyers was usually assessed by reference to margins achieved with the result that decisions were taken 'more often on "hard" criteria such as cost'. It is unlikely that the power of the apparel retailer relative to that of the manufacturer will decline in the near future so the attitudes and behaviour of the retail buyer will remain of interest. In addition, as the proportion of the market supplied offshore goes up and the role of domestic assembly declines, buying offices in areas of low labour costs are likely to achieve greater importance in the supply chain in the future – see, for example, the report by Magretta (1998) on the role of buying offices in Hong Kong.

It is also conceivable that the increased use of electronic marketplaces within the textile pipeline may result in buyers reducing their supplier base (if only because larger suppliers may be more equipped to participate) with a consequent rise in the power of a limited number of large purchases – as has been described by Mortishead (2000) in relation to British Airways and by Baker (2000) in relation to the World Wide Retail Exchange, headed by an ex-Courtaulds Textiles executive. Specialist textiles marketplaces already exist as demonstrated by Textiles Solutions.com based in Gothenburg (Bengtsson, 2001).

The future structure of apparel retailing in the UK

At the present time it can legitimately be argued that (Murphy, 1998, p. 380) 'substitutes to the High Street . . . currently are relatively unimportant in terms of market share' but it is also true that the market exhibits signs of unrest and transformation with, in particular, some of the previously most successful and important (in terms of market share) companies, such as Marks & Spencer and Arcadia, showing signs of a loss of direction and vitality.

The retailing of apparel is the fourth cell of the pipeline described in Fig. 1.1. Apparel has, after manufacture, to be delivered to the consumer. This can be achieved by a variety of mechanisms such as conventional high street stores, out of town shopping malls, traditional mail order or electronic home shopping.

The accepted doctrine is that this fourth cell in the pipeline has had the power to capture a disproportionately high proportion of the value added generated within the pipeline as a whole (see Chapter 2). The relative strength of each cell can be assessed using the concept of buyer power from the Five Forces Model outlined in Chapter 1. In this case it will be useful to picture the pipeline horizontally (see Fig. 10.1) so as to highlight the buyer–seller relationships throughout the pipeline. As product moves from left to right each element sells to their customer. The manufacturer's customer is the retailer personified by the retail buyer; the retailer's customer is the final consumer.

In this context the present author must strongly disagree with other published versions of this model as outlined in Murphy (1999) and Cox (2000). In these two sources the concept of the bargaining power of buyers applied to the retail sector is related to the strength of the retailers themselves. Cox (2000, p. 32), for example, gives as an illustration of the power of a customer to force down supplier prices the power of Marks & Spencer as the UK's third biggest retailer; Murphy (1999) likewise (using Cox as the justification) argues that the power of buyers in the Five Forces Model should be represented by the 'bargaining power

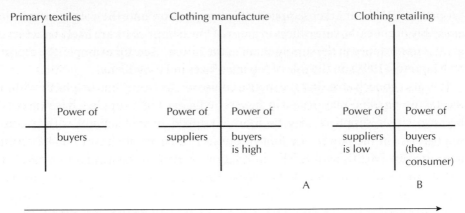

Fig. 10.1   The textiles–fashion supply chain and the power of the consumer.

of retailers'. This seems to be quite indefensible. It is clear that the large retailers exercise tremendous power in the pipeline so that a retailer like Marks & Spencer can be, as Cox puts it (2000, p. 32) 'in a stronger position to force down supplier prices' but this force must, by definition, be applied by the retailers to *their* suppliers, namely the manufacturers at A in Fig. 10.1. The customers of the retail sector who might apply strong or weak bargaining power as the *buyers* of the output of the retail sector are the final consumers (at B) – they cannot be the retailers themselves exerting bargaining power as the buyers of their own output! Porter (1998, p. 35) argues that powerful 'buyers or suppliers bargain away the profits for themselves' and that 'buyer power . . . is a function of such things as the number of buyers, how much a firm's sales are at risk to any one buyer . . .'. The suppliers to the retailer are the apparel manufacturers; the purchasers are the final consumers. Clearly the proportion of an apparel retailer's sales which are at risk to any one consumer is negligible. The only exception to this rule would be cases in which powerful consumer groups organised to boycott a specific apparel retailer. It is, of course, true that each consumer wields the ultimate sanction of deciding not to buy a product and it is possible that, over time, consumers could turn away from apparel purchases towards, for example, electronic products or consumer services. An illustration of the exercise of this power 'not to buy' would be the experience of the motor vehicle trade at the end of 1999. However, it seems to the present author unlikely that the biggest threats to the ability of the fourth cell in the textile pipeline to capture a large share of the total profit generated by the pipeline are likely to come from an increase in consumer power. The consumer can prevent prices being raised but provided that the fourth cell remains powerful relative to the other cells in the pipeline and provided that adversarial rather than co-operative relationships prevail, this 'problem' can be passed back down the pipeline and, for example, the manufacturing cell can be forced to absorb the pressure. There is little or nothing in current developments to suggest that the power of the retailer relative to the manufacturer is declining as was noted in the introduction to this section. The potential impact of the creation of electronic marketplaces on the internet for intermediate products upon the relative power of different elements in the supply chain is problematic but Mortished (2000) argues that the power of purchasing managers will rise and business will be channelled 'only to those whose electronic systems can be integrated sufficiently with those of an all powerful [retail] buyer' and that the advantage will lie with larger businesses. In the textile–apparel supply chain this would simply confirm the existing power of the retail buyer.

In relation to the question of shifts in the balance of power between alternative forms of business *within* a particular cell of the supply chain it seems most likely that the greatest threat to the position of the traditional apparel retailer will be manifested through other elements of the Five Forces Model such as, in particular, the threat of New Entry into the market by overseas retailers such as Benetton, Morgan, Kookai, Gap, Diesel and Zara and the threat of substitutes such as the evolution of non-traditional methods of shopping.

Substitution of non-apparel products in the overall expenditure of consumers has already been seen to be another threat. In Cox's words (2000, p. 31) 'different forms of retail channel compete for custom and a new and growing threat is from the Internet . . . Again, there is a gain in convenience as in mail order shopping. E-commerce is continually improving its accessibility and performance and this will attract more personal computer users to link up to it'.

The major unknown in this context is the extent to which consumers will differentiate between types of products in which e-commerce will really take off and those in which it will not because, for example, they wish to inspect the product or regard conventional shopping for a product as a social event. Williams (1997, p. 164) argues that teleshopping 'has the potential to effect major changes in shopping patterns. Its impact on the retail fashion market will develop over the coming years influenced by consumer acceptance and its own cost effectiveness'.

The ability of home shopping to capture a significant share of the market has been trumpeted many times in the past, e.g. Brenninkmeyer (1986) but, as Murphy (1998, p. 380) observed, while the traditional high street has 'had some competition from substitutability by conventional mail order catalogue companies . . . none of these has had more than a peripheral effect on mainstream UK retailing'. The wide availability of access to the internet via PC and TV has revived claims that the age of electronic shopping is about to dawn. It is difficult to be objective about the size of the electronic shopping market in the UK because, first, a wide range of estimates of current access appear in the literature and, second, many of the statistics quoted are forecasts – which also differ alarmingly. Most authorities estimate that in 2004 in the UK around 60% of homes had access to a PC and around 50% to the internet. However, Mintel (2005) estimates that apparel sales via the internet in the UK were a small part of the total while Goldsmith (2002) puts the figure in the USA at around 3% of the total. Mintel (2002, p. 50) concluded that e-commerce sales of apparel 'had yet to become significant'. Corporate Intelligence (1997) estimated that in the six months up to March 1997, 250,000 UK customers made an on-line purchase.

Most commentators are making very optimistic forecasts for the growth of electronic home shopping. Verdict Research predict (Verdict Research, 2000) that the internet's share of the total market will rise from 0.3% in 1999 to 3% in 2004. Therefore, much of the enthusiasm is based on future expectations rather than current experience and much is based on a comparison with the USA where it was estimated (Euromonitor, 1996a), in the mid-1990s that some 28% of retail sales were already made by the so-called 'distance' mode. The forecast for the USA in 2006, for example, is as high as $81 billion for all goods (Monsuwe, 2004) while Kim (2004) estimates that for France, Germany and the UK combined on-line sales may reach $168 billion by 2007.

There is clearly a demand for a home shopping facility – it has been provided over many years by the traditional mail order route which usually holds 75% of the UK home shopping market (*Corporate Intelligence*, 1997). Weeks (1998) confirmed that catalogue shopping was still the preferred non-store option among female consumers but argued that electronic shopping did pose a significant threat in the future. In the present context the crucial issue is the extent to which the pattern of shopping for apparel in the UK will, in the future, be modified by the advent of electronic shopping. It is difficult to be prescriptive in the absence of a model of fashion behaviour but it is possible to indicate factors which will influence the impact e-commerce might have on the fashion retailing sector, e.g. the extent to which consumers regard shopping for apparel as a social event and the extent to which customers require to actually see, touch and try on the product (Parsons, 2002).

A survey by the Future Foundation (1999) found that apparel was towards the bottom of a list of products which consumers said they purchase via the internet. As Corporate Intelligence (1997) conclude, not 'all products are suitable for selling through electronic shopping channels and those goods that consumers like to see, touch, feel . . . are likely to remain sold face to face'. The impact of electronic shopping will also depend on a number of non-product-specific factors such as efficiency of delivery and fears about the security of payment systems (Parsons, 2002).

There is no doubt that the growth of electronic home shopping is seen as a major issue by existing retailers. Thus, according to *Marketing* (1999) 46% of retailers believe this is the biggest challenge faced by the retailing sector. The full impact is probably some way into the future and, as Murphy (1998) notes, while 'a number of fashion retailers have made big investments in the internet – Arcadia, Marks & Spencer and Austin Reed to name just a few – most have been testing the water'. Bickerton (1999) concluded his survey of fashion retailing in Europe by arguing that electronic shopping 'will never replace personal selling, which holds a strong attraction for most European consumers, particularly young women'. Murphy (1998) concluded her survey of UK apparel retailers' use of the net with the words 'the future of electronic retailing is not about substituting software for human interaction . . . but rather how to use the WWW to create new kinds of interactions between consumers and businesses'. If this is correct then the challenge to existing face-to-face retailers will be to also create a new experience for the shopper; in the words of *Marketing* (1999) 'no-one believes that virtual shopping will make shops obsolete but retailers will need to justify and adapt their physical presence in order to survive'.

Electronic home shopping has also attracted a lot of academic interest. There is a huge body of research into the attributes of home shoppers (Lee, 2002; Goldsmith, 2002, 2004); into their profiles (Goldsmith, 2002; Karayanni, 2003; Kau, 2003) and into their purchase intentions (Park, 2003; Kim, 2004, 2005). There may, therefore, be uncertainty about the relative future strengths of various modes of apparel distribution but other features of the textile–apparel supply chain appear to be firmly established. First, the chain will continue to be retailer driven because, as Mattila (1996, p. 21) expresses it, they have 'become much bigger and more powerful in product sourcing' as they pursue their aim of going 'direct to the source themselves and subcontract production of their collections'. Second, the role of own label seems set to rise to the detriment of traditional manufacturers who will (Mattila, 1996, p. 23) 'face increasing competition in the future as retailers' own label sales increase and as the products are primarily sourced from outside the EU'.

C. Social, cultural and demographic factors in the evolution of the apparel market

Although the main focus of the present chapter is an economic one, it would be inappropriate not to recognise that there have been a number of extremely significant social, cultural and demographic changes which have had the potential to affect significantly the demand for apparel. These include changing gender roles in society, reflected in the rising proportion of women going out to work which rose from 49% in 1984 to 53% in 1994 (CSO, 1996, p. 17); the increasing proportion of the workforce in the service sector (see Chapter 1); the increased availability of credit; the growth of out-of-town shopping centres and the sheer availability of shops which encourage shopping as a leisure activity; the emergence of younger children as fashion consumers and the trend towards a more casual styled dress.

While it is true that (Chisnall, 1985, p. 16) explanations of consumer behaviour 'based solely on economic theory are clearly inadequate' and too narrow in focus there is, in a real sense, no necessary conflict between arguing that the size of the apparel market is primarily driven by economic factors and recognising the importance of social change. This is because many social changes have had the effect of increasing the affluence and economic independence of various groups, enabling consumers to indulge their desire for change and their wish to purchase something new and stimulating – the social and economic trends thus work in tandem.

A useful summary of the impact of social and cultural influences on the marketplace is produced by Palmer (1992) who demonstrates, for example, that there is a body of evidence showing the relationship between social class and consumer behaviour. Families represent a vital reference group and as the number of one-parent families increases it must be expected that this will be reflected in the demand for various categories of products in the same way as the proportion of people living alone impacts upon the demand for food products packaged in smaller quantities.

Cultural changes may also influence consumption behaviour. Palmer (1992) shows how the ethnic make-up of the population of the UK has changed over time and how it varies as between regions. This may affect the demand for ethnic foods and apparel. Other important social and cultural changes which can be identified as potentially influencing the demand for products include an increased amount of time devoted to leisure; the raised awareness of healthy living and 'green' issues; the trend towards greater informality and the casualisation of modes of dress, to name but a few. It is not being argued here that these issues do not matter. Rather it is contended that economic affluence is a prerequisite or a facilitator through which these various and disparate social trends are often expressed.

One of the most important social changes to have taken place in the recent past has been a demographic one, i.e. the ageing of the population. The potential importance of this for the apparel market has been widely recognised in the literature as is exemplified by the comment of the *UK Fashion Report* (EMAP/MTI, 1988/9, p. 23) that the 'population will become gradually older with the mean age expected to rise from 38.4 in 1996 to 42 by 2021' and (Anon, 2000, p. 84) that 'future retail spending will be affected by the demographic profile of the UK' which exhibits clear peaks in the 40–54 age group of post-war baby boomers and the 25–39 age group which consists of the children of the early baby boomers. Table 10.11 confirms that the younger age groups will decline while the 45–64 age group, on the other hand, is expected to gain 3 million people, based on an estimated total UK population in 2011 of 61 million.

Table 10.11   UK Population 1971–2011 (age groups as percentages of population).

Age group	In 1971	In 1997	In 2021 (projected)
0–14	24.1	19.2	22.1
15–29	21.1	19.9	17.7
30–44	17.5	22.3	19.4
45–64	24.0	22.8	26.2
30–64	41.5	45.1	45.7
65+	13.3	15.7	20.1
45+	37.3	38.5	46.4

Source: Annual Abstract of Statistics (ONS, 2004).

As Coleman and Salt (1992, p. 5) conclude, 'Business demographics is becoming big business in the USA and the ideas are now catching on in Britain. The centre of gravity of the baby boom in 1990 is still in the 15–29 group . . . By the 1990s it will have moved into the 30–44 age group; around the end of the century it will have made the latter middle aged group of over 45s the most potent force in the market place'. It is inevitable that by 2025 the people born in the two baby boom periods of the 1940s and 1960s will all be over 55 years of age. It is also a matter of record that many UK apparel retailers have targeted their customers by age. As Easey (1995, p. 102) states, 'the idea of segmentation has been taken on board by most of the high street retailers'. The Behling (1985) model reviewed below utilises the median age of the population as one of the independent variables. Therefore the view expressed by TMS (1996, p. 1) that 'age remains the biggest discriminator in clothing' has to be taken seriously.

It is also generally accepted in the literature that the younger age groups have been the fashion leaders. Easey (1995), for example, argues that innovators tend to be more open minded younger people and that the strength of feeling of group affiliations is greater in the young. The same point is made by Goldsmith (1992). Key Note (1998) showed that apparel spending also varies with age and income. ONS (1999) data show that in absolute terms (in £s) expenditure by age group is highest in the under-thirties age segment of the population. Therefore, changes in either or both the age distribution of the population and the proportion of income/wealth controlled by each age group could reasonably be expected to have a significant impact on the apparel market. In the words of Johnson (1990a, p. 59) the changes in demand in the market 'will not be simply from young to old . . . The booming teenage market of the 1960s and 1970s is a thing of the past and the new growth area will be people in later middle age'.

Verdict Research (2000) considers that retailers have been slow to respond to demographic changes, arguing that those retailers who continue to be fixated by younger consumers will lose out compared to those who target the older, more mature consumers who have real spending power. Verdict noted that by 2010

Table 10.12   Changes in population and income shares in UK 1986–1994 (as percentages).

Age group	Population change	Share of income change
16–25	−2.6	−0.8
26–45	+12.2	+12.5
46–64	+6.6	+5.6
65+	+1.9	+0.5
16–45	+9.6	+11.7
26–64	+18.8	+18.1
46+	+8.5	+6.1

Source: Jones, R.M. (1999) Demographics, the Distribution of Income and Wealth and the Marketing of Fashion in the UK. *Journal of the Textile Institute* (Part 2), Vol. 90, 1999, pp. 1–14.

there will be 2 million fewer 25–39 year-olds in the UK, for example. The 20–24 group is also small following the low birth rate in the 1970s. Unfortunately, the implications of these changes for apparel purchases are, upon closer inspection, far less straightforward than might initially be expected.

Jones (1999) concluded that most age groups lost or gained income share in line with changes in their share of the population (see Table 10.12). In the UK, in the period 1986–1993, one age group emerged as significantly increasing their share of income, namely the 26–45 age group. However, McAdam (1996) concluded that in that period the strongest fashion influence remained with the young – despite the fact that the median age of the population was steadily rising and that the share of both population and income represented by the younger age group (16–25) was also falling. Therefore it may well be the case that the young will always have the greatest interest in, and influence upon, fashion trends irrespective of trends in income or population shares. As Evans (1989) noted, the 'future dwindling size of the youth markets will not detract from their importance' because the concept of the youth market is so firmly entrenched in marketing analysis. Of almost equal interest to income distribution is the distribution of wealth. Unfortunately, as Dilnot (1994) points out, there is almost no empirical evidence concerning the distribution of wealth at the household or individual level in the UK. Jones (1999) secured some age-specific data for the periods 1991/2 and 1997/8 and found that changes in the shares of wealth and population by age group were not particularly well correlated.

Over the period, two age groups noticeably increased their share of the UK's wealth – the 30–34 group and, more especially, the 45–49 group. The latter controlled 39% of the nation's wealth in 1991/2 and is predicted to account for 21% of the population in 2011. In 1991 the over-50s constituted 31% of the population but controlled 54% of the nation's wealth. The main conclusion drawn by Jones (1999) was that the use of predicted changes in the shares of the population accounted for by various age groups to act as a guide to the economic strength of these groups and, by implication, the desirability of retargeting the product offer towards the expanding groups is a much less straightforward matter than might have been anticipated.

Palmer (1992, p. 172) records the efforts made by the (then) Burton Group to re-align their shops towards an older age group which was entirely in line with demographic forecasts but, as events early in 2000 have shown, this by itself was insufficient to prevent the collapse of the (now) Arcadia Group. The issue of demographic change and its impact on the apparel market is further complicated by uncertainty about what might best be described as the behavioural (as opposed to the chronological age) of the middle-aged consumer in the early twenty-first century.

Dychtwald (1997), in fact, argued that we already have a new idea of what 'old' means in that it is recognised that many over 65 years of age are still active. Morchis (1997) stresses that 'ageing is multi-dimensional, that is people gradually grow old biologically, psychologically and socially'. The second so-called 'baby boomer' group (of the 1960s) grew up under radically different social, economic and cultural circumstances to earlier generations – in particular, their experiences contrast vividly with those of the first 'baby boomer' period of the 1940s. Leventhal (1997) concluded that the second 'baby boomer' group was relatively more willing to try new products; was more widely read; more cynical; had a greater understanding of values and had a greater desire to obtain facts than earlier generations.

Bellan (1998, p. 106) in a study of age-related attitudes towards apparel in the USA suggested that 'many older people see themselves as younger than their chronological age' and that while there did not appear to be significant variations in the attitudes of younger and older women towards apparel there were great differences in their attitudes to media messages. Her conclusion was (Bellan, 1998, p. 111) that 'older women make up a large market with large discretionary income. They are willing to spend ... on apparel that fits appropriately and appeals to them'. In the women's wear market, however, there is considerable evidence (Jackson, 1994; Pruim, 1999) that irrespective of how women view themselves, body shape and size does change with age. Therefore, providing the correct balance between aspirations and practicability may represent a severe retailing challenge. The 'older' market is not homogeneous and is complex. Morchis (1997), for example, subdivides older consumers into four groups (healthy indulgers, ailing outgoers, healthy hermits and frail recluses) which would need to be served by entirely different marketing mixes. Therefore, as the above brief review has demonstrated, there is no escaping the fact that social, cultural and demographic changes all represent potentially significant variables in the evolution of the apparel market particularly when attention is focused upon the fashion process as opposed to the size of the market. It has proven to be extremely difficult to incorporate these factors in a workable model of the fashion process, as will be explained in the next section.

D. *Theories of fashion and the limits of economic determinism in the apparel market*

(i)   *A model of expenditure on apparel in the UK*

It has been noted above that there is a well established and close relationship between income and aggregate expenditure. This was confirmed by Mills' (1997) study of household spending. Jones (1997) has tested a model of consumer expenditure on apparel in which the independent variables are the trend in real disposable income and the price of apparel relative to the movement in all prices. The rationale behind the model was that in developed economies the demand for apparel can no longer be regarded as primarily a basic need. In Maslow's terms (Easey, 1995, p. 58) it is not a necessity in that most consumers have more garments than are required for functional purposes. Indeed it is imperative for the apparel industry that they are willing to replace garments which are not worn out.

Demand in these circumstances depends primarily on the amount of real disposable income available. The model has been tested for both the UK and Sweden. In both cases the model worked in the sense that changes in the two independent variables explained over 90% of the change in consumption upon apparel (see Fig. 10.2). In both cases it was possible to omit the price variable without significantly reducing the ability of the model to predict consumption but it was not possible to leave out the income variable without damaging the efficiency of the model. Therefore it can be confirmed that the most important variable determining variations in expenditure upon apparel is the trend in income. The income elasticity of demand in the UK was +0.9223 while price elasticity was −0.3733. These results (for the period 1974–1991) contrast vividly with those recorded by Briscoe (1971, p. 51) for the period 1946–1964 – when the income elasticity was calculated as +0.5 and the price elasticity as −1.11. Stone (1966) estimated that the income elasticity of demand for apparel in the 1930s was 1.4. The latest research by Jones (2002) found that income elasticity in the period 1997–2000 had risen to +2.0 while price elasticity had returned to −1.1. This suggests that, in the UK, over time apparel has changed from being a necessity to a luxury. In the USA, Fadiga (2005) estimated that expenditure elasticity for apparel ranged from +0.4 to +2.5 while price elasticities ranged from −1.0 to −2.0 so that classification as a luxury or necessity depended on garment type. Norum (1999) confirmed the crucial role of income in determining the consumption of apparel and fashion accessories in which case income elasticities were positive but less than one.

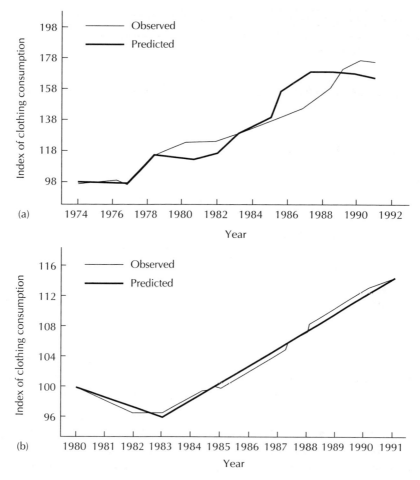

Fig. 10.2 A demand model tested for the UK and Sweden. Source: Jones, R.M. & Robb, P. (1997) The Demand for Clothing in the UK and Sweden. *Journal of Fashion Marketing and Management*, **1**, 113–125. Reproduced with permission. The top chart is the UK.

In a real sense, therefore, the likely future health of the UK apparel market can be predicted by examining trends in real personal disposable income which act as a leading indicator. The current trend is quite healthy (see Table 10.4) which bodes well for the market in the near future. The most important fact is that in relation to the overall size of the market – a very important fact to most businesses – there is a reliable leading indicator, namely income.

As Balkwell (1992) concluded:

'Economic and demographic variables are but part of the total fabric of culture. Consequently, they explain part of the major changes in dress dimensions and leave part unexplained.'

Economic independent variable	R^2%
Vogue data	
RPI	0.5
FT index	7.6
Rate of interest*	12.6 .
% unemployed	6.5
GDP	0.2
Littlewoods data	
RPI	4.9
FT index	0.3
Rate of interest**	1.3
% unemployed	10.5
GDP	0.0

Notes: * The regression *was* significant at the 5% level.
** The regression *was not* significant at the 5% level. The author wishes to acknowledge the assistance provided by Paul Robb, Departmental Statistical Assistant, who undertook the above computations.

Fig. 10.3   Summary of relationships between skirt lengths and economic variables.

Variations in skirt lengths illustrate the problems caused by the absence of an accepted model of the fashion process. In fact it is relatively easy to demonstrate that, for the UK at least, there is no relationship between the state of the economy and at least one specific dimension of fashion change viz skirt length. The assumption of cause and effect seems flawed in that there is no logical reason why skirts should be long in a recession and vice versa as has been argued by Mabry (1971) and many commentators since that date, such as Quant (1997). A test which takes skirt length ratios from Curran (1993) and correlates them against a range of standard economic indicators produces the results shown in Fig. 10.3. The extent to which the fashion cycle (as illustrated by variations in skirt length) can be explained by economic fluctuations is clearly refuted by the evidence and this particular idea can be disposed of once and for all. Economics has relatively little to contribute in this area of analysis but unfortunately rival constructs (which often incorporate some economic variables) have been slow to emerge.

(ii)   Alternative theories of the fashion process

The trend in the size of the apparel market can be explained by reference to economic factors – primarily income and price. However, in relation to the other dimensions of the apparel market identified in the introduction to this chapter – the direction and process of fashion change and the sources of new fashions – achieving a sound theoretical base for examining these issues has been far more difficult. As Sproles (1981, p. 117) observed, fashion theory 'includes a loosely organised array of *descriptive* (present author's emphasis) principles and propositions but it is not formalised in that it does not specify a detailed structure of concepts, variables and relations'. The passage of time has only – in the works of Behling and Nagasawa – partially remedied these shortcomings. Although the focus of this text (and chapter) is the economic dimension, it is important that models of change in the apparel market be reviewed even though they fall outside the strictly defined field of economics because, first, they often incorporate an economic dimension and, second, because it is useful to grasp the difficulties which have been created by the absence of a thoroughly validated model of fashion change.

There is a large literature base in the area widely defined as theories of fashion or models of the fashion process which will now be reviewed. First, a number of descriptive frameworks have been developed. The concept of the fashion cycle, for example, is well established in the literature (Easey, 1995, p. 127) and marketing theorists have devised classification systems which categorise consumers according to how likely they are to adopt new products (Easey, 1995, p. 67). The classic theory of innovation diffusion is attributed to Rogers and Shoemaker (1971). According to this theory consumers can be allocated to one of five groups: (a) innovators; (b) early adopters; (c) early majority; (d) late majority; and (e) laggards. Behling (1992, p. 40) has identified the fashion innovators as having the following profile: 'is a relatively young individual, is not married . . . has no children, has a relatively high income and occupation level, is likely to be female . . . and is mobile'. Goldsmith (1992) has, in contrast, argued that age was the most important factor in identifying fashion leaders and that, in his sample, neither income nor education was significant.

Finally, a number of theories have been produced to describe the diffusions of fashions through society. The so-called conspiracy theory is based on the contention that fashions are forced upon consumers by the industry. According to Sproles (1981, p. 118) there is 'little empirical documentation to support this idea although there can be little doubt that regular change is necessary to the survival of the apparel industry'. Goldsmith (1992, p. 176) does argue that 'industry is the more powerful change agent for fashion, not consumers'. The alternative models are consumer-based and include the following:

(1) *Trickle down theory*. This is the oldest model and was in vogue at the turn of the century. It contends that fashions spread downwards through society from an older, more affluent consumer in the higher social classes. Investigations by King (1981) and Field (1981) suggested that it had little empirical support. This, it must be stated, would not in itself reveal a fatal flaw in that, as will be seen, none of the so-called theoretical constructs enjoy much empirical verification.

(2) *Trickle up theory*. This proposes that fashions evolve at street level and move upwards through the social classes. Initially the young were seen as the origin of these upward movements but Field (1981) suggested that other groups, such as blue-collar workers or the ethnic minorities might also be sources of inspiration for new fashions. This is sometimes known as the Status Float Phenomenon (Field, 1981).

(3) *Trickle across theory*. This suggests that fashions spread laterally within each social class promoted by improvements in both mass production and communication.

(4) *The theory of collective selection*. This proposes that designers capture the spirit of the age.

(5) *The theory of sub-cultural innovation*. This suggests that ideas spread from disparate sub-cultural groups and are toned down, modified and adopted into mainstream fashion.

A useful summary of these concepts can be found in Curran (1991) but in reality none of these ideas constitute theories which have been subjected to any sort of rigorous testing although they have been supported by the use of selected examples, usually after the fact. Sproles (1981, p. 119), for example, concluded that in relation to the theory of sub-cultural innovation, 'research was non-existent' and that the 'mechanism of collective selection . . . is vague'. None of the above provides a means by which fashion change can be forecast with any degree of confidence and several are mutually exclusive. The result is that the fashion process has not lent itself to definitive explanation.

Two theoretical models have, however, been developed to an advanced stage and are worthy of attention. The oldest of the two models of fashion change and diffusion is that due to Behling (1985). It will be important to review this model because it features so prominently in the literature. The model isolates two independent variables – age and affluence – and relates changes in them to changes in two dependent variables – the direction and speed of fashion change. The independent variables are both clearly defined and objectively measured. However, one of the dependent variables is not precisely defined and neither are measured (and may not be measurable) in numerical terms. The direction of change is defined in terms of the trickle up or trickle down and the prediction is that the median age of the population determines whether or not fashions trickle down from the older groups or up from the younger groups. It is (Behling, 1985, p. 23) the median age 'which determines who the role models for our society will be, is a critical component of this theoretical model and determines whether or not fashion flows up or down from the young or from an older, wealthy' group of people. The degree of affluence 'may speed up the fashion change process or slow it down as the amount of discretionary income of large numbers of the population decreases or increases'. The concept of 'speed of fashion change' is not defined precisely.

Behling (1985, p. 23) concluded that the model worked in that it 'enables us to explain changes in fashion which have occurred over the past six and a half decades' and, additionally, would predict that in the future (up to the year 2000) that 'fashion influence should continue to trickle down from an older, affluent and visible class for the remainder of this century'.

There are, however, a number of serious problems in using this model, most of which derive from the difficulties noted in the introduction to this chapter of mixing research philosophies. First, the selection of the variable to measure affluence (the proportion of consumer spending financed from income as opposed to saving) offers no advantage over a more straightforward measure such as the trend in disposable income. Second, using the example of such a unique event as the Great Depression to demonstrate the validity of the argument that consumers dis-save in a recession is also counterproductive because it is simply not the case – either in the USA or the UK – that the savings ratio always goes up when incomes are rising and *vice versa*. In fact, most mainstream economists regard the official savings ratio data as almost totally unreliable. Harbury (1996, p. 234), for example, states that it is dangerous to read too much into the meaning of trends in the savings ratio which is a national income statistic known with remarkable little accuracy. In the UK the savings ratio peaked in 1980 and fell to 5% in 1988 at the height of the boom (Curwen, 1997). Artis (1992) points out that the traditional relationship between savings and the business cycle was no longer visible in the 1970s and 1980s. In the USA between 1960 and 1996 the savings ratio hardly moved in the affluent period 1960–70, remained constant in the mid-70s when incomes fell and then fell in the boom period of 1992–1996. Curwen (1997) argues that in the USA, the country within which the Behling model was developed, the official savings figures are regarded as something as a joke. Therefore, relying on the role of saving or dis-saving to generate an explanation of any trend is probably unwise.

Third, the two dependent variables are very difficult to define and measure objectively so that the mixing of objective data (on income) with more subjective analysis of fashion trends produces severe difficulties in that the result is a model which embodies the concept of casual relationships but cannot be tested by standard regression techniques because some of the variables are not measurable numerically. In effect the end product is a sort of hybrid model which employs the language of casual relationships but is not, in fact, a regression model in the real sense of the term.

Fourth, in both the UK and the USA the trend in affluence was, in the long period, almost exclusively upward (see Table 10.13 for the UK). It is true that minor and short-term recessions, for example in 1981 in the UK, correspond with short-term downturns in expenditure on apparel (Jones, 1997) but this does not discredit the observation that over the long term a steadily rising tide of affluence has remorselessly pulled up consumer expenditure. The same picture is revealed by the US Department of Commerce (1997) data for the post-1960 period.

Table 10.13   Lone term income trends in the
UK (£ millions, 2001 prices).

Year	Value (£ millions)	Index (2001 = 100)
1950	164,753	23.4
1960	223,531	31.8
1970	289,548	41.2
1972	317,431	45.2
1973	337,375	48.0
1974	334,654	47.6
1975	338,001	48.1
1976	336,678	47.9
1977	329,835	46.9
1978	354,004	50.4
1979	374,879	53.3
1980	381,136	54.2
1981	379,302	54.0
1982	377,984	53.8
1983	385,704	54.9
1984	400,106	57.0
1985	413,758	58.9
1986	430,863	61.3
1988	471,068	67.0
1989	493,163	70.2
1990	510,387	72.6
1991	520,698	74.1
1992	535,255	76.2
1993	549,995	78.3
1994	558,145	79.4
1995	571,105	81.3
1996	584,951	83.3
1998	610,691	86.9
1999	630,828	89.8
2000	670,109	95.3
2001	702,774	100.0
2002	713,235	101.5
2003	728,089	103.6

Source: Economic Trends (2004) Annual Supplement.

Therefore, while Behling (1985) identifies periods of greater and lesser prosperity the fact is that affluence has been rising steadily during the last four
decades and that this, as has been seen, has been largely responsible for the rise
in expenditure on apparel observed in both countries. If a graph of the trend in
disposable income is superimposed upon the graph used by Behling to show the
switch from trickle down to trickle up it adds very little to the analysis because it
is almost a straight line (see Fig. 10.4), indicating that variations in affluence
cannot contribute towards an explanation of the change in the fashion process
from trickle up to trickle down.

The search for an explanation of changes in the direction of fashion change
cannot, therefore, be carried out in the economic arena. The basic argument in

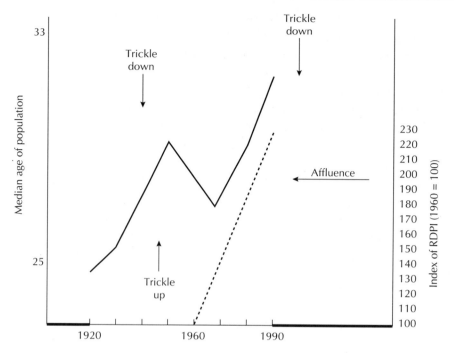

Fig. 10.4   A model of the fashion process (adapted from Behling (1985)).

the Behling model is that the direction of change is normally trickle down from an older, more affluent social class. This direction of flow can be reversed if the economy is (1985, p. 23) 'unusually depressed' and especially if the median age of the population is low or falling. It is true, as was shown in Section C above, that in the UK, for example, older people do own a high proportion of the nation's income and wealth. Therefore, it could reasonably be argued that what really matters is what age groups are able to participate in the marketplace although the literature does indicate that older people spend proportionately less of their income on apparel (Key Note, 1998).

The concept of the speed of the fashion process is also not precisely defined in the Behling model but it could be equated with a greater amount of spending on apparel in which case it would be correct to argue that this is positively associated with changes in affluence. If it is accepted that most apparel purchases in a developed market economy are not motivated by considerations of functionality, it would be logical to argue that spending on apparel will be greater in periods of affluence when consumers have larger amounts of disposable income and may be more inclined to take risks in their spending pattern. The consumers' ability to satisfy a desire for change is enhanced by rising prosperity. In the same way if fragmentation is defined in terms of individuality then in periods of rising affluence more people will be able to indulge in a desire to purchase something new and stimulating. Behling's argument (1985, p. 23) that the 'state of the economy may speed up the fashion change process . . . as the amount of discretionary income of the population decreases or increases' would be entirely correct in these terms.

The conclusion must, therefore, be that the Behling model cannot be regarded as a particularly satisfactory representation of the process of fashion change and diffusion. It does isolate some of the crucial variables such as levels of affluence and the age distribution of the population. McAdam (1996) applied the model to the UK and found that it was only partially successful in explaining trends and that, specifically, there were great difficulties in reconciling the steady increase in the median age in the UK population with the remaining influence of youth culture on the apparel market. It was shown above (Jones, 1999) that in the UK between 1986 and 1993 the younger age groups decreased as a proportion of the population while the 26–45 age group gained heavily in terms of their share of income, but fashion trends (McAdam, 1996) continued to favour the young and youthful styles. It could be argued, therefore, that the young will always be more interested in fashion because of the social role played by dress and the lack of demands upon their income from such things as mortgages and dependent children.

It is probably unreasonable to expect any one model to be able to explain so many dimensions of the apparel market. The size of the market depends primarily on economic factors but other issues such as the direction of fashion influences remain difficult to explain within a testable model.

The second model does not attempt to explain all the dimensions of the fashion market and makes little or no reference to demographic or economic factors. The Symbolic Interactionist model of fashion has been developed by Nagasawa (1995; 1996). The model is cast within a post-modernist framework and claims to result in the formulation of 'principles and theoretical statements in order to construct a theory of fashion' which will allow the 'development of scientific hypotheses' which can be tested. The model is built around five basic principles:

(1) *Cultural ambivalence* – that people entertain mixed emotions about their identities, e.g. a youthful appearance as opposed to chronological age.
(2) *Heterogeneity in appearance modifying commodities* – that in a capitalist, market economy products will be developed to cope with cultural ambivalence.
(3) *Symbolic ambiguity* – that this is fostered by the ability to manage appearance.
(4) *Meaning negotiation and style adoption* – that the meaning of existing ambiguities has to be negotiated and that those styles which become acceptable and meaningful through this process will be adopted and will be fashionable.

(5) *Ambivalence and style change* – that if the latter stage of adoption by a majority does not coincide with a resolution of cultural ambivalence then there will be further and, possibly, continuous change in fashion.

In the final paper (Nagasawa, 1996) the theory is tested against a feature of the apparel market (which has to be taken as correct) that youth styles exhibit more ambiguity and change than adult styles. The test is carried out by comparing the changes which take place in adolescents' appearances and the stability exhibited by the traditional, male business suit. The theory is able to explain both these circumstances by reference to the basic concept of cultural ambivalence. The model has the great virtues of being cast within a traditional scientific framework and of setting out to produce a testable hypothesis from the number of hypotheses that can be drawn out of the model. If cultural ambivalence increases for example, the range of fashion products will increase but that if styles clarify ambivalence they will not change. However, a starting point is that it has to be accepted that (1995a, p. 175) 'ambivalence is a basic human condition' and, as far as the present author can ascertain, no guidance is given as to how this is to be measured. Therefore, while it is stated (Nagasawa, 1995b, p. 243) that 'the theory should be testable empirically . . . the theory should allow the derivation of observational statements both to predict and explain' it does appear that the model is rather better at explaining than predicting – other than to predict that if ambivalence increases (and if this can be measured and recognised) certain consequences will follow, of which the most important seems to be increased unpredictability in the apparel market. The model is, however, relatively new and may hold out more promise for the future than any alternative. Two innovative approaches have been suggested by Law (2004) utilising 'chaos' theory and by Cholachathinyo (2002) in the so-called 'conceptual model of the fashion process'.

Many studies of fashion change do not employ model-building techniques at all. The comprehensive study of fashion change in the UK between 1900 and 1999, carried out by Mendes (1999) for example, is entirely descriptive and contains no model or theory of fashion change of any sort. The range of forces which is called upon to explain the observed changes in fashion is extremely wide, ranging from the impact of war with its impact on the availability of raw materials and the demand for practicality as well as the need to reflect more sombre times (or maybe to cheer people up!); changes in the level of affluence such as were experienced in the 1980s (when more ostentatious styles, power dressing and conspicuous consumption became the rule) or less sensationally so in the mid-1950s as economies recovered from post-war austerity; demographic changes as epitomised by the growing disposable income of young people in the 1960s which (Mendes, 1999, p. 157) 'would shortly bring about significant and irreversable changes in both fashion design and . . . retailing'; changes in gender values which, it is claimed, prevented men from being fashion aware in the 1940s but encouraged them to be preoccupied with appearance in the late 1960s; the role of film, theatre and music; the increased importance of sub-cultural influences as fashion became increasingly eclectic in the late 1990s, even extending to (Mendes, 1999, p. 256) the development of an all-white style which 'epitomised the desire for spiritual enlightenment'.

Models are an abstraction which simplify the real world through isolating a few variables which generate predictive power. The problem with the all-embracing, descriptive approach is that it sacrifices predictive power for descriptive realism. Therefore, it can be concluded that while economic theory can provide an explanation of the size of the apparel market, the search for a predictive theory of fashion change and processes remains elusive. Behling (1992, p. 40), for example, concluded her exhaustive study of fashion adoption research with the warning that, although a profile of the early fashion adopter can be generated from the research a new model may still be required and that even that would 'not be a substitute for theory' but only an 'interim step towards one'.

It must be concluded, therefore, that while it is possible to make predictions from a sound theoretical base (and utilising a proven leading indicator) about the size of the apparel market the same cannot be said about the process of fashion change on other than an *ex post facto* basis. The reason that this matters is that it makes prediction of future trends in the marketplace extremely difficult. A good example of this problem is the frequently expressed view that the UK apparel market is becoming more difficult because it is increasingly fragmented. Sorensen (1995, p. 14), for example, wrote that the 'demand for clothing is now more fragmented' while Atkinson (1995, p. 133) noted that the trend 'in the 1990s is towards the desire for considerably more diverse ranges of products'.

The implication drawn is that this increased fragmentation makes the market more difficult to operate in. The *UK Fashion Report* (EMAP/MTI, 1998/9) and the *UK Retail Report* (Retail Intelligence, 1999) both stress this aspect of the marketplace. It is, however, rare to find a definition of what exactly becoming more fragmented actually means and what the marketing implications of this process might be – even if there were a sound theoretical model of the fashion process within which increased fragmentation could be assimilated. Clearly, the division of the apparel market into fragments or segments is not new. Nor is this a unique characteristic of the apparel market. As Chisnall (1985, p. 262) comments, 'practically every market is capable of refinement into significant sub-markets'.

Target marketing has been the norm in the UK apparel market for many years (see Easey (1995, Chapter 5), for example) and the definition of a fragment is very close to that of a segment – 'a part separable from other parts'. Therefore, fragmented could just mean segmented. Does greater fragmentation mean that the number of target markets is increasing while their size is decreasing? And, if so, how do we know? It appears that the standards of verification acceptable in discussions of 'fashion' are simply different from those usually encountered in mainstream economics or marketing.

One group of reseachers who do deal with the concept of fragmentation are the so-called 'sub-culturalists' who stress that the increased cultural plurality in post-modern Western societies (Bauman, 1996) results in consumers having greater freedom to express their own desires in a way which is relatively unconstrained by more traditional conventions. Post-modernism refers to a body of thought or a set of beliefs about the nature of contemporary society which rejects the idea that modern industrial society gradually changes for the better and that these changes are guided or driven by rational or scientific forces. Morgado (1996, p. 50) argues that fashion can be seen as the most visible expression of post-modernism in that 'the diversity of contemporary styles and the increased speed of fashion cycles illustrate the sense of fracture and discontinuity characteristic of post-modern culture'. Post-modernism rejects the intrinsic value of traditional hierarchies and rules with the result that apparel markets would display (Morgado, 1996, p. 46) a 'highly volatile and accelerated rate of fashion change as compared with the rhythmic cycles of change in modern culture; an unstable aesthetic code in contrast with modernist rules' of appropriateness or co-ordination. In Kaiser's words (1990, p. 165) post-modernism when 'connected with advanced capitalism, spawns cultural ambivalence and a range of clothing styles that emerge, in part, to clarify and lend expression to ambivalence'.

It has been shown above that a new model of the fashion process has emerged from a consideration of post-modernist influences and, in particular, concern with this concept of ambivalence. One of the main implications of this model is that (Nagasawa, 1995a, p. 180) because society no longer sends out unambiguous messages as to what is appropriate or fashionable it follows that the apparel market must be characterised by increased 'stylistic eclecticism'. Mendes (1999, p. 192) also notes that the apparel market has become increasingly eclectic during the last 30 years. It can be argued, therefore, that a definition of fragmentation is emerging from this work in that it implies that, as Evans (1989) put it, the era of the fashion dictate is over so that a sensible marketing response would be to concentrate on building 'longer term brand images in a more segmented, pluralistic society'. This view would be confirmed by McAdam (1999, p. 6) who argued that 'the Paris catwalk dictate gives way to a more fragmented democratic fashion influence from a variety of sources, such as street fashions, subcultures and immigrant cultures' and this leads 'to a pluralistic, decentred fashion system that permits the mixing of texts in the construction of multiple identities for multiple occasions'.

As McAdam (1999) points out, elements of subcultural style may then become incorporated into mainstream fashion. Greater individuality will produce greater fragmentation in the sense of extreme and unpredictable product differentiation. As society becomes more affluent consumers may become more demanding and discerning – they will demand and be able to obtain infinite variety to suit their individual needs. This would, it can easily be appreciated, make the market a difficult one in which to operate and would place a high premium on the ability to respond rapidly to unexpected changes in demand. It could be argued that this conclusion is well illustrated by the decision (Simpkins, 2000) taken by C&A to withdraw from the UK market. It may also be significant (Section E below) that one of the contributory factors in the failure of C&A was the decision taken to buy centrally on a European basis. This resulted in the achievement of significant economies of scale but did not generate products acceptable to the British market.

If the post-modernist view of society is correct, the best prediction which can be made is that nothing is predictable! Lowson (1999, p. 4) reflected this view when he wrote 'a splintered society with its growing fragmentation and increasingly diverse consumer requirements' produces a future which is 'open ended, chaotic' and in which 'forecasting is . . . almost worthless'. This clearly would make the market an extremely difficult one in which to operate.

E.   The EU as the home market

It could be argued that, since 1993, the correct designation of the domestic market is the EU and not the UK. As has been seen in Chapter 5, some 70% of UK apparel exports go to other members of the EU. This concentration can be explained by reference not only to the geographic proximity of the EU market but also to the concept of psychic or cultural distance (Lee, 1997, p. 9) which can be defined as the 'perceived sociocultural distance between the home and target markets in terms of language, business practices, legal and political systems and marketing infrastructure'. Lee (1997) concluded that there is evidence that export performance is negatively associated with cultural distance. Paradoxically, as the population of the EU grows with expansion towards 455 million, diversity may increase and income per head fall.

The EU apparel market is extremely large, standing at 263,179 million euros in 2000 (Mintel, 2002). The UK is the third largest apparel market in the EU after Germany and Italy (Mintel, 2002). In terms of the proportion of consumer expenditure devoted to apparel and expenditure per head on apparel, however, the UK has been down the list of the member states and prompted the *UK Fashion Report* (EMAP/MTI, 1998/99, p. 37) to comment that while many interpretations can be put upon these statistics, 'that the UK is the best dressed nation in the EU is not amongst them'. In 2001, however, the UK ranked sixth (Mintel, 2002).

The EU apparel market is extremely valuable but is becoming less homogeneous as it expands and probably cannot be treated from a marketing point of view as 'one' market. The structure of distribution, for example, varies greatly from one member state to another with the role of the independents being far greater in Southern Europe than in the UK (Mattila, 1996). McGoldrick (1995) points to the relatively greater importance of department stores in Germany; their unimportance in Italy and the remaining role of the variety store in the UK are examples of the variation to be found within the EU. The differences in apparel markets in the individual members of the EU have been comprehensively summarised by Curran (1990). In addition, despite the claims of the globalists, there is evidence that patterns of spending within the EU do vary greatly. Spending on apparel ranges from a low of 3.5% of expenditure in Finland to a high of 8.5% in Portugal (Euromonitor, 1998).

It is also well documented that the national markets are structurally diverse within the Single European Market (SEM) – see, for example, Bickerton (1999) and Tordjman (1995). The questions of the degree of homogeneity in apparel markets, the extent to which this is increasing and the methods by which fashions spread within the SEM are extremely difficult to resolve in large part because of the absence of a validated theory of the fashion process. Tordjman (1995, p. 25) concluded that while there were some convergent trends in international retailing (such as the rise of discount stores) the convergence 'remains partial and marginal' relative to that achieved by the internationalisation of production. As Curran (1991, p. 49) argued, 'it is very difficult to establish whether garments should be adapted for different countries . . . The available literature does not give any indication of how long any convergence of styles across geographical boundaries might take and what variables might influence the speed of any convergence'.

Brown (1981) has described the geographic approach to the distribution of innovation in which new ideas are seen as spreading from larger to smaller population centres. In a European context it could, therefore, be argued that the larger centres of population such as London, Paris, Milan and Berlin could be recognised as primary centres of fashion innovation. The concept of global homogeneity of consumer demand will be fully discussed in Chapter 11 but it can be noted here that the evidence for a convergence of spending patterns is not strong. Selvanathan (1993), for example, concluded that the hypothesis 'that tastes are the same across countries was tested . . . and it was found that the OECD data do not support' this hypothesis. Nevertheless it will be seen that some authors, in particular Levitt (1983), argued that consumers are becoming more homogeneous over time. On *a priori* grounds it might be argued that if this idea has any force it would be stronger within a trading bloc like the EU than between a European and an Asian grouping.

The main factors which, from a survey of the literature, might be expected to influence the acceptance of a particular fashion include: the impact of religion;

the strength of feeling of national identity; the openness of a society as measured by such factors as foreign travel; and the impact of the mass media. Curran (1993, p. 6) attempted to provide an objective test of the variation between the UK and France in the fashionability of different skirt lengths over time and concluded that while fashion cycles seemed to be largely in conformity with one another in the two countries, data revealed 'significant discrepancies between prevailing skirt lengths in the eighties' and the degree of conformity had in fact declined over time.

The same author (Curran, 1999) compared trends in both skirt lengths and widths in Germany and the UK. In this case it was found that there was a great degree of similarity, especially in the case of skirt lengths, between trends in the two markets. It was seen in Chapter 5 (Table 5.2) that the vast majority of UK apparel exports go to the EU and it will be recalled from Chapter 1 that Owen (1999) argued that one of the main reasons for the poor performance of the UK manufacturing industry was early exclusion from the huge market represented by the EU. Clearly this alleged defect can no longer be detected in the pattern of UK apparel trade but the rate of growth exhibited in the recent past by the EU has, by global standards, been unimpressive.

Jamieson (2000) shows that the rate of growth in the EU every year since 1992 ranged from 48% to 80% of that exhibited by the American economy. The absolute size of the EU and NAFTA trading areas in 1996 was, in fact, rather similar in that both had populations of around 380 million and Gross Domestic Products of around $8,000,000 million (Euromonitor, 1996b). As Moore (1999, p. 41) observed, the UK has a large positive balance on services and investment income with NAFTA so that, in effect, 'she is paying off most of the negative balance she is incurring with the EC (EU) by what she is earning from the rest of the world'. The delayed entry of the UK into the Community probably never did result in her catching up on the alleged lost opportunity (Owen, 1999) because as Moore (1999, p. 372) concludes 'imports from the other EC member states ousted her home produced goods from her home market . . . So far from participating in a rapidly growing market her rate of growth fell'.

It would be the ultimate irony if (assuming Owen's analysis was correct) the UK has at a late stage joined the wrong trading bloc in respect of future growth so that UK manufacturers are, again, excluded from those markets which are currently or in the future the engines of global expansion. In this regard it has to be noted that the American apparel market – which takes only 5.7% of UK exports – stood at some $200,000 million (Euromonitor, 1996b) in terms of consumer expenditure in 1993. It should also be noted that according to Dickerson (1995, p. 208) expenditure on apparel in the USA was both rising more quickly than general consumption and as a proportion of consumer expenditure between 1973 and 1992, which was a complete contrast to the position of Europe. Therefore, while the apparent concentration on European markets exhibited by the UK industry is in many respects understandable it is by no means obviously desirable as a long-term strategy. The identification of potentially attractive future markets is considered in Chapter 11.

References

Anon (2000) Clothing Retailing in the UK: Forecasts to 2004. *Textile Outlook International*, **86**, 82–103.

Artis, M. (1992) *The UK Economy*. Weidenfeld and Nicholson, London.

Atkinson, S. (1995) Design and Marketing Fashion Products. In: *Fashion Marketing* (Ed. M. Easey), pp. 107–34, Blackwell Science, Oxford.

Bainbridge, J. (1999) Top 100 Advertisers. *Marketing*, 25.2.99, 26–8.

Baker, L. (2000) Retailers B2B International. *Independent*, 29.8.00, 13.

Balkwell, C. & Ho, S. (1992) A Quantitative Analysis of Dress Dimensions. *Clothing and Textiles Research Journal*, **10**, 47–53.

Bauman, Z. (1996) From Pilgrim to Tourist. In: *Questions of Culture and Identity* (Eds S. & P. Du Gay), pp. 18–36. Sage, London.

Begg, D., Fischer, S. & Dornbusch, R. (1991) *Economics*. McGraw Hill, London.

Behling, D. (1985) Fashion Change and Demographics: a Model. *Clothing and Textiles Research Journal*, **4**, 18–23.

Behling, D. (1992) Three and a Half Decades of Fashion Adoption Research. *Clothing and Textiles Research Journal*, **11**, 34–41.

Bellan, B.D. (1998) A Comparison of Older and Younger Women's Attitudes towards Apparel and Media. *Journal of Fashion Marketing and Management*, **1**, 10–18.

Bengtsson, A.K. (2001) Textile Solutions Starts a Virtual Fabric Market. *Journal of Fashion Marketing and Management*, **5.1**, 82–3.

Bickerton, I. (1999) *Fashion Retailing in Europe*. Financial Times, London.

Brenninkmeyer, B., Gibson, W.G. & Lowe, J. (1986) Electronic Shopping in the Clothing Sector. *Hollings Apparel Industry Review*, **3**, 103–19.

Briscoe, L. (1971) *The Textile and Clothing Industries of the UK*. Manchester University Press, Manchester.

Brown, L. (1981) *Innovation Diffusion*. Methuen, New York.

Chisnall, P. (1985) *Consumer Behaviour*. McGraw Hill, London.

Cholachathinyo, I., Padgelt, M., Crocker, M. & Fletcher, B. (2002) A Conceptual Model of the Fashion Process. *Journal of Fashion Marketing and Management*, **6.1**, 24–35.

Coleman, D. & Salt, J. (1992) *The British Population*. Oxford University Press, Oxford.

Conyan, M. & Machin, S. (1991) The Determination of Profit Margins in UK Manufacturing Industry. *Journal of Industrial Economics*, **4**, 369–83.

Corporate Intelligence (1997) *Clothing Retailing in the UK*. Corporate Intelligence, London.

Cox, R. (2000) *Retail Management*. Prentice Hall, London.

CSO (1996) *Key Data*. HMSO, London.

Curran, L. (1990) *The Marketing of Clothing in the Single Market*. MMU, Manchester.

Curran, L. (1991) Theories of Fashion and the Euro Consumer. *Hollings Apparel Industry Review*, **8**, 39–60.

Curran, L. (1993) The Search for the Euro Consumer. *Journal of Clothing Technology and Management*, **10**, 1–11.

Curran, L. (1999) An Analysis of Cycles in Skirt Lengths and Widths in the UK and Germany 1954–90. *Clothing and Textiles Research Journal*, **17**, 65–72.

Curwen, P. (1997) *Understanding the UK Economy*. Macmillan, London.

Davies, F. (1992) *Fashion, Culture and Identity*. University of Chicago Press, Chicago.

De Silva, R., Davies, G. & Naudé, P. (2000) Marketing to UK Retailers. *Journal of Fashion Marketing and Management*, **4**, 162–73.

Dickerson, K. (1995) *Textiles and Apparel in the Global Economy*. Merrill, New Jersey.

Dickson, M. (1999) US Consumers' Knowledge of and Concern with Apparel Sweatshops. *Journal of Fashion Marketing and Marketing*, **3**, 44–56.

Dilnot, A., Banks, J. & Low, H. (1994) *The Distribution of Wealth in the UK*. Institute of Fiscal Studies, London.

Dychtwald, M.K. (1997) Marketplace 2000. *Journal of Consumer Marketing*, **14**, 271–6.

Easey, M. (1995) *Fashion Marketing*. Blackwell Science, Oxford.

Economist (1985) *Economic Statistics 1900–1983*. Economist, London.

EMAP/MTI (1998/9) *The UK Fashion Report*. EMAP, London.

Euromonitor (1996) *European Marketing Data and Statistics*. Euromonitor, London.

Euromonitor (1996) *World Economic Facts 1996/97*. Euromonitor, London.

Euromonitor (1998) *European Marketing Data and Statistics*. Euromonitor, London.

Evandrou, M. (1997) *Baby Boomers: Ageing in the 21st Century*. Age Concern, London.

Evans, M. (1989) Consumer Behaviour Towards Fashion. *European Journal of Marketing*, **23**, 7–16.

Fadiga, M., Misra, S. & Ramirez, O. (2005) U.S. Consumer Purchasing Decisions and the Demand for Apparel. *Journal of Fashion Marketing and Management*, **9.4**, 367–80.

Fairham, A. & Fiorito, S. (1990) Retail Buyers' Decision-Making Processes. *International Review of Retail Distribution and Consumer Research*, **1**, 88–99.

Field, G.A. (1981) The Status Float Phenomenon. In: *Perspectives of Fashion* (Ed. G.B. Sproles), pp. 44–48. Burgess, Minneapolis.

Future Foundation in Jardin, A. (1999) Traditional Retailers Face their High Noon. *Marketing*, 16.9.99, 22–3.

Gereffi, G. (1999) International Trade and Industrial Upgrading in the Apparel Commodity Chain. *Journal of International Economics*, **48**, 37–70.

Goldsmith, R. & Flynn, L. (1992) Identifying Innovators in Consumer Product Markets. *European Journal of Marketing*, **26**, 42–56.

Goldsmith, R. & Goldsmith, E. (2002) Buying Apparel over the Internet. *Journal of Product and Brand Management*, **11.2**, 89–102.

Goldsmith, R. & Flynn, L. (2004) Psychological Drives of On-line Clothing Purchase. *Journal of Fashion Marketing and Management*, **8.1**, 84–95.

Harbury, C. & Lipsey, R. (1996) *An Introduction to the UK Economy*. Blackwell Publishers, Oxford.

Harris, R.J. & Heppel, J. (1991) Apparel Sourcing: A Survey of Retail Buyers' Attitudes. *Textile Outlook International*, **38**, 87–96.

International Metal Workers Federation (1998) *The Purchasing Power of Working Time*. IMF, Geneva.

Jackson, H.O. & O'Neil, G.S. (1994) Dress and Appearance Responses to Perceptions of Ageing. *Clothing and Textile Research Journal*, **12**, 8–14.

Jamieson, B. (2000) Don't Close Our Options Down. *Sunday Telegraph*, 30.01.2000, 48.

Jardine, A. (1999) Traditional Retailers Face Their High Noon. *Marketing*, 16.9.99, 22–3.

Johnson, P. (1990) Economic Trends in Population. *Admap*, 26.3.90.

Jones, R.M. (1994) The Demand for Clothing in the UK 1974–91. *Journal of Clothing Technology and Management*, **11**, 111–31.

Jones, R.M. (1996) Editorial. *Journal of Fashion Marketing and Management*, **1**, 5–6.

Jones, R.M. (1999) Demographics, Distribution of Income and Wealth and the Marketing of Fashion in the UK. *Journal of the Textile Institute*, **90**, 1–14.

Jones, R.M. & Hayes, S.G. (2002) The Economic Determinants of Clothing Consumption in the UK, 1987–2000. *Journal of Fashion Marketing and Management*, **6.4**, 1361–2026.

Jones, R.M. & Robb, P. (1997) The Demand for Clothing in the UK and Sweden. *Journal of Fashion Marketing and Management*, **1**, 113–25.

Kaiser, S. (1990) *The Social Psychology of Clothing*. Macmillan, New York.

Karayanni, D. (2003) Web Shoppers and Non-Shoppers. *European Research Journal*, **15.3**, 141–52.

Katics, M. & Peterson, B. (1994) The Effect of Rising Import Competition in Market Power. *American Economic Review*, **88**, 107–20.

Kau, A., Tang, Y. & Chose, S. (2003) Typology of Online Shoppers. *Journal of Consumer Marketing*, **20.2**, 139–56.

Key Note (1998) *Clothing Manufacture*. Key Note Ltd, Hampton, Middlesex.

Kim, E.Y. & Kim, Y.K. (2004) Predicting On-line Purchase Intensions for Clothing Products. *European Journal of Marketing*, **38.7**, 883–93.

Kim, M. & Park, J. (2005) A Consumer Shopping Channel Extension Model: Attitude Shift Towards the On-line Store. *Journal of Fashion Marketing and Management*, **9.1**, 106–21.

King, C. (1981) Fashion Adoption. In: *Perspectives of Fashion* (Ed. G.B. Sproles), pp. 44–8. Burgess, Minneapolis.

Law, K., Zhang, Z. & Leung, C. (2004) Fashion Change and Fashion Consumption: the Chaotic Perspective. *Journal of Fashion Marketing and Management*, **8.4**, 362–75.

Lee, D.J. (1997) The Effect of Cultural Distance on the Relational Exchange Between Exports and Imports. *American Economic Review*, **11**, 7–18.

Lee, M. & Johnson, K. (2002) Exploring Differences Between Internet Apparel Purchasers, Browsers and Non-Purchasers. *Journal of Fashion Marketing and Management*, **6.2**, 146–57.

Leventhal, R.C. (1997) Dress and Appearance Responses to Perceptions of Ageing. *Journal of Consumer Marketing*, **14**, 276–81.

Levitt, T. (1983) The Globalisation of Markets. *Harvard Business Review*, **LXI**, 92–103.

Lowson, B., King, R. & Hunter, A. (1999) *Quick Response – Managing The Supply Chain to Meet Consumer Demand*. J. Wiley, Chichester.

McAdam, A. (1996) The Value of Demographic Trends in the Process of Fashion Change. *Journal of Clothing Technology and Management*, **13**, 58–84.

McAdam, A. & Heam, G. (1999) *Fashion as Identity*. Unpublished research monograph, Manchester Metropolitan University, Manchester.

McGoldrick, P. (1990) *Retail Marketing*. McGraw Hill, London.

McGoldrick, P. & Davies, G. (1995) *International Retailing*. Pitman, London.

Mabry, M. (1971) *The Relationship Between Fluctuations in Hemlines and Stock Market Averages*. University of Tennessee. Unpublished thesis.

Magretta, J. (1998) Supply Chain Management H.K. Style. *Harvard Business Review*, **76**, 102–16.

Manning, C. (1999) Interest Greats. *Daily Mirror*, 5.2.99, p. 9.

Marketing (1999) The Top 50 Brends. *Marketing*, 12.7.99.

Martines, E., Polo, P. & Flavian, C. (1998) The Acceptance and Diffusion of New Consumer Durables. *Journal of Consumer Marketing*, **15**, 323–40.

Matila, H. (1996) European Garment Retailing. *Textiles Magazine*, **2**, 20–24.

Mendes, V. & De La Hague, A. (1999) *20th Century Fashion*. Thames and Hudson, London.

Mills, D. (1997) A Household Study of the Determination of Income and Consumption. *Economic Journal*, **107**, 1–25.

Mintel (2000) *UK Clothing Market (Special Series Review)*.

Mintel (2002) Clothing Retailing in Europe.

Mintel (2005) The Clothing Market in the UK.

Mitchell, B. & Deane, P. (1962) *Abstract of Historical Statistics 1900–1983*. Cambridge University Press, Cambridge.

Monsuwe, I., Dellaert, B. & de Ruyter, K. (2004) What Drives Consumers to Shop On-line? *International Journal of Service Industry Management*, **15.1**, 102–21.

Moore, C. (2000) To See Ourselves as Others See Us. *Journal of Fashion Marketing and Management*, **4**, 81–5.

Moore, L. (1999) *Britain's Trade and Economic Structure*. Routledge, London.

Morchis, G.P., Lee, E. & Mathur, A. (1997) Targeting the Mature Market. *Journal of Consumer Marketing*, **14**, 282–90.

Morgado, M. (1996) Coming to Terms with Post Modernism. *Clothing and Textiles Research Journal*, **14**, 41–54.

Mortishead, C. (2000) How the Internet is Playing the Lead Role in the Death of a Salesman. *Times*, 7.4.2000, p. 31.

Murphy, R. (1998) The Internet: A Viable Strategy for Fashion Retail Markets. *Journal of Fashion Marketing and Management*, **2**, 209–17.

Murphy, R. & Bruce, M. (1999) The Structure and Organisation of UK Fashion Retailing. *Journal of Fashion Marketing and Management*, **3**, 377–83.

Nagasawa, R., Kaiser, S. & Hatton, S. (1995a) Construction of an S.I. Theory of Fashion. *Clothing and Textiles Research Journal*, **13**, 172–84.

Nagasawa, R., Kaiser, S. & Hatton, S. (1995b) Construction of an S.I. Theory of Fashion: From Discovery to Formulation. *Clothing and Textiles Research Journal*, **13**, 231–45.

Nagasawa, R., Kaiser, S. & Hatton, S. (1996) Construction of an S.I. Theory of Fashion: Context and Explanation. *Clothing and Textiles Research Journal*, **14**, 54–63.

Newman, O. & Foster, A. (1995) *The Value of A Pound*. Gale Research International, Andover, Hants.

Norum, P. (1999) The Demand for Accessories, Footwear and Hosiery. *Journal of Fashion Marketing and Management*, **3**, 55–66.

ONS (1997) *Social Trends*. HMSO, London.

ONS (1999a) *Consumer Trends*. HMSO, London.

ONS (1999b) *Economic Trends*. HMSO, London.

ONS (1999c) *Annual Abstract of Statistics*. HMSO, London.

ONS (1999d) *Sector Review – Clothing, Leather and Footwear*. HMSO, London.

ONS (2000) *Social Trends*. HMSO, London.

Owen, G. (1999) *From Europe to Empire*. Harper Collins, London.

Palmer, A. & Worthington, I. (1992) *The Business and Marketing Environment*. McGraw Hill, London.

Park, C. & Kim, Y. (2003) Identifying Key Factors Affecting Consumer Purchase Behaviour in an On-line Shopping Context. *International Journal of Retailing and Distribution Management*, **31.1**, 16–29.

Park, J. & Stoel, L. (2005) Effect of Brand Familiarity, Experience and Information on On-line Apparel Purchase. *International Journal of Retailing and Distribution Management*, **33.2**, 148–60.

Parsons, A.C. (2002) Non-functional Motives for On-line Shopping. *Journal of Consumer Marketing*, **19.5**, 380–92.

Porter, M. (1998) *The Competitive Advantage of Nations*. Free Press, New York.

Pruim, F. (1999) *Consumenten Ontevreden over Kledigmaten*. De Telegraaf Den Haag, 10.2.99.

Quant, M. (1997) The Meaning of the Mini. *Daily Telegraph*, 18.10.97, 1–2.

Retail Intelligence (1999) *UK Retail Report: Clothing (No 111)*. Corporate Intelligence Group, London.

Robinson, N. (1999) *A Study of Working Time and Apparel Purchases*. Unpublished Manchester Metropolitan University research paper.

Rogers, E.M. & Shoemaker, F.F. (1971) *Diffusion of Innovations*. Free Press, New York.

Schiffman, L. & Kanulz, L. (1994) *Consumer Behaviour*. Prentice Hall, New Jersey.

Selvanathan, S. & Selvanathan, E. (1993) Cross Country Analysis of Consumption Patterns. *Applied Economics*, **25**, 1245–59.

Sigsworth, E.M. (1990) *Montague Burton – the Tailor of Taste*. MUP, Manchester.

Simpkins, E. (2000) Out of Fashion and Out of Britain. *Sunday Times*, 18.6.2000, p. 8.

Sorensen, C. (1995) The Fashion Market and the Marketing Environment. In: *Fashion Marketing* (Ed. M. Easey), pp. 13–42. Blackwell Science, Oxford.

Sproles, G.B. (1981) Analysing Fashion Life Cycles – Principles and Perspectives. *Journal of Marketing*, **45**, 116–24.

Sternquist, B., Tabbot, S. & Davis, B. (1989) Imported Apparel: Retail Buyers' Reasons for Foreign Procurement. *Clothing and Textiles Research Journal*, **7**, 35–40.

Stone, R. & Rowe, D.A. (1966) *The Measurement of Consumer Expenditure and Behaviour in the UK 1920–38*. Cambridge University Press, Cambridge.

Textile Market Studies (1996) *Boom, Bust, Better – the UK Clothing Market 1987–96*. TMS Partnership, London.

Tordjman, A. (1995) European Retailing. In: *International Retailing* (Ed. P. McGoldrick), pp. 25–49. Pitman, London.

US Department of Commerce (1997) *Statistical Abstract of the US – the National Data Book*. US Department of Commerce, Economic and Statistics Administration, Bureau of Census, Washington.

Verdict Research (2000) *The Retail Industry and Demographics*. Verdict Research, London.

Waterston, M.J. (1999) *Advertising Statistics Year Book*. The Advertising Association, London.

Weeks, W., Brannon, E. & Ulrich, P. (1998) Non-Store Shopping. *Journal of Fashion Marketing and Management*, **2**, 113–24.

Williams, J. (1997) Department Stores: An Enduring Retail Format. *Journal of Fashion Marketing and Management*, **1**, 145–50.

Zuhone, L.M. & Morganosky, M. (1995) The Relative Power of Retailers. *Clothing and Textile Research Journal*, **13**, 57–64.

Chapter 11

Emerging Markets and the Globalisation of the UK Apparel Industry

A. Introduction

It will be recalled (Table 5.2) that the vast majority of UK apparel exports go to other member states of the EU. Jones (1998, p. 252) studied the global reach of the UK apparel industry and concluded that in 'terms of direct exports from the UK the clothing industry's global credentials are very poor' and that there was little sign of this view being altered by investment flows which were also quite restricted geographically. The extent to which it is felt that over-concentration upon a particular market is a weakness depends upon whether or not those markets are fast growing and large.

The proportion of apparel produced in the UK which is exported has fallen sharply to 19% (ONS, 2004) compared to the UK average of 34%. Two-thirds of these exports go to the EU, i.e. roughly 13% of UK apparel production. Eighty-one per cent of apparel produced in the UK must by definition stay in the domestic market. Therefore, some 93% of apparel produced in the UK depends for a market on consumers in the EU (including UK). The industry is, therefore, heavily reliant on the old, established economies in Europe. In the recent past these economies have been relatively slow growing (Walwyn, 1997). In addition it is generally accepted that apparel markets in the developed world are saturated. The demand for apparel also tends to be income-inelastic (see Chapter 10). The share of total consumer expenditure devoted to apparel purchases has tended to fall over time in the richer, developed countries (Dickerson, 1995, p. 209) although this was not true of the USA between 1973–1992. Finally, demographic changes in the developed world – in particular the ageing of the population – tend to be potentially unfavourable to the evolution of apparel markets. Therefore, the fact that the UK apparel industry does not currently display a particularly impressive pattern of connections either via exports or outward investment with non-European markets elevates the issue of the future role of new markets to one of some interest.

This seeming lack of global credentials appears strange when contrasted both with the historical role of the textile sector as one of the first manufacturing sectors to achieve a wide spread of geographic activity and with the current dispersion of apparel manufacture across the globe. A partial explanation for this apparent paradox lies in the extremely casual way in which the word 'globalisation' is used. Sometimes, for example, it is used to indicate dispersed activity; sometimes it is virtually equated with free trade; and at other times it is used by a specific group of authors in a rather specialised way as clarified in Chapter 6. It will be the aim of this chapter to consider the role of newly emerging markets for apparel in the future.

B. Emerging markets

Global patterns of consumption were reviewed in Chapter 3. The aim of this section is to consider future markets for apparel. Emerging markets can be defined as countries in which, due to anticipated increases in income, a substantially enlarged market for apparel can be expected to appear in the future. It is recognised that other definitions are conceivable which do not depend, as Kolodko (2003, p. 15) puts it, on the creation of 'a new sales market for others'. They tend to be of two types: former planned economies making the transition to market economies in which frustrated consumption is being released and the countries of the Pacific Rim in which a substantial number of affluent consumers are emerging.

In a recent paper Zhang (1997) has studied apparel trade flows *from* the developed countries *into* the developing countries (which he entitles 'counter-trade'). He pointed out that some of the developing markets for clothing are quite large in that (in 1992) there were 11 developing countries which imported in excess of $100 million worth of clothing from the developed countries. In his words 'these represent a substantial market for apparel producers in the developed countries to pay attention to'. There is a remarkably wide variation in the size of these markets as indicated by per capita imports, e.g. from $79 in Kuwait to $0.01 in India. Zhang used a multiple regression model to attempt to identify the factors which determine these trade flows. His conclusion was that (1997, p. 238) 'only per capita GNP has a significant impact on apparel imports and the impact is positive . . . None of the market condition variables, however, is significant. Remarkably, the index of market barriers is insignificant'. He also concluded that imports into the developing countries were income-elastic and that distance did not seem to be an issue.

In Chapters 10 and 3 the established link between the demand for apparel and levels of income was demonstrated. The present author has (Jones, 1994) utilised this association to highlight the growth of potential future apparel markets. The

Table 11.1   Income per head as percentage of USA in 2013.

Japan	91
NAFTA	84
EEC (12)	67
EEC[1]	67
EEC[2]	65
Pacific Rim[3]	44
NEC[4]	20
NIC[5]	112
E. Europe	32
Asia	21
Africa	9
Ex-USSR	43
China	24
Brazil	54

Source: Jones, R.M. (1994) The Identification of New
Markets. *Journal of Clothing Technology and
Management*, **11**, pp. 111–131.

Key: (1) EEC and Sweden, Finland, Norway, Austria,
Switzerland.
(2) The above plus Turkey.
(3) Hong Kong, Singapore, Malaysia, South
Korea, Taiwan, Indonesia, Thailand and the
Philippines.
(4) China, Indonesia, Thailand, Malaysia, India
and Pakistan.
(5) South Korea, Taiwan, Hong Kong and
Singapore.

results of this research are summarised in Tables 11.1 and 11.2. The figures are based on forecasts of income levels up to the year 2013 and expressed as a proportion of the figure for the USA. Table 11.1 is based on calculations of income per head (taking into account forecasted population growth) while Table 11.2 is based on forecasts of total national income. It can be seen that the choice of income indicator substantially influences the result, e.g. the small group of NIC countries appears very attractive in terms of income per head but not so interesting in terms of national income while the position of China is the reverse.

As with all marketing statistics careful interpretation is required so that, for example, a company selling an expensive, niche product might find Table 11.1 more useful while a company selling a basic product might utilise Table 11.2. As recent experience in South-East Asia and South America has demonstrated, long-term forecasts of income growth can be rapidly rendered obsolete by events but, nevertheless, as Dicken (1998, p. 39) points out

'we should not forget the other side of the import penetration coin. The East and South East Asian NIEs [new industrialised economies] are not just export generators. They are increasingly important as markets for imports. In fact they make up one of the fastest growing markets in the world. In 1984 the East

Table 11.2 Income as
percentage of USA in 2013.

Japan	41
India	46
China	116
Ex-USSR	54
NAFTA	129
EEC (12)	85
EEC[1]	93
EEC[2]	108
Pacific Rim[3]	85
NEC[4]	219
NIC[5]	33
E. Europe	14
All Asia	260
Brazil	38

Source: As Table 11.1.
Key: As Table 11.1.

and South East Asian NIEs constituted less than 10% of the world market; in 1994 this had increased to 17%. In comparison, the combined market size of North America, the European Union and Japan fell from 52% to 47%. Hence, we must lose the habit of seeing East and South East Asian NIEs as merely the generators of cheap exports. Not only are the first tier NIEs producing increasingly sophisticated goods but also they and their neighbours are now major global markets'.

Emerging markets represent a considerable and expanding volume of business – both for apparel manufacturers and retailers. They are attractive by virtue of their size and because, in most cases, they represent unsaturated markets. Garten (1996) identified as Big Emerging Markets the so-called Chinese Economic Area (China, Hong Kong, Taiwan, South Korea); Indonesia and India; South Africa; Poland and Turkey; and, in Latin America, Mexico, Argentina and Brazil.

It is important to recognise – before a commitment is made either to invest in a structure to supply these markets or to plan a diversion of marketing effort towards them – that very substantial problems can be encountered in new and emerging markets. As Zhang (1997, p. 236) observed, care needs to be exercised 'as the market is relatively unstable'. In addition, the market can be very slow to develop; business infrastructures are often severely underdeveloped; rates of inflation are frequently high and domestic currencies weak; and crime rates can be a severe problem. Coker (1997) has made forecasts of fibre consumption by country/region up to the year 2005 (see Table 11.3). These figures suggest that per capita consumption in SE Asia will, by 2005, still only amount to 15% of the EU level. This is not surprising because Jones (1994) showed that if an economy has a level of income one-third of that enjoyed by a developed country it would

Table 11.3   World fibre consumption forecasts for 2005.

	Final consumption (000 tons)	Self-sufficiency index	Consumption per head (kg)
USA	9,575	66	32.5
EU	8,321	47	21.5
Japan	3,411	52	26.0
Total Western developed and Japan	24,109	54	24.9
E. Europe and Former USSR	5,932	91	14.4
China	8,736	150	6.4
Latin America	4,407	100	7.6
S Asia	4,732	175	3.3
E. and SE Asia	4,031	190	9.0
Total developing world	26,019	145	5.2

Source: Coker, J. (1997) World Textile and Clothing Consumption Forecasts to 2005. *Textile Outlook International.*

take 20 years for the former to catch up even if it grew at three times the speed of the latter. It must be remembered that the TOI figures do not relate to final consumption of garments but to the consumption of fibre in the textile pipeline.

The main lesson to be derived from the above statistics is that, while the new markets represent substantial potential, the old markets do remain attractive. Therefore, despite all the problems associated with the slow growth of apparel markets in the developed world it remains probable that, while the emerging markets cannot be ignored because of their potential size, the realisation of this potential does lie some way into the future and that any decision to divert resources to supplying these markets must be a long-term one. As was noted in Chapter 6, the process of globalisation has not been even and, while the subject of global economic development is beyond the scope of this text, it has to be recognised that in many countries progress to the levels of discretionary income needed to produce a viable market for wants-driven products such as apparel may never occur (Kolodko, 2003, p. 20).

The time horizon for the emergence of profitable trading in the emerging markets can be extremely long and the risks correspondingly high. As Foster (1997, p. 593) noted in relation to the evolution of the Chinese market, 'overseas enterprises minded to join the explosive growth of the region should not under-estimate the difficulties of working in an alien environment'. The current preoccupation of the UK apparel industry with the EU market may not, therefore, be quite as unexpected or as unhealthy as it initially appears with the proviso that, as was noted in Chapter 1, at least one author (Owen, 1999) has argued that the main reason for the poor performance of the UK economy during the last 50 years was a failure to participate in the fastest growing markets. Clearly it would not be desirable to repeat this (alleged) error. The role of China, with its production of 1.3 billion, will be reconsidered in the final chapter. Bootle (2003) notes that less than 1% of total UK exports go to China and India despite the growth of these two economies.

It has also to be noted that the culture gap between the UK and the other member states of the EU is likely to be less pronounced than that between the UK and the developing markets. This gap is frequently described as the psychological distance between markets or the perceived similarity of potential markets relative to the decision-maker's market. Lee (1999, p. 9) defines psychic distance as the 'perceived socio-cultural distance between home and target market in terms of language, business practices, legal and political systems and marketing infrastructure' and it has been argued in Chapter 6 that apparel is an example of a relatively culture-bound product. These issues will be considered in Section C below but before moving on it must be recorded that it is not being argued that income is the only factor which has to be taken into account when devising an international marketing programme – only that in identifying future apparel markets it will be one of the most crucial factors. Other important factors would include population growth and demographics; employment participation rates; unemployment; inflation; political stability; geographic distribution of the population; the tax regime; ease of entry; the extent of existing and potential competition and the structure of the distribution system. It is clearly beyond the scope of the present text to investigate these issues and they are covered in all major international marketing texts such as Onkvisit (1989) and texts on international business practice such as Daniels (1998).

C. The concept of globalisation and the remaining role of culture in global marketing

Culture can be defined as (Terpstra, 1985, p. 6) 'a learned, shared, compelling, interelated set of symbols whose meaning provides a set of orientations for members of a society'. Cultural differences can influence international business activity in a variety of ways, e.g. acceptable ways of conducting business transactions; the role of gender in business; the acceptability of standard products; and standardisation of elements of the marketing mix such as advertising. Apparel is an important and highly visible element of a society's cultural landscape. It is also an important cultural signifier as was demonstrated by Dodd (2000) in an exploration of fashion as a means of forming group identities.

An extreme but widely accepted view of the role of culture in determining demand has been expressed by Levitt in his seminal paper (1983) in which he argued that different 'cultural preferences, national tastes and standards . . . are vestiges of the past' and that 'accustomed differences in national or regional tastes' are gone forever so that the world's 'needs and desires have been irrevocably homogenised'. The strategic implication of this thesis is that companies should 'operate as if the world were a large market – ignoring superficial regional and national differences'. Successful global companies, it is argued, will only bow to regional variations reluctantly and as a last resort and will concentrate on 'what everyone wants rather than worrying about the details of what everyone thinks they may like'.

This thesis has, as was seen in Chapter 6, been built into the wider theory of globalisation but has not gone unchallenged. It is clearly sensible to accept the argument that (Levitt, 1983, p. 92) everyone wants 'the most advanced things the world makes and sells – goods of the best quality and reliability at the lowest price'. It is a large leap of faith from this position to the statement that cultural variations can more often than not be ignored. The application of the positivist approach to the search for evidence on these issues leads to the uncovering of a mass of research which contradicts the globalisation/homogenisation thesis. A thorough review of this research is to be found in Usunier (1993) who concludes that while competition has been globalised, markets have not. An important distinction must be made between culture-free products and culture-bound products. The former represent cultural universalities and need not be modified to suit local tastes, while the latter are products the demand for which is still greatly influenced by local traditions and culture.

It has been suggested in Chapter 6 that apparel is an example of a culture-bound product. Onkvisit (1989, p. 221) argues that 'consumption patterns, living styles and the priority of needs are all dictated by culture. Culture prescribes the manner in which people satisfy their desires'. Selvanathan's (1993) study of consumption patterns revealed quite substantial differences between countries and concluded that the thesis that 'tastes are the same across countries' was not supported by the data. A later paper by Whitelock (1997, p. 45) did uncover 'evidence to support the growing trend towards product and brand standardisation' from the point of view of achieving economies of scale but also observed, importantly, that it is 'difficult to find evidence that traditional barriers are breaking down; cultural influences on the purchasing process seem to be persistent'. Shoham (1996a, p. 101) also concluded an extensive review of the literature with the opinion that 'the empirical evidence suggests that markets are not homogeneous at this time . . . Furthermore they indicate that over time markets are diverging rather than converging'.

The impact of culture upon consumer demand can be expressed in a number of ways within the marketing mix. First, and most importantly, the product may have to be modified to suit local tastes. In the context of the apparel industry this would include anthropometric, colour and climatic variations. In the case of women's apparel these may be religious barriers to the wearing of certain types of garments. Garments may need to be modified in respect of fabric type, size, colour, fit and features to take account of variations in body size, skin colour, climate and cultural preferences.

The argument for standardisation relies mainly, but not exclusively, upon cost considerations (Usunier, 1993, p. 224) although in the case of products, such as apparel, which have significant symbolic attributes, globalisation can introduce other dimensions – Usunier (1993, p. 231) argues that 'ethnocentrism is instinct-ive in all symbolic thought . . . The inappropriate (or even just poor) use of backgrounds that diffuse symbolic images which are not adapted to the local consumer is a danger for international marketers'. Secondly, and strongly related to the last issue, promotional activities can be severely compromised in their effectiveness by cultural barriers, e.g. certain promotional activities are illegal in some countries; much advertising relies on language and there are numerous examples in the literature of slogans and brand names which did not translate successfully from one language to another. As Usunier (1993) makes clear, different cultures have different attitudes to comparative, informative and persuasive advertising and strongly contrasting attitudes to such issues as the portrayal of gender roles and the use of nudity in advertising messages.

Media availability varies greatly from country to country. A major study of international advertising by Onkvisit (1987) found little support for the argu-ment that standardised advertising programmes were successful or that con-sumers were homogeneous. The conclusion drawn was (1987, p. 53) that the key 'is to determine when and where a limited measure of homogeneity exists for some level of standardised advertising'. Similarly, Alden (1996, p. 140) studying advertising in Japan, while concluding that similar humour structures to the West were observed there remained quite substantial though subtle differences, so that it was 'crucial that global managers remain sensitive to subtle cultural differences'.

Thirdly, in relation to distribution the suitability of a particular channel can vary from country to country. In the UK, for example (see Table 10.9), little apparel is sold through supermarkets although both Asda and Tesco are increasing apparel sales. In France the proportion has always been higher. Fourthly, pricing strategies may have to be adapted upon entry into new markets because acceptable or normal price levels vary for the same product from country to country. As Usunier (1993, p. 283) observes 'price is a significant element of communication between buyer and seller'. In some societies haggling is considered usual. The relationship of price to perceived value is influenced (Usunier, 1993, p. 291) by cultural attitudes to ostentatious or conspicuous consumption. Shoham (1996b, p. 67), while conceding that some aspects of the market mix can be standardised in certain regions, drew the conclusion that 'the data mostly supports the positive effect of adaptation of the 4Ps on performance'. It has to be reaffirmed that, on the basis of accumulated evidence, the support for the global standardisation thesis is not (as was indicated in Chapter 6) particularly strong.

Two general market-related issues have also to be taken into account when considering culturally diverse markets. First, and particularly in relation to the fashion sector, the speed at which new ideas spread throughout society varies between countries, as may the identity of opinion leaders. Onkvisit (1993, p. 300) argues that rather than simply recognising that consumer behaviour is affected by culture it is

'more important to specifically list the cultural norms in a country and to understand why those norms vary from country to country. It is thus important to appreciate how these norms are shaped by reference groups, social class, family, opinion leadership, and the diffusion process of innovation'.

As was seen in the previous chapter, a widely accepted and tested model of the fashion process has yet to be developed which renders this task quite difficult.

Secondly, the entire question of conducting market research across cultures is fraught with difficulties. It is usually argued that the formulation of research objectives must take into account cultural contexts   the so-called 'emic' approach (Usunier, 1993). Among the main problems identified are a reluctance to answer questions because of variations in attitudes to privacy and the existence of 'courtesy bias' in some cultures. Flynn (2000, p. 118), in relation to fashion research, did, on the other hand, find that some techniques 'could be used in cross-cultural fashion research with the same confidence' in both Korea and the USA.

Finally, in view of the global changes taking place in the role of developing regions in the textile–apparel supply chain (as revealed in Chapter 3) it will be appropriate to briefly consider the role of culture upon design influences in the context of moves on the part of Asian suppliers to achieve a role in the supply chain other than simply acting as a low cost production centre. In the words of Au (1997, p. 190), 'Hong Kong clothing manufacturers are seeking to engage in more value-added activities within the clothing pipeline . . . many of the leading manufacturers have developed their own brands and this will be an accelerating trend in the future'. Au (2000) contends that Eastern and Western designers think differently and have different design theories and inspirations: while Western designers rely 'on historical resurrection' and hold to a 'strong sense of Western culture and sexuality', in contrast, Eastern designers are motivated by a different sense of aesthetics and femininity. Au concluded that 'Japanese design theory hardly exists in Western terms . . . Japanese designers have never worked on the same basis as Western designers (and) . . . do not have an endless appetite for change in the Western sense'. They have a more evolutionary attitude to design, rooted in deep-seated philosophical, cultural and religious values. It remains to be seen whether or not these ideas and design concepts will be permanently assimilated into apparel design for global markets. De Long (2005,

p. 178) found that US students 'perceived Chinese elements of dress less desirable to purchase than those perceived as American, European or Japanese'.

Supplying these new markets profitably will, however, present a substantial challenge. As Anson (1999, p. 4) notes, countries such as India 'do appear to offer substantial market potential . . . for Western producers of relatively low volume, high added value products'. Zhang (1999) found that young Chinese consumers of denim wear would pay a 50% price premium for imported goods and that brands were becoming more important. Fit, comfort, style, colour and workmanship were all important attributes in the consumer purchasing decision. Moore (1999) also noticed a trend for UK-based apparel manufacturers to supply products from 'units which they may own in Asia . . . They may supply the design and the material according to the location. But since some of the fastest growing markets are in Asia, they now appear to be willing to locate clothing production in a developing country provided that they gain in return some access for their upmarket products into that country'. This may be true but as yet, as was seen in Chapter 5, the investment flow statistics do not reflect this. The possible link between attitudes to trade liberalisation (Chapter 9) and access to, and interest in, emerging markets is also of interest (Anson, 1994).

Clearly, it is not possible to give a review of apparel markets in a wide range of countries but it is possible to note that a great deal can be learned about foreign apparel markets from secondary sources. Fong (1999), for example, studied the market for men's suits in Hong Kong; Uppal (1999) reported on the opportunities for apparel retailing in the massive Indian market, pointing in particular to the rather special nature of the 'middle class in India'; Goveia (1999) likewise considered the apparel market in Brazil, highlighting anthropometric variations and the need for garments to be capable of frequent washing because of the climatic conditions. Grasson (1997) found that African-American mothers had some unique needs in relation to fit, colour and fabric in regard to children's clothing in the USA while Liu (1999, p. 265), in a study of the market for business wear in Taiwan, found that based 'on their unique cultural background, Taiwanese male consumers . . . emphasised fit, colour and price over ease of care, fibre content and brand . . . for their business apparel purchases'.

The magazines *Textile Outlook International* and the *Journal of Fashion Marketing and Management* regularly produce reports on the textile and apparel industry and market in different countries. *Textiles Eastern Europe* produces regular reports on the emerging markets of Central and Eastern Europe and the former Soviet Union. Finally, a wide range of market research agencies produce reports on the market for consumer goods in countries and regions around the world. The volume and quality of this information does, it must be recorded, tend to be in inverse proportion to the state of economic development of the countries concerned.

References

Alden, D. & Martin, D. (1996) Global and Cultural Characteristics of Humour in Advertising: the Case of Japan. *Journal of Global Marketing*, **9**, 121–42.

Anson, R. (1994) The MFA and Implications for Marketing Towards 2000. *Journal of Clothing Technology Management*, **11**, 1–39.

Anson, R. (1999) Who Wants Free Trade in Textiles and Apparel? *Textiles Outlook International*, **83**, 3–5.

Au, K.F. (1997) The Current Status of the Hong Kong Clothing Industry. *Journal of Fashion Marketing and Management*, **1**, 185–90.

Au, J., Taylor, G. & Newton, E. (2000) East and West Think Differently. *Journal of Fashion Marketing and Management*, **4.3**, 223–43.

Bootle, R. (2003) Welcome the Rise of China and India. *Daily Telegraph*, 12.10.03, 4.

Coker, J.D. (1997) World Textile and Clothing Consumption Forecasts to 2005. *Textile Outlook International*, **70**, 35–77.

Daniels, J.D. & Radebough, L. (1998) *International Business.* Addison Wesley, Harlow.

De Long, M., Wu, J. & Bao, M. (2005) The Influence of Chinese Dress on Western Fashion. *Journal of Fashion Marketing and Management*, **9.2**, 166–80.

Dicken, P. (1998) *Globalshift: Transforming the World Economy.* Paul Chapman, London.

Dickerson, K. (1995) *Textiles and Apparel in the Global Economy.* Prentice Hall, New Jersey.

Dodd, C., Clarke, I., Baron, S. & Houston, V. (2000) Looking the Part – Identity, Meaning and Culture including Purchasing. *Journal of Fashion Marketing and Management*, **4**, 41–9.

Flynn, L.R., Goldsmith, R.E. & Kim, W. (2000) A Cross Cultural Validation of Three New Marketing Scales for Fashion Research. *Journal of Fashion Marketing and Management*, **4**, 110–21.

Fong, L.A. & Fan, J. (1999) Hong Kong Consumers' Expectations in Suit Quality and Price. *Journal of Fashion Marketing and Management*, **3**, 191–9.

Foster, M. (1997) China: Are the Rewards Still Worth the Risk? *Long Range Planning*, **2**, 585–94.

Garten, J. (1996) The Big Emerging Markets. *Columbia Journal of World Business*, **31**, 6–32.

Goveia, C. (1999) Brazil – the real deal? *Journal of Fashion Marketing and Management*, **3**, 188–90.

Grasson, M. & Wright, R. (1997) African–American Mothers' Needs, Search and Evaluation of Children's Clothing. *Journal of Fashion Marketing and Management*, **2**, 41–55.

Jones, R.M. (1998) The Global Reach of the Clothing Industry. Part I. *Journal of Fashion Marketing and Management*, **3**, 137–53.

Jones, R.M. (1994) The Identification of New Markets. *Journal of Clothing Technology and Management*, **11**, 111–31.

Kolodko, G.W. (Ed.) (2003) *Emerging Market Economies.* Ashgate, Aldershot.

Lee, D.J. (1999) The Effect of Cultural Distance on the Relational Exchange Between Exports and Imports. *American Economic Review*, **11**, 7–18.

Levitt, T. (1983) The Globalisation of Markets. *Harvard Business Review*, **LX1**, 92–103.

Liu, K. & Dickerson, K.G. (1999) Taiwanese Male Office Workers: Selection Criteria for Business Apparel Purchase. *Journal of Fashion Marketing and Management*, **3**, 255–67.

Moore, L. (1999) *Britain's Trade and Economic Structure: The Impact of the EU*. Routledge, London.

Onkvisit, S. & Shaw, J. (1987) Standardised International Advertising: A Review and Critical Evaluation of the Theoretical and Empirical Evidence. *Columbia Journal of World Business*, **22**, 44–53.

Onkvisit, S. & Shaw, J. (1989) *International Marketing: An Analysis Strategy*. Merrill, Columbus.

ONS (2004) *Business Monitor*, M10.

Owen, G. (1999) *From Empire to Europe*. Harper Collins, London.

Selvanathan, S. & Selvanathan, E. (1993) Cross Country Analysis of Consumption Patterns. *Applied Economics*, **25**, 1245–59.

Shoham, A. (1996a) Global Marketing Standardisation. *Journal of Global Marketing*, **9**, 91–121.

Shoham, A. (1996b) Market Mix Standardisation Determination of Export Performance. *Journal of Global Marketing*, **10**, 53–74.

Terpstra, V. (1985) *The Cultural Environment of International Business*. South Western Publishing Co., Cincinnati.

Uppal, A. (1999) Apparel Retailing in India – Myth or Reality? *Journal of Fashion Marketing and Management*, **3**, 187–8.

Usunier, J.-C. (1993) *International Marketing – A Cultural Approach*. Prentice Hall, New York.

Walwyn, S.S. (1997) A Vision of Sourcing for a Global Market. *Journal of Fashion Marketing and Management*, **1**, 250–60.

Whitelock, J. & Pimblett, C. (1997) The Standardisation Debate in International Marketing. *Journal of Global Marketing*, **10**, 45–58.

Zhang, Z. (1997) Counter Flow of International Trade in Apparel. *Journal of Fashion Marketing and Management*, **1**, 223–39.

Zhang, Z., Ching, G., Ging, G., Moody, J. & Liu, W. (1999) An Investigation of Denim Wear Consumption in China. *Research Journal of Textiles and Apparel*, **3**, 60–4.

Chapter 12
Conclusions and Lessons for the Future

A. *Summary of UK experience*

- The apparel production cell within the textile–apparel pipeline is not and probably never was the dominant player.
- In the UK – as in most developed economies – the contribution to national output and trade currently made by apparel manufacture is very small. It is not regarded as a strategic industry, nor as a knowledge-based industry, at a point in the development of mature economies when the non-manufacturing, and particularly the knowledge-based service sector, is emerging as the engine of growth.
- The apparel manufacturing industry's industrial structure is almost uniquely disadvantageous to the generation of large profits and/or market power in that the level of seller concentration is extremely low; the degree of capital investment is low; the degree of labour intensity is abnormally high; there is little diversity; barriers to entry are low and the size distribution of companies is still somewhat biased towards the small end of the spectrum.
- The structure of the textile–apparel pipeline is also inimical to the possibility of the apparel manufacturing cell capturing any significant proportion of the profits generated by the pipeline as a whole – in particular the buyer power faced by the sector is very high. The pipeline is retail led. There is little prospect that this will change.
- In the UK – over a very long period of time – relationships within the pipeline have been adversarial rather than co-operative in nature.
- The forces of global shift in the sector are extremely powerful, reflecting a natural tendency for apparel manufacture to act as an engine of development in newly industrialising nations.
- The industry at the assembly stage has remained stubbornly labour-intensive. The labour cost gap between the developed and developing world remains large and there is no sign of any immediate technological breakthrough which could mitigate the impact of this gap upon costs. In the words

of Byrne (1995) 'the philosophy of total automation has been shelved for the foreseeable future'. There is no possibility of a large-scale relocation of the industry to developed, high labour cost centres. Anson's (1995) observation that an 'intensification of UK industry's delocalisation may be needed if manufacturing firms are to survive' has proven all too prophetic.

- Export performance deteriorated badly after 1998 and the sector displays a huge trade deficit a high negative trade balance on apparel trade. Import penetration of the domestic market has risen rapidly to 92%. The removal of the system of managed trade embodied in the MFA in the year 2005 has increased the pressure on the domestic industry. Price competition is severe – consumer demands are, in a sense, the real problem.

- The global spread of the UK industry is extremely limited – nearly 70% of direct exports are destined for other EU member states while, until very recently, the use made of outward processing arrangements has been low. The UK domestic market is large but extremely competitive and dominated by a small number of large retailers who have traditionally been dominant partners in any quasi-supply chain agreements which have existed. In the 1990s a sea change took place in their commitment to domestic sourcing. It is not possible to foresee where the collapse in employment will end but the prospects do not appear favourable. The IFM (2004) report concluded that, in the UK, 'it may be expected that the clothing industry remaining will rapidly close or de-localise' while Anson (2005) argues that 'a huge % of the world's textile and clothing capacity outside China would appear to be at risk'.

- In the period after 1995 the trend in UK output and employment entered a new phase in that both data series have turned down together. This represents a significant break with the experience of the last two decades – within the textile pipeline the apparel manufacturing industry in the UK continued to prosper, or at least to survive, long after the decline in the primary textile sector but this very survival may now be under threat.

In summary it would be difficult to devise a more daunting scenario than the one faced by UK-based apparel manufacturers. In many respects these problems are common to all developed (high labour cost) locations. However, there have been variations in experience as between developed nations. Structure and external environmental forces are not the sole determinants of success or failure – there is a role for strategy.

B.   *The role of strategy in the evolution of an industry*

The literature makes it clear that the industry in different countries did react in a variety of ways to what were relatively common external pressures. In brief, the

Italian industry followed a path of relying on supply chain collaboration and networking partnerships between very small firms to generate the competitive advantages of flexibility and rapid responsiveness to changes in fashion. This has been extensively documented by Belussi (1997, p. 129) who stresses the ability of the industry to fight back against low cost competition: 'through differentiation, time to market, flexibility and fashion'.

The German apparel manufacturing industry, while suffering a severe fall in employment between 1974 and 1994 of some 270,000 (Alder, 1997, p. 131) used Outward Processed Trade (OPT) to compensate for the loss in domestic production. In Alder's words (1997, p. 137) the

> 'generic strategy appears to be one of using outward processing for non-fashionable garments, while continuing to use domestic production for garments of high quality and client-oriented, just-in-time production lines'.

In contrast, the approach adopted in the UK was to rely on the construction (usually by merger) of relatively large vertically integrated textile–apparel producers and to concentrate on relatively long production runs, domestically produced, for the large retailer. This system was then buttressed by a mild system of protection. In smaller companies, de-skilling and attempts to reduce costs traditionally prevailed – especially in the ethnic sector which was the main source of increasing employment in the UK. Unfortunately this policy has proven over time to be singularly out of step with the demands of the evolving apparel marketplace. The dominant feature of the market has been its increasingly volatile and multi-faceted nature.

Obviously, it is easy to be wise after the event and there is no way of telling whether or not this should or could have been anticipated at the time, but a system which stressed long runs for a middle of the road market turned out to be virtually the opposite of what was required, which was flexibility, increasing short runs, more frequent and rapid change and quick response.

This point was neatly captured by Nolan (1997, p. 279) when he wrote that the Italian system (my emphasis) *'appears to match* the needs of the business environment, allowing flexibility, responsiveness and control of quality to coexist in a most efficient way' and that in the Italian case the 'constant drive to de-integrate where in other parts of the world companies were actually becoming larger . . . suggests that a *different mind set* existed across the Italian industry'.

As Anson (1998a) put it, the fashion in the UK in the 1960s and 1970s

> 'was to build large vertical firms through merger and acquisition in the belief that companies would benefit from economies of scale and would therefore be better able to withstand the threatening tide of import competition . . . but two or three decades on, big companies are no longer in fashion'.

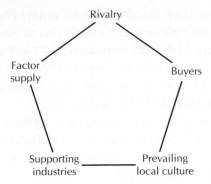

Fig. 12.1   A Pentagon Framework showing the effect of culture.

It can, therefore, be argued that the business culture prevailing in the UK at the time when adjustment was needed was, unfortunately, not conducive to the selection of the best strategies. Landes (1998) has examined the role of culture in the evolution of national economies and argues that (1998, p. 175) the 'inner beliefs that inspire populations in their daily lives are intimately linked to worldly success' and that if any lesson is to be learned from 'the history of economic development it is that culture makes all the difference'.

This may make it difficult to transfer a successful strategy from one culture to another – if cultures vary in their degree of openness or respect for co-operative work, for example. Bull (1993) highlighted this aspect of the evolution of entrepreneurial textile communities in Italy and the UK: in the latter it was found that success was identified with self-sufficiency and there was a deep-seated reluctance to co-operate with other local firms. This made it unlikely that policies which had worked in Italy could be transported successfully to the UK.

On a more global scale the reluctance in the past of China to accept and embrace foreign ideas has been identified by Jay (2000) as a major reason behind the historical inability of that country to assume world economic leadership. In effect, therefore, the Porter Diamond may need to be turned into a pentagon (Fig. 12.1) with prevailing business culture being the additional factor. It may simply not be possible for a country to copy the policies adopted elsewhere. If a country's prevailing business culture is in line with the demands of the optimum strategy it will succeed. Alternatively, if a country is conservative and resistant to change while the market demands continuous change then problems will occur. In Taplin's (2000, p. 17) words it is likely that 'institutional factors . . . predispose firms in certain countries to pursue certain types of strategies'. It may turn out to be impossible for China to copy Western corporate culture.

This possibility was recognised by Porter (1998a, p. 129) although it was not built into the classic Diamond framework:

'cultural factors are important as they shape the environment facing firms . . . social and political history and values create persistent differences among nations that plan a role in competitive advantage in many industries'.

C. Potential survival strategies

Initially, it will be assumed that the supply chain remains largely as outlined in Fig. 1.1. What conclusions can be drawn about the future of the apparel manufacturer based in developed countries? First, there appears to be no evidence to suggest that power relationships within the supply chain are likely to change in favour of the apparel manufacturer. Second, while there is a little evidence that the traditional adversarial links are being replaced by more co-operative ones in the context of evolving supply chain management, it is clear that there is still a long way to go to achieve the levels secured in other sectors. Third, it was shown in Chapter 2 that the structure of the apparel manufacturing sector was almost uniquely unfavourable to its ability to capture a large part of the profit generated by the supply chain – there is no evidence that this situation is about to change drastically. Fourth, there seems to be (Chapter 4) little chance of any revolutionary breakthrough which will reduce the labour-intensive nature of the assembly operation. Fifth, it is clear that the EU is committed to trade governed by collective rules within the WTO. There is no possibility that the EU would move on trade barriers outside the WTO rules and there is no sign that the latter would ever consider re-establishing anything like the MFA (Anson, 1992).

Finally, it seems improbable that the sector can expect governments, in the West, to provide substantial aid. Therefore, in relation to the range of potential strategies outlined in Fig. 7.1 the first five can be virtually discounted as plausible strategies for the majority of the sector. The following options remain.

(i) Import a successful domestic strategy from elsewhere

It is clear that choice of strategy does make a difference (Chapter 7) and that (Chapter 3) the developed world does still remain a significant producer of many types of apparel. In the case of the UK it is clear, with the benefit of hindsight, that the twin strategies of relying on a mild form of protection allied to support for domestic production of relatively long production runs were, in the long run, doomed to failure, particularly as they served to repress the utilisation of offshore production. It was unlikely, of course, that the textile sector in the UK could be divorced from the prevailing industrial mood of the times. To this extent it is probably the case that the mindset in other countries was simply more in tune with what turned out to be the requirements of the market. The classic example of this difference in approach remains the Italian model reviewed in

Chapter 7. The biggest single impediment to importing such a policy into the UK is probably one of prevailing business culture, as was discussed above.

Therefore, it appears difficult to make a case for a UK solution based on local clusters of firms in line with the Italian model. It must be recalled that Porter (1990, p. 494) in his initial work on successful clusters in a range of countries concluded that 'Britain lacks comparative advantage in . . . most areas of textiles/apparel' and that, therefore, although the UK government has expressed (Buckley, 2000) an interest in focusing industrial policy upon 'clusters' and Porter (1998b) has reaffirmed his belief in the importance of such geographic concentrations of interconnected companies in promoting global success, it seems barely credible that this could result in a concentration upon the assembly of apparel. Kilduff (2006) has shown that the UK continues to lose competitive advantage in apparel production.

(ii)   Niche marketing solutions

There is (as was seen in Chapter 7) a limited amount of evidence that concentrating on high value added niche products when linked to the development of flexible and responsive manufacturing systems and the use of offshore production can enable producers in high cost centres to compete. There does not seem to be any logical impediment to UK firms adopting this strategy.

(iii)   Added value, quick response and lean manufacturing principles

These policies were explored in Chapter 7 and, clearly, there can be little argument but that banishing waste and time from the supply chain must be seen as desirable. Therefore, it can safely be concluded that these policies offer some competitive advantage to those who can take advantage of them. This is particularly true given that, as was seen in Chapter 2, historically the level of productivity achieved in the UK apparel sector had not compared favourably with that secured elsewhere. This appears still to be the case in that Hart (1992), for example, found that, in a UK–German comparison, the biggest productivity gap out of 23 industries studied was in clothing. The downside of reliance on these policies is that, in so far as can be judged from the evidence, the adoption rate is rather low and there is virtually no direct or hard evidence on the distribution of the gains from quick response policies as between the players in the supply chain.

This conclusion would be supported, for example, by the study of BhS suppliers reported by Smith (1999) who commented on the remaining resistance to change and lack of trust within the pipeline. In this context it is possible to virtually dispose of the argument that apparel manufacturers (as a group) could seek to capture a greater share of the profits generated in the chain. There is no evidence that the balance of power will switch from the retailers back to the manufacturing branch of the supply chain. Indeed there is, in the UK, continuing evidence of the dominance of the retailer as exemplified by the decision of Marks & Spencer (Mills, 2000) to arbitrarily cut prices paid to suppliers. In addition, there are numerous examples in the literature sufficient to demonstrate the viability of offshore sourcing in a time-sensitive environment. A number of examples can be considered here. Tait (1999) described the growth of the American company Duck Head apparel which produced 200 new styles per season on a rolling basis as an average cycle of 30–40 days, despite having only 5% of production located in the USA. Design and cutting is retained in or near to the company's headquarters in Georgia. Distribution for the US market is also handled centrally.

Black (1991) outlined the evolution of Nautica to the stage where some 500 lines are produced, mainly in the Far East and the Caribbean with a small proportion produced in the USA – all via contract manufacturing because they argue their business is design and marketing. The major American producer, MAST Industries, while taking a different stance on the organisation of offshore production in that it utilises joint ventures, produces a turnover of over $1 billion in some 35 countries – of which only 5% is conducted in the USA with some 70% being sourced in China, Sri Lanka, Hong Kong, Taiwan and Korea. Trust (1999) argues that the key drivers of the success of the company are migration (having the correct mix of global manufacturing capacity to meet customer demand); integration and technology (to control resources and provide efficient communication and collaboration) and talent – and that it is the latter which is the limiting factor on future growth. Therefore, it is unlikely that QR can be seen, of itself, as a route to substantial relocation of manufacturing capacity to high cost centres other than in those sections of the apparel market where retailers value locally responsive suppliers highly.

On the other hand, there do not appear to be any substantial negative aspects of these policies so that, to the extent that they can be adopted to the benefit of the apparel manufacturer as well as to the retailer, they clearly should form part of future strategies wherever possible. Therefore, the conclusion which is inexorably emerging is that – other than in small sections of the industry where either the technological input is unusually large or the need for very rapid response is paramount – the probability of a largely domestically based strategy succeeding is rather low. Attention must be focused on international solutions.

(iv)   External solutions

As has been seen in Chapter 4, the labour cost gap between different countries is vast. It is likely, therefore, that apparel manufacturers worldwide will continue to take advantage of the availability of cheap labour by moving garment assembly operations to low cost regions. The argument over the desirability of utilising offshore facilities is – despite the continued protestations about hidden costs – effectively over. This can be seen from the statistics in Chapters 3 and 8. As Anson (1998b) expressed it, companies 'will have to source overseas to remain competitive so as to preserve at least some of what remains of the UK clothing industry'.

Taplin (1999) concluded that 'if trade barriers continue to fall . . . more and more of the low value added and less time sensitive products will be shifted to low cost areas of the world'.

If further proof were needed the many pronouncements in the trade press detailing decisions taken to move production offshore provide dramatic supporting evidence. Rush (2000) and Tait (1999) both document these changes.

Finally, it can be concluded that this rush offshore will occur because the major retailers demand it. The only issue is whether or not this development has to be viewed in an entirely negative light. Clearly, from an employment point of view, the short-term effects are entirely negative. However, there is (as was seen in Chapter 7) some limited evidence that the industry in those countries which adopted offshore production most comprehensively did enjoy relatively greater success in world markets than those which did not. Ohmae (1994) argues that companies which won market share through a policy of exporting assembly jobs were able to employ more people in the so-called higher value added jobs – such as design, finance, marketing – retained domestically. This effect was confirmed for the USA for the period 1979–90 by Feenstra (1996) who concluded that 'outsourcing has contributed substantially to the increase in demand for non-production labour'.

It would have to be recognised that in the case of apparel manufacture with its extremely high ratio (Chapter 2) of operatives to total employment this effect would probably be less pronounced than in other sectors. Therefore, it has to be concluded that, partly because of the labour cost structure in the sector and partly because other options have a limited capacity to generate solutions, the offshore option will figure prominently in most future strategies. It is true that the use of offshore sources does introduce a number of administrative obstacles to be cleared – a wide range of documentation needs to be dealt with in order to comply with regulations dealing with issues such as customs clearance, duty payments, origin rules and import licensing, but companies can relatively easily learn to deal with these issues. Guides exist (Humphrey, 1996) or the task can be outsourced.

In Porter's (1998a) words:

'Companies have to spread activities globally to source inputs and gain access to markets. Failure to do so will lead to competitive disadvantage. And for stable, labour intensive industries such as assembly . . . low cost factors are often decisive in driving locational choices'.

In a sense this could be regarded as an opportunity to exploit some of the clusters which were found by Porter (1990) to represent UK strengths – distribution, financial services and advertising. UK-based companies should be capable of organising and financing global operations. In the absence of a concern over assembly jobs the Diamond framework becomes more favourable.

Sewing capacity and capability is not in scarce supply – it is unlikely to form the basis of sustainable competitive advantage. Nor is it likely to be the limiting factor upon commercial success. Design capability and the possession of an understanding of the marketplace allied to the supply chain management, logistical and quality control capabilities to produce apparel that sells, are in far less plentiful supply. Additionally, many of these skills are in far greater supply in the developed countries. In the case of the UK, for example, Porter (1990) identified a number of successful 'clusters' in the general area of international financing, banking and global advertising. Therefore it would be sensible to exploit whatever favourable trends exist in the wider UK economy to support a strategy for the industry.

If companies could reorganise their structure and tasks to reflect these strengths they might have a greater chance of success. To move down this road does require a substantial change in attitude towards the importance of the assembly operations, but such a move would recognise that the assembly operation is not the main value-adding operation in the garment production process. This kind of flexibility of approach is being demonstrated by countries previously associated with the sewing process.

As Au (1997) puts it, the

'Hong Kong manufacturers are seeking to engage in more value-added activities within the clothing supply pipeline . . . many of the leading manufacturers have developed their own brands and this will be an accelerating trend in the future'.

A limited number of apparel manufacturers may be able to exploit technological advances in fabric so as to produce performance garments from within a developed country base – in effect they would be overcoming the industry's well-known non-scientific nature. In addition there will probably always be the demand for some quick response capacity. For the rest (and majority) of the industry it seems clear that no survival will be possible in the absence of a move to offshore production as a basic element in overall company strategy. In effect, this solves the basic problem of high labour costs.

It does not, of course, solve any of the other problems such as relative power relationships within the pipeline, although it will call for the development and deployment of superior logistical and supply chain management skills within the evolving global supply chain. It is this belief that has driven the conclusion drawn in Chapter 2 that the UK industry had by 1998 reached a second crucial period and that substantial losses of jobs and UK output can be anticipated into the future.

The effect upon total employment in the apparel sector was expected to be unusually severe because of the high ratio of operatives to total staff. Therefore, it was predicted that (Jones, 2002) employment in the sector in the UK could be expected to fall towards 75,000 by the year 2005. This prediction was based upon the rapid growth in OPT, the rising rate of import penetration, the simultaneous collapse of output and employment reported in Fig. 2.1, and the rash of closures and movements offshore reported at the end of 1998 through to the beginning of 2000 by such companies as Bairds, Dewhirst, Courtaulds, T.J. Hughes, New Look, Dawson International and, most spectacularly, Coats Viyella. This prediction is validated by the latest figures for 2005 which indicate that employment had fallen to 46,000 (ONS, 2005).

D. Solutions involving reconfiguration of the supply chain

If the straightjacket of the concept of the traditional textile–apparel supply chain is relaxed a wider range of options opens up and some more imaginative solutions can be envisaged. For example, in the traditional scenario a range of functions have to be carried out and companies who undertake design, cutting and assembly are labelled manufacturers. There is nothing sacrosanct about this. De Meyer (1998, p. 270) argues that European manufacturers will increasingly be forced to 'break down the ways that activities were constructed around the manufacturing task' so as to allow a more service-orientated approach to business to evolve. In Chazen's words (1996) the question of 'who is a manufacturer and who is a retailer is getting a little fuzzy'. The assembly stage does not necessarily contribute to the greatest proportion of value added. Magretta (1998) argued that it was becoming so difficult to squeeze any additional profit out of the manufacturing process that it was becoming correspondingly less important to be involved with that part of the value chain. Singhal (2004) estimated that 57% of the value added for a typical garment was created at the retail stage (compared with 23% at the manufacturing stage) and that potential cost reductions as a percentage of final value were three times as likely at the retail stage than at the manufacturing stage. Therefore, it may just be that the best way forward for apparel manufacturers historically based in the high cost centres is to let go any lingering loyalty to assembly-type operations and to become sourcing facilitators and merchandisers.

As Au (1999) has shown, the Hong Kong industry has an impressive record of reinventing itself as cost conditions change. Miller (1997) describes the latest trend as from a manufacturing base to a fashion centre.

The upshot of these developments is that the debate over the appropriateness of offshore production is over – despite the occasional argument over 'hidden costs'. The key questions now are 'where?', 'who does what?' and 'what form will the offshore network assume?'. Two new threats to the industry in high-cost countries have emerged as the evolution of dispersed supply chains progresses viz industrial upgrading (Gereffi, 1999) and direct retailer sourcing bypassing the domestic manufacturer (KSA, 2005). As Gereffi (1999, p. 45) observed, whereas in the past the 'retailers were the apparel manufacturers' main customers . . . now they are increasingly becoming their competitors' and the analysis of Chapter 2 makes it clear who would win in that battle. In addition, it is probably true to say that the retailers did not see the end of the MFA as a threat but as an opportunity which (IFM, 2004, p. 285) 'will make their sourcing a lot easier and probably cheaper'. Not for the first time do the interests of the retailer and the domestic manufacturer diverge. There would be no reason, in principle, why a combination of Western retailer and low-cost supplier could not carry out most of the tasks in the supply chain, effectively cutting out the developed country manufacturer. Many 'offshoring' experts are already arguing (Aldrick, 2004) that activities such as computer graphics, programming, design engineering and research are being outsourced to offshore locations which are 'nearer-to-needle'. The implication of these developments is that a few years ago it could be argued (Jones, 2002) that the future for the apparel industry in the UK could be seen as reducing the emphasis on assembly and manufacturing and focusing on other areas of value creating activity, (such as design, marketing, supply chain management and logistics) so as to provide the flexibility and responsiveness which retailers demand and thereby obtaining a competitive advantage. Magretta (1998) described this as dispersed manufacturing. Fung (1998) contended that a new type of company would then emerge which would actively avoid anything to do with manufacturing but which would produce

> 'a new type of value added, a truly global product. The label may say "made in Thailand" but it is not a Thai product. We dissect the manufacturing process and look for the best solution at each stage. . . . We're pulling apart the value chain an optimising each stage'.

The problem is that that if offshore suppliers move into these areas there is correspondingly less for the UK-based company to do.

The rapid decline in activity in the UK as described in Chapter 2 has not been confined to the UK, of course. Similar trends have been observed in the USA, for example, as has been dramatically described by Kilduff (2005, 2006), Shelton (2005), Nelson (2006) and Oh (2006). These developments will normally give rise to the growth of more modern and complex supply chain networks with varying configurations, some of which are discussed in Appendix C. These changes are also associated with the evolution of so-called lean and/or agile supply chains which aim to minimise waste and increase flexibility of response to changes in the marketplace as was seen in Chapter 7. Gereffi (1999) has described the emergence of industrial upgrading in Asia as a movement from mere export-oriented assembly operations through OEM (Original Equipment Manufacture) which means full package supply (incorporating developing sources of inputs and supplying components) to OBM (Original Brand Name) operations which involve using own brand names and selling branded goods both domestically and internationally. He argues that East Asia moved through this process because it succeeded in developing close links with the retail buyers who were driving the supply chain. He found that in apparel chains the types of networks which evolved varied with the type of retailer leading the chain. For example, retailers and marketers tended to rely on OEM supliers to buy ready-made apparel via, for instance, Hong Kong and China, whereas the so-called branded manufacturers created networks which focused upon apparel assembly using imported inputs often on a regional basis, such as the EU to North Africa and Eastern Europe. Over time a learning process resulted in industrial upgrading. Additionally, because in the apparel sector sources do change with changes in labour costs, the supply network continually spreads out and this also contributes to upgrading because the higher price point work normally involves more complex products and styles.

Gereffi (1999) also champions the second change mentioned above, i.e. direct sourcing. In a sense, retailers who move to this are catching up with the branded marketers who always operated as manufacturers without factories and always relied on offshore sources. These companies are content to pass increasing functions (such as pattern and marker making) to their suppliers. In effect they are recognising (Gereffi, 1999, p. 47) 'that overseas countries have the capability to manage all aspects of the production process'. The result is, of course, as was predicted by Jones (2002), that apparel manufacturers in developed countries are squeezed from all directions. There is no study for the UK which identifies particular retailers following specific supply chain models in the way Gereffi (1999) does for the USA but Chen (2005) does provide an insight into the relationship between six UK retailers (anonymously) and their Chinese suppliers. He distinguished between the so-called traditional model (Appendix C) and various forms of streamlined models which, in effect, lead to direct sourcing (Appendix C). He found that the latter tend to evolve over a long period and also that the Hong Kong offices were typically undertaking much more of the non-sewing operations in the chain. The major problems identified related to communication problems along the supply chain.

Oh (2006) studied the evolution of fast and responsive (agile) chains and concluded that China had frequently outperformed nearer to market suppliers despite the apparent disadvantage of distance – citing the example of the failure of the Mexican apparel industry to upgrade. In his view (Oh, 2006) 'in the quota free era, what rules the sourcing game is the development of fast and flexible supply chain networks that reduce the risks . . . for retailers' and concluded that there was no doubt 'that China will dominate world apparel markets without quotas since China has the most responsive and efficient supply chain networks'. This confirms the scepticism expressed in Chapter 8 that quick response was so incompatible with offshore sourcing that it could be invoked as a potential saviour of domestic jobs in developed countries. Oh (2006) also explores the options for the industry in the USA and concludes that it is essential that the remaining producers develop collaborative networks on a regional basis – clusters in effect. Can regional clusters save jobs in developed countries? Porter (1998a) continues to argue that the existence of self-supporting clusters remains crucial and he had already drawn the conclusion that there were few successful textile clusters in the UK. The UK does, however, have strength in international finance trade and advertising. In addition, good design has been emphasised by Kingswell (1998) and Smith (1999) so that the best hope for the future may still lie in a reconfiguration of activities away from an overbearing concern with assembly and towards a focus on marketing, design, sourcing and supply chain management. A number of researchers have investigated this possibility; for example, Blair (2001) examined clusters in Mexico and their importance has been promoted by Doeringer (1995), Feser (2000) and Hill (2000). The main drawback from the point of view of the developed country is that most of the labour-intensive parts of the operation would take place in those parts of the cluster which lie in the low-cost regions within the cluster so that this policy would not lead to any large-scale recovery of employment in developed countries. It is clearly and demonstrably true that sources of imports into a developed country such as the UK do change over time as can be seen in Table 12.1 but these changes represent trade diversion not trade reduction and do not imply any return to domestic sourcing. As Anson (2005, p. 166) observed, trade policy interventions 'continue to exert a predominant influence on trade *flows*' but not on volumes as one source simply replaces another. The impact of rising imports of apparel upon employment and production in the UK has been dramatic as has been shown in Chapter 2 As Jones (2005) observed, in the period 1997–2004

Table 12.1   Sources of UK apparel imports (%).

	1996	2003
EU	30.7	25.3
Rest of W. Europe	4.7	11.7
E. Europe	3.7	7.1
N. America	2.1	1.1
Other Americas	0.4	0.2
M. East and N. Africa	6.7	6.2
SubSaharan Africa	2.6	1.7
Asia and Oceania	49.1	46.7

Source: As Table 5.1.
Note: The rise in the share taken by W. Europe is entirely due to the increase in imports form Turkey.

some 88,000 jobs were lost (66% of the total as opposed to a 17% fall in manufacturing as a whole); exports fell by 22%; production fell by 54%; and the
number of enterprises in the sector by almost 50% with virtually no comment
in the press or from any politicians. It is not possible to blame these reductions
on either increased productivity (which fell 32% between 1995 and 2001) or on
a lack of demand in the UK market (see Chapter 10) so the prime cause must
have been the rise in imports. Somewhat paradoxically, on a European scale the
accession of the Eastern and Central European countries will increase the EU's
share of global production (as would the accession of Turkey, of course). This
represents a statistical oddity rather than any sign of recovery of the sector, of
course, and there is no prospect of a major recovery of employment in the
apparel sector in the older members of the EU such as the UK unless there was
to be a catastrophic and irreversible collapse in the world trade system.
Prosperous niches will remain but the era of mass production is gone forever. It
can be argued that difficult conditions provide the opportunity to learn important, if unpalatable, lessons. The process of learning in the global apparel sector
as trade controls have been removed has been slow and represents as Dickerson
(1995) observed many years ago the biggest challenge facing the developed
world as global shift proceeds. Ahmad (2004, p. 155) correctly observed that the
aim of both the EU and the USA after 1995 was 'to retain as high a share of . . .
production and trade as possible for as long as possible' by using non-quota
instruments so as not to have to learn the lessons. This position is simply not tenable in the long run and merely – in so far as they are ever successful – serves to
postpone the inevitable adjustment that has eventually to be made. The events in
the EU of July 2005 provide a perfect illustration of how far there is still to go to
come to terms with the realities of shifting competitive advantage in the global
apparel supply chain with China employing 1.3 million in the apparel industry
in 2002 (ILO, 2006).

E. The role of China

China's role is now clear despite the statistical problems described in Chapter 3.
There have been huge surges in imports of apparel from China into both the EU
and USA since 2001. China is also the major supplier to Japan and Australia.
There is little doubt, therefore, that China will be the major supplier of apparel
to the developed markets unless there is a major retreat into isolationism as
discussed below or a total collapse in the world trade system due to political
problems in the region. As Phillips (2004, p. 43) noted, the 'Chinese Government
has always considered the development of the textile and apparel industries
to be a key factor in the social and economic advancement of the people as a
whole'. There is no doubt that China's entry into the WTO was equally as
significant as the phasing out of the MFA. The remaining question is which

other suppliers will succeed with China and which will fail. In terms of a market China represents an enormous potential customer for the future with its population of 1.3 billion. However, as Storey (2003) points out, while China has some 21% of the world's population it currently has only 3% of the world's wealth. Studwell (2003) provides cautionary examples of Western entrepreneurs who failed in their attempts to exploit this potential market. The process of negotiating with Chinese businessmen is notoriously difficult (Bloch, 2004).

Meyerand (1996) of General Motors calculated that if only 1% of the population of China could afford cars it would give a market roughly the size of his company's total European market. As Ma (2000, p. 2) points out, GDP rose by almost five times between 1980–1997 which was 'considered a miracle by many observers' while the ratio of trade to GDP rose from 9% to 36% reflecting the increasing opening up of China to the rest of the world. In effect China is in an almost unique position of trying to achieve two transformations – from command to market economy and from rural to urban society – in an extremely short space of time. However, supplying the market represents an enormous business and cultural challenge (Nolan, 2000).

The normal relationship between consumption and income highlighted in Chapter 10 does, according to Song (2000), exist in China but it is unstable and 'highly sensitive to policy changes and structural breaks' over time. Cook (2000) argues that the transformation of Chinese big business stands at a crossroad and that 'the future pattern of the relationship between multinational business and emerging big business in China will be powerfully shaped by international relationships, especially that between China and the USA'.

Landes (1991) points to the fact that, in the past, Chinese cultural inhibitions – such as a rejection of outside ideas – have hindered development. Menzies (2002, p. 405) in his acclaimed analysis of Chinese maritime activity in the 15th century concluded that in 1423 'China was entering . . . its long night of isolation from the outside world' and that had she not 'retreated into xenophobia and isolation, China, not Europe, would have become the mistress of the world'. Jay (2000) quotes the opinion of the Chinese Emperor in 1793 that China 'had no need to import the manufactures of outside barbarians' so that although China was, in the eighteenth century, probably the most powerful society in the world, it contributed little to the global network of sea routes pioneered by others and in the nineteenth century 'did not industrialise, turning its back for a second time on the opportunity to seize an unchallengeable world leadership . . . The reasons for this apparent reluctance . . . lie . . . partly in the structure of Chinese society'. As Jay (2000, p. 311) argues, the country has a long history of 'centrally organised rejection . . . of economic opportunity'. Will it fail for a third time?

Similarly, it is possible that the demand for constant change in the apparel market may not be in tune with Eastern values – in Russell's (1984) words, while the 'typical Westerner wishes to be the cause of as much change as possible, the typical Chinese wishes to enjoy as much and as delicately as possible'.

The differences between design inspirations as between Western and Eastern cultures have been explored in Chapter 11. Therefore, it is not possible to determine with any great degree of exactitude whether the future role of China in the global apparel industry will be predominantly benign – as a major new market and source of cost-efficient production – or will assume the role, in Walden's (1999) rather colourful words, of 'an imported Mercedes driven by a demented peasant . . . (so that) anyone who gets in its path would be crushed under its wheels'. Storey (2003) also sees a clash between a benign China focused upon raising the living standards of the population and an assertive power driven by an inflated view of its correct status in the world. The provenance of the so-called Chinese curse that it should be 'your fortune to live in interesting times' may be in doubt but its appropriateness to the global apparel industry in the early twenty-first century is not.

References

Ahmad, M. (2004) Trade in Textiles and Clothing: the Way Forward from 2005. *Textile Outlook International*, **112**, 150–94.

Alder, U. & Brutenacher, M. (1997) Production Organisation and Technological Change. In: *Rethinking Global Production* (Eds I. Taplin & J. Winterton), pp. 131–56. Avebury, Aldershot.

Aldrick, A. (2004) Outsourcing Going to Hit Professionals. *Daily Telegraph*, 11.11.04, 33.

Anson, R. (1992) The Demise of the MFA. *Manufacturing Clothier*, **73**, 16–19.

Anson, R. (1995) Delocalised Production. *Manufacturing Clothier*, **76**, 6–7.

Anson, R. (1998a) Editorial, *Textile Outlook International*, **76**, 3–5.

Anson, R. (1998b) A Green Light to Move Operations Offshore. *World Clothing Manufacturer*, **79**, 62–3.

Anson, R. (2005) Editorial: Post-2004 Strategies. *Textile Outlook International*, **111**, 3–9.

Au, K. (1997) The Current Status of the HK Clothing Industry. *Journal of Fashion Marketing and Management*, **1**, 185–91.

Au, K. (1999) Production Shift for the HK Clothing Industry. *Journal of Fashion Marketing and Management*, **3**, 166–79.

Belussi, F. (1997) Dwarfs and Giants. In: *Rethinking Global Production* (Eds I. Taplin & J. Winterton), pp. 77–131. Avebury, Aldershot.

Black, S. (1991) Nautica: Its Ship Has Come In. *Bobbin*, **32**, 52–6.

Blair, J. & Gereffi, G. (2001) Local Clusters in Global Chains. *World Development*, **29.11**, 1885–1903.

Bloch, B. (2004) West Struggles to Learn 'Cunning Tricks'. *Daily Telegraph*, 11.11.04, 13.

Buckley, C. (2000) Byers to Outline New Strategy for DTI. *The Times*, 17.7.2000, p. 26.

Bull, A., Pitt, M. & Szarka, J. (1993) *Entrepreneurial Textile Communities*. Chapman and Hall, London.

Byrne, C. (1995) The Impact of New Technology in the Clothing Industry. *Textile Outlook International*, **58**, 111–40.

Chazen, J. (1996) Notes from the Apparel Industry. *Columbia Journal of World Business*, **31**, 40–43.

Chen, Z. (2005) *Quality Management in International Clothing Chains.* Unpublished PhD Thesis, MMU, Manchester.

Cook, S., Yao, S. & Zhuang, Z. (2000) *The Chinese Economy Under Transition.* Macmillan, Basingstoke.

De Meyer, A. (1998) Manufacturing in Europe: Where Do We Go Next? *European Management Journal*, **16**, 262–71.

Dickerson, K. (1995) *Textiles and Apparel in the Global Economy.* Prentice Hall, New Jersey.

Doeringer, P. & Terpzla, D. (1995) Business Strategies and Cross Industry Clusters. *Economic Development Quarterly*, **9**, 225–37.

Feenstra, R.C. & Hanson, G. (1996) Globalisation, Outsourcing and Wage Inequality. *American Economic Review*, **86**, 240–46.

Feser, E. & Bergman, E. (2000) National Industrial Clusters. *Regional Studies*, **34.1**, 1–20.

Fung, V. (1998) quoted in Margretta, J. (1998) Supply Chain Management Hong Kong Style. *Harvard Business Review*, **September–October**, 102–16.

Gereffi, G. (1999) International Trade and Industrial Upgrading in the Apparel Commodity Chain. *Journal of International Economics*, **48**, 37–70.

Hart, P. & Shipman, A. (1992) The Variation of Production Within British and German Industries. *Journal of Industrial Economics*, **4**, 417–27.

Hill, E., Brennan, J. (2000) A Method for Identifying the Drivers of Industrial Clusters. *Economic Development Quarterly*, **114**, 65–96.

Humphrey, A. (1996) *International Trade Procedures for the Clothing and Textile Industries.* MMU, Manchester.

IFM (2004) *Study on the Implications of the 2005 Trade Liberalisation in the Textile and Clothing Sector.* Institut Français de la Mode, Paris.

ILO (2006) Statistics supplied to author by ILO, Geneva.

Jay, P. (2000) *The Road To Riches.* Weidenfeld and Nicholson, London.

Jones, R.M. (2002) *The Apparel Industry.* Blackwell Science, Oxford.

Jones, R.M. (2005) Editorial. *Journal of Fashion Marketing and Management*, **9.3**, 253–55.

Jones, R.M. (2006) Editorial. *Journal of Fashion Marketing and Management*, **10.1** (forthcoming).

Kilduff, P. (2005) Patterns of Strategic Adjustment in the US Textile and Apparel Industries since 1979. *Journal of Fashion Marketing and Management*, **9.2**, 180–95.

Kilduff, P. & Chi, T. (2006) Longitudual Patterns of Competitive Advantage in the Textile Market. *Journal of Fashion Marketing and Management* (forthcoming).

Kingswell, V. (1998) Dealing with the Trouble Ahead. *Drapers Record*, 1.8.98, ii–iii.

KSA (2005) *Global Sourcing Reference* (7th edition), Manchester.

Landes, D.S. (1998) *The Wealth and Poverty of Nations.* W.W. Norton and Co., New York.

Ma, J. (2000) *The Chinese Economy in the 1990s.* Macmillan, Basingstoke.

Magretta, J. (1998) Supply Chain Management Hong Kong Style. *Harvard Business Review*, **September–October**, 102–16.

Menzies, G. (2002) *1421: the Year China Discovered the World.* Bantam Press, London.

Meyerand, M.G. (1996) quoted in Ehrlich, H. (1998) *The Wiley Book of Business Quotations.* J. Wiley, New York.

Miller, L. (1997) What Future for the UK's Clothing Manufacturing? *Drapers Record*, 6.9.1997, 12–13.

Mills, L. (2000) M & S Tells Suppliers to Cut Prices. *Sunday Telegraph*, 24.7.2000, 1.

Nelson, N. & Karpona, E. (2006) Employment in the US Textile and Apparel Industries. *Journal of Fashion Marketing and Management* (forthcoming).

Nolan, P. & Xiaoqiang, W. (2000) Reorganisation Among Turbulence. In: *The Chinese Economy Under Transition* (Eds S. Cook, S. Yao & J. Zhuang), pp. 1–15. Macmillan, Basingstoke.

Nolan, T. & Condotta, B. (1997) Close Knit Relationships Hold Key to Italian Fashion Industry Success. *Journal of Fashion Marketing and Management*, **1**, 274–83.

Oh, H. & Kim, E. (2006) Strategic Planning for the US Textile Industry in the Post-Quota Era. *Journal of Fashion Marketing and Management* (forthcoming).

Ohmae, K. (1994) *The Borderless World*. Harper Collins, London.

ONS (2005) *Labour Market Trends*. HMSO, London.

Phillips, P. (2004) Textiles and Apparel in China: Preparing for Quota Free Markets. *Textile Outlook International*, **109**, 13–46.

Porter, M. (1990) *The Competitive Advantage of Nations*. Free Press, New York.

Porter, M. (1998a) *The Competitive Advantage of Nations*. Free Press, New York.

Porter, M. (1998b) Clusters and the New Economics of Competition. *Harvard Business Review*, **76**, 77–92.

Rush, D. (2000) UK Textiles: an Industry Left in Rags. *Sunday Times*, 20.2.2000, 4–6.

Russell, B. (1984) quoted in *A Dictionary of Political Quotations*. Europa, London.

Shelton, R. & Wachter, K. (2005) Effects of Global Sourcing on Textiles and Apparel. *Journal of Fashion Marketing and Management*, **9.3**, 318–30.

Singhal, A., Sood, S. & Singh, V. (2004) Creating and Preserving Value in the Textile and Apparel Supply Chain. *Textile Outlook International*, **109**, 135–56.

Smith, N. (1999) BHS Suppliers Need to Focus Design and Flexibility. *Drapers Record*, 10.4.99, 6.

Song, H., Liu, X. & Romilly, P. (2000) Aggregated Consumption and Income. In: *The Chinese Economy Under Transition* (Eds S. Cook, S. Yao & J. Zhuang), pp. 300–21. Macmillan, Basingstoke.

Storey, J. (2003) *China: the Race to Market*. Prentice Hall, London.

Studwell, J. (2003) The China Dream. Profile, London.

Tait, N. (1999) Duck Head Apparel. *Clothing World*, **March**, 27–31.

Taplin, I. (1997) Continuity and Change in the US Apparel Industry. *Journal of Fashion Marketing and Management*, **3**, 360–69.

Taplin, I. & Winterton, J. (1997) Restructuring Clothing. In: *Rethinking Global Production* (Eds I. Taplin & J. Winterton), pp. 1–18. Ashgate, Aldershot.

Taplin, I. & Winterton, J. (2000) Diversity in Global Restructuring of Garment Manufacture. *Strategies for Competitive Success: Responses to Global Restructuring in the Clothing and Textile Sector*, Conference Papers, Sheffield Hallam University, 16.6.2000.

Trust, M. (1999) *Mast Industries, Inc: The Winning Combination*. Mast Industries, Andover, USA.

Walden, G. (1999) *Lucky George: Memories of an Anti-Politician*. Penguin, London.

Appendix A

Statistics in the UK Clothing Sector and the PRODCOM System

The majority of UK official industrial data is published using a system of categorisation based upon the Standard Industrial Classification (SIC). Unfortunately, for those users of statistics who are interested in plotting trends over time, the SIC is periodically revised – we have had a SIC (1968), SIC (1980) and an SIC (1992). We now have a fourth variant in existence – SIC (2003). The problem introduced by the change from one system to another is that the categories within each system frequently do not correspond with any degree of exactitude. It is, therefore, quite difficult to produce time series data which involve a change from one system to the next without encountering a break in the series.

Another significant change has taken place with the introduction of the PRODCOM system. This is a Europe-wide system of data collection based upon manufacturer product sales enquiries. PRODCOM is a European Community-wide initiative to harmonise the *collection and publication* of data about *products*. The great advantage of PRODCOM is that it will provide a definitive list of products (and data about them) which directly links to international trade data. It will, therefore, provide *direct compatibility* between production and trade data for the twelve EU Member States. As is stated by ONS (2002) the SIC has always followed the same principles as the relevant international systems and post-1980 revisions have been necessary to bring it into line with the European Commission's NACE system.

The SIC (2003) is a hierarchical five-digit system, e.g. D is manufacturing; DB is textiles and apparel (SIC 17 and 18); 18 is apparel; 18.2 is the manufacture of wearing apparel; 18.23 is underwear; 18.23/1 is other men's underwear. The new (2003) classification is identical to the 1992 classification in the case of SIC 18, the apparel sector, and contains no major changes.

The new SIC (2003) which defines clothing is 18 'Manufacturing of Wearing Apparel; Dressing and Dyeing of Fur'. This breaks down as follows:

18.1   Manufacture of leather clothes.
18.2   Manufacture of other Wearing Apparel and Accessories.
18.21   Workwear.
18.22   Manufacture of other outerwear.
18.22/1   Other men's outerwear.
18.22/2   Other women's outerwear.
18.23   Underwear.
18.23/1   Men's underwear.
18.23/2   Women's underwear.
18.24   Other wearing apparel and accessories, not elsewhere specified.
18.24/1   Hats.
18.24/2   No longer in use.
18.24/3   Cut Make Trim.
18.24/9   Other (includes babywear, tracksuits, swimwear, gloves, belts, ties etc.).
18.3   Fur.

Knitted and crocheted hosiery and other articles of apparel (pullovers, cardigans etc.) are classified in textiles.

A comparison between the SIC (1980) and the SIC (1992) can be found in Jones (2002, p. 307) for those readers interested in historical comparisons. A full guide to the new SIC can be found in ONS, National Statistics (2002).

Appendix B

Employment and Output Statistics

Output data: manufacturing of wearing apparel (SIC Division 18)

Base year 2001 = 100

Year	Index Number
1978	172.4
1979	175.1
1980	156.7
1981	145.0
1982	144.9
1983	149.7
1984	155.2
1985	163.5
1986	164.6
1987	166.1
1988	163.5
1989	158.0
1990	159.3
1991	143.8
1992	147.7
1993	147.3
1994	154.0
1995	149.4
1996	146.4
1997	137.1
1998	127.2
1999	115.3
2000	114.0
2001	100.0
2002	91.0
2003	86.4
2004	74.5

Source: ONS, Newport – I am grateful to the ONS for supplying these statistics free of charge.

Note: The use of a base near to the present date does disguise the extent of the fall in output over the period. If a 1985 base is used the 2004 figure becomes 45.6.

Employment data: SIC 18

Year	Numbers Employed
1978	294,157
1979	292,905
1980	258,074
1981	228,486
1982	216,913
1983	213,380
1984	214,380
1985	220,131
1986	215,214
1987	216,874
1988	216,501
1989	206,940
1990	187,210
1991	156,771
1992	147,044
1993	154,823
1994	149,056
1995	144,575
1996	140,674
1997	134,037
1998	123,841
1999	108,000
2000	104,300
2001	95,000
2002	84,000
2003	54,600
2004	46,400
2005	41,200

Source: ONS, Labour Market Trends, various editions (Table B13).

Note: (1) On a 2001 base to make these figures comparable with the output index the figure for 2004 is 48.8. If a 1985 base is used the figure for 2004 would be 21.0.

Notes on sampling procedure

It is important to realise that both sets of data are produced from samples. The primary data source for the output data is the Monthly Production Inquiry of Manufacturing Industries. This is taken from a sample of approximately 6% of the businesses in the sector covered. Large companies remain in the sample, but smaller ones are rotated. The data covers only output physically produced in the UK (i.e. it does not include OPT data – see Chapter 8). The employment data is derived from the Annual Employment Survey which covers approximately 30% of the work sites in the UK. It is important to realise that the employment figures – although appearing very precise – are not based on a head count or a procedure similar to the Census of Population. The sample of firms supplying data is not constant over time and the figures from each size band which supplies data are weighted according to the importance of the size band they represent.

Appendix C
A Model of Exchange Rate Fluctuations

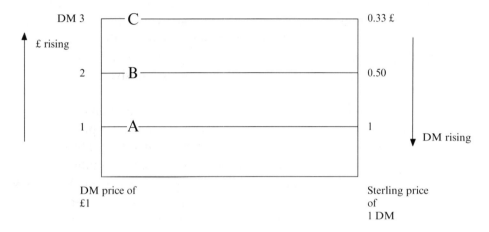

Notes: (1) DM represents German currency; £ represents UK currency.
(2) On the left scale at A it costs 1 DM to buy £1. At point C it costs 3 DM so that each DM is buying fewer £s. Therefore, the DM is falling and the £ rising.
(3) On the right scale at A it costs £1 to buy 1 DM. At point C it costs 33p. This means that at C it costs less to buy each DM and that each £1 spent purchased more DMs. Therefore, the £ is rising and the DM is falling.

Appendix D

Supply-chain Configurations in the Apparel Sector

There is no doubt that the nature and configuration of international (if not global) supply chains in the apparel sector is changing under the twin pressures of industrial upgrading by the low-cost countries in their search for higher order competitive advantage and the search for ever more responsive production networks by the retailer.

The traditional supply chain in the apparel sector was based on the assembly model. In Gereffi's (1999) terms this was the first stage and preceeded the so-called Original Equipment Manufacture (OEM) model. It usually consisted of a developed country retailer, a developed country apparel manufacturer and a low-cost manufacturer. The latter simply assembled the garment. There may or may not have been the involvement of some intermediary (such as an agent or agency) in the chain working either for the developed country manufacturer/retailer or as a representative of the low-cost producer. This model corresponds very closely to what Gereffi (1999) described as a buyer-driven chain which he defined as 'those industries in which large retailers (such as Wal Mart), branded marketers (such as Liz Claiborne or Nautica), and branded manufacturers (such as Sara Lee and Levi Strauss) play the pivotal role in setting up decentralized production networks in a variety of exporting countries, typically located in the Third World'. These arrangements produced aggressive sourcing activities around the world. According to Gereffi (1999) these simple chains evolve into OEM operations in which an increasing range of non-assembly functions are transferred to the low-cost producer. This is sometimes known as 'full package' supply and incorporates such functions as material and component sourcing and even design. The last stage of evolution is known as Own Brand Manufacture (OBM) which, as the name implies, involves the use of own design capabity and the sale of branded goods at home and abroad on the part of the (originally) low-cost supplier.

The main problem introduced by these models is that they leave progressively less for the apparel manufacturer in the developed country to do. Similarly, a move to direct retailer sourcing as identified by Chen (2005) in his 'streamlined model' will further erode the position of the manufacturer in high-cost locations.

In effect these newer models reflect what is sometimes called inadvertant technology transfer or the training of future competitors. This was foreseen in the first edition of this book (Jones, 2002, p. 298).

The changes described above are related to questions of 'who does what' in the supply chain (see p. 297) but there is also concern over how long it takes to progress through the chain. This has been described in the evolution of the so-called 'agile chains' which have been introduced in Chapter 8 above. These developments are more concerned with collapsing the supply chain and making them more responsive to the vagaries of an ever more fickle consumer (Christopher, 2004) than where the tasks are carried out. However, the two strands do come together because the advocates of the agile chain tend to argue that they are incompatible with distant sourcing and, therefore, offer some hope of a recovery in domestic production in developed countries if only sourcing managers would cease to be so short-sighted. As has been made clear in Chapter 8, the present author does not subscribe to this view. There seems to be little evidence that reasonably agile chains cannot evolve with far-away partners. According to Araujo (2005), even Zara can afford to ignore nearby Portugal in favour of China. Finally, it is worth noting that semi-agile chains can be seen in a variety of regional settings involving cooperation between a developed country partner and a low-cost supplier in a range of offshore options, e.g. USA–Mexico; EU–N. Africa and EU–E. Europe. This concept of a regional cluster (Blair, 2001) seems to bear a close relationship to Gereffi's (1999) concept of triangulation in which a developed country partner works with an agency in a newly industrialised country who subcontracts to an even lower-cost country. None of these new models offers any real prospect of relocalisation of substantial employment back to the developed countries. Fogarty (2006) rejects the 'hidden cost' case and demonstrates a saving of $1.30 per garment.

References

Araujo, M. (2005) Private correspondence with Professor Mario De Araujo, University of Minho, Portugal.

Blair, J. & Gereffi, G. (2001) Local Clusters in Global Chains. *World Development*, **29.11**, 1885–903.

Chen, Z. (2005) *Quality Management in International Clothing Supply Chains*. Unpublished PhD, MMU, Manchester.

Christopher, M., Lowson, R. & Peck, H. (2004) Creating Agile Supply Chains in the Fashion Industry. *International Journal of Retail and Distribution Management*, **32.8**, 367–76.

Fogarty, A. (2006) Domestic vs Offshore Manufacturing (Editorial). *Journal of Fashion Marketing and Management*, **10.2** (forthcoming).

Gereffi, G. (1999) International Trade and Industrial Upgrading in the Apparel Commodity Chain. *Journal of International Economics*, **28**, 37–70.

Index

Dec 17/07